Rubel on Karl Marx

Rubel on Karl Marx

Five Essays

EDITED BY
JOSEPH O'MALLEY
AND
KEITH ALGOZIN

*Marquette
University*

CAMBRIDGE UNIVERSITY PRESS

Cambridge
London   New York   New Rochelle
Melbourne   Sydney

Published by the Press Syndicate of the University of Cambridge
The Pitt Building, Trumpington Street, Cambridge CB2 1RP
32 East 57th Street, New York, NY 10022, USA
296 Beaconsfield Parade, Middle Park, Melbourne 3206, Australia

First published 1981

Printed in the United States of America
Typeset by Huron Valley Graphics, Ann Arbor, Michigan
Printed and bound by Vail-Ballou Press, Inc., Binghamton, New York

Library of Congress Cataloging in Publication Data
Rubel, Maximilien.
Rubel on Karl Marx.
Bibliography: p.
Includes index.
1. Marx, Karl, 1818–1883 – Addresses, essays,
lectures. I. O'Malley, Joseph J. II. Algozin, K. W.
III. Title.
HX39.5.R7966   335.4   80–21734
ISBN 0 521 23839 0

Essay 1 originally published in French as "La légende de Marx ou Engels fondateur," *Etudes de marxologie*, no. 15 (December), 2189–99, I.S.M.E.A., Paris, © 1972 Maximilien Rubel.

Essay 2 originally published in French as "Introduction" to Vol. 1 and "Avant-propos" to Vol. 2 of *Pages de Karl Marx pour une éthique socialiste* by Payot, Paris, © 1970 Maximilien Rubel.

Essay 3 originally published in French as "Introduction" to Karl Marx, *Oeuvres: Economie II*, by Gallimard (Bibliothèque de la Pléiade), Paris, © 1968 Maximilien Rubel.

Essay 4 originally published in French as "Plan et méthode de l''Economie'," *Etudes de marxologie*, no. 16 (October), 1777–820, I.S.M.E.A., Paris, © 1973 Maximilien Rubel.

Essay 5 originally published in German as "Nachwort" in Karl Marx and Friedrich Engels, *Die russische Kommune. Kritik eines Mythos*, by Carl Hanser Verlag, Munich, © 1972 Maximilien Rubel.

Contents

Preface

This volume contains five essays by the French Marx scholar
Maximilien Rubel, together with a bibliography of his publications to date. Rubel is one of the world's foremost authorities
on Marx: There are few people currently writing in any language about the controversial figure and doctrines of Marx
who approach Rubel's experience of nearly forty years of con-
tinuous and often pioneering scholarship in the published and
unpublished texts of Marx or who can match Rubel's overall
knowledge of the corpus of Marx's writings and the facts of
his life. Rubel's views on Marx are not, however, as well
known in the English-speaking world as are those of some
other commentators whose interpretations rest on lesser scholarship. It is hoped that the present volume will help change
that. Rubel is first and foremost a scholar whose primary aim
has always been to bring to light through historical and critical
text research exactly what Marx said and held, including
Marx's own perception of his accomplished work and of his
intellectual and political tasks. That primary aim has, however, been constantly linked to a second one, that of clarifying
the genesis and nature of the historical phenomenon called
Marxism, which Rubel considers – in all of its varieties – to be
a dangerous mythification of Marx's thought. Rubel's views
regarding both Marx and Marxism are controversial, at times
highly so, but they have always been argued on a basis of
thorough scholarship and profound reflection on the significance both of Marx's thought and of recent social and political
history. For that reason, his views deserve the careful consideration of anyone seriously interested in who Marx was, what
he was trying to demonstrate, and what his relationship continues to be to the movement, parties, and doctrines that lay
claim to his name. Moreover, one may disagree with some of
Rubel's views without denying the crucial importance of his
scholarly work. Like that of Franz Mehring, David Riazanov,
and Carl Grünberg, to name just three of his best-known pre-

decessors, Rubel's scholarship has contributed in an indispensable way to the advance of knowledge about Karl Marx.

The translating and other work on this volume has been a
cooperative effort involving the editors, Mary Algozin, and
Margaret Manale (under Rubel's supervision). Keith and Mary
Algozin did the first translation of Essay 5, "A visionary legacy
to Russia," and I did the same for Essay 3, "A history of
Marx's 'Economics.' " Ms. Manale revised these translations,
making changes in consultation with Rubel, and did the first
translation of Essay 1, "The Marx legend, or Engels, founder
of Marxism"; Essay 2, "Socialism and ethics"; and Essay 4,
"The plan and method of the 'Economics.' " I then revised
these and the remaining essays and with the help of the Algo-
zins made some final changes, mostly stylistic. I prepared the
Bibliography of Rubel's publications and the Introduction, and
Mary Algozin did the Index.

Thanks are due to Ellen Murphy of the Memorial Library at
Marquette University and J. Duxbury of the Memorial Library
at the University of Wisconsin, Madison, for bibliographical
help provided; to the Marquette University Committee on Research for grants in support of preparation of this volume; and
to Barbara Olson and Grace Jablonsky for help in preparing
the typescript.

JOSEPH O'MALLEY

Milwaukee, Wisconsin
February 1981

Abbreviations used in footnotes

MEGA   Karl Marx/Friedrich Engels, *Historisch-kritische Gesamtausgabe*, Erste Abteilung, Bände 1–7 (Marx-Engels-Institut, Moscow), Frankfurt a/M and Berlin, Marx-Engels-Verlag, 1927–35.

MEW   Karl Marx/Friedrich Engels, *Werke* (Institut für Marxismus-Leninismus beim Zentralkomittee der Sozialistischen Einheitspartei Deutschlands), Bände 1–39, Berlin, Dietz Verlag, 1957–68.

Grundrisse   Karl Marx, *Grundrisse der Kritik der politischen Oekonomie (Rohentwurf), 1857–1858,* Berlin, Dietz Verlag, 1953.

Oeuvres, vol. 1.   Karl Marx, *Oeuvres, Economie,* t. I, ed. M. Rubel, Paris, Editions Gallimard (Bibliothèque de la Pléiade), 2nd ed., 1965.

         vol. 2.   Karl Marx, *Oeuvres, Economie,* t. II, ed. M. Rubel, Paris, Editions Gallimard (Bibliothèque de la Pléiade), 1968.

MESW   Karl Marx/Frederick Engels, *Selected Works in Two Volumes.* Moscow: Foreign Languages Publishing House, 1955.

CW   V. I. Lenin, *Collected Works.* 45 volumes. Moscow: Progress Publishers, 1970.

Introduction

Maximilien Rubel was born in 1905 in Czernowitz, at that time an Austro-Hungarian city, capital of the Bukowina, which passed to Rumania in 1918 and to Russia in 1947. He attended secondary schools in Vienna and Czernowitz, receiving a Rumanian degree in law in 1928 and a second one in philosophy in 1930. In 1931 he moved to Paris to do German Studies at the Sorbonne, and he received a *Licence-ès-lettres* there in 1934. He remained in France, supported himself by teaching German and law in private schools, and obtained French citizenship in 1937. The following year, he started a small literary magazine called *Verbe – Cahiers humains*, of which just two issues appeared before he was mobilized in 1939 in the ambulance corps of the French Army. Following the defeat of France and his demobilization, he returned to Paris and resumed teaching, living under the German occupation semiclandestinely because of his Jewish origins.

In these circumstances, in 1941, he was approached by a group of French Marxists in the resistance movement who asked him to translate into German a political text to be distributed in a handbill to the occupying German forces. He agreed, but when he asked to see the text he was told that it had yet to be written. In the end, although all professed to be Marxists, those charged with composing the text differed so greatly in their interpretations of Marx that they were unable to agree on its formulation. Astonished at this confusion among so many followers of what was claimed to be "scientific" socialism, Rubel undertook serious study of the literature of Marxism and the writings of Marx. Under difficult circumstances, he located, among other materials, a copy of the *Marx-Engels-Gesamtausgabe* (MEGA), which had been published in the period 1927–35, and he studied it thoroughly. He was greatly surprised to find that no complete edition of Marx's writings existed and that not even a complete bibliography of the writings had ever been published. Moreover, he

I

found that the existing biographies of Marx were incomplete and unsatisfactory: One had to compile several of them to begin to get a clear picture of Marx's intellectual life and political activities. He then began composing his own bibliography on file cards as he searched out and studied additional materials. By the end of the war, after four years of such work, he had reached the paradoxical conclusion that what is called Marxism is actually anterior to the knowledge of Marx: Marxism, he concluded, has only the thinnest of relations to Marx's basic teachings and is in fact a kind of mythification of Marx's person and work. He thus conceived of the need for, and initiated, a special research discipline with a two-fold subject matter: first, Marx's thought in its origins and development, considered both intrinsically and in relation to contemporary times; and second, Marxism viewed as a trend of thought that, referring itself to Marx's theoretical and political work, has engendered a multitude of currents and schools, parties and sects, theories and doctrines. He coined the name *Marxologie* (as the French equivalent for the German *Marx-forschung* or *Marxismus-Forschung*) for this discipline, which he considered to be in the tradition of the scholarly periodical *Archiv für die Geschichte des Sozialismus und der Arbeiterbewegung,* published in the years 1910–30 under the direction of Carl Grünberg, and of the research work done by the Russian Marx scholar David Riazanov before he was dismissed from his functions and sent into exile in 1931 by Stalin.

After the end of the war, Rubel continued to teach privately and to pursue the kind of research he had been doing since 1941, in view now of presenting a doctoral thesis. His first publications on Marx appeared in 1946. In 1954 he received the *Doctorate-ès-lettres* from the Sorbonne for two theses on Marx, the principal one being a study of Marx's intellectual development, subsequently published under the title of *Karl Marx. Essai de biographie intellectuelle* (1957). As the title indicates, this work was not intended to be a complete or definitive biography of Marx – something that Rubel believes has yet to be written and would have to be at the very least the size of Gustav Mayer's multivolume biography of Engels. His secondary thesis was an annotated bibliography of Marx's writings, including a list of Engels's writings as well, published in 1956 as a *Bibliographie des Oeuvres de Karl Marx*. Both of these works aimed to fill serious gaps, which Rubel's earliest research had shown to exist in the body of knowledge about Marx. Indeed, the bibliography, published more than seventy years after Marx's death and long after the establishment of Marxism, represented the first serious effort to inventory Marx's writings in a reasonable manner. Today, more than twenty years later and almost one hundred years after Marx's death, it remains the only available catalog of his writings that approaches completeness and can be said to be generally reliable. Together with its supplement, published in 1960, this bibliography has proved to be a most valuable research tool for a generation of specialists and students.[1]

While working on his doctorate in 1947, Rubel joined France's *Centre national de la recherche scientifique* (CNRS), taking a post as *Attaché de recherche* in the *Centre d'études sociologiques* in Paris. He has remained with CNRS ever since; he was promoted to *Chargé de recherche* in 1954 and to *Maître de recherche* in 1959. He retired in 1970 as *Maître de recherche honoraire*. Intermittently since 1950, he has done research in Amsterdam at the International Institute for Social History, depository of the bulk of the original manuscripts of Marx and Engels. He is a longtime member of the French Institute of Social History, the French Institute of Sociology, the International Association of French Language Sociologists, and the French Political Science Association. Among his teaching activities over two decades, he has conducted advanced seminars and directed doctoral theses at the University of Paris, has been visiting professor at the University of Nice (1976, 1978) and at the Universities of Munich in Germany (1973) and Aalborg and Copenhagen in Denmark (1979), and he has been Visiting Fellow in the History of Ideas Unit of the Australian National University in Canberra (1971). He has also lectured at the *Karl-Marx-Haus* in Trier (1968), at the Universities of Aarhus and Roskilde in Denmark (1979), and at Harvard University (in the Russian Research Center), the

---

[1]The supplement corrected errors and filled gaps that the 1956 publication inevitably contained, given the vicissitudes of the literary remains of both Marx and Engels (the dispersal of their libraries, feuds among the literary heirs, losses and thefts of manuscripts during the operations that saved the materials from the threat of destruction by the Nazis, etc.), the ground-breaking nature of Rubel's work of compilation, and the generally unfavorable circumstances in which the work was carried out, especially the inaccessibility of the archives in the possession of the Moscow Institute for Marxism-Leninism, then as now holder of the most complete set of photocopies, as well as some originals, of the manuscripts of Marx and Engels.

University of California at Berkeley, and Ohio Wesleyan University in the United States (1961, 1966). He participated in the First World Congress of Sociology in Washington, D.C. in 1962; the Franco-German Colloquium held in Bochum in 1965; the Symposium on Marx and the Western World at Notre Dame University in 1966; the Conference on the Russian Revolution at Harvard University in 1967; the Conference to commemorate the one hundred fiftieth anniversary of the birth of Friedrich Engels in Wuppertal in 1970; and the Symposium on Varieties of Marxism held at the Van Leer Jerusalem Foundation in Israel in 1974.[2]

Rubel's list of publications on Marx, beginning in 1946, contains over eighty titles, including books, articles, translations, and editions of texts. He remains today as active as ever and is presently preparing an important *Marx Lexicon* (together with his frequent collaborator Louis Janover), supervising the forthcoming third volume of his French language edition of Marx, about which more will be said, and preparing a forthcoming issue of *Etudes de marxologie*, one of the series of *Cahiers* published by the *Institute de sciences mathématiques et économiques appliquées*, which is associated with the CNRS and directed by Professor François Perroux. Rubel has edited the *Etudes de marxologie* since the founding of the series in 1959. Many of his publications reflect what has always been one of his principal concerns: the lack of a complete and critical edition of Marx's writings. He pointed out the need for such an edition in early articles; he lamented Stalin's purge of the scholarly Riazanov and criticized the subsequent effects of Stalinism—the "abusively political use of Marx's thought," its "mummification and falsification," the "purification" of certain texts and the suppression of others in inferior editions prepared by confused and fearful people. Stalinism thus revealed itself as "the absolute negation of all culture."[3] On

[2]Rubel's controversial paper on Engels's role in the creation of Marxism, prepared originally in German for the 1970 Wuppertal Conference and subsequently read in English at the 1974 Symposium in Israel, is included in the present volume as Essay 1.

[3]Rubel made these charges in "La Vie posthume de Karl Marx" (1948) and "Marx auteur maudit en U.R.S.S.?" (1951) as well as other places. (For bibliographical details of these and all other writings of Rubel to date, see the bibliography of his works included in this volume.) His severe criticism of the Soviets' treatment of Marx's writings provoked predictably hostile responses from representatives of the Moscow Institute for Marxism-Leninism. His work was branded as "falsifying revisionism" and he was accused of using "suspect," "anarchist," "anti-Marxist," and "enemy" sources in preparing his bibliography; see Rubel's foreword to the 1960 supplement to his bibliography.

these themes he found a sympathetic but pessimistic correspondent in Karl Korsch, who wrote:

The need for a complete edition of Marx's published and unpublished writings ... has been my preoccupation for the last thirty years more or less – for the falsification of Marxian thought dates back as far as that and, in other forms, began even during the lifetime of Marx and Engels. (Perhaps this phenomenon is inevitable in the case of truly revolutionary theory as in every other kind of religious or quasi-religious movement.) I share your profound hope that the present crisis, after having destroyed nearly all the possibilities, will finally give rise to a wider recognition of this need to reconstitute Marx's actual theory in its integrity. But I think that the difficulties are greater than you imagine. First of all, it is impossible (and barring a new revolution in Russia, which is very highly improbable, it will always remain impossible) to have access to the Moscow manuscripts, and you know better than anyone else the extent to which the thirty volumes of the Russian edition have been cut, mutilated and falsified. You are also no stranger to the other hundred-odd obstacles which make it impossible to realize this great task even if the financial means could be found – which is not the case either in the U.S. or in Western Europe. The most that could be accomplished by a select group of nonpartisan Marx scholars would be a *critical edition* encompassing in the original or in translation all of the texts and text variants that are actually available to us today with detailed descriptions of those texts to which we have no access. However, the fact that the majority of the unedited or poorly edited manuscripts remain in Moscow, either in the original or the form of photocopies, is a hindrance to such an enterprise and gives the advantage to the falsifying monopolists. Therefore, the situation for restoring the texts of Marxism after only one century is worse than it had been for the restoration of Chinese philosophy two thousand years after the great "burning of the books" of the Ch'in dynasty – or worse than for the restoration of the Manichaean dogmas after the total destruction of the written documents belonging to this "heresy."[4]

The problems and obstacles mentioned by Korsch continue to exist today and set limits to what independent scholarship can achieve in publication of Marx. Still, Rubel has persisted in the effort to "reconstitute Marx's actual theory," if not in its integrity at least as far as possible, by bringing to light and making more widely available essential texts and by providing didactic

[4]K. Korsch to M. Rubel, July 7, 1951; cf. *Etudes de marxologie*, no. 18 (Apr.–May 1976), 937–8.

commentary on them. Two of his earliest publications were
selections of texts taken from throughout Marx's writings presented in translation, French in one case, English in the other,
including many first translations, some extracted from unpublished manuscripts. Most of his earliest articles were translations or descriptions of texts that were at the time unavailable
or little known, for example, the first French translation of
parts of Marx's 1844 Paris manuscripts, and descriptions of
Marx's *Grundrisse* of 1857–8 and of his research notebooks
from the 1840s and 50s. These were extremely valuable contributions at the time and some of them still have not been supplanted by subsequent scholarship. Since the series' inception
in 1959, the *Etudes de marxologie* has been Rubel's principal
vehicle for these kinds of contributions and for communicating
a mass of valuable bibliographical information; it has also been
a forum for text editions, interpretive studies of texts and historical essays by a number of independent scholars, including
Miguel Abensour, Bert Andréas, Shlomo Avineri, Siegfried
Bahne, Yvon Bourdet, Olivier Corpet, Hal Draper, Loyd
Easton, Louis Janover, Margaret Manale, Paul Mattick, Henry
Mayer, Niel McInnis, Marian Sawer, Fred E. Schrader, Jeanine
Verdès, Marc Vuilleumier, and others.

There have been disappointments. In the early 1970s, for
example, in anticipation of the 1983 centennial of Marx's
death, Rubel tried to stimulate formation of an international
editorial board of nonpartisan Marx scholars that would produce a historical and critical (and of necessity partial) "jubilee" edition of Marx. The Moscow Institute of Marxism-
Leninism, however, had already announced a renewed effort
to produce a full *Marx-Engels-Gesamtausgabe*, a new MEGA
in more than one hundred volumes, and in collaboration with
the Institute for Marxism-Leninism in East Berlin had published a sample volume (1972) exemplifying the features of the
projected edition. Rubel's efforts encountered a lack of support owing in large part to the opinion held by certain Western
scholars that his project was essentially the negative one of an
"anti-MEGA" – a judgment that completely neglected both
the positive features of all of Rubel's previous work and also
the advantages of the kind of historical and critical edition he
was proposing.[5]

[5]At this writing Rubel is still attempting to organize production of a centennial
edition. He envisages an edition of thirty-five volumes of 600–800 pages each and

Rubel's efforts to produce critical editions of Marx's texts have been crowned by his superb French edition of Marx, published in Paris by Gallimard in the *Bibliothèque de la Pléiade*. To date, two massive volumes of Marx's economic texts have been published and gone through several editions; a third volume, devoted to Marx's philosophic and critical essays of 1838–46, is now in press and due to appear in the near future. The first volume of economic texts is composed of writings published during Marx's lifetime and features the first truly critical French edition of Book I of *Capital*. The second volume, about which more will be said, contains texts that Marx left unpublished and that Rubel has selected and arranged in keeping with his own concept of the structure and contents of Marx's broader "critique of political economy." Rubel considers this a pilot edition to serve serious students as well as specialists pending eventual publication of all of Marx's manuscripts. At the same time, in its introductory material, notes, appendixes, and critical apparatus, in its overall presentation of texts and in its overall concept, it is a great scholarly achievement and, as its most serious reviewer has pointed out, a work of historical importance: "It can henceforth be said that if some day a complete edition of Marx's materials is realized, Rubel, who proceeds in a way similar to Riazanov, will have marked with his editorial work an important intermediary stage – and this stage is all the more important in that it reveals an unknown Marx."[6]

The "unknown Marx" who is revealed in Rubel's edition, and throughout his other writings, is almost the exact opposite

having a number of remarkable features. For example, Marx's writings would be presented in three sections or series, in accord with the methodological criteria of the author's three-fold critique – (1) the critique of ideology, (2) the critique of politics, (3) the critique of political economy; each volume would contain, along with the appropriate main works of Marx, the correspondence, source materials, and contemporary documents bearing on those works; the presentation of texts, while respecting the regular canons of scholarly editing, would be designed not for specialists (as in the case of the ongoing critical edition of Hegel) but for the broader category of readers and researchers whom Marx aimed to reach. Recently, after agreeing to undertake publication, a Swiss publisher had to abandon the project because of the production costs. Rubel is now proposing the constitution of an international society of scholars and other interested persons, the principal purpose of which would be the realization of the Marx Jubilee Edition.

[6]Miguel Abensour, "Pour lire Marx," *Revue française de science politique* 20, no. 4 (Aug. 1970), 777.

of the mythic figure found in popular consciousness and Marxist orthodoxy. He is a thinker whose doctrines combine utopian ethics and social science, a writer whose literary remains are but fragments of the masterwork he projected, and a political man who neither founded nor wished to found any system, party, or movement. Yet, he was a man whose view of things, for all of its peculiarities, remains of unique value today and therefore must be permanently disengaged from the distortions of Marxist (and anti-Marxist) mythology. In the balance of this Introduction we will briefly treat these points in Rubel's interpretation of Marx.

Ethics and science

For Rubel, Marx's doctrines contain both utopian-ethical and rigorous scientific elements. The ethical element is comprised of a vision and a demand: the socialist-utopian vision of a universally human community, and the demand – formulated as a Kantian categorical imperative – that it be realized. The scientific element, on the other hand, is a descriptive and analytic account of the modern system of economy and its social and political structures; this account takes the form of a critique of the "science of modern society" (political economy), and it shows modern society to be in the process of destroying itself while simultaneously generating the material and spiritual prerequisites for the kind of society envisaged by the utopians. In Marx therefore, as Rubel understands him, an ethical impulse motivates the scientific endeavor, and the scientific results support an ethical vision: the critique of political economy demonstrates the historical viability of the utopian ideal. Quoting Rubel:

Ethics does not constitute the basis of the Marxian theory; rather socialist ethics – which is anterior to Marx – received scientific reinforcement in the theoretical teachings of the author of *Capital* . . . Marx preserved the substance of the ethical demand for the socialist utopia in order to put it into a sociological account of the capitalist relations of production, an account he referred to rather modestly as a "scientific conception of social conditions" (letter to F. Lassalle, 12 Nov. 1858). It is a science of the coming-to-be and passing-away of a mode of man's exploitation by man; and it is the utopia of a universally human community willed and realized by the class comprised of the most numerous and most poor, to whom Marx attributed the consciousness of this emancipatory mission.[7]

While insisting on this dual character of Marx's thought, at once descriptive and visionary, combining a theory of realized history with the image and project of a history to be constructed, Rubel stresses the utopian-ethical over the rational-scientific side of Marx's doctrines. In opposition to the view of Marx as founder of a system of thought and of a unique scientific *Weltanschauung*, Rubel's interpretation tends to underline the emancipatory aim behind Marx's teachings, highlighting the stimulating ambiguities and frequent invectives that are so little in conformity with the strictly scientific spirit attributed to Marx in Marxist literature.

After reading Rubel's *Karl Marx. Pages choisies pour une éthique socialiste* (1948), Karl Korsch endorsed Rubel's stress on the utopian-ethical side of Marx, which Korsch took as equivalent to making "social *praxis* rather than science or theoretic dogma" the heart of Marx's message.[8] For Miguel Abensour, the same stress on the ethical-utopian over the scientific aspect of Marx's thought is reflected in Rubel's Pléiade edition of Marx; the edition, according to Abensour, represents a conception of Marx's thought as essentially *Zukunftstheorie*, that is, a "theory of the future which is animated by the vision of a

[7]*Etudes de marxologie*, no. 18 (Apr.–May 1976), 921. Quoted is Rubel's précis of one of his letters to the Dutch socialist, Anton Pannekoek (1873–1960), with whom he corresponded frequently in the period 1951–5, in large part about the relationship between ethics and science in Marx's thought. Pannekoek's letters and summaries of Rubel's replies are in the issue of *Etudes de marxologie* just cited, pp. 840–932.

[8]To quote from Korsch: ". . . the *very fine* anthology enabled me to understand fully your point of departure in dealing with the problems we face in common. I think I can say that on the whole all of my ideas on Marxian theory and its history (past, present, and future) are much closer to yours than one might have expected in view of our differences in generation and, especially, experience, both theoretical and practical, which could hardly be more divergent. On certain points our differences are more terminological than real. For example, I must confess that there is something unacceptable in the title 'Pour une éthique socialiste' in the eyes of an old Marxist who can recall so many attempts to reduce Marx's theory to empty conventional morality, or rather to translate this morality into the revolutionary language of Marxism. Even now, after having read your Introduction, I am still not thoroughly convinced that it is appropriate to equate the ethics of Kierkegaard, Nietzsche, and Marx . . . Nevertheless, I fully agreed with the actual contents of your presentation, which I take to be an interpretation of Marxism as social *praxis* rather than science or theoretic dogma." Letter of July 7, 1951; *Etudes de marxologie*, no. 18 (Apr.–May 1976), 935–6. Rubel's introduction to which Korsch refers is included in the present volume as Essay 2 under the title of "Socialism and ethics."

classless society and has as its project a workers's socialist revolution and the building by the proletariat of a new world."[9] Referring also to the Pléiade edition, and specifically to Rubel's Introduction to Volume 2 of Marx's economic texts, Louis Dumont writes: "Maximilien Rubel stresses forcefully what he calls the ethical conviction of Marx's initial stand and sees in it the great shaping force that determined the general outline of Marx's thought forever afterward. The fact is so obvious that it is hard to understand that Rubel's thesis is not universally admitted."[10] What prevents some from admitting Rubel's thesis is their insistence, in the face of the textual evidence, on dividing Marx's intellectual life into prescientific (or nonscientific) and scientific periods, in the fashion of Louis Althusser. Others unlikely to accept Rubel's thesis are those holding narrower conceptions of science and ethics who tend to consider the two incompatible, and those who, perhaps uncomfortable with the idea of ethics or that of utopia, want to locate the value of Marx's doctrines exclusively in their scientific character. Those who stress the scientific side of Marx, however, usually ignore or deny what for Rubel is a demonstrable matter of fact: Marx's projected scientific work went largely unwritten.

The "Economics"

Marx intended to write a six-part critique of political economy, but this work, which he referred to as his "Economics," remained at his death largely unwritten. The work was to have been elaborated according to a plan that Marx formulated and announced in the period 1857–9 and that he neither abandoned nor significantly altered thereafter.[11] Of the projected six parts, Marx himself completed and published only a portion of the first, what we know today as Book I of Capital, leaving at his death a mass of more or less rough manuscripts and raw research data. Engels, and subsequently Karl Kautsky, produced out of these materials the remaining parts of Capital, Engels editing Books II and III and Kautsky editing Book IV ("Theories

[9]Abensour, "Pour lire Marx," 788. Rubel promises to present, in his introduction to the forthcoming Vol. 3 of his Pléiade edition of Marx, a more elaborated interpretation of the ethical implications inherent in Marx's teaching.

[10]Louis Dumont, From Mandeville to Marx. The Genesis and Triumph of Economic Ideology (Chicago & London: The University of Chicago Press, 1977), p. 216, n. 9.

[11]See Essay 4, "The plan and method of the 'Economics.' "

of Surplus Value"). The common view, which is also the view propagated by orthodox Marxism, that *Capital* sets forth Marx's full political economic doctrine, is wrong on two counts. First, *Capital,* even taken altogether in its four books, is not equivalent to what Marx projected as his "Economics," but only to its first part; and second, Books II and III of *Capital* in the form we have them as edited by Engels are not really finished treatises, as Engels let them appear to be, but rather are an assemblage of Marx's more or less raw materials selected and arranged, at times arbitrarily, by Engels. Hence, there is a much less finished character about Marx's theoretical work in political economy than is ordinarily supposed or than orthodox Marxism pretends. This sets a two-fold task for an editor of Marx who wishes to remain true to the author's intentions and concept of his work. First, instead of being presented as a self-sufficient work, *Capital* must be published together with other texts that Marx considered to be closely related to his "Economics"; most of these are texts that Marx left unpublished, and some of them, including the very important *Grundrisse* of 1857–8, Engels seems to have been unaware of. Second, Books II and III of *Capital* have to be redone with critical scrutiny of Engels's choice of materials and in such a way as to eliminate the false finished appearance of Engels's version. This is what Rubel has done in the first two volumes of his Pléiade edition, the second volume of which is especially controversial. There Rubel has selected and arranged Marx's draft manuscripts for Books II and III of *Capital* differently than Engels did – one result being that Rubel's edition includes texts published nowhere else; moreover, he includes Marx's first draft of a critique of political economy, written in Paris in 1844 (the so-called Economic and Philosophic Manuscripts) among the preliminary draft materials for the "Economics" – in effect again rejecting the thesis of a "break" between Marx's early and mature thought; and he freely selects and rearranges material from the *Grundrisse* so as to reflect Marx's ground plan for his "Economics." These are controversial steps, the kind of daring moves that can be taken with success only by an editor who is profoundly in touch with his author's thought and intentions and also thoroughly familiar with the mass of relevant manuscripts.[12] For Rubel, there is

[12]Rubel justifies these moves and deals at length with the subject of Marx's "Economics" in his introduction to Vol. 2 of the Pléiade edition, which is included in this volume as Essay 3 under the title of "A history of Marx's 'Economics.' "

more at stake here than a mere choice between possible arrange-
ments of Marx's texts: Rather, it is a matter of fundamentally
different conceptions of the character of Marx's doctrines and
his way of thinking. *Capital*, in Rubel's view, is a work that is
not only unfinished but amendable: Marx's manuscripts for the
unfinished Books II and III are more often attempts at critical
reasoning and preliminary conclusions than ironclad and apodictic constructions. Furthermore, Marx's broader plan for his
"Economics" indicates not a rigid system but a pattern of
thought open to corrections and extensions. In sum, instead of
the monolithic Marx with a closed, perfected, and axiomatic
system, Rubel proposes a living Marx whose doctrines are
open, unfinished, and faithful to their author's critical spirit.[13]

Marx and Marxism

Marx, as Rubel presents him, propounded neither a philosophy
of history nor a scientific *Weltanschauung;* moreover, he
founded no party, school, or movement of either an ideological
or a political nature. What Marx's self-styled followers have
elevated into a supposedly scientific *Weltanschauung*—his "materialist conception of history"—was for him merely a "guideline" for research and study. The pretense of Marxism to be a
scientific theory and unique interpretation of human history
based on the words and works of a prophet is therefore false. So
too is the pretense of the "Marxist" states to embody the realization of Marx's social message. Their revolutions could not
have been either proletarian or socialist, because they resulted
in the creation of proletarian masses and state-capitalist production relations. "Moreover, they could find in Marx's writings no political recipe intended for statesmen desirous of 'making a revolution.' "[14] Both in its theoretical claims and in its
political practices, Marxism mystifies facts, propounds and
feeds on mythology.[15] And that mythology, moreover, is shared

---

[13]Cf. Abensour, "Pour lire Marx," 773 ff.

[14]"Le parti de la mystification et la dictature du prolétariat," *Etudes de marxologie,* no. 19–20 (Jan.–Feb. 1978), 428. A full treatment of these questions will be
found in Essay 5, "A visionary legacy to Russia." See also the sensible review of
Rubel's *Die russische Kommune* (Munich: 1974) by Helmut Hirsch, in *Erasmus,*
1974, coll. 315–20.

[15]Margaret Manale has carried out this line of Rubel's thought, tracing the genesis
and early development of Marxism; see her three-part study: "Aux origines du concept
de 'marxisme,' " *Etudes de marxologie,* no. 17 (Oct. 1974), 1397–1430; "La constitution du 'marxisme,' " Ibid., no. 18 (Apr.–May 1976), 813–39; and "L'édification d'une
doctrine marxiste," Ibid., no. 19–20 (Jan.–Feb. 1978), 163–215.

and promoted by most species of anti-Marxism, as for example that of France's *nouveaux philosophes:*

Marx, who set out to show the force of fate in the development of human history and so the lack of control and responsibility on the part of the individual subjected to the "productive forces" – a concept he extended also to the actions of social classes – this Marx has had foisted onto him the role of a superman capable of giving birth to revolutions and terrors, empires and inquisitions. The fact that Marx himself renounced philosophy in favor of scientific research into the matter of social evolution did not forearm him against the excessive judgments of those pseudophilosophers who, fanatical "Marxists" only yesterday, now try to shift the blame for their own misfortunes onto Marx, the very thinker whose entire effort was to denounce and frustrate the play and triumph of unbridled ideology. Of all the intellectual fashions that have appeared in France since the imaginative liberation of May 1968, the most recent one, foolishly baptized as the "new philosophy," is incontestably the most stupifying. The ignorance it displays in attacking Marx is matched only by the impudence with which it rejects today the Marxism that only yesterday it accepted and venerated as the truth of salvation.[16]

For Rubel, establishing the truth about Marx and Marxism is more than a matter of historical and scholarly accuracy: It is a matter of freeing ourselves from a potentially fatal misunderstanding of the forces at work in our contemporary world. "The regimes of false socialism are no less inhuman than are those of true capitalism . . . these apparently antagonistic systems of government are in reality accomplices in one and the same enterprise of man's material destruction and moral debasement."[17] Expanding on this startling conception, Rubel indicates why in his view the study of Marx is important and also what he sees to be at stake in the ideological, economic, and political strife of our time; for what the following text says about these things, and for what it tells us about Rubel himself, it is an appropriate quote with which to conclude this introduction:

Out of the conflict between machine and man, between profit-economy and general interest, between state and society, there progressively emerged a revolutionary teaching and social theory that found in Marx a most convincing spokesman. His teaching consti-

---

[16]Avant-propos to *Etudes de marxologie,* no. 19–20 (Jan.–Feb. 1978), 4.
[17]Avant-propos to *Etudes de marxologie,* no. 17 (Oct. 1974), 1395.

tutes in fact the most coherent critical theory of the crisis that grips the modern world, and as such it is the negation of all political ideologies and so also of Marxism in all of its varieties, whether revolutionary or reformist. According to this theory, the present crisis represents a necessary stage in the transition of the capitalist mode of production towards a human community free of commodities, money, and State, a society in which the economic and political forms of human alienation are unknown. This era of transition is the era of the bourgeoisie creating man in the bourgeois image: a mutilated being serving capital and the State ... The historic mission of the bourgeoisie is to develop the productive forces, both material and intellectual, through science and technology. This being the case, the contemporary regimes that call themselves socialist or communist and that have only recently attained the level of modern civilization in fact fill the same historic function which the bourgeoisie filled in the Western nations; they develop a system of state capitalism that combines the traits of the most advanced industrialism with the characteristics of the most inhuman political absolutism. The bourgeois nature of these "Marxist" regimes is fully revealed in the priority they give to the development of their industries of death, the material arm of the military totalitarianism they practice and cultivate with the aim of maintaining the balance of terror between themselves and the powers of the so-called "free" world, a balance of terror which is the *conditio sine qua non* for imposing by terror the economic and social *status quo* that assures their own privileges as the dominant minorities. As an authoritarian ideology, Marxism, particularly in its social-democratic, Leninist, and Maoist versions, is an accomplice to the system of political and economic domination that threatens to plunge our human societies into a new world cataclysm. In other words, this Marxism is one of the things – and not the least dangerous one – that help keep the exploited and dominated masses of mankind in a permanent state of intellectual and moral resignation.[18]

We have been able here only to touch on some facets of Rubel's work. That will have been enough, however, if by now the reader suspects that Rubel is special among Marx commentators, and so is stimulated to study the essays that follow with an open and critical mind and with the expectation of gaining new knowledge. Such a reader will not be disappointed.

[18]Avant-propos to *Etudes de marxologie*, no. 18 (Apr.–May 1976), 770–1. For another contemporary judgment of Rubel's career and work, which appeared in print as the present volume was going to press, see Bruno Bongiovanni, "Maximilien Rubel," *Estratto da Belfagor* 35 (May 1980), 279–305.

I

The "Marx legend," or Engels, founder of Marxism

Note to the reader: In May 1970 the city of Wuppertal (German Federal Republic) organized an international scientific conference to mark the one hundred fiftieth anniversary of Friedrich Engels's birth. This event attracted the participation of nearly fifty Engels specialists from more than ten European countries, Israel, and the United States. Their task was to resume modern research into the thought of this man who was the closest friend and collaborator of Karl Marx and who is universally considered one of the founders of Marxism. I was among those invited to participate in this conference, and I submitted for discussion a paper consisting of eight critical "theses" or "viewpoints" centered on Engels's responsibility for the foundation of what has now become the dominant ideology of the twentieth century. Because I had assumed that this celebration would be more scientific than commemorative in spirit, I thought it imperative to pass on my critical reservations to an audience of social scientists informed of the problems that have been generated during the course of this century's own particular events and upsurges by the evolution of ideas. Consequently, I sent the organizers of the conference my paper, written in German and entitled "Gesichtspunkte zum Thema 'Engels als Begründer'."

My surprise was great, on arriving in Wuppertal, to be received by the conference officials who immediately informed me of our predicament: My Soviet and East German colleagues felt personally offended in reading my "Viewpoints" and threatened to leave the conference unless my contribution were withdrawn from the debates. After tedious negotiations we came upon a formula that seemed to mitigate the irritation of the "scientific" representatives from the so-called socialist countries; henceforth the papers would no longer be read from the podium but simply commented upon and discussed.

There is little interest in recounting here the details of the debate provoked by the "Viewpoints." The objections made *against them were wholly void of any "scientific" quality, while the conduct of certain participants betrayed their categorical refusal to engage in any discussion that might engender doubts about that scheme of ideological positions known as Marxism-Leninism. Moreover, this obstinate, if not simply insulting, refusal of discussion was an adequate confirmation of the validity of my critique of the use of the concept of Marxism. I conceived of my "Viewpoints" precisely as a denunciation of the illogical use of this concept, of the fanaticism and mythology to which it is attached.[1] The epilog to the conference again emphasized the relevance of my denunciation, which through a simple exercise in semantics actually defends Marx's social theory against Marxist mythology. The organizers did not scruple to violate the elementary rules of editing policy generally respected in bourgeois democratic states: The text (that had been submitted* at the request of the officials) was not included in the volume dedicated to the contributions received in advance of the conference.[2]* Habent sua fata libelli. . . .

[1] A summary of the Wuppertal debates is given in the article written by Henryk Skrzypczak "Internationale wissenschaftliche Engels Konferenz in Wuppertal" in *Internationale wissenschaftliche Korrespondenz zur Geschichte der Deutschen Arbeiterbewegung* (IWK), no. 10, Berlin (June 1970), pp. 62 ff. A résumé of the "Viewpoints" is found on pp. 81 ff.

[2] *Friedrich Engels, 1820–1970. Referate – Diskussionen – Dokumente.* Internationale wissenschaftliche Konferenz in Wuppertal vom 25–29 Mai 1970. Hanover, Verlag für Literatur und Zeitgeschehen, 1970. We find the following comments on my "position" on pp. 255 f.: "In order to be able to fulfill the program foreseen for the final day, the conference council decided to dispense with discussion following the VIth session and to begin with the general debate immediately after the VIIth session. First of all, Maximilien Rubel was to continue [?] the exposition of his conception. He had submitted to the conference a text formulated in polemic terms and attacking Engels but did not present it subsequently to the assembly [and with reason!]. His eight theses which, according to the author's original intention, were to provoke a debate on the actual significance of Marxism today, may be summarized as follows: After Marx's death Engels devoted much effort to the task of transforming the term "Marxism," which had been coined by Marx's adversaries, into an intelligible and definable concept. In so doing, Engels unwittingly founded a system of hybrid thought which had nothing in common with Marx's own intentions. Following Engels's death the germs of this ideological system developed into a conceptual methodology necessarily dependent on certain class relations."

The report then mentioned a polemic from a preceding session in which my views confronted those of an East German Marxist, Erich Hahn, regarding the concept of "historic mission," a debate "in which Engels played only an indirect part" (ibid., pp. 255 ff.).

Much could be said about this "abridged report" summarizing my theses and the "polemic" that they provoked. However, I only wish to emphasize that my text was

The following is an English rendition, amplified by a number of comments, of the German manuscript that was turned down by the organizers of the Wuppertal conference.

Viewpoints on the theme of "Engels as founder of Marxism"

For the ultimate triumph of the ideas set forth in the Manifesto Marx relied solely and exclusively on the intellectual development of the working class, as it would necessarily ensue from the united action and discussion.

F. Engels, Preface to the 1890 German edition of the *Communist Manifesto*

I

Marxism is not an original product of the Marxian way of thought but was conceived in the mind of Friedrich Engels. Insofar as the term "Marxism" embraces a theoretically apprehensible subject matter, the responsibility lies not with Marx but with Engels. Moreover, if the problem of understanding Marx is still an actual concern in today's world, it is for the most part related to questions that Engels resolved only partially or not at all. If these questions admit of an answer, it is only by returning directly to Marx that we can find it. This is not to say that Engels should be excluded from the current discussion on Marx, but we may justly ask if and to what extent Engels's statements should be taken into account in dealing with writings of Marx that entirely escaped his friend

not intended as an "attack on Engels" but rather, through its criticism of a gesture that proved to be historically negative, was directed against a particular school of Marxist thought whose very existence constitutes the negation of all that Marx and Engels had done for the working-class movement and for socialist thought. And I continue to maintain that my contribution, more than any other, honored the scientific spirit of this conference: Was it not our task to pay our respects in a scientific manner to the originator of "scientific socialism," a concept, moreover, that he equated with "critical socialism"? The only true homage the conference might have paid to the man it was celebrating would have been to adopt as its guideline and the basis of its debates the following statement from a letter of Engels to Gerson Trier (Dec. 18, 1889): "The working-class movement is founded on the most rigorous critique of existing society. Critique is its vital element. How could it dispense itself from self-criticism and prohibit debate?" (*MEW* 37, p. 328).

Engels's attention. In more general terms: What is the extent of Engels's competence, as the unchallenged executor of Marx's intellectual legacy, in answering the material and intellectual questions evoked by Marx's writings?

II

This interrogation leads us to examine a central topic, that of the intellectual relationship between Marx and Engels, both of whom are considered to be the "founders" of a contradictory system of political ideologies and concepts with scientific pretentions, artificially subsumed under the label of Marxism. That this problem is today more urgent than ever points to a phenomenon, highly characteristic of our era, that may be termed twentieth-century constructions in mythology. The "founders" themselves referred more than once to mythological figures when characterizing the particular nature of their friendship and intellectual collaboration: Marx had ironically invoked the example of the "Dioscures" and that of Orestes and Pylades; Engels was amused by the rumor that "Ahriman-Marx had led Ormuzd-Engels" astray of the path of virtue.[3] The opposite is equally possible. Efforts have been made, and with increasing frequency, to oppose Marx and Engels: The former is held to have been the "true founder," the second merely a "pseudodialectician."[4]

III

If we are to investigate the relations between Marx and Engels, we will make no progress until we rid ourselves of the

[3]See the letters from Marx to Engels, Jan. 20, 1864, and Apr. 24, 1867; from Engels to Bernstein, Apr. 23, 1883 (*MEW* 30, p. 387; 31, pp. 290–1; 36, p. 15.) There are even instances where the two friends are referred to as if they were one: i.e. "Marx and Engels says" (see Marx's letter to Engels, Aug. 1, 1856; *MEW* 29, p. 68).

[4]See for example the opposition established by Iring Fetscher between Marx's "proletarian philosophy" and that of Engels. Fetscher also investigates their different ways of interpreting the "negation of philosophy," the relation between human history and natural history and, further, the notion of an "objective" dialectic of history and of thought as a reflection of reality, conceptions necessarily unacceptable for Marx. See I. Fetscher, *Karl Marx und der Marxismus. Von der Philosophie des Proletariats zur proletarischen Weltanschauung* (Munich: 1967), pp. 132 ff. (English ed: *Marx and Marxism* [New York: Herder & Herder, 1971], pp. 162 ff.). See also Donald C. Hodges, "Engels's Contribution to Marxism," *The Socialist Register* (1965), 297–310; Vladimir Hosky, "Der neue Mensch in theologischer und marxistischer Anthropologie," *Marxismusstudien* 7 (1972), 58–86.

legend of a foundation and until we recognize in the rationally indefinable concept of Marxism our methodological point of departure.

To his great merit, Karl Korsch submitted Marxism to a critical examination twenty years ago, prior to a radical revision of his own intellectual positions. Although this critique was so severe as to verge on belligerency, Korsch left it unfinished, for he failed to liberate the concept of Marxism from its mythological elements. Instead, he tried to remove the difficulty by using linguistic artifices designed to save important aspects of the Marxian doctrine for the "reconstruction of a revolutionary theory and *praxis*." In "Ten Theses on Marxism Today" Korsch speaks at random of "the teaching of Marx and Engels," "Marxist doctrine," "Marx's doctrine," "Marxism," and so forth.[5] In the fifth thesis, concerning the predecessors, founders, and continuators of the socialist movement, Korsch omits the name of Engels, Marx's so-called alter-ego.[6] He was not far from discovering the essence of the problem, however, in writing that: "All of the attempts to reestablish Marxist teachings as an entity and restore them in their primary function as the theory of social revolution for the working class have today proved to be reactionary utopias."[7] Korsch might well have spoken, and more appropriately, of "erratic mythologies" rather than "reactionary utopias."

IV

The impossibility of finding a rational definition of the concept of Marxism leads us, consequently, to abandon the term despite its frequent and universal usage. The word has been abused so flagrantly that, today, it is no more than a mystifying catchword; and indeed it has borne the stigma of confusion since its inception.

Toward the end of his life, as he began to acquire a certain reputation for his theoretical and scientific work, Marx engaged in a sustained effort to divorce himself from this concept and repeatedly and peremptorily declared: "All I know is that

[5]"Dix thèses sur le marxisme aujourd'hui," in *Arguments* 2, no. 16 (1959), 26 ff. This text was originally mimeographed and dated "Zürich, September 4, 1950." See also the letter of Korsch to Rubel quoted in the introduction.

[6]Cf. James Guillaume, *La Première Internationale. Documents et Souvenirs* 2 (Paris: Stock, 1907), p. 303.

[7]2nd thesis, Korsch, "Dix thèses . . . ," p. 26.

I am not a Marxist."[8] It is to Engels's credit that he passed on this portentous warning to their sectarian disciples and to posterity, yet this does not relieve him of the responsibility for having ultimately sanctioned the terms "Marxist" and "Marxism" with his authority. As guardian and continuator of a theory that he recognized as having been "discovered" and elaborated by someone other than himself,[9] he was convinced

[8]Engels noted that Marx's declaration was provoked by the "Marxism" rampant "among certain of the French" around 1879–80, but that his reproach also applied to a certain group of intellectuals and students within the German party. The latter, together with all of the "oppositional" press, brandished a "convulsively distorted 'Marxism' " (see Engels's letter to the editors of the *Sozialdemokrat* dated Sept. 7, 1890 and published in this same paper on Sept. 13, 1890; *MEW* 22, p.69). Each time the opportunity arose, Engels made reference to Marx's retort (see his letter to Bernstein, Nov. 3, 1882; to Conrad Schmidt, Aug. 15, 1890; to Paul Lafargue, Aug. 27, 1890; *MEW* 35, p. 388; 37, pp. 436, 450). After discussing with Engels the perspectives of revolution in Russia in September 1883, G. A. Lopatin recounted the essence of their talks in a letter to a member of the *Narodnaiia Voliia*: "I once told you, you will remember, that Marx himself was never a Marxist. Engels reported that at the time of the conflict between Brousse, Malon & Co. and the others Marx remarked with a laugh: 'I can say only one thing, that *I am not a Marxist!*' " (see the passage from Lopatin's letter to M. N. Ochanina, Sept. 20, 1883, translated from the original Russian, in *MEW* 21, p. 489).

There is, however, little amusement in the tone of Marx's letter written to Engels while on a trip to France. Here he shares with his friend his impressions of the quarrels engaged in by the socialists who attended the two simultaneous congresses held at St. Etienne and Roanne ("possibilists" v. "guesdists") in autumn 1882. " 'Marxists' and 'anti-Marxists',," he wrote, "*both kinds* have done their best to spoil my stay in France" (Marx to Engels, Sept. 30, 1882; *MEW* 35, p. 100).

Concerning Marx's differences with the Russian "Marxists" on the subject of the Russian peasant commune and its future see his letter to Vera Zasulitch, March 8, 1881 (in the original French in *Oeuvres*, vol. 2 pp. 1561ff.; in English translation in Marx and Engels, *Selected Correspondence*, Moscow: Foreign Languages Publishing House, n.d, pp. 411ff.). Marx's and Engels's relations with their Russian followers are dealt with in Essay 5 on the Russian commune in this volume.

[9]Such was Engels's formal declaration on numerous occasions. Because space prevents us from enumerating all of them here, let us simply note that he left no doubts whatsoever about the authorship of the great "scientific discoveries" that he attributed to Marx alone.

The most significant of these declarations is perhaps the footnote Engels joined to his text on *Ludwig Feuerbach and the End of Classical German Philosophy* (1888), the object of which was to show the continuity of German philosophy, raising its most distinguished heir, Karl Marx, to the rank of a founder of a system (the German text is found in *MEW* 21, pp. 259–307; English in *MESW* 2, pp. 359–401; see Engels's footnote on p. 385). It is in this writing that Engels formally names the theory after Marx: "Out of the dissolution of the Hegelian school still another tendency developed, the only one which has really borne fruit. And this tendency is essentially linked with the name of Marx" (Ibid., p. 291). Engels repeated the act of christening "Marxism" in a footnote, where he remarked that "what Marx accomplished, I would have been unable to achieve. [. . .] Marx was a genius; we others are at best gifted. Without him,

that in glorifying Marx's name he would be righting a wrong. In so doing, however, he promoted the development of a myth whose devastating intellectual consequences he had by no means anticipated. Today, we can measure the full effect of his questionable consecration. When Engels decided to adopt the designations "Marxist" and "Marxism," forged by his and Marx's adversaries as pejoratives for use in moments of polemic, and to put the followers of "scientific socialism" in defiance of their adversaries by transforming these terms into titles of glory, he hardly expected that his act of defiance (or was it resignation?) made him the spiritual father of a mythology destined to dominate the history of the twentieth century.

V [10]

We can trace the genesis of the Marxist myth beginning with the conflicts within the International Workingmen's Association that first provoked the pejorative use of this term. In the early 1870s Marx's opponents in the IWA, the "antiauthoritarians" headed by Bakunin, were sufficiently motivated in their fight against Marx's influence to create terms such as *marxides, marxistes,* and *marxisme* with which they calumniated their adversary and his supporters. [11]

The word "Marxism" seems to have been used for the first time in the title of a writing in 1882, when Paul Brousse published his polemic brochure, entitled *Le Marxisme dans l'Internationale,* which attacked the "Marxists" in the French socialist party. Gradually, however, the French disciples grew accustomed to the new titles, which they had done nothing to create, and helped develop them from sectarian labels to concepts with political and ideological content.

the theory would not be by far what it is today. It therefore rightly bears his name" (Ibid., p. 292).

After such statements, we can hardly be surprised that the conclusion to this writing declares Marx to be both heir and founder of a philosophical school: "The German working-class movement is the heir of classical German philosophy" (Ibid., p. 307). Engels thus consummated the mésalliance between metaphysics and proletariat, between "Marxist" philosophy and the radical critique of all aspects of existing society.

[10]This thesis or viewpoint is not found in the original version but has been elaborated from the "Introduction" to the German text.

[11]See Margaret Manale, "Aux origines du concept de 'marxisme'," *Etudes de marxologie,* no. 17 (Oct. 1974), 1397–1430; "La constitution du 'marxisme'," Ibid., no. 18 (Apr.–May 1976), 813–39; and "L'édification d'une doctrine marxiste," Ibid., no. 19–20 (Jan.–Feb. 1978), 163–215.

At the outset Engels appears to have been disinclined to use such terminology. More than anyone else, he was aware that it risked corrupting the essential meaning of Marx's writings, which Marx himself considered to be the theoretical expression of an actual social movement and in no sense a doctrine invented by an individual for the use of a political and intellectual elite. Engels resisted the temptation to use such terms until 1889, when the dissensions between possibilists and broussists, on the one side, and collectivists or guesdists on the other, threatened to cause a definitive rupture in the French working-class movement. Engels recognized the manifest danger in employing the terms "Marxist" and "Marxism" and therefore attempted to forestall the risk of confusion and ideological corruption by using quotation marks around them or speaking of the "so-called Marxists." When Paul Lafargue expressed his fear that their group would come to be known as just one "faction," Marxist, within the working-class movement, Engels replied: "We never called you anything but 'the so-called Marxists' and I wouldn't know what else to call you. If you have another name just as short, let us hear it, and we shall duly apply it, with pleasure."[12]

VI

If Nietzsche published *Ecce homo* to prevent unwanted disciples from canonizing him one day, for Marx such a precaution did not appear to be necessary, although he had not been able to finish and to publish more than a fragment of his planned works. All of his printed and unprinted writings alone represent a formal and rigorous interdiction: *his name* was not

[12]Letter from Engels to Lafargue, May 11, 1889; in Friedrich Engels, Paul and Laura Lafargue, *Correspondence*. Vol. II (1887–1890). Paris: Editions Sociales, 1956, p. 251. Once engaged in this sort of verbal concession, Engels could no longer turn back and finally had to go the whole length. He did so at a moment when he thought victory to be assured for the "collectivists" led by Guesde and Lafargue: "But the position we conquered over the Anarchists after 1873 was now attacked by their successors, and so I had no choice. Now we have been victorious, we have proved to the world that almost all Socialists in Europe are 'Marxists' (they will be mad they gave us that name!) and they are left alone in the cold with Hyndman to console them" (Ibid., p. 286).
The irony of fate would have it that the same Hyndman had received a letter from Marx in which the latter advised against using his name in the party program of the newly formed English socialists: "In party programs, care must be taken to avoid everything that might show a direct dependence on any particular author or any particular book" (July 2, 1881). *MEW* 35, p. 203.

to be given to the cause for which he had fought and to the teachings that he had believed himself mandated to elaborate in the name of the *anonymous masses* of modern proletarians. Had Engels respected this interdiction, he would have vetoed the use of Marx's name, and Marxism, that fatal worldwide, ersatz religion, might never have come into being. However, Engels committed the inexcusable error of approving this abuse and thus acquired the doubtful honor of being the first Marxist. Although he thought himself to be Marx's heir, he was in fact the founder of the Marxist school, albeit involuntarily—and we are tempted to see in this the revenge of history. Indeed, destiny seems to have played a bad trick on Engels, with the same irony that he often took pleasure in invoking: In spite of himself, Engels proved to be prophetic in writing the following words relative to a celebration in honor of his seventieth birthday: "My fate would have it that I harvest the honour and glory sown by a man who was much greater than I—Karl Marx."[13] On his one hundred fiftieth birthday we are obliged to accord Engels the problematic honor and rank of "founder of Marxism."

VII

Engels occupies the forefront in the history of Marxism as the cult of Marx. The human, quasireligious aspect of Engels's friendship with Marx is sufficiently well known for us to dispense with a special examination of their relations. By contrast, we should investigate in detail the effects of his behavior on Marx, on his followers, and on more distant disciples. In his desire to act as a pioneer of Marx's ideas, Engels wrote much that Marx no doubt was unable to accept uncritically. However, Marx kept silent on these occasions, out of respect for the friendship that bound them in solidarity until the last. We have no way of knowing whether Marx accepted all that Engels thought independently, for instance regarding the "dialectics of nature." Nevertheless, this problem is relatively minor, for we do know that Marx admitted admiration for his friend's talents and even considered himself to be Engels's disciple.[14]

[13]Letter to the editors of the *Berliner Volksblatt*, Dec. 5, 1890. *MEW* 22, p. 86.
[14]Cf. Marx's letter to Engels, July 4, 1864: "You know, primo, that I am always slower in getting onto things and, secundo, that I follow in your footsteps." *MEW* 30, p. 418.

What Marx did not permit himself to do has therefore become a strict duty for those who are studying the works of both men: The task is to break the spell of the mythology surrounding Marx and discover the role of Engels's writings both in developing the intellectual heritage of socialism and in determining the course of the working-class movement.

VIII

Only if we recognize that Engels had the makings of a founder is it possible to understand why he worked at his tasks as editor and continuator of Marx's writings in a way that offers, today more than ever before, serious grounds for criticism.[15] Engels neglected or overlooked a whole series of Marx's writings (such as the preliminary writings for the doctoral dissertation, the Kreuznach critique of the Hegelian philosophy of right, the Paris and Brussels manuscripts, the voluminous first draft of the "Economics" dating from 1857 to 1858 (*Grundrisse*), numerous study notebooks, and his correspondence with third parties), which present new problems of interpretation to the researcher and specialist; what is more, they interest new categories and generations of readers who no longer can and should content themselves with the stereotyped phraseology and orthodoxy of professional Marxists. Their interest is heightened by the imperative of understanding, living, and acting in an era in which ideology, mechanization, and the manipulation of mind and consciousness are associated with political power and pure violence, changing the modern world into a vale of tears.

§

These points are intended as an introduction to a debate to be oriented around the problem of Marxism as the mythology of our modern era. The question of Engels's responsibility in creating this universal process of mystification is of course part of this debate, yet secondary, if we recognize the validity of

[15]See the appendix to essay 3 in this volume, a list in abridged form of Marx's discoveries in political economy that he recognized as his own. Marx never credited himself with the "founding" of "historical materialism" nor with the "discovery" of "surplus value." Engels attributed these innovations to his friend, who appeared to have approved this gesture by his silence. See, for example, Engels's reviews in *Das Volk* of Marx's 1859 *Critique of Political Economy* as well as the biographical article on Marx published in *Volkskalender*, Braunschweig, 1878 (*MEW* 19, pp. 96–106).

Marx's lesson in materialism, which tells us that ideologies—of which Marxism in all its variants and offshoots is one—do not appear as bolts from the blue. They are basically dependent on class interests, which are power interests. If we acknowledge Engels's claim to the Marxian intellectual legacy as legitimate, no other justification is necessary to denounce, in his name and to his honor, all forms of institutionalized Marxism, a school of confusion and illusions for our cataclysmic age of iron.

2

Socialism and ethics

The Marxian dream: utopia and revolution

Seldom have men remained faithful to their adolescent dreams and inspirations with the passionate conviction evidenced by Karl Marx. When, in a German essay written for his final examination in the *Gymnasium* (1835), he proposed that man can reach fulfillment and real humanity only in a truly human milieu, he was anticipating the thesis that would subsequently underlie the teachings of *Capital*. Marx had drawn up early in his career an ambitious plan of work that constantly prompted him to recommence and to undertake more profound study of the original topics whose treatment he had left unfinished. "Self-alienation" and "total man," themes the young Marx had treated in both published and unpublished writings, recur in *Capital*, thus illustrating the author's fidelity to the ethical problems that had first stimulated his genius.

Thanks to the discovery and publication, in 1927 and 1932, of his writings from the period 1844–6, we now have sufficient information to permit an exact definition and evaluation of Marx's "materialist" theory of history. Researchers concerned with historico-critical examination of the Marxian texts are no longer justified in identifying Marx's theory of history with a so-called proletarian *Weltanschauung*, as Engels put it, nor in defining it as speculative "materialism," regardless of how dialectical this might be. There is even less justification for reducing his theory to a doctrine of party strategy and tactics, whether labeled Marxist or not. Moreover we discover that Marx's social utopia, far from contradicting his later economic theories, should be considered the central motivation of his entire life's work. As the proponent of a view of man restored to full humanity, Marx merits a rank among the greatest of the social utopians. Unlike those utopians who propounded visionary means for achieving their socialism, however, Marx gave socialist utopia a rational basis by linking the *ethical postulate* of socialism's realization to the scientific law of capitalism's destruction and the immanent consequences of this for human behavior.

Marx shared with many other liberal minds of the pre-1848 period the notion of an impending socialist revolution in the advanced industrial countries of the Western world. This prospect was so vivid for him that he was led irresistibly to imitate the utopians and elaborate, in a style still strongly marked by the influence of Ludwig Feuerbach, a vision of man in the community of the future. Yet Marx's conception was no fantastic anticipation of a particular social system but simply the image of "integral" or "total" man – man given the opportunity to develop his capacities in the rightful human environment of nonalienated society.[1]

Marx's writings did not abolish utopia; on the contrary, they renewed and enlarged the scope of its meaning. In his thought utopia became a movement with two stages: revolution and creation. Earlier, the utopians had pictured the creation of the New Community independently of its actual construction, and they had generally counted on an elite group to effect the creation. Marx, on the other hand, was primarily concerned with the men who were to build the new world: "We know that to work well the new-fangled forces of society, they only want to be mastered by new-fangled men – and such are the working men."[2]

Initially a disciple of Robert Owen and Charles Fourier, Marx was drawn into direct political activity at an early date, yet he never broke the spiritual ties that bound him to utopian socialism. To confirm this fact, we need only read the statement he prepared two years before his death in answer to the Russian populists who had requested his opinion on the prospects for developing the peasant commune in Russia, which was then menaced by the threat of capitalist penetration. Not once during his long and arduous meditation on this question did Marx dwell on strictly political questions such as the composition of social classes or party organization. His thought was concentrated instead on the particular characteristics of the archaic rural commune as an institution and its importance as the "mainspring of social regeneration in Russia" and a

[1]Cf.the "Paris Manuscripts" of 1844 and *The Holy Family* (1845).
[2]Speech delivered on the anniversary of the *People's Paper*, April 14, 1856; in *MESW* I, p. 360

"source of superiority over the countries enslaved by the capitalist regime."[3]

In his apologia for this "localized microcosm," as Marx called the Russian commune, we can readily detect a last tribute to Robert Owen, the pioneer of cooperative and communal socialism. Like Owen, Marx put all his confidence in the creative spontaneity of those who produce society's wealth without themselves sharing in it. He bestowed upon the primitive commune the virtues of a social microcosm, and his idealization of this obscure institution doubtless bears traits of wishful thinking. It is therefore no accident that Marx sympathized with Owen's utopia as well. Marx envisaged a cooperative commune that would solve the problematic opposition between the Jacobin conception (a political one) and what one might term the communist notion of the working-class movement. According to the former, political avant gardes, who are the first to develop a consciousness of purpose and to initiate action, guide the easy-to-manage masses; in the latter, political elites are deemed superfluous because the smaller size of the action groups permits long-term, and hence "professional" leadership to be dispensed with. Here, the delegation of power does not signify the relinquishing of a right but rather the conferring of a temporary and necessary mandate for explicitly defined tasks of representation.

In a sense Marx is the most utopian of the utopians: Apparently little concerned with the appearance of future society, he is bent chiefly on destroying the existing order and exalts this revolution to an ethical exigence necessitating the total engagement of the modern wage slave. It is the mechanics of this imagined or imaginary revolution that are tinged with utopian elements, for it presupposes men who are capable of comprehensive social criticism, of grasping all aspects of socialist thought, men who are thoroughly conscious of their "gilded" misery. In fact, Marx establishes the economic law of a kind of impoverishment that is more difficult to comprehend than plain and simple privation. Animating the daily struggle of the working class with a utopian outlook, he formulates the dialectics of the proletarian revolution: If the workers are able to desire and to accomplish *their* revolution, they shall get socialism in the bargain. In other words, consciousness of their state of alienation—in the profound sense

[3] *Oeuvres*, vol. 2, pp. 1558, 1573.

that Marx ascribed to this term borrowed from Hegel – gives the working men the strength to destroy capitalist society and construct utopia, that is, a stateless, classless, moneyless society. Marx's conception thus contains a strange paradox. At the apex of destitution the workers are expected to become conscious of the necessity to attain social renewal by means of a cataclysmic *total* revolution. It is indeed a strange sort of "materialism" that conceives of a spiritual metamorphosis in the slaves who have been broken by a pitiless machine and reduced to mere cogs in the immense industrial mechanism that serves the unique goal of profit making.

The law of accumulation, through the agency of the capitalists, condemns the wage laborer to an "accumulation of misery," which is not always translatable in monetary terms and consists of an "agony of toil, slavery, ignorance, brutalization and moral degradation." Yet out of this very accumulation of distress the will to total contestation must arise, the "resistance of the constantly expanding working class, itself ever more disciplined, united and organized by the very mechanisms of the capitalist production process."[4]

The conclusion to *Capital*, Book I, from which the preceding phrases are taken, is written in a style that deliberately parodies that of Hegel and presents the "negation of the negation," that is, the "triumph of the proletariat," as a kind of law inherent in the development of big industry. But actually this triumph is an act of will whose fulfillment is attended by the total subversion of the existing system. What is more, it demands of the proletariat, reduced to an abject condition, a clear consciousness of its creative mission, which embraces the vision of a New Community, the future classless society freed from the chains of capital and the state.[5]

Marx makes no attempt to "compensate" for what might seem to be an illogical element in his dialectics of misery by adding the notion, or theory, of a conscious and knowledgeable elite to offset the lack of consciousness and the ignorance of the disinherited masses. Quite to the contrary, the idea of

[4]*Capital*, Book I; *MEW* 23, pp. 675, 790 ff.

[5]As for "established socialism," Marx would have immediately reorganized its mystifying ideology as just one historically determined variant of that particular mode of production and domination that he often referred to as "oriental despotism." On the characteristics of capitalist society in its different forms, see *MEW* 25, pp. 479, 842, 907. For a discussion of "oriental despotism," see Essay 5 of the present volume, "A visionary legacy to Russia."

the creative spontaneity of the proletariat, *Selbsttätigkeit* in the language of the *Communist Manifesto,* is the central axiom of a dialectics founded on absolute confidence in the emancipatory will of the proletarian class. Although its labor secures the material existence of the entire community, this category of man incorporates "absolute wrong" within society itself. The "real movement" of history is to be understood as the development of modes of production simultaneously with and parallel to the evolution of the forms of collective consciousness, which are by no means simple "reflections" of the former. To produce the revolutionary phenomenon there must be an alliance between "suffering humanity which thinks and thinking humanity which is oppressed."[6] By sublimating their instinctive awareness of distress to the level of *theoretical* consciousness, the working men will be able to recognize the absurdity of the abysmal servitude into which they have fallen, this in an era of lustrous triumphs in science and technology. In their struggle the working men may profit from the assistance of intellectuals who have espoused their interests without actually belonging to the proletarian class and who introduce into it not a ready-made theory or philosophy, nor esoteric doctrines concerning the ends and means of history, but what Marx called "elements of culture." When organizing its struggle, the proletariat constitutes itself as a class; however, the individual workers must never relinquish their initiative to elitist groups or parties that presume to guide them and to prescribe their political and social objectives. As forms of working-class organization, trade unions, parties, and councils are justified only insofar as they are the spontaneous and conscious creations of the working men themselves. The position of the communists is a special one, for they are the "most advanced and resolute faction of the working-class parties in every country" and speak for the movement as a whole. This endows them with a viewpoint that is above the specific interests of the proletarians in any particular country. In his manner of characterizing the communists Marx plainly introduces a normative factor: These men are the "theorists" who, thanks to fortuitous circumstances, "have over the great mass of the proletariat the advantage of clearly understanding the conditions, the course, and the general consequences of the proletarian movement."[7]

[6]Marx to Arnold Ruge (May 1843); *MEW* 1, p. 343.
[7]*Das kommunistische Manifest* (Berlin: 1955), p. 63.

In this context we distinguish "communist party" in the "eminently historical sense" of the term as the indivisible and enduring party of men who adhere to the cause of the modern proletariat and dedicate all their affective and mental energies to it. This "historic party" must not be confounded with any existing working-class parties whose politics are subject to temporal and regional contingencies and that have immediate practical objectives to fulfill. Marx affirmed his fundamental allegiance to the historic party and expressed a certain disdain for the "ephemeral" organizations that can be effective only insofar as they are created spontaneously by the working men in full awareness of the revolutionary aim of their struggles.[8]

Even granted a certain tendency on Marx's part to idealize *la classe la plus nombreuse et la plus misérable,* to use the expression formulated by Saint-Simon, such idealization could only provoke the dissidence of those who have failed to grasp the essence of Marx's vision of the proletariat as a social movement in which all revolutionary initiative emanates from the laboring masses themselves and not from sharp-witted elites who sympathize with their misery.

In the writings that outline his materialist conception of history Marx gave a frankly idealist presentation of the relations between the working class and those who join with it in order to attain for themselves a more thorough comprehension of the proletariat's revolutionary calling. In this relationship not the knowledgeable intellectuals but the conscious working men dominate. Whatever the role of the former, it should in no way resemble a directory avant-garde that determines for or dictates to the others their modes of behavior. Engels thus correctly confirmed Marx's intentions when he stated that to realize the principles expressed in the *Communist Manifesto,* Marx relied exclusively on the intellectual maturity of the working class as it "necessarily had to ensue from united ac-

[8]After the split in the Communist League, Marx, who was living in exile in London, wrote to Engels: "I quite enjoy living in isolation from the public as is now the case with both of us. This is entirely in keeping with our position and our principles. The system of mutual concessions, of superficialities tolerated for propriety's sake, and the obligation of having to publicly assume one's portion of ridiculousness in the party together with all those asses – all this has finally come to an end" (Feb. 11, 1851). In his reply Engels damned the corrupting influence of the political emigration and said he preferred "the position of the free-lance writer who doesn't care a rap about the so-called revolutionary party" (Feb. 12, 1851). (*MEW* 27, pp. 184–5, 186).

tion and discussion."[9] Marx saw these "principles" as deriva-
tions from the "real movement" of the working class. And
because he believed he had deciphered the secret of human
history and had discovered the "economic law" of modern
society, he attributed to the "historic party" of the working
class an essentially educative role. "Communist consciousness"
must emanate from the disinherited masses, and not from an
intellectual "elite."[10] Bourgeois intellectuals cannot become
communists until they have attained the level of revolutionary
consciousness native to the enslaved working men.

Thus we have the paradox of the working-class movement.
Nevertheless, Marx's theory retains its coherence: He distinguishes between socialist consciousness and socialist science,
the latter being possible and necessary only as a function of
the real proletarian movement, which must progress on two
fronts simultaneously, through the growing class consciousness of the proletariat and through political action. When
appointing spokesmen for its political representation the
proletariat voices its will to use the force of law (within the
limits of given institutions) in order to reverse the existing
system; under other circumstances it is obliged to resort to
the law of force. In the Communist Manifesto we read: "The
proletariat constitutes itself as a class and thus as a political
party." In other words, the workers are spontaneously
aroused to group self-consciousness and themselves create
their selfhood instead of joining political parties constituted
outside their own ranks. The bourgeoisie, as a social class, is
united in the pursuit of profit, whereas the cohesion and
unity of the proletarian class is forged in the immediate
struggle for its well being and in its conscious pursuit of a
single revolutionary goal. Marx, and before him, in 1843,
Flora Tristan, formulated this thought in a proposition that
continues to serve as the implicit basis of all genuine socialist
thought: "The emancipation of the working classes must be
conquered by the working classes themselves."[11]

The real problem of the working-class movement is not
therefore the conflict, real or not, between Marxism and

[9]F. Engels, Preface to the 1890 German edition of the Communist Manifesto;
MESW I, p. 31.

[10]The German Ideology; MEW 3, p. 69.

[11]Documents of the First International 1864–66 (Moscow: Foreign Languages
Publishing House, n.d. [1963]), p. 288.

anarchism,[12] Marxism and reformism or revisionism, and so on, but the antagonism between Jacobinism and self-emancipation, which is summarized in the following question: Can social classes retain their autonomy of action and consciousness while relying on representative bodies that have been chosen to express and to defend their collective interests? Socialist thought before Marx was essentially preoccupied with solving this problem, and its response was a description of the "ideal society" in many different versions. Marx not only enriched this legacy of the utopian socialists, he also criticized it, challenging not its fundamental premises but some of the eccentric aspects of these utopian visions. Producers' communes, cooperative enterprises, the unity of labor and culture – in short, the future community liberated from the state and from money – meant for him the revival of the archaic rural commune, the cradle of primitive communism, on the level of modern technological society.

Although Marx often overestimated the political factor in the working-class movement, never did he think that this class should become a passive instrument answering to the dialectical wisdom of a party or an elite group of professional politicians. As we shall see, the utopian element of the revolution according to Marx is contained in *the ethics of proletarian behavior*. The workers' mental and physical alienation is the chief cause of their revolutionary activity and consequently the principle motivating force behind their creative activity in establishing a new social order as well. The proletariat is not only the agent of this transformation, but its subject as well, because it will abolish itself in abolishing wage labor.

Utopia and revolution are the two historical dimensions of the working-class movement, the two perspectives of socialist thought. Utopia is its spacial element, revolution its temporal one. The socialist movement, in other words, must develop in both directions in order to attain fulfillment. Revolution and utopia represent the inseparable, normative bases of socialist ethics – the desire for both revolution and utopia, for the abolition of all existing social orders and the creation of a New Community. This ethical principle is implicit in most socialist doctrines and is the hallmark of numerous thinkers who professed an adherence to communism, socialism, or anarchism.

[12]Cf. M. Rubel, "Marx, théoricien de l'anarchisme," *L'Europe en Formation*, Nos. 163–4 (Oct.–Nov. 1973), 39–54.

To varying degrees it nourished the thought of Owen, Fourier, Saint-Simon, Marx, and Engels no less than that of J. P. Proudhon, M. A. Bakunin, Georges Sorel, Petr Kropotkin, Rosa Luxemburg, and Gustav Landauer.

Socialist ethics, however, must not be confused with the explicit or implicit thought of any particular individual, regardless of how genial he may be or have been, for it expresses the *spirit* of the entire movement. To confound it with the thought of any single person would mean a betrayal of its impersonal nature. Socialist humanism thus signifies the ethics of revolution and utopia. Only when willed and conceived of as an ethical necessity does socialism really become a historical imperative. This is what Marx wanted to convey when he declared: "The proletariat is revolutionary or it is nothing!"[13] Let us add, in order to restore to socialist ethics its fullest meaning, that socialism is either consciously utopian or it is nothing.

Marx's ethics of the social revolution

Kierkegaard, Nietzsche, Marx

Nineteenth-century Europe provided the backdrop for more than one ambitious scheme to furnish a new code of values for advancing industrial society, to give men new reasons for living, new behavioral norms corresponding to the modern way of life. Briefly, in other words, various efforts were made to produce a new ethic. That certain of these attempts continue to attract considerable interest in our times is tangible proof of our failure so far to discover viable principles to guide our actions in this new environment or to give our lives a rational style and establish harmony in a world that, although our own creation, apparently eludes human control. Lacking its own "apostles of truth," or insensible to them, the twentieth century finds itself obliged to exploit the spiritual legacy of its predecessor.

Three thinkers of genius of the previous century, as authors of powerful ethical messages, have left an indelible mark on the remnants of moral consciousness in today's world. Contemporaries, yet unknown to one another, Søren Kierkegaard, Karl Marx, and Friedrich Nietzsche may well be spoken of as severe and incorruptible judges of their age, men who expected

[13]Letter to J. B. von Schweitzer (Feb. 13, 1865); *MEW* 31, p. 446.

that age to achieve fresh tasks oriented toward the new goals of modern times. Each encountered at the start of his intellectual career the same singular phenomenon that was evidently crucial for his mature development: Hegel's "system." In each, this encounter provoked uncompromising opposition to both Hegel and his disciples and inspired a personal *Weltanschauung,* a critical outlook on human existence and human destiny. Rejection of this disappointing thinker, their erstwhile master, facilitated the discovery of their own genial paths. They needed Hegel in order to recognize how not to think and how not to live. Although all three developed fundamentally different conceptions of man and society, past and future, and although their interpretations of the fact of man's existence are indeed irreconcilable, their underlying opposition to Hegel was rooted in a common judgment: In Hegel's so-called philosophy of *becoming* (*Philosophie des Werdens*) they readily perceived an anchylotic and stagnant doctrine that condemned men to submit calmly and consciously to the yoke of a historic fatality whose oracle was proclaimed to be the "system." *Ducunt volentem fata, notentem trahunt.* However, these three critics were endowed with the ability to dissipate the tenebrae of the Hegelian construction, which impeded their view of our teeming, pulsating world and to observe this world, shorn of all embellishments, in its magnificence no less than its wretchedness. Acting according to his own particular genius and temperament, each selected the field best suited for him to participate in the material and spiritual battles of a mankind now standing at the crossroads of its destiny.

In the works of Søren Kierkegaard we find frequent attacks on Hegel. One of his principal writings, the *Afsluttende uvidenskabelig Efterskrift til de Philosophiske Smuler* (1846; Eng. trans. as *Concluding Unscientific Postscript*) contains a scalding critique of Hegelian thought for its original sin, the absence of any ethics. According to this eminent Danish theologian and scholar, Hegel's gross fault is to be found in his philosophy of history: "In spite of all that Hegel says about process, he does not understand history from the point of view of becoming, but with the help of the illusion attaching to pastness understands it from the point of view of a finality that excludes all becoming."[14] Real *becoming* (*Werden*) is the activ-

[14]*Kierkegaard's Concluding Unscientific Postscript,* trans. D. Swenson and W. Lowrie (Princeton; 1941), p. 272.

ity of present generations of living men who ask questions about the future course of their world; however, those with questioning minds who desire to learn how they should act will find no answers in Hegel. Hegel can only teach them about "what is past and finished" – obviously unsatisfying for a living being whose real existence, not his comprehension of a dead past, is at stake. "Hegelian philosophy, by failing to define its relation to the existing individual, and by ignoring the ethical, confounds existence."[15]

Kierkegaard judges Hegel with particular severity for having treated the problem of Christianity as if it were a topic of abstract speculation: For the true Christian the message of his own existence is in question. Strange as it may seem, Kierkegaard evidences sympathy for Ludwig Feuerbach, the "scoffer" who "attacks Christianity and at the same time expounds it so reliably that it is a pleasure to read him."[16] The alienation of religious man that Feuerbach denounced as an impoverishment is for Kierkegaard a true Christian virtue, and he exhorts the Christian to emulate the representation Feuerbach gave in *Das Wesen des Christentums* (1841). Those who call themselves Christians should *become* Christian, should "die to the self." Like Feuerbach he concedes that official Christianity no more resembles the Christianity of the New Testament than the square resembles the circle; but whereas Feuerbach condemned the imitation of Christ, Kierkegaard held it to be the sole postulate of ethics.

No critic ever attacked the Church and Christendom with the intention of destroying Christianity as fiercely as Kierkegaard did in the hope of saving it. He tried to be a "witness for the truth," that is, a person for whom truth was so thoroughly a "heartfelt matter of inwardness" that he became an occasion for scandal in "the established order."[17] It is therefore hardly astonishing to find that in our day as well Kierkegaard remains a subject of controversy in academic and speculative circles. Desirous neither of founding a new philosophic school nor of establishing new ethical norms, he postulated the imitation of Christ as the criterion of noble life. Thanks to his inimitable mastery of language, he succeeded, moreover, in lending new

[15]Ibid., p. 275.
[16]Ibid., p. 543.
[17]From *Indøvelse i Christendom* (1850); Eng. translation: *Training in Christianity*, trans. W. Lowrie (London: 1941), p. 88.

vitality to the fundamental principle of all ethics: the mediation between the Ideal and real existence.[18]

Hegel's star had not yet faded from the intellectual horizon of Bismarckian Germany when Friedrich Nietzsche launched his first appeals to the Western world for a radical renewal of human values, appeals that were at the same time calls for revolt against the bourgeois civilization of superabundance. While still very young, Nietzsche had come under the intellectual influence of Arthur Schopenhauer, the first philosopher to unmask the "Hegelian harlequinade" and the first European advocate of the Buddhist virtues of self-denial and compassion. However, Nietzsche's only heritage from his earliest teacher was a certain contempt for academic philosophy. As he wrote to Erwin Rohde, "A completely radical institution for *truth* is not *possible* here. Above all, from here nothing really revolutionary can come."[19] At this time he was himself preparing to forge these truths and to assume the role of philosopher-legislator. One of Nietzsche's finest essays, *Vom Nutzen und Nachtheil der Geschichte für das Leben* (1874), is an attack on historicism, the illness of his century, and its keenest critical blows are reserved for Hegel:

History understood in this Hegelian way, has been contemptuously called God's sojourn upon earth – though the God was first created by the history. He, at any rate, became transparent and intelligible inside Hegelian skulls, and has risen through all the dialectically

[18]After having voided the Kierkegaardian message of its ethical and religious contents, Martin Heidegger developed into an ardent proponent of a philosophy adaptable to any cause – even that of Hitler. In his Hegel critique, Kierkegaard anticipated that judgment that, in our times, might well be passed on similar abuses: "Why has Hegel treated conscience and the conscience-relationship in the individual, as a 'form of the evil'? Why? Because he deified the established order" (*Training in Christianity*, p. 88). And while we are dealing with the latter-day tergiversations of philosophic Marxism, we should by no means overlook the following remark – a veritable challenge to rational, dialectical, or nondialectical thinking: "Marxism is history itself in the process of attaining consciousness of self" (Jean Paul Sartre, *Critique de la raison dialectique*. Vol. 1: Théorie des ensembles pratiques. Paris: 1960, p. 142). Can the author of this statement possibly be unaware that in representing Marx's teachings as purely metaphysical substantialization he is committing the gravest offense possible against the latter? Equally unworthy of the ethical exigencies postulated by the thinker who produced both *Capital* and the 1844 "Economic and Philosophic Manuscripts" is a certain critique of the above verbal fiction that questions its compatibility with a "dialectic philosophy of nature in the sense of Hegel and Marx" (cf. Raymond Aron, *Histoire et dialectique de la violence*. Paris: 1973, p. 235).

[19]Letter of Dec. 15, 1870, in *Selected Letters of Friedrich Nietzsche*, ed. and trans. C. Middleton (Chicago & London: 1969), p. 73.

possible steps in his being up to the manifestation of the Self: so that for Hegel the highest and final stage of the world-process came together in his own Berlin existence.[20]

The cult of history implies resignation to fait accompli, mechanical submission to whatever has triumphed and to established power. Nietzsche condemned this cult as a new mythology and protested as well against its priests for their sacrifices to the "power of history." He demanded the creation of a new concept of history, one that would be opposed to Hegel's and would serve life and life's values. Historic truth according to Nietzsche should reflect a judgment of the world; historians should be the judges of the past and the builders of the future. Henceforth history must be a challenge to the future not a remembrance of the past, a call to action instead of dispassionate contemplation: Man must cease dreaming of the new world and set out to conquer it. What sort of world will this be? It will be the world of Olympian man, of the exceptional individual. History as the history of the masses will come to a close, introducing a new era of men gifted with enlightened genius and unbending will, which will ultimately lead to history as the product of Caesars blessed with the soul of Christ.

Kierkegaard and Nietzsche, both opposed to the Hegelian system for its failure to challenge their spirits eager for creative expression, chose divergent paths toward that attainment of the human ideals they wished to equal.[21] Without an ethic, Hegelian philosophy of *becoming,* as a philosophy of freedom, proved sterile. Kierkegaard, Nietzsche, and Marx recognized this fact; to remedy the deficiency, the first proposed the imitation of Christ; Nietzsche called for the imitation of Caesar. It was Marx's vocation to establish the ethics of man created in the image of Prometheus, the god who challenged Jupiter.

In our times Marx's personality and his writings have nourished more political and philosophical controversy than any other intellectual figure or any other works of the kind. The dispute centered around Marx erupted shortly after the death

[20]*The Use and Abuse of History* in *Thoughts Out of Season,* Part II, trans. A. Collins (New York: 1964), p. 71. In *Die fröhliche Wissenschaft* (1882) Nietzsche judges Hegel more indulgently, according him the virtue of having been the first to introduce the notion of "evolution" in science: "Without Hegel there would have been no Darwin." (English trans.: *The Joyful Wisdom,* trans. T. Common. New York: 1964, p. 306.)

[21]On the intellectual affinity between these two thinkers, see Karl Jaspers, *Psychologie der Weltanschauungen* (1919).

of Friedrich Engels, who had been the faithful guardian of his friend's intellectual heritage; and, as the theories Marx presented in *Capital* and the political principles he established as inspirer of the International Working Men's Association have become more and more deeply involved in the worldwide economic and social struggles of the proletariat, they have engendered ever greater controversies. After more than half a century of "Marxism" and "anti-Marxism" we are forced, therefore, to acknowledge that neither the personality nor the teachings of this man so devoutly worshipped by his admirers and mercilessly attacked by his detractors have been elucidated as yet in any definitive way.[22]

Is Marxism a philosophy or a method of scientific investigation? An economic theory or the canon law of revolutionary or reformist political behavior? Is there a Marxist epistemology, and, if so, is it materialist or idealist, parallelist or epiphenomenalist? Is Marxism monist or pluralist? Humanist or amoralist? Is the validity of the concept of historical materialism limited strictly to the domain of history or does it extend

[22]Marx's would-be biographers, past and present, have been greatly handicapped by the lack of a complete edition of his extant writings. The first project for a *Marx-Engels-Gesamtausgabe* (MEGA) was begun in 1925 by David Riazanov under the auspices of the Marx-Engels Institute in Moscow. However, publication of the material collected by this prominent scholar came to a stop in 1931, when he was deprived of his position and deported. The reasons for his disgrace have never been divulged. His successor, Victor Adoratski, assumed the task of editing what remained of the forty-four volumes originally projected by Riazanov. A total of eleven volumes had appeared by 1935, at which time publication once again broke off. In 1939 and 1941 the Marx-Engels-Lenin Institute published, surprisingly enough, the so-called "Fundaments of a Critique of Political Economy" (*Grundrisse*), certainly Marx's most decisive work prior to *Capital*.

(1969) We call the reader's attention to the existence of a German edition, hitherto the most complete, of the works of Marx and Engels: the *Werke* in thirty-nine volumes, published in East Berlin between 1956 and 1968; two complementary volumes have also been published recently.

(1978) A new MEGA was begun in 1972, projected at one hundred volumes and announced by a "specimen volume" elaborated jointly by the Soviet and East German Institutes for Marxism-Leninism. To date, six volumes have appeared, at least three of which contain new, previously unedited material. Characteristic of the spirit in which this edition is conceived is the following passage from the "Preface to the Complete Works": "Such an edition answers to urgent demands of science and revolutionary praxis in the present era, as the Marxist-Leninist theory gains increasing importance in social life and as the historical greatness of Marx's and Engels's achievement in founding scientific communism appears with ever greater persuasiveness" (vol. I, 1, Berlin: Dietz Verlag, 1975, p. 19). No less indicative of the general orientation and the method of this enterprise—termed an "ideological task"—is the fact that this same preface speaks of Marx and Engels as the "founders of Marxism."

to all scientific disciplines, to biology, physics, psychology, and even ethics, in the form of dialectical materialism? Our problem is how to reconcile the many diverse and contradictory interpretations of Marxism, each one elaborated on the basis of actual writings of Marx. Indeed, it appears justifiable to conclude a priori that any such effort toward conciliation must inevitably fall short; even worse, it could lead to a new exigesis, thereby increasing the number of Marxisms and augmenting the existing ideological chaos.

There is but one way to salvage the unity of Marx's thought: to identify and expose the basic inspiration and orientation of his many political activities and theoretical endeavors. We must extricate the central impulse, the leitmotiv, of his life-work from its intellectual matrix and its operational context.

Marx's genius, his originality and uniqueness, derives quite simply from the fact that he sought and found the elements of his teachings at the heart of his own humanness. Herein, then, lies the true key to the significance of the Marxian message.

Marx and Marxism

At Marx's graveside Friedrich Engels delivered a brief and moving funeral oration in which he sketched an intellectual portrait of his lifelong friend, unaware, however, that his words contained the germ of a new social ideology, of still another deceptive intellectual pitfall. Under the label of Marxism this ideology has ultimately swelled to encompass a veritable babel of divergent interpretations, all claiming to represent Marxian thought. What, then, were Engels's remarks? Beginning with a summary of Marx's theoretical accomplishments as the author of *Capital,* he praised his friend's two "discoveries" – the "law of the development of human history" and the "specific law of motion governing the present-day capitalist mode of production." He proceeded next to pay homage to Marx the publicist and the propagandist of the International – the "revolutionary" in contrast to the "man of science" who was "not even half the man."[23] In thus attributing to Marx a "double personality," so to speak, Engels, who had been his close collaborator for nearly four decades, presumably wanted to eulogize the universality and richness of his best friend's

[23]*Reminiscences of Marx and Engels* (Moscow, n.d.), p. 349.

genius, and saw no harm in separating the theorist in Marx from the revolutionary. Because his "two souls" harmonized so perfectly, there was evidently no Faustian enigma to be solved there.

Until his death in 1895 Engels served the first generation of Marxists as executor of Marx's literary testament, and through his firm counsel and encouragement showed himself to be an alert mentor, giving when necessary his own commentary and making essential rectifications of certain Marxian theses that tended to ambiguity. Thanks to his efforts, both the image of the Marxian personality and the works were protected from bias and distortion, and Engels's own writings were readily accepted as the legitimate continuation of Marxian teachings.

However, this situation changed radically after Engels's death. Initiated by Eduard Bernstein, one of Engels's direct disciples, Marxist heresy arose under the sign of "revisionism." Bernstein attacked precisely the most vulnerable point in Marxian teaching: its dualism. He attempted to separate "systematically" what he termed "the pure science of Marxist socialism" from its "applied aspect,"[24] maintaining that a critical revision of the latter had to be undertaken. Marx's political errors, Bernstein stressed, resulted from the fundamental flaw in his theory, namely, the dialectical method adopted from Hegel.[25] Using quotations taken from various Marxian texts, or when necessary from the writings of Engels, Bernstein succeeded with apparent facility in proving that Marx had contradicted himself, and thereby justified his elimination of the truly revolutionary elements in Marx's teachings.

It is no secret what became of Bernsteinian revisionism: Although officially rejected by the German Social Democrats, it in fact continued to inspire political praxis until the eve of World War I and even thereafter, despite serious attacks leveled at it by Karl Kautsky and Rosa Luxemburg.[26] Using a heavily metaphorical idiom, Rosa Luxemburg took Bernstein to task for his remark that theorizing should remain the affair of an "academic elite." "The entire strength of the modern labor movement rests on theoretic knowledge . . . ," she wrote,

[24]*Die Voraussetzungen des Sozialismus und die Aufgaben der Sozialdemokratie* (Stuttgart: 1899), p. 11.

[25]"Marx and Engels attained greatness in their work not thanks to Hegelian dialectics but in spite of it" (Ibid., p. 36).

[26]K. Kautsky, *Bernstein und das sozialdemokratische Programm* (Stuttgart, 1899).

"only when the great mass of workers take the keen and dependable weapons of scientific socialism in their own hands will the petty bourgeois inclinations, all the opportunist currents, come to naught . . . Quantity will do it!"[27]
For his part, Kautsky refuted only superficially the Bernsteinian critique of Marxian thought, which claimed to have discovered a gross dualism of irreconcilable contradictions in Marxism. Kautsky countered that this dualism was a pure figment of Bernstein's imagination and that Marx's merit lay in his creation of a "superior" synthesis between utopian socialism and the revolutionary movement. In other words, Marx had given socialism a scientific basis. It was Rosa Luxemburg, however, who proved to be profoundly intuitive in commenting that the Marxian dualism is nothing other than "the dualism of the socialist future and the capitalist present," "of capital and labor," "of the bourgeoisie and the proletariat," or, "the scientific reflection of the dualism existing in bourgeois society, the dualism of the class antagonism writhing inside the social order of capitalism."[28]
This discussion provoked by Bernstein at the heart of German social democracy generated currents within Marxist circles in other countries as well. In France it found a noteworthy polemicist in Georges Sorel, who immediately welcomed Bernstein's efforts as a "return to Marxist *esprit*."[29] Sorel, in turn, also tried to clarify the dualist aspect of Marx's theories, drawing attention to the purpose underlying this "dualism": Revolutionary socialism could not in fact dispense with the *social myth*. Marx's presentation of the proletarian revolution as the inevitable outcome of a historical process was formulated in the language of an activist and not that of a critical historian.[30] Arturo Labriola in Italy set himself against Marx the economist for having authored a sterile metaphysics of economy, yet emphasized Marx's importance as a socialist and inventor of the "definitive research method for investigat-

[27]Rosa Luxemburg, *Sozialreform oder Revolution?* (Leipzig: 1899); quoted from *Reform or Revolution*, trans. Integer, 2d ed. (New York: Pathfinder Press, 1973), pp. 9–10.
[28]*Sozialreform oder Revolution?* 2d ed. (Leipzig: 1908); *Reform or Revolution*, p. 40.
[29]"Les Polémiques pour l'interprétation du marxisme," *Revue internationale de sociologie* (1900).
[30]*La Décomposition du marxisme* (Paris: 1908), 3d ed. (Paris: 1926), pp. 58 ff. Sorel developed the topic of social myth in his *Réflexions sur la violence* (Paris: 1908).

ing the essential characteristics of human societies."[31] Like Sorel, Labriola considered revolutionary syndicalism to be the true continuation of the Marxian tradition.

During the early part of this century it was Lenin who carried on the Russian version of the revisionism quarrel in a theoretical battle first against the Mensheviks. In addition to the extensive internal opposition within the Russian Marxist camp itself, Lenin also had to face the incisive criticism voiced by Rosa Luxemburg.[32] As these discussions on the real significance of the Marxian message intensified and the number of its interpreters continued to grow, new clouds gathered around the image of this thinker whose name has been used to designate one of the most widespread modern ideologies. Marx gradually became a kind of oracle whose sibylline revelations had to be painstakingly investigated by a new hermeneutics. Eschewed by his enemies and distorted by those interested in exploiting him, Marx's thought has continually provoked the most contradictory interpretations and has been demonstrated, with equal incisiveness and equal vigor, to be both completely impotent and thoroughly valid.

This unusual situation might well be interpreted as proof of the enormous vitality in Marx's thought. In reality, however, if we judge according to the attitude of those for whom his message was originally destined, Marx was never less alive than he is today. The world's proletariat remains indifferent to his fundamental appeal while the ideological disputes over his intellectual legacy are conducted *pro domo,* so to speak, among specialists who are far removed from the scenes of conflict where the disinherited masses are fighting for material security while remaining ignorant of their "historic mission."

This controversy over Marx stems from a fundamental misunderstanding that has marred all previous interpretations of his life work, irrespective of whether they refuted the contention of a dualism in Marxian thought or reduced this dualism to a theoretic variance in order to reconcile more adeptly the inherent contradiction. Engels's sharp and arbitrary dissection of his friend's personality showed an evident lack of foresight. Marx, the man of science, was not even "half the man"; "before all else" he had been a revolutionary. Was Marx, then, not a revo-

---

[31] *Karl Marx, l'économiste, le socialiste* (Paris: 1909), p. 196.

[32] "Organisationsfragen in der russischen Sozialdemokratie," *Iskra* and *Die neue Zeit* (1904).

lutionary theorist? Did he himself attribute less revolutionary significance to his own scientific "discoveries" than to the technical inventions of someone like the physicist Marcel Deprez, for instance? Had he not contributed more as the author of *Capital* to the emancipation of the modern proletariat than as editor-in-chief of the *Rheinische Zeitung* or as correspondent to the *New York Daily Tribune* or even as the inspirer of the International Working Men's Association? It would of course be unreasonable to attach excessive importance to a funeral oration delivered three days after Marx's death by his closest friend; unreasonable, that is, if it were only possible to overlook the manner in which Engels sacrificed the basic integrity of his friend's personality to an ambiguous description of his various titles of glory. Despite his great talents, or perhaps because of them, Engels lacked that particular gift of intuition that would have enabled him to detect the touch of genius that highlighted Marx's revolutionary career.[33]

The key to the problem of the evident dualism in Marx's teachings can be found only in an understanding of the true originality that characterized his genius. We shall never arrive at a solution if we cling to the traditional method of interpreting his theory, a method that permits everything to be proved without clarifying anything. We must of course make reference to his writings and even use them as aids in grasping the uniqueness of Marx's personality. Yet instead of limiting ourselves to an investigation of theoretical propositions, and thereby creating an artificial corpus of speculative doctrines, we shall try to approach and understand this particular type of man, a poetic genius of social science.

More than his other writings, Marx's autobiographical remarks disclose both the orientation and inspiration of his work. In his correspondence, for example, we find numerous allusions to the psychological factors that motivated his theoretical endeavors and political activity. The following excerpt is taken from a letter written to a friend shortly after he had finished preparing the manuscript of *Capital* (Book 1):

[33]At Marx's graveside Engels reportedly pronounced a second remark that attests to a "Marxist" way of thinking and would have been energetically rebuked by his friend. Speaking of Marx's "real mission in life," that is, to "contribute to the liberation of the modern proletariat," Engels proclaimed that "*he* was the first to make [the proletariat] conscious of its own position and its needs, conscious of the conditions of its emancipation" (*Reminiscences* ..., p. 349). Contained in this statement is the germ of future "Leninism."

Well, why didn't I answer you? Because I was constantly hovering at the edge of the grave. I therefore had to use *every* moment when I was able to work to finish my book, to which I have sacrificed health, happiness and family. I trust that this explanation needs no postscript. I must laugh at the so-called "practical" men and their wisdom. If one chose to be an ox, one could of course turn one's back to the sufferings of mankind and look after one's own skin. But I should really have considered myself *impractical* if I had checked out without completely finishing my book, at least in manuscript form.[34]

Paul Lafargue reported the following words of Marx regarding scientific work and the scholar's responsibility: "Science must not be selfish pleasure: those who have the good fortune to be able to devote themselves to scientific pursuits must be the first to place their knowledge at the service of humanity."[35]

Although abuse of the epithet "idealist" has gradually stripped it of any positive connotation, we are at a loss to choose another qualifying term in designating statements such as these, which reveal the profound personal convictions of their author.[36] Their inspirational source is evident: A powerful ethical persuasion motivates such disclosures. It would, however, surpass the limits of our inquiry were we to seek a definition of the specific ethical orientation of Marx's thought or its relation to any moral system, as has been the aim of numerous Marxist ideologues.[37] Marx's own account of the influences that had been essential to his intellectual development was explicit enough for us to conclude to the uselessness of trying to affix the label of any specific moral philosophy to Marx's thought at the risk of flagrantly mutilating it.

Promethean materialism

Marx discovered his own intellectual path while trying to flee the false charms of Hegelian philosophy. Several arduous years of struggle passed before he finally disengaged himself entirely from the captivating hold of the "system" whose "craggy mel-

---

[34]Letter to Siegfried Meyer (Apr. 30, 1867); *MEW* 31, p. 542.

[35]*Reminiscences . . .* , p. 72.

[36]"Marx's own life with its ostracisms, grinding poverty, refusal to compromise truth and revolutionary honor, is an illustration of what his ethical values were." Sidney Hook, *Towards the Understanding of Karl Marx* (London: V. Gollancz, 1933), p. 92.

[37]Cf. Max Adler, *Marxistische Probleme* (Stuttgart: 1913) and Karl Vorländer, *Kant und Marx*, 2d ed. (Tübingen: 1926).

ody" he compared to a siren's seductive song. Even before he had finished his university studies, in his doctoral thesis on Democritus and Epicurus, Marx seemed to have been preoccupied with Hegel the "mystifier." In his thesis, stress was placed on the ethical aspect of Epicurus's doctrines: His opposition to all ideologies and myths and his exaltation of contingency as a possibility open to man to escape divine fatality and attain freedom. Marx made no secret of his preference for the Epicurean concept of nature, which rejects objective causality and restores individual consciousness to the active principle of human experience. Democritus was the philosopher who renounced a royal crown in order to devote himself to the search for a new etiology and in the end committed suicide, despairing of his goal. Epicurus, by contrast, showed only disdain for universal determinism and considered the senses to be the heralds of truth: He sought *ataraxia* in the consciousness of self.[38]

In the preface to his thesis Marx attempted to enliven Epicurus's libertarian philosophy with Prometheus's titanic insolence. Henceforth he adopted the Promethean creed "I detest all gods" as his own, and he therefore defended his own cause when he affirmed that motto as philosophy's challenge "to all the gods of heaven and earth who fail to acknowledge human consciousness as the supreme divinity."[39] At the conclusion of the preface Marx assigned Prometheus a place of honor among the saints and martyrs of the philosophic calendar, thus marking his choice of a view of life that conceives man's existence as a gigantic battle against the forces of barbarism and as the terrestrial mission of constructing the City of Brotherhood.

Thus, beginning with his first philosophical writings, Marx subscribed to the viewpoint that thought is a function of active life, and he aspired, confronting a world in decay, to be the herald of a new world. This desire soon led him to turn his back on Hegel, the idolater of the established order. While he was preparing the preliminary notes for his thesis, Marx silently combated the "system," leaving unnamed the philosopher whom he would soon denounce openly for his dangerous "mystification." In these notes he contrasts philosophy with

[38]Auguste Cornu, *La Jeunesse de Karl Marx* (Paris: 1934). Cornu underscores the reasons for Marx's attraction to Epicurus, in particular, that the latter's physics "does not constitute an end in itself as in Democritus, but is the basis for an ethics which it serves to confirm" (Ibid., p. 120).

[39]*On the Difference between the Philosophies of Nature in Democritus and Epicurus* (1841); in *MEW*, supp. vol. 1, p. 262.

the real world, and comments on the emptiness that this contrast leaves in the heart of a man possessed by the desire for self-realization and driven by a "consuming flame" that compels him to turn toward the "exterior world." Marx insists on the necessity of eliminating the chasm between the real world and philosophy and employs here, for the first time, that characteristically Marxian formula that he retained even in his most mature works: *The realization of philosophy is at the same time its subversion.* As Marx's thought matured, this phrase, once removed from the stifling context of Hegelian scholastics, was to assume a profoundly ethical significance.

After exiling himself from Germany in late 1843, Marx began his life as a pariah, voluntarily abandoning his status in the bourgeois world.[40] He chose this crucial moment for an act of intellectual self-examination aimed at disengaging, for incorporation into his own concept of history, what he considered to be the fundamental element in Hegelian phenomenology: the idea of man's self-creation. During this period of soul searching he also made a first critical study of political economy and elaborated his conclusions in a series of unpublished manuscripts, now commonly referred to as the "Paris Manuscripts." Summarizing the results of these studies, he wrote:

Thus the chief merit of Hegel's *Phenomenology* and of its final result – the dialectic of negativity as the moving and creative principle – is first of all that Hegel conceives of man's self-creation as a process and of objectification as . . . alienation and transcendence of this alienation. He thus grasps the true nature of *labor* and understands objective man – true man because real man – as the product of his *own efforts.*[41]

However, Hegel's man is not a real human being with all his faculties, but just a partial aspect of this being, for Hegel transformed the consciousness of self, a human *predicate,* into the subject itself. He therefore does not conceive of human labor as concrete, sensuous activity but simply as abstract speculation; for Hegel, man's life and action are matters only of

---

[40]"Marx shared the lot of the modern proletariat not only in the wretchedness of his material life but also in the total insecurity of his existence." Franz Mehring, *Karl Marx. Geschichte seines Lebens* (Leipzig: 1918), 5th ed. (Leipzig: 1933), p. 263. See also the excellent biography of Boris Nicolaievsky and Otto Maenchen-Helfen that contains documents unknown to Mehring: *Karl Marx, Man and Fighter* (London: Allen Lane The Penguin Press, 1973).

[41]*MEW,* supp. vol. 1, p. 572.

speculative thought, and consequently his conflicts with the
world are merely collisions between categories of thought; triumphs and defeats are nothing more than manifestations of
the dialectical vicissitudes of ideas. Self-creation is for Hegel a
purely formal and abstract act of human thought; alienation
(*Entfremdung*) is therefore a speculative operation that can be
overcome by another operation of the same order, that is, by
the negation of the negation. Hegel reduces total reality and
the real totality of man to a function of the human mind. And
this mind is, par excellence, the eminently encyclopedic mind
of Hegel himself.

At a later date Marx again took up Hegel's *Logic* and,
caught by the allure of Hegel's "method of writing," he felt "a
desire to make intelligible . . . to the average mind the *rational*
element of the method discovered and at the same time mystified by Hegel."[42] When he wrote these lines to Engels, he could
hardly have forgotten that during the period in which he first
espoused the cause of communism, he and Engels had together
begun the work of "purifying" Hegel in *The Holy Family*
(1845) and *The German Ideology* (1846). In the former work
Marx had exposed the extreme conservatism of the Hegelian
system, which paraded behind a revolutionary mask. He nevertheless recognized that the "Hegelian phenomenology, despite its speculative original sin, provides in more than one
respect the necessary elements of a true description of the human condition."[43] On the other hand, the Young Hegelians
(Bruno Bauer and his consorts) had produced merely an empty
caricature of their master's thought by substituting "criticism"
for "absolute knowledge" and "categories" for "ideas." *The
Holy Family* is marked throughout by an intense preoccupation with questions of ethics, a preoccupation that shows itself
both negatively and positively: negatively in a condemnation
of both the master morality represented by the elite "critical"

[42]Letter to Engels (Jan. 16, 1858); *MEW* 29, p. 260. At the time Marx was writing
his *Contribution to the Critique of Political Economy*. In view of such remarks, Pierre
Naville's contention that "Marx spoke time and again of a book on Hegel" seems
unfounded. *Psychologie, marxisme, materialisme* (Paris: 1946), p. 174. In fact, Marx
wrote such a book in 1843 to unmask Hegel the "sophist," but this manuscript, the
"Critique of Hegel's Philosophy of the State," was not published until 1927. Furthermore, Marx held Joseph Dietzgen's work on *Das Wesen der menschlichen Kopfarbeit*
(1869) to be a masterful and rational exposé of dialectics, although the author was at
the time not yet familiar with Hegel's philosophy.

[43]*MEW* 2, p. 205.

cult of Hegel's followers and the slave morality apotheosized in Christian resignation, and positively in a profession of faith in the theses of eighteenth-century French materialism concerning the importance of man's empirical milieu for the development of human personality. Following Feuerbach's example, Marx adopted from Paul Henri d'Holbach the notion that "for man the most essential of all beings is man himself" and made this the fundamental principle of his concept of society. Moreover, Marx was simply paraphrasing C. A. Helvetius when he wrote: "If man is not free in the materialist sense—free, that is, not in the negative sense of being able to avoid this or that, but in the positive sense of being able to realize his own personality—then we have no right to punish crime in the individual, but instead we must destroy the antisocial wards of crime and provide each individual with the social latitude he needs to develop his life to the fullest."[44]

Hoping to close the most important gap in Hegelian philosophy, the Young Hegelians had instead become the proponents of a moral doctrine whose postulates were the logical consequences of the "system" itself: Because reality is a function of self-consciousness, which thus is responsible for the fetters and illusions that bind the individual, a simple metamorphosis of consciousness is all that is needed to change the world. The most resolute spokesman for such faith in the omnipotence of creative consciousness was Max Stirner. His eccentric book, *Der Einzige und sein Eigentum* (1845), was written in defiance of all philosophies, religious faiths, and moral and political doctrines, and it propounded an intellectual nihilism that denies the existence of everything except the ego of the author himself, who arrogantly asserts in the form of an epilog, "I have founded my cause on *nothingness*."[45]

Stirner's book received such acclaim that Marx and Engels felt it necessary to devote a lengthy pamphlet to it. The manuscript of this pamphlet was then incorporated into *The German Ideology,* forming its largest section; but for lack of a publisher the entire manuscript was ultimately abandoned to

[44]*MEW* 2, p. 138. On the materialist morality of the encyclopedists the reader is referred to Pierre Naville's instructive work: *d'Holbach et la philosophie scientifique au XVIIIe siècle* (Paris: 1943).

[45]For a perceptive account of the relationship between Stirner's book and the thought of Marx and of Engels, the latter independently of his friend and collaborator, see R. W. K. Paterson, *The Nihilistic Egoist Max Stirner* (New York, London, & Toronto: Oxford University Press, 1971), in particular pp. 105–22.

the "gnawing criticism of the mice." It is here nonetheless that we find the clearest and most methodical exposition of the materialist conception of history as conceived by its principal author, Marx,[46] who seems to have wanted to distance himself entirely from Hegel and the Hegelians by denying any autonomy or creative function whatsoever to human consciousness. The various manifestations of man's mental activity are depicted as "direct emanations from material behavior." Marx summarized this extreme standpoint in the following formula: "It is not consciousness that determines life, but life that determines consciousness."[47] In 1859, when reviewing the outcome of his 1844–5 studies in Paris and Brussels, Marx again employed this formula in a slightly different wording.[48]

Can we therefore describe the originality of Marxian thought as a "reversal" of Hegelian dialectics, as Marx stated in his 1873 afterword to the second edition of *Capital*, Book I? Was he interested only in "putting back on its feet" the dialectic he found "standing on its head" in Hegel? Had he not accomplished more than simply overturning the pedestal that Hegel and his disciples had erected as a prop for man's *self-consciousness*, that same self-consciousness on behalf of which Epicurus had rebelled against religious superstition? Had Marx done no more than substitute a materialist philosophy for Hegel's idealistic one?

The 1873 afterword appears to offer a definitive answer to these questions, an answer authored, however, not by Marx but by a Russian critic whose interpretations of the dialectical method used in *Capital* Marx quotes with approval. One sentence taken from this rather lengthy quotation presents an evidently fatalistic solution to the problem at hand. According to the commentator – and hence by inference according to

---

[46]Before 1932, when the first edition of *The German Ideology* was published thanks to the editorial efforts of David Riazanov, it was only possible to deduce this conception from a number of lapidary passages scattered throughout the various writings of Marx and Engels. The exigesis focused on this sparse material represents one of the least glorious chapters in the history of Marxist ideology. As for the origin of the conception, Marx himself never spoke of "historical materialism"; indeed, it was Engels who attributed its discovery to Marx without, however, disavowing his own role in the "elaboration of the theory" (cf. Engels's Preface to *Ludwig Feuerbach and the End of Classical German Philosophy*, 1888).

[47]*The German Ideology; MEW* 3, p. 27.

[48]"It is not the consciousness of men that determines their existence, but, on the contrary, their social existence determines their consciousness" (Preface to *A Contribution to the Critique of Political Economy*, 1859; *MEW* 13, pp. 8–9).

Marx as well—human consciousness and will are subject to the immutable determinism of historic laws: "Marx conceives of the social movement as a natural sequence of historical phenomena governed by laws which are not only independent of men's will, consciousness and designs but which, on the contrary, determine their will, consciousness and designs."[49] Marx added the following postscript to the quoted exposé, as if his purpose were to substitute a kind of materialist metaphysics for Hegelian panlogism:

Not only is the basis of my dialectics different from the Hegelian, but my method is its direct opposite. For Hegel, the thought process, which he even transforms into an independent subject called the "Idea," is the demiurge of reality, which is itself viewed as nothing more than the phenomenal form of the Idea. For me, however, ideas simply represent the material world as transposed and expressed by the human mind.[50]

Historical possibility—ethical necessity

It seems therefore that Marx's teachings are marred by an insoluble contradiction: On the one hand, he presents the rise of a truly human society as the inevitable outcome of the no less fatal collapse of the capitalist system; on the other, he conceives of the social revolution that is to effect the radical transformation of the human condition as the accomplishment of highly conscious individuals who assume a specific historic mission. In one instance Marx wrote: "What one proletarian or another or even the proletariat as a whole momentarily considers to be its aim has little import; what counts is the real life condition of the proletariat which imposes on it its historic mission."[51] Its historic goal and action are "manifestly and irrevocably prescribed" to the proletariat "in its own life situation and in the whole of present-day bourgeois society."[52] Capitalism engenders its own negation, that is, socialism, with the same "fatality that guides the metamorphoses of nature."[53] Yet we also read in Marx that "history does nothing . . . rather, it is real *living* man who accomplishes all that . . . Nor is *history* a separate being that uses man as a means for realiz-

[49]*Capital,* vol. I (Moscow: 1959), p. 18.
[50]Ibid., p. 19.
[51]*The Holy Family* (Moscow; 1956), p. 53.
[52]Ibid.
[53]*Capital,* vol. I, p. 763.

ing its own ends. History is *nothing but* the activity of man pursuing his own goals."[54] In other words, "it is the mass that prescribed history's *tasks* and its *action*."[55]

Our particular theme – that of historic necessity – is probably one of the most controversial of those problems that have incessantly generated discord among the ranks of Marxist ideologues. As noted earlier, the problem was first touched upon by Bernstein, who thought he perceived the "snare" of the Hegelian dialectic method in the Marxian theory of capitalism's fatal demise; and today the same problem is no less central to the discussions carried on by proponents of the various currents of Marxist thought.

In the texts just quoted a rigidly fatalist conception of historic development is conjoined to a contrasting absolute faith in the "historic initiative" of the oppressed class that is invested – by whom? – with a "historic mission." Is it possible to reconcile such thoroughly contradictory viewpoints without betraying the basic unity of Marx's genius and without forcibly relying on the alleged esotericism of his message? The problem has never before been examined from this angle; instead Marx's teachings have been perennially subjected to the most far-fetched political and ideological travesties, and relevant texts have been invoked with certitude in support of one or another of the divergent judgments about his work.

How, then, are we to reconcile the thesis of capitalism's inevitable disappearance – an intrinsic element of the "economic law of modern society," which Marx was convinced he had demonstrated – with the idea of a political revolution as the eminently heroic task proposed to proletarian consciousness in the form of an ethical exigency, that is, as a "categorical imperative."[56] The easiest and therefore the most conve-

[54] *The Holy Family*, p. 125.
[55] Ibid., p. 108.
[56] Marx's critique of religion closes with the following statement: "The critique of religion ends in the doctrine that man is the supreme being for man; thus it ends with the categorical imperative to overthrow all conditions in which man is a debased, enslaved, neglected, contemptible being . . ." *A Contribution to the Critique of Hegel's Philosophy of Right. Introduction,* 1844; in *Karl Marx: Critique of Hegel's Philosophy of Right,* ed. J. O'Malley (Cambridge: Cambridge University Press, 1970), p. 137. "The social principles of Christianity preach cowardice, self-contempt, debasement, submission, humbleness, in short, all the qualities of a miserable wretch. Yet the proletarian who refuses to let himself be treated as a miserable wretch needs his courage, his self-esteem, his pride and his taste for independence much more than he needs his bread" ("Communism and the *Rheinischer Beobachter,*" 1847; MEW 4, p. 200).

nient way of quietly extricating ourselves from this dilemma would be to reject one of the two postulates and thus reduce the Marxian teachings either to a system of political economics alone or to a doctrine of political action. This is precisely what Bernstein did in elaborating his conception of reformist socialism: Because capitalism is not fatally destined to collapse and because there is a gradual improvement of the economic situation of the proletariat under capitalism, Bernstein necessarily transformed the revolutionary fight, which Marx linked to the proletariat's conscious acceptance of its historic mission, into a campaign for political and economic reforms. Step by step, these reforms would convert capitalist society into a new socialist one.

After Bernstein, the question of the validity of Marx's "theory of crises" (*Zusammenbruchstheorie*) provoked a veritable mountain of Marxist literature. Of all the efforts made to preserve the coherence of Marxian thought the most interesting for our topic was that of Rosa Luxemburg. Her theoretical work, *The Accumulation of Capital* (1913), embodies both a serious attempt to reestablish the materialist foundations of Marxian ethics as well as a masterful critique of those doctrinaire economists, before and after Marx, who tried to prove the objective possibility of unlimited capitalist accumulation and therefore the permanence of our subjection to the present system. We are not concerned here with the validity of Rosa Luxemburg's critical analysis of the Marxian scheme of expanded reproduction;[57] her presentation interests us instead as a revolutionary vision of socialism's genesis, conceived as the only alternative to mankind's otherwise fatal decline into an unspeakable barbarism.[58] It is, according to Rosa Luxemburg,

[57]In his work *Das Akkumulations- und Zusammenbruchsgesetz des kapitalistischen Systems* (1929) Henryk Grossman develops this topic over some six hundred pages in order to prove the validity and importance of Marx's crisis theory in capitalism. In contrast to Rosa Luxemburg, Grossman demonstrates that, according to the Marxian schema as elaborated by Otto Bauer, capitalism's decline is fatal.

[58]By ignoring this alternative that Marx began elaborating in 1848, James Burnham was able to develop his specious theory on capitalism's recent metamorphosis with the concomitant transition from capitalist to managerial society (*The Managerial Revolution.* New York: The John Day Co., 1942). Marx himself had, however, foreseen the totalitarian dimensions of the technocratic state and maintained that this phenomenon would be an inevitable consequence of capitalist concentration, inseparably linked to the transformation of "personified" capital into "abstract" capital. In *Capital,* Book III, we find numerous explanations of this conversion by which individual capital becomes "social power, alien to and independent of man" and of the

this historical alternative that dictates to the proletariat its
revolutionary behavior and imbues it with the strength to in-
tervene actively in the blind interplay of the forces of capital:

The more violent the militarist methods with which capital endeavors, both from within and without, to stamp out the noncapital-
ist classes of society, thus intensifying the misery under which the
working population must live, the more extensive becomes the transformation in world-wide dimensions of capitalist accumulation into
an unbroken chain of political catastrophes and social convulsions.
This, in addition to the periodic economic catastrophes which appear
in the form of crises, shall finally prove itself an insurmountable
obstacle to further accumulation and necessitate the revolt of the
international working class against the domination of capital, even
before this economic system will have attained its natural, self-
defined limits.[59]

Although her writings contain many insights of genius, Rosa
Luxemburg failed to derive from them a coherent conception
of Marxian ethics. Nonetheless, her attempts to reconcile the
apparent antinomy between economic determinism and proletarian spontaneity were strong in comparison to what is found
in the Marxist ideologues, whose efforts in this regard are but
a weak echo of hers. It is by reason of their exemplary value
rather than any real effectiveness, therefore, that her life and
work represent the only purposeful attempt made so far to
refute the fatalist interpretation of Marx's message. This
woman, who was both witness to and victim of the barbarism
of World War I, achieved what might be called a "revelation":
She recognized not only that socialism is not inevitable but
also that "historical necessity" may engender a chaos that
threatens the very survival of humanity, should the proletariat's "historical initiative" founder at the decisive moment.
From the first moment she entered the debate over Bernsteinian revisionism she grasped the essential relationship between

contradictions thus entailed. Marx even speaks of the "suppression of private
property" and "private labor" "within the framework of capitalist production itself"
(*Capital* vol. 3; *MEW* 25, pp. 379 ff., 429 ff.). He considered the "direct relationship
between the owners of the means of production and the immediate producers" to be
the "profound secret, the hidden basis of every social formation" and of the "particular form of the state" as well (Ibid., p. 842). Even given the correctness of Burnham's
thesis, it could be damaging only to orthodox Marxism and in no way impairs the
validity of Marxian *ethics;* the imperative of a social revolution remains as compelling
in our time as it was during the nineteenth century.
[59]*Die Akkumulation des Kapitals* (Berlin: 1923), pp. 379 ff.

modes of action and abstract goals; in this she was more discerning than Lenin, who realized only too late that there is nothing dogmatic about the Marxian teachings.[60] And although she was less faithful than Georges Sorel to the letter of Marxian thought, she contributed a conception of revolutionary syndicalism that did much to clarify one of the most important problems facing the working-class movement.[61]

In 1926, under the pretext of "liquidating" Marxism, Henri de Man attacked the very foundations of Marx's teachings, insisting however that his target was not Marx's personality but rather a flagrant gap in his writings: the absence of a moral etiology for socialism.[62] De Man maintained that Marx had deliberately limited his investigations to the domain of economic etiology, that is, to an examination of the objective causes of the working-class movement, where, moreover, his research had been superbly successful. Nonetheless, according to de Man, Marx had consciously refrained from treating socialism's ethical motivation and had even gone so far as to "repress" his own feelings of morality. In short, Marx's socialism was the result of a "repression" of ethical drives rather than a direct manifestation of them.[63]

Sidney Hook's work belongs to that category of efforts that examines the ethical aspects of Marxian thought without presuming its "obsolescence" in light of modern psychological theories. Hook's writings are distinguished by their interest in

---

[60]"Marx used to say to Engels: 'Our theory is not a dogma but a guide to action' " (V. I. Lenin, *A Letter on Tactics*, Apr. 1917). However, Lenin was thinking less of proletarian class action than of the initiative taken by an "avant garde" – and his program is therefore strangely reminiscent of the practices of bourgeois political parties.

[61]"There are not two different class struggles of the working men, one economic and the other political; there is but *one* struggle whose objective is to check the expansion of capitalist exploitation within bourgeois society while at the same time abolishing both this exploitation and bourgeois society." *Massenstreik, Partei und Gewerkschaften* (Leipzig: 1906), new ed. (Leipzig, 1926), p. 57.

[62]*Zur Psychologie des Sozialismus* (Jena: 1926).

[63]For a discussion of Henri de Man's writing and that of Max Eastman (*Marx and Lenin: the Science of Revolution*. London: G. Allen & Unwin, 1926) see Pierre Naville in *Psychologie, marxisme, matérialisme* (Paris: 1946). Eastman held that Marx was a "victim" of Hegel and attributed very little importance to the "Theses on Feuerbach." He presented Lenin as the prototype of a non-Marxist revolutionary. De Man, on the other hand, proposed Bergsonian philosophy as the ethical basis for socialism. He believed that Marx "viewed his program of action as a description of what history was itself in the process of accomplishing," and that Marx "left to history the ungrateful task of defining the goal to be attained" (De Man, *Marx and Lenin*, p. 150).

harmonizing the scientific postulates of Marxian thought with the pragmatic principles that crown it. Commenting on the Marxian thesis of communism's historical inevitability, Hook remarks:

Communism is not something fated to be realized in the nature of things; but, *if society is to survive,* communism offers the only way out of the impasse created by the inability of capitalism, despite its superabundance of wealth, to provide a decent *social* existence for its own wage-earners. What Marx is really saying is: either *this* (communism) or *nothing* (barbarism) . . . The objectivity of Marxism is derived from the truth of the disjunction; the subjectivity, from the fact that *this* is chosen rather than *nothing*. Normally a recognition of the truth of the disjunction carries with it a commitment to communism. But the connection is not a *necessary* one any more than the knowledge that milk is a wholesome drink makes one a milk drinker. One might accept the economic analyses of Marx, recognize the existence of the class struggle, and apply historical materialism to the past. That does not make him a Marxist. Bourgeois thinkers have done so since Marx's day, and some even before. It is only when one accepts the first term of the disjunction – which is a psychological, and, if you please, an ethical act – that he has a right to the name . . . The objective truth of Marxism realizes itself in the informed revolutionary act. Marxism is neither a science nor a myth, but a realistic method of social action.[64]

Marxian ethics are characterized negatively by their amoralism and positively by their essentially pragmatic method of reasoning. Via Feuerbach, Marx's ethical thought enjoys a common bond with the ethics of Spinoza, the greatest amoralist of all times. The ethics of both thinkers are existential messages rather than speculative systems; both assign man a place in the eternal cycle of infinite nature and charge him with the task of realizing ideal perfection through the development of the totality of his faculties. Our analogy must end there, however, for to carry it further would lead only to absurdity. We can, nonetheless, attribute hypothetically to Marx the startling avowal that Nietzsche made one day upon discovering his own affinity with Spinoza:

I am completely surprised, utterly enchanted! I have a *predecessor*, and indeed what a predecessor! I was hardly acquainted with Spi-

[64]Sidney Hook, *Towards the Understanding of Karl Marx* (London: 1933), pp. 102–4.

noza at all; it was an "act of instinct" to have sought him out *now*. Not only have we the same basic orientation – to make knowledge the *most powerful passion* – but moreover I rediscover myself in five essential points of his doctrine. This most exceptional and solitary thinker resembles me most closely in *these* respects: he denies freedom of will, finality, a universal moral order, selflessness, evil. Our dissimilarities are undoubtedly very great, but they are due primarily to differences in our times, sciences and cultures.[65]

Marx strongly disliked the moralizing verbalism of the doctrinaire socialists and in his own writings avoided as pure phraseology and mythology references to "justice," "duty," "morality" – terms that were constantly abused by other socialists, Proudhon in particular.[66] Nevertheless, the most objective of Marx's own trains of thought are tied to value judgments of one kind or another. He condemned this "modern mythology" simply because it served to camouflage injustice and immorality.[67]

A perennial example of what may be called the ambivalence in Marxian thought is the preface to his 1859 *Contribution to the Critique of Political Economy,* in which Marx presented the most concise account of the "materialist" conception of history to be found in his writings. After first sketching the relations between society's economic infrastructure and its ideological superstructure, he notes that the asiatic, ancient, feudal, and bourgeois modes of production may be considered as "progressive" epochs of society's economic evolution. On a note of conviction he concludes:

The bourgeois production relations are the last antagonistic form of the social production process . . . The productive forces developing at the very heart of bourgeois society simultaneously create the material

[65]Letter to Franz Overbeck (July 30, 1881); in Friedrich Nietzsche, *Werke in drei Bänden,* ed. Karl Schlechta (Munich: 1956), vol. 3, pp. 1171–2.

[66]One example among others is furnished by Marx's sally against Proudhon in a footnote to *Capital* (*MEW* 23, pp. 99 f.). The ideal of social justice, Marx held, derives from the juridicial relations that obtain under the system of commodity production. "What would we think of a chemist who, rather than studying the actual laws of molecular changes in the metabolism of living matter and basing his solution to definite problems thereon, pretended to regulate this metabolism using the 'eternal ideas' of '*naturalité*' and '*affinité*'? Do we really know more about usury when we say that it contradicts '*justice éternelle*,' '*équité éternelle*,' '*mutualité éternelle*' and other '*verités éternelles*' than did the Church fathers when they said that it was incompatible with '*grâce éternelle*,' '*foi éternelle*' and '*la volonté éternelle de Dieu*'?"

[67]Cf. Marx to Engels (Aug. 1, 1877) and Marx to Sorge (Oct. 19, 1877); *MEW* 34, pp. 66, 303.

conditions for solving this antagonism. With this social system, therefore, the prehistory of human society comes to a close.[68]

It would be utterly unfounded to speak of contradiction in connection with this passage or the many others that could be quoted in its place. Marx presents the coming of socialism as both an economic possibility and an ethical necessity. When, in *Capital* and the *Communist Manifesto*, he announced the fall of the bourgeoisie and the triumph of the proletariat as "equally inevitable," he was simply formulating a rationally valid hypothesis based on scientific analysis of the economic laws governing capitalism and on his direct observation of the actual conflict that pits modern society's two principal classes against one another, a conflict in which Marx was personally engaged as the theorist and educator of the proletariat. His prediction of a socialism-to-come is not so much a scientific truth as a rational argument based on an ethical conviction and orientation and nourished by objective knowledge of the given material, economic, and historic conditions that render possible the total reversal of present society and the founding of "social humanity" (Tenth Thesis on Feuerbach). This statement concerning the inevitability of socialism belongs, in other words, to that category of truths that require active *participation, moral* engagement, in order to become "objective" (Second Thesis on Feuerbach). Socialism, as Marx conceives of it, *can* become reality *if* the modern proletariat, that is, the class whose historic position favors socialism's realization, adopts and accomplishes this historic task in full awareness of its responsibility to itself and with the courage to conquer its human dignity through its own effort. What is the socialist movement if not the proletariat's conscious acceptance of a revolutionary task that effects its own transformation while simultaneously changing the world and putting an end to its own moral and material destruction?

Objective possibility and ethical necessity – Marx himself clearly recognized this "dualism" in his message, a dualism that his critics insist is irremediable and his less discerning disciples prefer to deny rather than look for its key and justification in the "Theses on Feuerbach," the *vade-mecum* of Marxian thought. We have evidence that Marx perceptively anticipated

[68]Preface to the *Contribution to the Critique of Political Economy* (1859); *MEW* 13, p. 9.

the reactions his teachings could not fail to stimulate among his more hostile readers, thanks to a remarkable document: a letter to Engels, written shortly after the publication of *Capital*, Book I, in which Marx outlined an "objective" critique of his book. These notes were intended to serve Engels in reviewing *Capital* for a periodical edited by a close friend of the reknowned Karl Vogt, whom Marx had exposed some years previously as the "literary lackey" of Louis Bonaparte. Wanting to sport with this journal, Marx wrote a kind of self-parody and gave his imaginary critic, in fact Friedrich Engels, the key to the ostensible weaknesses of his work. *Capital*, its author confessed, proves to be at one and the same time scientific and "tendentious."

Marx's self-critique begins with a sally against Prussia for having killed "scientific initiative" with the result that the "German spirit" can manifest itself only in exile. He continues:

As for the book itself we must distinguish between the author's positive contributions ... and the tendentious conclusions which he draws. The former constitute a direct enrichment of science: he has produced a new analysis of real economic conditions using a materialist approach ... *Example* 1) the analysis of money; 2) the "natural" development of co-operation, the division of labor, the system of machinery and the corresponding social relations and social ties. As concerns the author's tendentiousness, it should be noted that: when showing how present society is, from an economic standpoint, pregnant with a new and superior social order, he merely points out for the social realm the same evolutionary process Darwin revealed in natural history. This is implied ... in the liberal theory of "progress," and the author deserves commendation for having shown that even where modern economic conditions entail the most intimidating immediate consequences, there is some degree of latent progress. With this critical interpretation the author has also – perhaps even *malgré lui* – put an end to all doctrinal socialism, i.e. to all utopianism.

On the other hand, the author's subjective tendency, i.e. the way he imagines or presents the final result of the present movement, of the real social process, has actually nothing to do with the analysis itself – he was perhaps morally obliged and committed to this standpoint by virtue of his political affiliation and his past. Providing there were space for a more detailed discussion, it could perhaps be shown that his "objective" analysis refutes his "subjective" biases.[69]

[69]Marx to Engels (Dec. 7, 1867); *MEW* 31, pp. 403–4.

When examined more closely, this apparently ironical judgment of Marx's life work turns out to be true "self-criticism." A born fighter, Marx felt a solidarity with all humanity that was shared by few thinkers before him. His vision of the possible rational restructuring of human society in no way obscured his immediate observation of the dismal reality of actual affairs, foreboding an unprecedented barbarism, which is the second term of our ultimate choice. Marx therefore championed a cause that is not necessarily a triumphal one but simply a possibility; this cause is the proletarian struggle, a single opportunity granted by merciless destiny.

The two apparently irreconcilable aspects of Marx's teachings, his "objectivism" and "subjectivism," are in fact the double manifestation of a single, indivisible genius, of a personality whose most trivial action was oriented toward one definite goal. We recognize in his epistemological approach to militancy an eloquent proof of the unity of Marx's thought:

In social life alone do subjectivism and objectivism, spiritualism and materialism, activity and passivity, lose their contradictory character, and only then do they cease to exist as antinomies. *Theoretical* antinomies can be solved only in a practical way, only by man's practical energy. Their resolution is therefore not a task of knowledge alone but a *real,* vital problem which philosophy has been incapable of solving precisely because it only considered the theoretical aspect.[70]

It would indeed be difficult to be more explicit than Marx was in this passage. The true significance of the materialist conception of history can therefore be understood only in light of this and similar affirmations: It is both a method for exploring all domains of historical development and a doctrine for social action as well, a tool for understanding history and an instrument of instruction in revolutionary behavior.[71]

[70]"Paris Manuscripts"; *MEW* supp. vol. 1, p. 573.

[71]In *The Economic Interpretation of History* (New York: Columbia University Press, 1902) E. R. A. Seligman dissociates these two aspects of the materialist conception of history, thus opposing socialism and "historical materialism." He defines the former as the "theory of what ought to be" and the latter as "a theory of what has been"; the one is "theological," the other "descriptive." In his book entitled *Karl Marx* (London: 1938) Karl Korsch defends the same standpoint as Seligman, maintaining that the "objective" description of the historic process as the development of productive forces, and the "subjective" description of history as class struggle are two independent lines of Marxian thought, equally original and developed independently of one another. "They culminate in an objective materialist theory to be used not only by the researcher but as a tool to aid the proletariat in its practical struggle as well." *Karl Marx,* ed. Götz Langkau (Frankfurt a.M. and Vienna: 1967), pp. 6 ff.

As a method for objective research, the materialist conception of history permits us to make a highly scientific analysis of the causal connections between historical *facts*. As an ethical valuation of human activity, it seeks to establish the principles for proletarian class action, directing the proletariat toward self-emancipation and the construction of a harmonious human community. Although past historical phenomena are governed by *causal determinism,* in the ethical sphere the immediate means employed to attain a future goal are governed by *choice:* Psychologically speaking, ends and means must coincide in *revolutionary praxis.* This means, in other words, that the world and men must be transformed simultaneously: "We can envisage and rationally comprehend the process of transforming the circumstances of human life as occurring simultaneously with human action, or man's self-transformation, only when we conceive of it as *revolutionary practice.*"[72]

Revolutionary praxis

The psychological aspects of revolutionary praxis are in principle the same as those of human action in general. In both instances behavior is determined in function of a given goal; realization then implies a process of activating psychomotive mechanisms that gradually elaborate the elements of the new reality. Projection of the goal is therefore a critical factor in the choice of means that are organically linked to it. "In the act of true intelligence pursuit of a goal precedes the discovery of means," notes Jean Piaget,[73] whose psychological investigations fully corroborate Marx's *Theses on Feuerbach.* At an elementary stage of intelligence, by contrast, little distinction is made between means and ends, the choice of means is left to chance, and actions lack any intentionality. "In so far as feelings guide conduct by attributing values to goals . . . they furnish the necessary energy for action, while knowledge lends it its form."[74]

Revolutionary praxis manifests its ethical character through perfect correlation of ends and means. We are justified in applying this correlative mechanism to the realm of social con-

[72]Third Thesis on Feuerbach. In *The German Ideology* we find a similar statement: "In revolutionary activity transformation of the individual is correlated with the transformation of the external conditions" (*MEW* 3, p. 19).

[73]*La Naissance de l'intelligence chez l'enfant* (Paris: 1935), p. 186.

[74]J. Piaget, *La Psychologie de l'intelligence* (Paris: 1947), p. 9.

duct because it is to be found in the very simplest operations of real human activity. Marx discussed its nature in *Capital*, in a description of the labor process in general. Labor being an act of exchange with nature, when man acts upon nature in order to transform it, he simultaneously changes his own nature by developing his inherent potentialities and subjecting the interplay of his faculties to conscious control. Marx stressed that his concern was specifically human labor, "an eternal condition of human life" and therefore "common to all social forms" regardless of the particular social relations between producers. He compared human labor to the activities of the spider or bee, remarking that in the construction of their wax cells the insects put many a human architect to shame:

But the factor which distinguishes the worst architect from the most highly skilled bee is that the former constructed his cell in his head before realizing it in wax. The labor process ends with a result that already existed at the outset in the worker's imagination, that is to say, in an *ideal* form.[75]

The human worker produces "not only a change of form in natural matter; he realizes at the same time his own conscious purpose which determines his mode of action with the force of law and demands the subordination of his will."[76]

Before Marx, Hegel had remarked that man acts according to self-imposed goals and that "he is determined by the mental images of what he is and what he desires." Herein we find the source of man's inner autonomy, the distinction between man and the animal, which "lacks these representations that appear ideal and real."[77] It was also Hegel who wrote that "man must create himself in order to be man," although he immediately qualified this statement by adding: "He must conquer everything himself because he is Spirit [*Geist*]."[78] Hegel therefore turns the thesis of human self-determination through the autonomous choice of goals into a doctrine of history as a delusive vision in which individuals and peoples are nothing more than emanations of an immaterial substance, that is, universal Spirit.

Hegelian thought nevertheless exerted a certain influence on

[75]*Capital*, vol. 1; *MEW* 23, p. 192.
[76]Ibid.
[77]G. W. F. Hegel, "Die Vernunft in der Geschichte" in *Vorlesungen über die Philosophie der Weltgeschichte*. Quoted from the edition *Recht, Staat, Geschichte*. Friedrich Bülow ed., 6th ed. (Stuttgart: 1964), p. 383.
[78]Ibid.

Marx in the elaboration of his method of historical investigation, and Marx openly acknowledged his debt to Hegel. The master had left him with a historic terrain cleared of all morality and imbued him with a faith in the rationality of historic events. Yet Marx himself repeatedly confirmed that this was the least significant aspect of his own dialectics. We recognize the profound originality of Marx's materialist view of history only in opposing it to Hegelian apriorism, thereby revealing its value as an instrument for understanding historic development, as an ethics of "conscious participation in the . . . historic process of social upheaval."[79]

Translated in terms of revolutionary behavior, the organic relationship between means and ends – which according to Marx, is the principal trait of human practice – may be expressed as the basic affinity between an ideal goal and the concrete means for its attainment. That ends play an integral role in the choice and employment of particular means is illustrated by Marx's use of the word "socialism" to designate both the social *movement* that strives to realize the new human community and the goal itself, namely, *social humanity*.[80]

There is no better illustration of Marx's uncompromising ethical attitude toward the use of revolutionary means than his hostile disapproval of Ferdinand Lassalle's *Realpolitik*.[81] A bitter enemy of the liberal bourgeoisie, Lassalle was induced to form a tactical alliance with Bismarck against the liberals. Still, no one was more aware than he – as founder of the first German working men's organization – of the tragic "dialectical contradiction inherent in revolutionary action."[82] In a letter to Marx that represents even today one of the most lucid analyses

[79]*Herr Vogt* (1860); *MEW* 14, p. 439.

[80]The interdependence noted here is qualitatively the same as that pointed out by Piaget when he speaks of an interdependence "inherent to all forms of organization, whether intelligent or biological" and manifested in the relations between the "ideal" and "value," between "totality" and "relationship." Piaget's explanation regarding the realm of psychic activity retains its validity when applied to that sphere of human action that is oriented toward a social goal.

[81]However, Marx had no idea of just how far Lassalle had really gone in his efforts to win the Prussian monarch to the proletarian cause; the correspondence between Lassalle and Bismarck was not published until 1928. In one of his letters Lassalle asserted that the working class "feels instinctively attracted to dictatorship" and is inclined to consider the crown as the "natural agent of social dictatorship" (Lassalle to Bismarck (June 8, 1863); in *Bismarck und Lassalle, ihr Briefwechsel und ihre Gespräche*, ed. Gustav Mayer (Berlin: 1928), p. 60).

[82]Lassalle to Marx (Mar. 6, 1859); in *Ferdinand Lassalle. Nachgelassene Briefe und Schriften*, ed. Gustav Mayer (Osnabrück: 1967) Vol. 3, p. 151.

to which this problem has ever been subjected, Lassalle explained his standpoint on the questions of revolutionary ends and means. Revolutionary movements, he wrote, derive their strength from "enthusiasm," from a belief in the omnipotence of particular ideas. This implies that the revolutionary masses neglect the means for and the difficulties of realizing their ideal, whence their complete ignorance of available practical means. Yet any revolution that trades its boundless enthusiasm for realist intelligence must necessarily miscarry. Only by harmonizing ends and means can this difficulty be overcome:

Just as old Hegel explained with such masterful profundity, a goal can be attained only with a means that is already imbued with the nature of the goal itself. This goal must therefore be developed and realized in the means themselves, which, in order to attain it, must share the nature of the goal. In Hegelian logic, consequently, the goal is not realized *with the aid* of the means but realized in the means themselves. It follows that no goal can be attained except through something which corresponds to its own inner nature, and that is why *revolutionary goals* cannot be accomplished by *diplomatic means*.[83]

"Historical materialism" – and Marx cannot be credited with having coined this designation for his conception of history any more than with the authorship of "dialectical materialism" – is a method for causal analysis of historical experience as well as an appeal to human initiative, to the "actors and authors of their own drama."[84] A kind of fatality seems to characterize the "historic necessity" of past events and it is the task of the materialist interpretation of history to unearth their causal laws. By contrast, this "necessity" as regards the present or the future stands for the realization of a goal according to norms established by the ethical-materialist doctrine of history. This second aspect of the materialist conception of history was emphasized by the French socialist Charles Andler, who remarked that the cessation of antagonisms between men "is not the inevitable result of fatal necessity but is due to the fact that men do not want to perish; historical materialism is an appeal to their will to live. It causes thought to be orientated towards practical life and practical life towards rationally conceived social organization."[85]

[83]Ibid., pp. 152–3.
[84]*La Misère de la philosophie* (1847), in *Oeuvres*, vol. 1, pp. 83 ff.
[85]Charles Andler, *Le Manifeste communiste de Karl Marx et Friedrich Engels* (Paris, n.d.), p. 208.

From a theoretical standpoint, therefore, the two aspects of Marx's materialist conception of history are not at all contradictory: They provide a rational foundation for revolutionary praxis, demonstrating how human emancipation depends on specific material conditions, in particular on the level of development of society's productive forces. Whereas in the past the material conditions of existence undeniably enjoyed supremacy over man, this supremacy *can*, in the era of fully developed productive forces, be superseded by man's domination over these conditions. However, this is a simple possibility – not the inevitable result of historical development. The objective possibility contained in the material conditions is correlated with an ethical task to be accomplished by creative human activity. "Prescribed by actual conditions," this task consists in "giving society a communist organization."[86]

It was Feuerbach and the major French eighteenth-century materialists who provided Marx with the inspiration for his pragmatic ethics. The severity with which Engels judged Feuerbach after Marx's death is therefore astonishing, as the contemporary reader of Feuerbach's *Wesen des Christentums* (1841), *Grundsätze der Philosophie der Zukunft* (1843) or *Das Wesen der Religion* (1845) cannot help but note. For Feuerbach just as for Marx: "Man is a product of man, culture and history."[87] Feuerbachian ethics, like the Marxian, is a doctrine of action and not contemplation:

The negation of the world beyond implies acceptance of this world; the negation of a better life after death implies the demand for a better life on this earth; thus this better life, otherwise a sterile and useless objective, becomes a matter of duty and of conscious human activity. There can be no doubt about the flagrant injustice of some having everything and others nothing . . . The only conclusion to be drawn from the present injustice and suffering in human existence is the will and effort to change these evils and not the belief in a sterile world beyond this one – a belief which allows these evils to subsist here and now.[88]

Feuerbach recognized that humanity does not stand still and that history is man's *becoming*. There is a history of human civilization: Even plants and animals are subjected to such

[86]*The German Ideology; MEW* 3, p. 424.

[87]Feuerbach, "Principles of Philosophy" (1843–44); in *Sämtliche Werke*, vol. 2, ed. W. Bolin and F. Jodl (Stuttgart-Bad Cannstatt: 1959), p. 389.

[88]"Vorlesungen über das Wesen der Religion"; in *Sämtliche Werke*, vol. 8, p. 358.

transformations and cultivation that in time we are incapable of retracing and distinguishing their ancestry.[89] In contrast to Engels, Marx never criticized Feuerbach's study of social relations from the standpoint of mutual affinity but stressed instead the positive aspect of the latter's writings: Feuerbach had shown how reason, affection, and unfulfilled desires become powers that encumber the individual. The sole point that elicited Marx's reproach was that Feuerbach had "ideally" isolated the phenomenon of human servitude from history's natural course "instead of considering it as the product of a transitory stage of historic development."[90] Marx found that Feuerbach had overestimated and idealized man's affective impulses at the expense of his energetic faculties, his creative ability, his capacity to transform the historic environment in which he moves. Marx nevertheless incorporated into his own world view a principle of the philosophy of the future revived by Feuerbach in 1843: "*Homo sum, humani nihil a me alienum puto.* This phrase, understood in its most universal and most eminent sense, is the maxim of the modern philosopher."[91]

Yet Marx owed his greatest debts to Helvétius and d'Holbach for the fundamental elements of socialist ethics that he outlined in *The Holy Family.* In these pages we find the clearest expression of socialism's spiritual heritage from French and English materialism; here Marx espouses the materialist theses of original goodness and the equality of human intellectual faculties, of the importance of human environment and education, and of the legitimacy of man's claim to the right of pleasure. What is more, from the lessons contained in these premises Marx deduces the following ethical postulates:

If man derives all his knowledge, sensation, etc., from the sensible world and the experience won in it, the empirical world must be so constructed that in it man experiences and assimilates true humanity, that he becomes aware of himself as a human being . . . If man is shaped by his surroundings, his surroundings must be made human.

If man's positive liberty consists in the realization of his true individuality, it follows that "each man must be given sufficient social breadth for the vital manifestation of his own being."[92]

[89]Cf. "Principles of Philosophy" (1843–4); in *Sämtliche Werke,* vol. 2, p. 389.
[90]*The German Ideology; MEW* 3, p. 86.
[91]Feuerbach, "Principles of the Philosophy of the Future" (1843); in *Sämtliche Werke,* vol. 2, p. 317.
[92]*MEW* 2, p. 138.

These imperatives result logically from eighteenth-century materialist philosophy and define the goals of the socialist movement in the most sublimely humanist terms. Later, Marx was to complete them with the doctrine of revolutionary means whose first postulate is the self-emancipation of the working class.

Proletarian self-emancipation

The postulate of proletarian self-emancipation is the leitmotiv of Marx's entire life work. It is the only key to a genuine understanding of his ethics; for it alone furnished the inspiration for all his theoretical and political activities beginning in 1844. At that early date, while engaged in work on *The Holy Family*, he remarked that "the proletariat can and must emancipate itself"; during the turbulent years of the International he proclaimed as that organization's slogan: "The emancipation of the working class must be the work of that class itself"; and finally, toward the end of his life, he developed an interest in the fate of the Russian revolution and placed his hope in the centuries-old *Obschina* and its peasant constituents.[93] The strength – or the weakness – of Marxian ethics is its faith in suffering and conscious man: in the average man who represents society's greatest number. It addresses itself to this man while at the same time calling upon the exceptional individual to contribute to the cause of his less fortunate brothers. At the summit of the power hierarchy is a third category of men: the minority of omnipotent oppressors, masters of the means of life and death, commanders of an endless array of servile scribes and soldiers whose mission it is to maintain or reestablish the status quo each time suffering and thinking men unite in hopes of destroying the established order and constructing not heaven on earth but merely a human community on human soil.

Marx did not envisage the alliance of suffering men and conscious men as an agreement between two groups of persons assigned different tasks, as if they had rationally divided the labor between them, the first being condemned to misery and blind rebellion against their human condition, the latter destined to think for their associates and furnish them with ready-made truths. On this question Marx spoke with a clarity that precludes any ambiguity. In a letter to Arnold Ruge

[93]Cf. "La Commune rurale et les perspectives révolutionnaires en Russie," in *Oeuvres*, vol. 2, pp. 1551 ff.

he explained that the alliance between those who suffer and those who think is in fact an alliance between "suffering humanity that thinks and thinking humanity that is oppressed." The working men must, in other words, sublimate their primitive feelings of distress to the level of *theoretical comprehension* and thus render their misery historically significant while simultaneously permitting the class as a whole to perceive the absurdity of its situation. If "the weapon of criticism cannot replace the criticism of weapons," if "material force can be overthrown only by material force," then it is no less true that "theory too changes into material force as soon as it has seized the masses."[94]

Described in this manner the revolutionary movement evokes not an image of suffering, unknowing masses guided by an elite of clairvoyants who sympathize with their distress, but a vision of the multitude in a permanent state of revolt and privation, conscious of its identity, its desires, and its actions. In most cases the radical aspirations of the proletariat emerge spontaneously under the shock effect of a particularly oppressing situation. At such moments those thinking men who experience the degradation of the masses as an offense to their own dignity also make themselves heard; they are the first to recognize and announce the possibility, the necessity, of a radical revolution that shall transform society's material bases and its spiritual countenance. They join with the proletariat, adopt its needs and interests as their own, and assume the role of Socratic educators who teach the working men to think for themselves. They explain first that the class struggle is not just a historical *fact*, that is, an unalterable phenomenon of the past, but also a historical obligation, a task to be accomplished in full awareness of its justification, an ethical postulate. Realized consciously, this postulate should permit mankind to avoid the ineffable miseries that technological civilization will inevitably provoke at the peak of its material power if it continues to develop according to its own laws, which are in fact the laws of chance.

While the various representatives of religious and moral systems preach to the disinherited of this world the consoling promise of redemption or purification in a world beyond in

[94]*Contribution to the Critique of the Hegel's Philosophy of Right. Introduction* (1844); *MEW* 1, p. 385.

return for voluntary acceptance of their suffering, socialist thinkers teach them to regard themselves as the victims of a social mechanism. Because they are the principle cogs in this mechanism, they have the possibility of making it function for the material and moral benefit of all mankind. At this moment historical development will have reached a point where *homo faber* can finally effectuate that "totality" of productive forces that promotes the appearance of "total man": "Of all the instruments of production the greatest productive force is the revolutionary class itself."[95]

Marx's conception of the working-class party permits us to demonstrate explicitly the ethical nature of his postulate of proletarian self-emancipation. It is common knowledge that none of the proletarian parties that arose during his own lifetime, either with or without his patronage, corresponded to his ideal. Less well known and, in the first instance, astonishing is the fact that even after the dissolution of the Communist League and before the founding of the International Marx continued to speak of the "party" as if of an extant body. On this score his correspondence with Engels and Lassalle contains many extremely significant passages. In numerous letters exchanged between the three friends there is talk of "our party" although there was no political organization of the working class at that time. Even more relevant are Marx's letters written during the period of the Vogt affair to Ferdinand Freiligrath, the poet of the 1848−9 revolution and former member of the Communist League. Freiligrath had contributed fervent verse to the *Neue Rheinische Zeitung* when that organ was under Marx's editorship, and now he was living, as was Marx, in London where he had an "honorable" position in a bank. After seeing his name introduced in the calumnious attacks on Marx and the so-called Marx Party by the reknowned naturalist Karl Vogt, Freiligrath made every effort to escape his responsibility to serve as a witness in the legal suits that Marx filed against Vogt in London and Berlin. Writing in a warm and friendly tone, which in no way compromised the rigor of his argument, Marx tried to persuade Freiligrath that the suits against his calumniator, Vogt, were "decisive for the historical revindication of the party and for its future position in Germany." Therefore, one could hardly remain on the sidelines:

[95]*La Misère de la Philosophie; Oeuvres*, vol. 1, p. 135.

Vogt is trying to profit politically from your name and makes it appear as if he were acting with your approval in muckraking the entire party which is proud to count you among its members . . . If both of us are conscious of having exalted the banner of the *classe la plus laborieuse et la plus misérable* over the heads of the philistines all these years, each in his one way and in spite of personal interests, motivated by the purest feelings, it would be a crime against history for us to fall out with one another because of trivialities all of which stem from misunderstandings.[96]

Freiligrath replied, while assuring Marx of his unerrant friendship, that he considered himself tacitly freed of any responsibility toward the "party" since the dissolution of the League, regardless of any loyalty he might still feel toward the proletarian cause. "My nature," he explained, "like that of any poet, demands freedom! The party, too, is a cage and the singing is better outside of it than inside, even *for* the party itself. I had been a poet of the proletariat and the revolution long before joining the League and the staff of the *Neue Rheinische Zeitung!* I therefore want to continue using my own wings to fly, I have no desire to belong to anything but my own self and I want alone to dispose of my own person!." Before ending his letter Freiligrath did not neglect the opportunity to allude to "all the questionable and base elements . . . which had crept into the party's ranks" and to note his satisfaction at no longer himself being a member, "if only out of a sense of purity."[97]

Marx's counterreply is interesting from several points of view. Together with the *Communist Manifesto* and the *Critique of the Gotha Program* it constitutes one of the rare documents that shed light on a question that is perhaps the most crucial for Marx's teachings, one that has continuously caused the greatest confusion among his disciples. He had himself proposed the disbanding of the League in 1852, Marx recalled to Freiligrath, adding that since that date he had joined no other organization, secret or public. "The *party* in this thoroughly ephemeral sense ceased to exist for me eight years ago," he wrote. After the publication of the *Contribution to the Critique of Political Economy* (1859) he had held lectures on political economy not for any specific society but for a small, select number of workers,

[96]Marx to Freiligrath (Feb. 23, 1860); *MEW* 30, pp. 461–2.

[97]Freiligrath to Marx (Feb. 26, 1860); *Freiligraths Briefwechsel mit Marx und Engels*, vol. I, ed. Manfred Haeckel (Berlin: 1968), p. 138.

including some former members of the League. When asked by American communists in 1858 to reorganize the old League, Marx had replied that for the past six years he had entertained relations with no association whatsoever: "I replied that . . . I was firmly convinced that my theoretical endeavors were of greater utility for the working class than my participation in any organization whose days were now over on the Continent." And he continued:

Since 1852, therefore, I have had *nothing* to do with any "party" in the sense expressed in your letter. You may be a *poet*, but I am a *critic*, and my experiences from 1849 to 1852 were enough for me. The *League*, like the *Société des saisons* of Paris and a hundred other societies, was but one episode in the history of the party *which is spontaneously rising from the soil of modern society* [italics added].[98]

Further on in this same letter we read: "The *only* action I continued after 1852, and continued as long as it was necessary . . . was the *system of mockery and contempt* [Eng. in original] . . . against the democratic duperies of the emigration and its bungling attempts at revolution." Turning to the topic of those dubious elements that, as Freiligrath intimated, had supposedly belonged to the League, Marx remarked that the individuals in question had never actually been part of their group; and he added:

During storms a lot of muck is stirred up, revolutions are not made of rose-water, at times one is spattered even by all sorts of scum – so much is certain . . . Yet when you consider the extent of the efforts directed against us by the whole official world which, in order to ruin us, does not stop with a perfunctory reading of the *Code pénal* but meticulously scrutinizes it; when you consider the calumnies spread by the "democracy of stupidity" which could never forgive our party for having more brains and more strength of character than it; if you are familiar with the *contemporary* histories of all the other parties; and finally if you ask yourself what *facts* can *actually* . . . be adduced against the party as a whole, you arrive at the conclusion that in this 19th century it is a brilliant example of *purity*.

Is it possible to escape being sullied when one engages in bourgeois relations or trade? In this trade, dirt has its natural habitat. . . In my opinion the honest infamy or the infamous honesty of solvent morality . . . is not a wit superior to the abject infamy which neither the first Christian communities nor the Jacobin Club nor our erstwhile League

[98]Marx to Freiligrath (Feb. 29, 1860); *MEW* 30, pp. 489–90.

were able to avoid completely. But only one who lives in a bourgeois milieu acquires the habit of insensibility towards either respectable infamy or infamous respectability.[99]

After subsequently answering a number of questions concerned in particular with the details of the Vogt affair, Marx concluded his letter with the words: "I have, moreover, tried to eliminate any sort of misunderstanding: as if I had meant by party either a League which died out eight years ago or an editorial staff that was disbanded twelve years ago. I understood party to mean party in the eminently historical sense."

The party *in the eminently historical sense:* To Marx this meant the historical but *invisible party founded on real knowledge* rather than any existing party with dubious knowledge of itself and of its goals. In other words, he did not presume that any working men's party, simply through the fact of its existence, could represent the "consciousness" or the "knowledge" of the entire proletariat.[100] During the years in which he abstained from all political agitation and devoted his entire energy to a grueling scientific project, he went on speaking, whenever the occasion presented itself, in the name of this invisible party, which he hoped in the end would include the entire working class and for which he continued to feel a sense of responsibility. Thus, in 1859, when visited by a delegation from the London Working Men's Educational Society, Marx declared without misgivings that he and Engels considered themselves the representatives of the proletarian party; their mandate, albeit self-attributed, was countersigned by the "unqualified and universal hatred" shown them by "all the old world factions and parties."[101]

When the Western world witnessed a revival of the labor movement in the 1860s, Marx thought that the moment had come for "the political reorganization of the working men's party" and for a new and open declaration of its revolutionary

---

[99]Ibid., pp. 491–2.

[100]Engels seems to have understood the concept of "party" in the same sense as Marx, judging from the letters he wrote to his friend during the League's critical period in the early 1850s. For instance, in one letter, dated February 13, 1851, he remarked: "What business do we have getting involved in a party, we who abhor official positions like the plague? We who detest popularity and begin to have doubts about ourselves when we start gaining popularity – what do we want with a party, or in other words, with a band of asses who swear by us because they think they are our equals?" (*MEW* 27, p. 190).

[101]Marx to Engels (May 18, 1859); *MEW* 29, p. 436.

goals. The International Working Men's Association was in spirit a continuation of the Communist League whose role Marx and Engels had defined on the eve of the February Revolution (1848). The League had not been conceived of as just one working-class party among others; its goal was more universal and therefore more eminent: The League was to represent at all times both the "interests of the whole movement" and "the movement's future" independently of the day-to-day struggles fought at national levels by the other working-men's parties. In 1864 the International was founded in London under infinitely more favorable circumstances than had accompanied the founding of the League in that same city seventeen years earlier. The IWA was designed to be the organ of the working men's common aspirations and the vital expression of their theoretical knowledge and political intelligence. According to Marx, it was *the* proletarian party, the concrete manifestation of working-class solidarity throughout the world. The working class, Marx wrote in the Inaugural Address, possesses one element of success – its numbers: "but numbers count in the balance only if united by combination and led by knowledge"[102] – "led by knowledge" and not by professional "know-it-alls" or revolutionaries!

The International symbolized for Marx "the alliance between science and the proletariat" launched by Ferdinand Lassalle shortly before his early death in 1864 as his most precious and final message. When, after the fall of the Paris Commune, the International proved unable to continue functioning in the role that Marx, as its spiritual mentor, had assigned it, he chose once again to return to his scientific work. Desirous of leaving the coming generations of working men and women a perfected tool of revolutionary self-instruction, Marx was one of the first to recognize that "ideas can never surpass the conditions of the world"; "to realize ideas, men are needed who exert a certain practical force."[103] If we admit that ideas can lead us only beyond other ideas, the ideas of the past, it follows that to transform the real world we must transform simultaneously both the things of this world and human consciousness as well; what is more, we must recognize that the man who lives in a permanent state of revolt and denial is in a sense the precursor of the

---

[102]*Documents of the First International. 1864–1866* (Moscow: Foreign Languages Publishing House, n.d. [1963]), p. 286.
[103]*The Holy Family; MEW* 2, p. 125.

"integral man," the human being who will populate the community of the future.

Marx's ethical challenge

Marx's passionate appeal to every human individual, to man's
humanity, resounds from his teachings as both an ethical challenge and a call for total change both within and without. Although addressed to modern man in general, to man deformed
by the universal gangrene Marx termed "self-alienation," this
appeal nevertheless implies a task that can be reasonably im-
puted only to the members of the industrial working class. Only
those in a state of moral and physical ruin can accomplish a feat
of revolt and denial that will definitively end man's progressive
degradation and bring to a close that era that, although called
"history," is in fact only mankind's long prehistory. Although
both the "proletarian and the propertied classes represent the
same state of human alienation," only the proletariat incorporates, in its ruin, the revolt against this general condition of
human degradation, "a revolt to which it is compelled by necessity due to the contrast between its human nature and its actual
life-conditions, which are the outright and direct negation of its
nature."[104]

Without a doubt, the economic and social structures of the
present-day world differ from those of the nineteenth century
that Marx investigated in his works. Strictly speaking and not
without reason, it might therefore be argued that we should
substitute a new semantics for that of Marx, provided such a
substitution would help us grasp more adequately the contemporary aspects of the phenomenon Marx held to be inherent in
the capitalist system of production – man's exploitation and
oppression by man.

Looking at the issues of today, we may ask, for instance,
whether the modern state is still an instrument of bourgeois
domination or whether it is being gradually transformed into
the tool of a new dominant minority, an anonymous, bureaucratic elite whose controls over social capital and individual
labor rival a despot's authority. From the standpoint of Marxian ethics, the true significance of this question only becomes
apparent when we consider it in light of Marx's pragmatic
postulate of 1844–5: "The existence of the state is inseparable

[104]*MEW* 2, pp. 36 ff.

from the existence of slavery";[105] or, as expressed in *The German Ideology:* "The proletarians ... are directly opposed to the form in which individuals in society have hitherto given themselves a general expression, that is to say, the state, and in order to realize their personalities they must destroy the state."[106] In the context of present-day politics an equally important issue is Marx's notion of the proletarian party; yet this critical question can be settled only in light of the fundamental postulate of proletarian self-emancipation. It is this postulate that distinguishes Marx's teachings on socialism from all varieties of conspiratorial ideology or Caesarism. The working men, when constituting themselves as a class and as a party, need not renounce the use of their native intelligence: There is no reason for them to turn over their historical initiative to an avant garde that claims to embody revolutionary consciousness and the so-called historical dialectic, and that reduces the problems of revolutionary ethics to matters of political strategy and tactics.[107]

In short, the proletariat must not expect its salvation to come from any other class, party, messiah, or church. "We imagine that the proletariat desires to be aided by others; we do not realize that it expects no one's aid but its own."[108] It is hostile to the social principles of Christianity, which preaches submission and humbleness; it refuses "to let itself be treated like a dog"; and it "has much greater need of its courage, self-esteem, pride and sense of liberty than of its bread."[109] The socialist ethic condemns this resignation and exalts heroism. The working men ridicule pedants who calculate the costs of war; *they* deduct the costs of the struggle against the bourgeoisie from their miserable subsistence wages and experience revolutionary activity as the "supreme satisfaction of their lives."[110]

[105]"Critical Remarks on the Article 'The King of Prussia and Social Reform'," in *Vorwärts!* (1844); *MEW* 1, pp. 401 ff.

[106]*MEW* 3, p. 77.

[107]Lenin and Trotsky both entertained this notion of the party. For the latter "problems of revolutionary morality are fused with the problems of revolutionary strategy and tactics." *Their Morals and Ours* (New York: 1942), p. 35.

[108]"Communism and the *Rheinischer Beobachter*" (1847); *MEW* 4, p. 194.

[109]*MEW* 4, p. 200.

[110]*Wage Labor* (1847); *MEGA* I, 6, p. 471. We can no longer question the fact that proletarian violence, a subject that inspired Georges Sorel's most enduring thoughts (cf. *Reflexions sur la violence.* Paris, 1908), bears signally ethical importance. The positive value of this violence is accentuated in contrast to the passivity and serviceableness of the proletariat in today's "civilized" countries, attitudes that favored

Although Marx always welcomed the founding of new working-class parties in the democratic countries, he nevertheless made a sharp distinction between the class movement as a whole and the political agitation conducted by such parties. In a letter to J. B. von Schweitzer, president of the German ADAV (General German Working Men's Union) after the death of its founder Lassalle, Marx outlined the principles he considered fundamental to the program of any serious working-class party. These were: "agitation for complete political freedom, regulation of the working day and the systematically planned, worldwide cooperation of the working class in accomplishing its historic task for the benefit of all society."[111] Marx therefore looked upon the successful passage of the ten-hour bill in England and the cooperative movement as two triumphs of proletarian political economy. He also felt that the 1871 Commune was an impressive example of the working class's historical initiative and that the cooperative factories were proof that "production on a large scale . . . may be carried on without the existence of a class of masters employing a class of hands."[112] If the workers' political struggle is to lead to political supremacy, they must, in the course of their fight for higher wages, acquire sufficient experience to organize the new social relations of the economy. When wresting from capital those legislative reforms that favor labor, the working class is merely fulfilling a basic responsibility to itself:

Time is the room of human development. A man who has no free time to dispose of, whose whole lifetime, apart from the mere physical interruptions by sleep, meals, and so forth, is absorbed by his labor for the capitalist, is less than a beast or burden. He is a mere machine for producing wealth for another, broken in body and brutalized in mind.[113]

the irrational horrors of two world wars and permitted a "concentration camp" nightmare to be established as a governmental system. Were we to expound here on this topic, we would be lead to examine the ethical problems raised by the current politics of the so-called working-class parties today. Although the scope of this essay precludes such a discussion, it should nevertheless be emphasized in passing that Marx, while considering values such as "justice" and "duty" to be historically conditioned and therefore quite relative, did employ concepts like "falsehood" and "dignity" in their most ordinary sense and without making any "dialectical" distinctions.

[111]Published in the *Social-Demokrat*, Aug. 28, 1868; *MEW* 16, p. 316.

[112]Inaugural Address of the IWA; in *Documents of the First International. 1864– 1866*, p. 285.

[113]*Wages, Price and Profit*; in *MESW* 1, p. 398. On Marx's and Engels's ideas of the cooperative movement, see Thomas Lowit, "Marx et Engels et le mouvement coopératif," in *Etudes de marxologie*, no. 6, *Cahiers de l'ISEA* (Sept. 1962), 79 ff.

It is therefore clear that the proletarian movement as a class movement must be strictly differentiated from the political agitation of parties that by definition divide the workers, sometimes even into hostile factions. In return, however, the working-class labor unions can implement this class movement if they remain consciously revolutionary and faithful to their responsibility of fighting the immediate consequences of the capitalist system. Without overestimating the result of the day-to-day struggle or letting themselves become absorbed entirely in the scrimmages provoked by capital's continual encroachments on labor, the unions must dedicate their forces to the primary task of combating the causes of the present system and of using these "organized forces as a lever for the final emancipation of the working class, that is to say, the ultimate abolition of the wages system."[114] They should function as "organizing centres of the working class in the broad interest of its complete emancipation."[115] As "schools of socialism" they must stay clear of political parties for "they alone are capable of constituting a barricade against the power of capital."[116]

For Marx the true working-men's party – "party" understood "in the eminently historical sense of the word" – is one

[114]*MESW* 1, p. 405.

[115]Instructions for the Delegates of the Provisional Council; in *Documents of the First International. 1864–1866*, p. 349.

[116]These phrases are extracted from a declaration Marx made to J. Hamann, functionary of a German metal workers' trade union, in reply to the question: "Must labor unions preferably be dominated by political associations in order to be viable?" Hamann summarized and published Marx's answer in the journal *Der Volksstaat*, edited by Wilhelm Liebknecht. The report quoted Marx as saying further: "What does Liebknecht, Schweitzer or my own self mean to you? In truth, nothing but the cause." Hamann added in his commentary that Marx "advised us never to attach ourselves to individuals but always to keep the cause in mind and orientate our judgments according to it" (*Volksstaat*, Nov. 27, 1869). A reply addressed to Liebknecht that same year, upon the latter's insistence that Marx participate in a forthcoming congress of the German *Volkspartei* to be held at Eisenach, reveals the extent of Marx's hostility to any kind of political messianism. Marx recapitulated his reply in a letter to Engels as follows: "I have no desire whatsoever to show myself to the German working men and I shall *not* go to their congress. Someday, when they have become part of the International and set up a decent party organization . . . only then will *by and by* [Eng. in orig.] the opportunity present itself. Furthermore, it should be clearly understood that the new organization must be neither a *Volkspartei* [Liebknecht-Bebel party] nor a Lassallean church. Were we to attend their congress now, we would have to speak out *against the Volkspartei*, and Wilhelm and Bebel would certainly be unhappy about it! And even if they were to admit this – *mirabile dictu* – we would be obliged to throw *our weight* into the struggle against Schweitzer and consorts rather than let the reversal result from the free action of the workers themselves." Letter to Engels (July 3, 1869); *MEW* 32, p. 332.

that never, at any stage in the proletariat's struggle for emancipation, betrays the socialist cause by resorting to *Realpolitik*. Although recognizing Lassalle's "immortal merit" for having revived the working-class movement in Germany, Marx was nevertheless unable to pardon his attempt to compromise the working class by manipulating a political alliance with the feudal powers-that-be under the guise of so-called political realism – to which Lassalle claimed to hold the key. Marx once said, speaking in the name of the Communist League: "For us the issue cannot be the smoothing over of class antagonisms, but the abolition of classes, not the improvement of existing society but the founding of a new one."[117] At moments when the workers are forced to side with the bourgeoisie in order to fight their common enemy, the forces of reaction, they "must at every opportunity present their own demands alongside of those of the revolutionary democrats"[118] without masking their final great objective: the overthrow of the bourgeoisie itself.

If we take, therefore, the ethical postulate of proletarian self-emancipation as our point of departure, the most controversial issues in Marx's teachings – issues such as the conquest of political power and the dictatorship of the proletariat – are seen in their proper perspectives. Marx understood the proletarian seizure of power to signify the outcome of a gradual process in which the working men would attain both political and intellectual maturation through revolutionary praxis, with a growing awareness of accomplishing a historical mission. This explains Marx's insistence on the bourgeois-democratic conquest of political rights, a feat that marks, in one respect, the disintegration of feudal society and, in another, the end of mankind's "bestial history" and the beginning of a new era that will be characterized by the masses' conscious and active participation in economic and political struggles.[119]

In both his *Critique of Hegel's Philosophy of the State*, written in 1843 but not published until 1927, and his essay "On the Jewish Question," which appeared in 1844 in the *Deutsch-*

[117]Address of the Central Committee to the Communist League; *MESW* 1, p. 102.
[118]Ibid., p. 104.
[119]When one considers the tragic history of the international working-class movement since 1914, one is inclined to regard the doctrine of revolutionary syndicalism advocated at the beginning of this period by the "new school" of Georges Sorel, Edouard Berth, and Arturo Labriola as one of the most interesting and promising forms in which Marxian thought has experienced a renaissance.

Französische Jahrbücher, Marx began a brief but pertinent analysis of the nature and historical significance of the bourgeois state and its legal system. The political emancipation gained by the bourgeoisie has led to a distinct split of each individual into two antithetical beings: the human person and the citizen. Whereas, on the one hand, man is reduced to a member of bourgeois society, to an egoistic being motivated exclusively by private interests, in his second aspect man becomes an abstract political being, "an allegorical and moral personality." We recall that Jean-Jacques Rousseau defined in his *Du Contrat social* (1762) the notion of the "man-citizen," a truly novel concept for his time and one that Rousseau justified with perfectly logical argumentation. This concept later provided the basis for the Declaration of the Rights of Man in 1791. To "institute a people," Rousseau proclaimed, it is necessary to change in a certain sense human nature and to replace man's real existence with a "partial and moral existence," robbing him therefore of "his own forces in order to give him others which are alien to him and which he can employ only with the aid of others."[120] Rousseau, apologist of the return to nature, was paradoxically enough the defender of unlimited *étatism* as well.

Bringing Rousseau's arguments to their natural conclusion, Marx argued that once the bourgeoisie has achieved full political emancipation, the proletariat can envisage human emancipation, the goal of its revolution. This final emancipatory step will be realized "only when the real individual and the abstract citizen are again one, when man in his empirical existence as an individual, in his individual labor, his personal relations, will have become a social being [*Gattungswesen:* generic being], when he will have recognized that his personal forces are social forces and will have organized them as such and will therefore cease to separate these social forces from his own being by projecting them into political power."[121] The path toward universal human emancipation begins with the conquest of bourgeois law by the working class and advances to a phase of dictatorship during which this class is compelled to exercise its authority over the minority of formerly privileged persons who are unwilling to renounce voluntarily their

[120]J. J. Rousseau, *Du Contrat social* (1762); in *Oeuvres complètes* vol. 3 (Paris: 1964), pp. 381–2.
[121]*On the Jewish Question* (1844); MEW 1, p. 370.

supremacy as the exploiting class.[122] In the *Critique of the Gotha Program* (1875) Marx stated explicitly that a "revolutionary dictatorship of the proletariat" would form the necessary transitional phase between capitalist and communist societies. Its own social antagonisms gradually destroy the capitalist system from within both economically and socially and at the same time prepare the ground for its successor. There is nothing accidental to such a phenomenon for the realization of a proletarian dictatorship presupposes a certain level of material and intellectual development at which regression is rendered altogether impossible. In other words, the postulate of proletarian hegemony in the state precludes any possibility of failure. To merit the name of "proletarian," therefore, a dictatorship must be succeeded by the new social form which that dictatorship was instituted for the purpose of creating; thus the existence of a *proletarian* dictatorship can be demonstrated only a posteriori. Consequently any dictatorship that is overthrown cannot have been a dictatorship of the proletarian majority.

As an ethical challenge Marx's thought has lost none of its validity and remains as intensely provocative and instructive for modern man as it was a century ago. The value judgments and moral imperatives Marx voiced to rouse the working men of the nineteenth century appeal in an equal measure to the revolutionary consciousness of our era. More than ever in the past, the present times are filled with horrors that defy even the most vivid imaginations; we, the builders of today, are well placed to recognize that Marx in no way exaggerated his account of the crisis theory in capitalism, a theory that in the early part of this century might well have been taken for the

[122]Without doubt Marx developed most definitively his ideas of the conquest and overcoming of the state apparatus by the proletariat in his writings on the Paris Commune, although here his conception differs from that elaborated in the *Communist Manifesto*. In any case, however, Marx never conceived of the proletarian dictatorship as meaning that the proletariat would ever abandon the fundamental liberties won by the bourgeois revolution or that a minority of "new" men would become society's dictators, manifesting their claims to political omnipotence and "dialectical" omniscience. Mention should also be made of the distortion to which this Marxian concept was subjected in the hands of Engels. It was the latter who, after Marx's death, first promulgated the legend that the Commune, in Marx's words "a government of the working class," was in fact his model for the future proletarian dictatorship; cf. Jules Andrieu, *Notes pour servir à l'histoire de la commune de Paris en 1871*, ed. with an introduction by M. Rubel (Paris: 1971), pp. xvi ff.

product of an obsessed mind. The manifold threats to our contemporary world not only confirm without reservations Marx's most pessimistic predictions but also add weight to their significance. Let us therefore discover and acknowledge in Marx the man he was fundamentally – not the scholar or the visionary, but the ethical theorist of the social revolution.

3

A history of Marx's "Economics"

From philosophy to political economy

The story of Marx's "Economics" is the story of a long obsession. At the outset, he chose political economy as but one of several subjects that he aimed to treat in a series of brochures. Yet after forty years of repeated efforts, each time beginning afresh, Marx was unable to finish the task of actually writing his "Economics." The burden was simply too heavy to be borne by one man alone, and Marx's "bourgeois poverty" only made it all the more crushing. In that work, which forcibly remained unfinished, everything was connected: Marx's personal distress was only a particular case of the poverty of a civilization whose theoretical negation was to be the prelude to its practical destruction and the birth of a new society. Marx's *Capital* is a history of a world in the course of self-destruction, a pathology of an inhuman society; but it is only a fragment of a collective work of criticism that will end only with the complete ruin of the economic system being analyzed. Marx nourished his work not only with ideas drawn from other authors but with their passion and hatred as well. He himself defined the meaning of his perennial reading: "I am," he once confided to his daughter Laura, "a machine condemned to devour books and then throw them in a changed form on the dunghill of history."[1] It is not necessary to read between the lines of *Capital* to discern in it, from the very beginning, an act of moral condemnation and rejection. The real target behind Marx's criticism of the science of political economy was a specific mode of existence, the mode of life and labor of humanity threatened by its own achievements, its technical inventions and institutions. *Capital,* itself a scientific work, is directed against a science whose pretext is the wealth of nations and whose raison d'être is the enslavement of "the poorest

[1] Letter written in English to his daughter, Laura Lafargue, Apr. 11, 1868; in *Annali,* Instituto Giangiacomo Feltrinelli, Milan, I (1958), 167.

82

and the most numerous class." For Karl Marx, political economy was the theory of evil, the science of the dominant social
order, and he undertook the study of economics with the
single, fixed purpose of censure and denunciation. Marx in-
tuited that evil before he had any theoretical certitude about it,
in fact even before he began the study of political economy. He
went from socialism to science, not from science to socialism.
His revolutionary faith preceded all scientific demonstrations,
and he did not intend, in writing *Capital,* to found a new
philosophy or a new economic science. What was needed was
not a new interpretation of the world, but a radical critique
that would destroy a science that, while giving the appearance
of objectivity, was actually the science of the means of obtain-
ing wealth by producing poverty. Marx aimed to give explanations in order to pillory the exploitation of labor; he aimed to
destroy delusions, to tear apart the deceptive veil of an ideology that justifies the exploitation of man by man. In short,
Marx's ambition was the critique of political economy. One
thing is certain: Prior to becoming a socialist, and before turning to economics with the goal of laying scientific foundations
to the movement of working-class emancipation, he had already established his scale of values and spontaneously condemned both the state and money.

However, this interpretation must be qualified: Only with
apparent suddenness did Marx adhere to the working-class
movement and to socialism. His already profound reflections
matured through experience. When forced to abandon his
plans for a university career he turned to journalism, but then
was condemned to silence by an arbitrary government hostile
to a free press. Moreover, prior to his marriage his family
refused him his share of the paternal inheritance that would
have allowed him to face more easily the hard test of exile.[2]
These successive obstacles made his studious retreat into the
calm setting of Kreuznach, in the spring and summer of 1843,
one of the decisive moments in his intellectual growth. The
meditation to which he devoted himself in Kreuznach, after the
suppression of the *Rheinische Zeitung,* bore fruit: His two
essays, which were finished a few months later in Paris, were
by far the most important pieces published in the *Deutsch-*

[2]For details concerning the obstacles that Marx's mother and Jenny von West-
phalen's family put in the way of the couple's marriage, see Marx's letters to Arnold
Ruge, dated July 9, 1842, Jan. 25, and Mar. 13, 1843; *MEW* 27, pp. 405, 415, 417.

Französische Jahrbücher (Franco-German Annals) in February
1844. These essays, *On the Jewish Question* and the *Introduction to a Contribution to the Critique of Hegel's Philosophy of Right,* are two facets of a single manifesto whose substance
would be reasserted four years later in the *Manifesto of the
Communist Party* (and twenty years after that in *Capital*). In
that period of 1844–48 Marx began the critique of political
economy, producing three important texts: the *Economic and
Philosophic Manuscripts, The Poverty of Philosophy,* and
Wage-Labor and Capital. In the same productive period he
conceived what is called the "materialist" theory of history
and explicitly formulated it for the first time in *The German
Ideology,* a collective work that also included the participation
of Moses Hess, the "father of German communism," and his
disciple, Friedrich Engels.

Thus Marx came to socialism through the two-fold motivation of the heart and the intellect, and his decision became all
the more firm as his work in his scientific project progressed.
The key to *Capital* is contained already in his writings of
1843–4: There we find the conclusion to the work that was
still to be written. The only way to understand both the scope
of Marx's "Economics" and the reason for its incompletion is
to follow the intellectual and affective course of a lifetime
spent in pursuit of a single aim.

The studies and meditations in Kreuznach

As a liberal journalist formed in the school of neo-Hegelianism,
Marx spent an entire year fighting for freedom of the press. In
the Prussian state, where religion was the state's spiritual substance and censorship had been made an all-powerful institution, public spirit was held strictly in tow. Against this state
Marx defended the idea of a state based on free reason. To
combat a regime whose morals coincided with the purpose of
the state and that subjected society to permanent espionage, he
chose to support the autonomous ethics that Spinoza, Kant, and
Fichte had opposed to religion based on the heteronomy of the
human spirit. The state appointed its servants as "spies of the
heart, omniscient men, philosophers, theologians, political men,
oracles of Delphi," in short, as a bureaucracy possessed of esoteric knowledge and strangely resembling the millenary organization of the Chinese state. Marx called for a nation of free

men educating one another, of citizens freely and consciously giving themselves public laws – the natural laws of their own reason, human reason.[3] In his quest for a rational state and in the name of the public interest he attacked the privileges of the great landowners, demanding on behalf of the victims of poverty the recognition of a property consecrated by common law, an inviolable legacy of the high Middle Ages. He questioned the argument enunciated by Proudhon two years before: "If every violation of property, without distinction or specification, is called theft, then is not all private property theft? Do I not by my private property deprive the other of that property?" Already an idea appeared to be taking shape that was later to be the keystone of Marx's political sociology: the idea of the state as instrument of the possessing classes. "The organization of the state, the role of the various administrative authorities, all have to be turned upside down in order to be nothing but an instrument of the property owner, whose interest must appear to be the soul that animates the whole mechanism. All the organs of the state become the ears, eyes, arms and legs with which the interest of the forest owners listens, watches, reckons, protests, grasps and pursues."[4] To this description of the real Prussian state Marx opposed an ideal vision that, sublimating the state, was in fact its negation: "The state radiates spiritual nerves throughout the whole of nature; and it must everywhere appear that it is not matter but form, not nature without the state but the nature of the state, not the *unfree object* but *free man*, which dominates."[5]

But before arriving at the negation of the state as such, Marx had to free himself from the spell of the philosopher who had been one of his principal teachers: His Kreuznach studies provided the occasion for a final confrontation with the political philosophy of Hegel.

In his preface to *A Contribution to the Critique of Political Economy* (1859) Marx relates how he had come fifteen years earlier, through a critique of Hegel's philosophy of right, to discover the "anatomy of civil society" in political economy.

[3]See Marx's articles in the *Rheinische Zeitung* (Cologne: 1842) and the *Anekdota zur neuesten deutschen Philosophie und Publizistik* (edited in Switzerland by Arnold Ruge, 1843); *MEW* 1, pp. 3–77.

[4]Cf. Marx's articles on the "Debates on the Wood Theft Laws"; *Rheinische Zeitung* (Oct. and Nov. 1842); *MEW* 1, pp. 109–47.

[5]Cf. the article on "The Estates Committees in Prussia"; *Rheinische Zeitung* (Dec. 31, 1842); *MEGA* I, 1/1, pp. 334–54.

Thus on Marx's own word it was in 1843, that is, *prior to* his first economic studies, that he discovered what he called, in the same preface of 1859, the "guideline" of his studies: precisely the materialist conception of history. "To resolve the doubts that assailed me [with respect to the French socialism and communism echoed in the *Rheinische Zeitung*] I undertook a first work, a critical revision of Hegel's philosophy of right. The Introduction to this work appeared in the *Deutsch-Französische Jahrbücher* published in Paris in 1844. My studies led to the following results," and so on.[6]

The incomplete text of that "critical revision" was published for the first time in 1927. Prior to that only Marx's introduction to it was available. It is a voluminous manuscript rich in insights that, despite their polemical tone, constitute altogether a meticulous exegesis both of Hegel's political thought and of his style as well. Marx points up Hegel's imaginary antinomies, his tautologies, feats of sophistry, and mystifications, in short, the speculative artifices used to support a central argument on which pivots the entire construction of Hegel's political system: The people and society are of themselves nothing, the state is everything. This is the quintessence of Hegel's philosophical effort, and one need only "translate it into prose" to uncover the entire hoax. In Hegel's "logical, pantheistic mysticism" the state – which is the reality of the moral Idea, the moral spirit – appears to be an unconscious emanation from the family and civil society; but at the same time, as the "real (or actual) Idea," this state generates the family and civil society within itself as its own "finitude." By a clever subterfuge Hegel makes the concrete mediation an "appearance" distinct from the "reality" of the Idea. Marx responds with the image of a reality composed of concrete relations subjected to the rule of arbitrariness: The family and civil society are the real subjects, the active elements of the state. He minutely dissects the construction of Hegel's speculative arguments and concludes that the philosophy of right is merely a "parenthesis" to the Hegelian logic. For Hegel "the Logic does not serve to verify the state, rather the state serves to verify the Logic." Marx discloses the true intention behind Hegel's sophisms: to demonstrate the necessity of the Prussian monarchic state and "to present the monarch as the true God-man, the veritable incarnation of the Idea." In the end the

[6] *Zur Kritik der politischen Oekonomie. Vorwort; MEW* 13, p. 8.

apology for hereditary power is reduced to a justification of animality pure and simple: "In this system, nature produces kings and peers just as it produces eyes and noses . . . . In this system, the highest social dignities are incarnated in particular bodies, predestined by birth."[7] The best pages of Marx's text are devoted to refuting this metaphysical axiom. He then proceeds to reveal a concept of democracy in which can be glimpsed the germ of his conception of socialism, or more precisely the reason for his adherence to the cause of the proletariat. This development, however, does not become explicit until the introduction to this unpublished critique of Hegel, subsequently drafted in Paris.

Critique of the state and defense of democracy

For Hegel, the monarch is a kind of ontological proof of the rationality of the state. No wonder then that he had a confused if not monstrous notion of popular sovereignty. The crux of the problem is an irreducible antinomy: sovereignty of the monarch or sovereignty of the people. Marx's choice is categorical: "Democracy is the resolved *enigma* of all constitutions" for only in democracy is man free to give himself a constitution. The concept of democracy thus implies the transcendence, indeed the negation, of the political sphere in the state, whether republican or monarchic.

Just as religion does not create man, but man religion, so the constitution does not create the people, but the people the constitution. In a certain sense democracy is to all other forms of the state what Christianity is to all other religions. Christianity is religion *par excellence,* the *essence of religion,* deified man as a *particular* religion. So also, democracy is the *essence of every state constitution,* socialized man as a *particular* state constitution; its relation to all constitutions is that of the genus to the species . . . All other forms of state are related to democracy as its Old Testament. Man does not exist for the sake of the law, but the law for the sake of man; democracy is *human existence,* whereas in the other forms man has only *legal existence.* This is the specific character of democracy.[8]

Here Marx transposes the Feuerbachian critique of religion into the realm of social relations. If it is true that man dehu-

[7]*MEW* I, pp. 216, 313.
[8]*MEW* I, p. 231.

manizes himself in relinquishing his attributes to an unreal being, then his dehumanization is more monstrous still when he betrays his social vocation to the advantage of a real being, namely the political state. In fact the democracy Marx envisioned here was realized in none of the existing forms of government, for in all of them man was separated from himself, alienated from himself and from others. "Until now the political constitution has been the *religious sphere*, the *religion* of popular life, the heaven of its universality as opposed to the *earthly existence* of its reality . . . . *Political* life in the modern sense is the *scholasticism* of the people's life. The monarchy is the perfected expression of this alienation. The republic is the negation of this alienation within its own sphere."[9] A political constitution has achieved perfection when the realms of private property have an independent existence; for example, once commerce and landed property are free. During the Middle Ages, which was the "democracy of non-liberty" and the "rule of absolute alienation," the people's life was identical with the life of the state whose real principle was subjugated man. Modern times have witnessed the abstraction of the political state; and since the French Revolution separated political life from society as a whole, private life assumed a separate existence and organized itself outside the political sphere: This was the case especially in the political republic, which is democracy within the abstract form of the state.

Hegel clearly defined the separation of bourgeois society and the political state as a rational truth. He "opposes bourgeois society as private estate [*Stand*] to the political state"; yet his intention was not to separate civil life from political life. After having "made the 'estates' the expression of that separation between the two modes of life" he wants them to "represent the identity, the synthesis" of the two. After having admitted their separation he wants the unity of bourgeois society and political state to be achieved within the state by making the "estates" of bourgeois society the legislative element of the state. As for these "estates," Marx notes, "it is private interest which constitutes their general interest, and not the general interest which constitutes their private interest." They are "the expression of the contradiction between state and society"; but for Hegel "they are supposed to effect the synthesis, though he refrained from explaining just how these contraries could be reconciled."

[9]*MEW* I, p. 233.

Political representation, police, tribunals, administration: These constitute the Hegelian "mediation" between the people and the governing power. Philosophy takes the form of the Prussian civil code; Hegel "gives his logic a political body."[10] Marx discerned, within Hegel's philosophy of the state, the nature of future bureaucratic society under evolved capitalism (a theme to which he later returned in his writings on the Second Empire—i.e., *The 18th Brumaire of Louis Bonaparte, 1852,* and *The Civil War in France, 1871*—and in *Capital*). We may suppose, therefore, that the phenomenon of bureaucracy would have constituted the major theme of the work he proposed to devote to the state.[11] Thus, an understanding of Marx's "Economics" would be incomplete without a reading of these masterful pages of the anti-Hegel manuscript, important fragments of which appear here.

The bureaucratic spirit is a fundamentally Jesuitical, theological spirit. The bureaucrats are the Jesuits and theologians of the state. The bureaucracy is *la république prêtre* . . . The bureaucracy identifies itself with the final end of the state. Making formal aims its content, it everywhere comes into conflict with real aims, which obliges it to present the form as the content and the content as the form. The purposes of the state are changed into the purposes pursued by the bureaus and vice versa. The bureaucracy is a circle from which no one can escape. Its hierarchy is a *hierarchy of knowledge* . . . The bureaucracy holds in its possession the state, the spiritual essence of society: the state is its *private property*. The general spirit of bureaucracy is that of secrecy, mystery: within, it is the hierarchy that preserves this secrecy, and without, it is preserved because the bureaucracy is a closed corporation. Hence, to the bureaucracy an open spirit of the state, as well as state awareness, appear to betray its spirit of secrecy. This is why *authority* is the principle of its knowledge and the idolatry of authority is its mentality. But within the bureaucracy itself this *spiritualism* turns into *crass materialism,* the materialism of passive obedience, of blind belief in authority, of mechanically fixed and formal practice, of rigid principles, concep-

[10]*MEW* 1, p. 250. Here Marx imitates his teacher, Feuerbach, who had "revealed" the inversion of the subject-predicate relationship as the source of speculative philosophy. In applying this critical method to Hegel's political philosophy, Marx surpassed the intentions of Feuerbach, author of the *Provisional Theses for the Reform of Philosophy* (1842) and *Principles of the Philosophy of the Future* (1843). Cf. Ludwig Feuerbach, *Sämtliche Werke,* vol. 2 (Stuttgart: 1959), pp. 222–320. Marx's criticism is directed in particular against §§ 267 and 269 of Hegel's work; cf. *MEW* 1, pp. 209–17.

[11]See the section "The method and themes of the 'Economics' " in this essay.

tions and traditions. As for the individual bureaucrat, he makes the state's aim his own private aim: the *pursuit of higher posts, careerism*. In the first place, he regards real life as *material* life, for *the spirit of this life has its proper and autonomous existence* in the bureaucracy ... The state exists only in the form of various rigid bureaucratic minds related one to another by subordination and passive obedience. *True* science appears devoid of content, just as real life appears dead, for this imaginary science and life are held to be real. This is why the bureaucrat must, whether consciously or unconsciously, act in a Jesuit-like manner towards the state. But as soon as their Jesuitism faces knowledge of this contradiction, it must become self-conscious and thus deliberate.[12]

Hegel distinguishes two kinds of "identities" between the interest of the state and the particular, private end. The first identity—election—is superficial: The election of those who rule in no way lessens the conflict between private interest and the "higher interest." Moreover, Hegel is candid enough to recognize within the state the "natural power of arbitrariness." The second identity lies in the chance that every citizen has to become a functionary. This, says Marx, is no less superficial, and he compares civil society and the state to "two hostile armies" and their "deserters."[13]

However, it would be inaccurate to conclude from this attack on the political state that thereafter Marx condemned the state as such. On the contrary, he continued to demand a "true" state, a "rational" state—in other words, a real democracy. But his allusions to this remain vague, and the negative element of his criticism, which is directed toward refuting Hegel's attempts at conciliation and compromise, greatly overshadows any positive anticipation of his own concepts. The Hegelian argument regarding the monarch's inherent sovereignty and that of the bureaucracy is a parody of Catholic theology and projects over the Church the unreality of the divine sovereignty. Political society, Hegel affirms, is an open society; each citizen can accede to it by chancing an examination, which is the objective bond between the knowledge proper to civil society and the knowledge proper to the state. In reality, Marx counters, this ascent within the hierarchy of power and knowledge is far from having the rational character

[12] *MEW* 1, pp. 248–9.
[13] *MEW* 1, p. 253.

Hegel ascribes to it. "The examination is nothing but the bureaucratic baptism of knowledge, the official recognition of the transsubstantiation of profane into sacred knowledge." To consecrate the public function a new element of chance appears: One accedes to the rank of political man by the grace of the prince. Examination and election are the objective and subjective factors of the citizen's political alienation: Two beings, the functionary and the man, struggle within the same individual without ever reaching agreement.

State, civil society, and the religion of private property

The mystifying character of the dialectical antinomies established by Hegel regarding legislative power prompted Marx to undertake a historical reexamination of the problem. Hegel managed to avoid the antinomy between the constitution and the legislature only at the cost of another antinomy: The state constitutes the realization of free spirit, but to muffle the collisions between the constitution and the legislature, Hegel is forced to invoke blind natural necessity, which is the negation of freedom. Now, all revolutions "of a general and organic character," including the French Revolution, have been the work of the legislative power, which represents the people and the collective will; all retrograde revolutions, on the other hand, have been the work of the executive governmental power, which represents the particular, subjective, and arbitrary will.[14]

History belies Hegel's idea of a gradual evolution of constitutions. Constitutions have only changed radically as a result of revolutions under the constraint of social conditions and social needs. If this transformation is to occur without violence, every future constitution must have progress as its principle and the people as its true support. If the constitution ceases to express the people's will, then they have the right to give themselves a new one. In Hegel's political system, neither the people nor the estates know what they want; they lack true political knowledge, for that is the monopoly of the functionaries. The state demands only one thing of individuals in exchange for the "objects" of legislative power: money, which is the value of objects and services. Real conflicts hide behind the

[14]*MEW* 1, pp. 257–60.

"organic unity" that Hegel postulates of the different powers, and his great respect for the state's moral spirit veils a profound contempt for the "many" and for the corporative element as delegated by bourgeois society. Marx now moves from a critique of the Prussian state idealized by Hegel to a critique of the *Idea* of the modern or constitutional state, within which "public affairs" are monopolized by the governmental power:

A constitutional state is one in which the public interest as the people's real interest has only formal existence. . .alongside the real state. . .It has become a mere formality, the *haut goût* of the people's life, a mere ceremony. The corporative element is the sanctioned, legal lie of constitutional states which decree that the state is the people's interest or that the people is the state's interest. The state's real contents will expose this lie which establishes itself as legislative power precisely because the contents of this power are the general interest, because it is an affair of knowledge rather than of will, because it is the metaphysical state power; whereas the same lie established as governmental power etc. would have to either break down immediately or else become a truth. The metaphysical state power was the most appropriate seat for the universal, metaphysical illusion about the state.[15]

Here the materialist interpretation of social phenomena begins to emerge. The general law applies to the individual: As a citizen he participates in a two-fold organization, the bureaucratic order, which is the emanation of the transcendent state, and the social order in which he is a private being outside the state. For Hegel, this atomism is part and parcel of the very nature of the people; for Marx, it is the condition that typifies bourgeois society: Man must effect a split within his own essence. In Marx's first economic works this condition of psychic bifurcation will be called "alienation," a term that here designates the separation of the individual from his real human and social being. In bourgeois society this alienation is expressed by the opposition between the political state and political life, the "ethereal region of civil society." By reducing the political differences of the Middle Ages to private differences devoid of political bearing, the French Revolution perfected and achieved the representative system that transformed political orders into social, bourgeois orders. Here Marx outlines the problem that Hegel treated in the section of his *Phi-*

[15]*MEW* 1, p. 268.

losophy of Right dealing with "Civil Society" (§182–256), and particularly in the chapter on "The System of Needs" (§189–§208). Marx intended to criticize this section as well, but abandoned that project in order to begin his critique of political economy. In fact, it is in the final pages of the Kreuznach manuscript that he first focuses his attention on the working class – "the estate of direct and concrete labor," the propertyless estate, which provides the "foundation" for the spheres of bourgeois society.[16] This incipient social analysis marks the shift toward political economy: Marx considers the social position of the members of the different professions in relation to the community and the classes, and he finds bourgeois society to be the "accomplished principle of individualism." As yet unfamiliar with the history of revolutions, Marx speaks exclusively of *Stände*, that is, social estates, and not "social classes," in this text. Nonetheless, we discover here already the elements of his future critique: The political constitution is the constitution of private property, and the "reality of the moral Idea" is merely the "religion of private property."[17]

From this point on, Marx's critical analysis centers on the material character of social conflicts. Thanks to that "mediation" that is the speculative mystery of logic, Hegel's philosophy – a syncretism of the basest coin – has succeeded in disguising antagonisms as harmonies. Woven with the aid of dialectical subterfuges, the romantic veil that identifies the state's will with that of the social orders masks the opposed interests of landed property and "wealth" (*Vermögen*). Primogeniture is petrified private property. Hegel inverts the causal relationship, holding that the political state dominates private property by means of primogeniture; for Marx, it is private property that dominates. The inalienability of landed property expressed in primogeniture severs the "social nerves" of private property by isolating it from civil society and even from family life, which is the state of natural morality: Primogeniture is the "barbarism of private property against family life"; it is the most abstract form of private arbitrariness. Hegel elevates this medieval institution, which is the seigneurial form of private property, above the "insecurity of a trade, the thirst for gain, the instability of property, the dependence of wealth," whereas Marx prefers the "true idealism" of private right, which limits

[16]*MEW* 1, p. 284.
[17]*MEW* 1, p. 307.

the arbitrariness of private property: "Compared to the brute stupidity of autonomous private property there is something elegiac in the insecurity of a trade, something pathetic (dramatic) in the thirst for gain, something gravely fatal (tragic) in the vicissitudes of property, something moral in the dependence on the state's fortune. In short, in all these emotions one hears the human heart beating through the property; it is a sign that man depends on man . . ." Those who benefit from primogeniture know nothing of man's innate rights. Further, Hegel exalts the vocation of legislator and public representative by virtue of birth while degrading a vocation by "the hazard of election." Thus, birth confers on certain individuals the right to personify the highest state functions. Hegel's political spiritualism is actually a vulgar materialism in which the highest social honors are held by title of birth and belong to "predestined bodies"; this is a zoological philosophy crowned by the science of heraldry: "The secret of the nobility is zoology."[18]

Hegel's merit lies in having exposed the morality of the modern state and modern private right as the morality of the illusory existence of abstract subjectivity and the right of abstract personality. The person of private right and the subject of this morality are precisely the state considered as person and subject. In wishing to emancipate morality and separate it from the state, certain critics of Hegel have simply shown that the separation of the modern state from morality is itself moral, that morality cannot be of the state, and that the state is not moral. "On the contrary," notes Marx, "his [Hegel's] great merit – though in a way . . . unconscious – is to have assigned its true place to modern morality."[19]

Marx makes a historical comparison between Roman, Germanic, and modern private rights, undoubtedly inspired by Proudhon's Mémoire sur la propriété.[20] With respect to the modern form of property rights Marx was particularly concerned with the French Constitution promulgated following the July Revolution; that constitution represented an "advance" in that it clearly set forth the political principle, the modern idea of the state as bourgeois society abstracted from

[18]MEW 1, p. 311. To criticize Hegel's ideas on primogeniture, Marx refers back to the first part of The Philosophy of Right, the first section of which treats property. Hegel's §§ 65 to 71 are devoted to the "alienation of property"; cf. MEW 1, pp. 305–11.

[19]MEW 1, p. 313.

[20]MEW 1, pp. 313–16.

itself. Hegel's political philosophy, on the other hand, did not succeed in freeing itself from the perspective of medieval institutions, of corporate right, in which the democratic element is no more than the formal principle of a state organism elevated to the rank of absolute Idea devoid of any material content. Hegel saw clearly the dilemma of popular participation in state affairs: Either civil society enters into political decisions by means of deputies, or *everyone* does so as an individual. But this problem, Marx notes, is only an abstract political problem intrinsic to the abstraction of the political state; the problem itself results from the separation of the political state from bourgeois society. "On the one hand, bourgeois society would disappear as such if all of its members were legislators; on the other hand, the political state which opposes it can accept it only in a form suitable to its, i.e. the state's, own standard." In short, the participation of bourgeois society in the political state by means of deputies is indicative precisely of its separation from, and strictly "dualistic" unity with, the state. In a really political civil society, by contrast, the legislative power is a social activity that expresses the needs of man as a species. "For example, the cobbler, insofar as he satifies a social need, is my representative. . .that is to say, a determination of my being, just as every man is representative of the other. He is representative not by virtue of something else which he represents, but by virtue of what he *is* and does."[21]

Marx now explains the struggles to reform the electoral laws in France and England by reference to the dualistic nature of the legislative power. From the standpoint of representative constitutionalism the question is not to decide whether bourgeois society should have recourse to deputies or whether each individual should exercise legislative power, but whether it is fitting to extend and generalize the right of suffrage, active and passive. Suffrage, therefore, is the true political interest of mature bourgeois society. In fact, democracy must lead to the abolition of the political state: "In universal active and passive suffrage, bourgeois society rises finally and really to its own abstraction, to political existence as its true universal essence. But achievement of this abstraction is simultaneously its negation. In truly making political existence its real existence, bourgeois society recognizes its bourgeois existence as inessential as

[21] *MEW* 1, pp. 324–5.

distinguished from its political existence; and when one of the separated elements disappears, so does the other, its opposite. Consequently, electoral reform within the abstract political state means the dissolution of this state and thus of bourgeois society itself."[22]

At this point Marx announces his intention to consider "later" the question of suffrage from the point of view of the various "interests" and their conflicts. However, here we reach the final pages of the manuscript, and as Marx's criticism grows more and more acid he finally brands as "abject" Hegel's servile, bureaucratic mentality. Marx never resumed this exegesis, but before turning to political economy he defined his new credo in *The Jewish Question* and the *Introduction to a Contribution to the Critique of Hegel's Philosophy of Right*. These two essays are in fact the conclusion of his interrupted critique of Hegel.

From speculation to revolution

Marx could not follow Hegel in his metaphysical flights without suffering a certain vertigo. What better remedy could there be than to read history while pursuing the philosophical exegesis? Marx's study of the bourgeois revolutions is, in a sense, the intermediate state between his critical revision of the Hegelian philosophy of the state and the study of the "anatomy" of bourgeois society, that is, political economy. His analysis of the great social struggles was to disclose to him the real source of the conflicts of interest and the class antagonisms that Hegel had disguised as oppositions and contradictions between ideas and principles at the heart of the absolute Idea. Hegel's own spirit of encyclopedic curiosity had been alerted to the problems of Germany's destiny, of its past and future. There is no doubt that the historical allusions that abound in *The Philosophy of Right* prompted Marx to study the origins of that "civil society," which was one of the essential themes in Hegel's work. Moreover, Marx had originally intended to include this theme as well in his critical revision. There is little doubt that history, more than any other scientific discipline, including political economy, was Marx's true intellectual passion, and was also the only field that allowed him to display his various talents as a

[22]*MEW* I, pp. 326–7.

thinker and writer. During the last decade of his life, when ill health kept him from completing his "Economics," he would while away the slow struggle with death by compiling extensive chronologies. That simple work of a copyist was to be his ultimate intellectual enjoyment.[23]

During the summer of 1843 in Kreuznach, Marx began to acquaint himself with the history of the French, English, and American revolutions and their consequences. His efforts are recorded in five study notebooks totaling more than 250 pages.[24] Among the works from which he made excerpts, three are not histories in the strict sense: Rousseau's *Du Contrat social* (103 excerpts), Montesquieu's *De l'Esprit des lois* (109 excerpts), and Machiavelli's *Discorsi sopra le Deche di Tito Livio* (20 excerpts from the 1832 German translation by Johannes Ziegler).

Marx's guides in studying pre-revolutionary French history were the best German historiographers of the time, C. G. Heinrich and E. A. Schmidt. In their works he examined principally the social and juridicial structure of Gaul, feudalism, the growth of towns and the birth of the bourgeois communes, the development of the peerage from Philip II to Philip IV, the Third Estate and the Assembly of Estates General, and the notables and the parliament, among other topics. For the period of the French Revolution itself, he relied chiefly on C. F. E. Ludwig's *Geschichte der letzten fünfzig Jahre;* he summarized his excerpts from Ludwig as follows: "Representation of wealth in the Constitutent Assembly, the Saint Bartholomew's Day of property. Division of the National Assembly on the subject of private property; the maximum; the Jacobins opposed to, the royalists in favor of popular sovereignty. Revolutionary government. The situation in France before the Revolution." From J. C. Bailleul's work, which refuted Mme de Staël's *Considérations* on the French Revolution, he drew material that focused especially on the differences relative to property between the feudal system and modern society. He

[23]On Marx as a historian, see M. Rubel, *Karl Marx devant la bonapartisme* (Paris/ The Hague: 1960), pp. 7 ff.

[24]Altogether Marx made more than seven hundred excerpts from twenty-four different books; this material includes two chronologies, one for France (from 600 B.C. to 1589), the other for Germany (from its origins to the end of the seventeenth century). See *MEGA* I, 1/2, XXIV–XXIX, 105–6, 118–36; also M. Rubel, "Les Cahiers de Lecture. 1840–1856" ("Les Cahiers d'étude de Marx"), in *Marx Critique du marxisme* (Paris: 1974), pp. 301–59.

carefully summarized Wilhelm Wachsmuth's work on the history of revolutionary France, paying particular attention to class conflicts, problems of liberty and equality, the agitation by the Hébertists, the great revolutionary personages, and the *sansculottes*. The works of C. de Lacretelle, two brochures of Chateaubriand, a book by K. W. von Lancizolle, and several studies of Leopold Ranke provided the material for his excerpts on the Restoration period and the July Monarchy; these excerpts are centered on constitutional history and the problems of administrative centralization and communal and corporative rights as well as on electoral law, the Charter, the property rights of the old nobility, the state religion, the sovereignty of the people, and the opposition between town and country.[25]

Several books on England furnished Marx with reflections on a wide variety of topics such as liberty and order in bourgeois society, the poor laws, unemployment and wages, parliamentary reform under Cromwell and the reform projects of Pitt, the Crown and Parliament, the refusal of all reform by evoking the specter of the French Revolution, the press, the consequences of the Norman conquest, the old Anglo-Saxon Constitution, the Magna Carta, the royalty and nobility, the history of the English Parliament, the development of cities and the bourgeoisie, the growth of the authority of the House of Commons, feudalism in England and France, political and civil liberties, landed property, the basis

[25]During the first months of his stay in Paris, which dated from late October 1843, Marx resumed his study of the French Revolution with the intention of writing a history of the Convention. Certain pages in his Paris writings attest to his interest in historical research. Commenting, for example, on the *Mémoires* of the ex-Conventionary R. Levasseur (1829), Marx noted with sympathy the initiatives to establish "popular power," those "improvised centres of government, the emanation of anarchy itself" that, from 1791 to 1792, led to the Convention. Marx introduced his notes with the following remark from Levasseur that reflects the essence of his future works as a historian and admirer of proletarian spontaneity: "Therefore, what is taken today as the delirium of a fanatical few was the common sentiment of an entire people, and in a way its manner of existing" (*MEGA* I, 3, p. 419). When he began studying political economy some months later, Marx nevertheless did not abandon his project of historical work, which was in fact his true intellectual vocation. Consequently, the pages devoted to the French Revolution in *The Holy Family* are very significant; he wrote, for example, the following characteristic passage in response to Bruno Bauer's remarks on the role of "ideas" in the French Revolution: "*Ideas* can never advance beyond an old world system; they can only surpass the ideas of the old world system. Ideas can *realize nothing* at all. To realize ideas, men who exert practical force are needed . . ." (*MEW* 2, p. 126).

of the nobility's strength and, in turn, that of the constitutional monarchy.[26]

Although his readings in the history of Germany, Sweden, Italy, Switzerland, and Poland count for little in the Kreuznach notebooks, Marx devoted a number of pages to material on America, excerpted from the work of an author who has unjustly fallen into oblivion today: *Men and Manners in America* by Thomas Hamilton.[27] Hamilton's book is the narrative of his voyage to North America, first published in 1833, hence prior to de Tocqueville's *De la Démocratie en Amérique*. In certain respects it surpasses the latter work in the vigor of its descriptions and the remarkable insight of its predictions. Perhaps unconsciously the Scottish traveler drew conclusions that were much more radical than those of his French successor. In illustrating the progress and tendency of opinion among the inhabitants of New York City, he sketched the principal traits of the social future of the United States and its class struggle. "In that city a separation is rapidly taking place between the different orders of society. The operative class have already formed themselves into a society, under the name of *The Workies*, in direct opposition to those who, more favoured by nature or fortune, enjoy the luxuries of life without the necessity of manual labour." One of the Workies' principal demands was for equal and universal schooling, because differences in education had created a practical aristocracy, and one "of the most odious kind – an aristocracy of knowledge, education, and refinement, which is inconsistent with the true democratic principle of absolute equality." All of their physical and mental efforts were oriented toward destroying this flagrant injustice, toward attaining the same educational level and acceding to the same offices in the state. An impossible thing, adds Hamilton, for this

[26]In his Kreuznach notebooks, Marx excerpted from the following works on English history: John Russell, *Geschichte der englischen Regierung und Verfassung von Heinrich VII. Regierung bis auf die neueste Zeit*, trans. from the English (Leipzig: 1825); J. M. Lappenberg, *Geschichte von England* (Hamburg: 1834); John Lingard, *Geschichte von England seit dem ersten Einfalle der Römer*, trans. from the English, (Frankfurt: 1827–8).

[27]Marx used the German edition prepared by L. Hout: Thomas Hamilton, *Die Menschen und die Sitten in den Vereinigten Staaten von Nordamerika* (Mannheim: 1834). This book by Hamilton – also author of a novel, *Cyril Thornton*, which enjoyed considerable contemporary success – passed in a short time through three German and two French editions. On North America, Marx also cited in his 1843–4 writings the work of A. de Tocqueville, *De la démocratie en Amérique* (1835), and Gustave de Beaumont's *Marie ou de l'esclavage aux États-Unis* (1835).

is to want "to reduce the richer to the same mental condition as the poor . . ." The radical wing of the Workies was not content to protest against this moral degradation; it demanded an "agrarian law and a periodical division of property." It denounced that monstrous iniquity, the division of rich and poor. "Only equalize property, they say, . . . a consummation worthy of centuries of struggle to attain." After this description of the growing opposition between classes, Hamilton foresees the industrial rise of the United States, accelerated urbanization, industrial concentration, wealth, abundance, crises, a new deterioration of morals and increased impoverishment: "When the pendulum vibrates in one direction, there will be an influx of wealth and prosperity; when it vibrates in the other, misery, discontent, and turbulence will spread through the land. A change of fashion, a war, the glut of a foreign market, a thousand unforeseen and inevitable accidents are liable to produce this, and deprive multitudes of bread, who but a month before were enjoying all the comforts of life."

Federalism and universal suffrage, the citizen's legal as compared to their real situation, conflicts of interest between North and South, the constitutions of the New England States: Such were the important problems that Marx discovered thanks to the striking tableau of American society painted by Hamilton. Behind the facade of democracy and quasiequality remarked on by de Tocqueville, Hamilton was discerning enough to note the revolutionary potentialities of American democracy. After weighing the possibilities of social change as provided by the Constitution and the possibilities of working-class politics in a country that, with its inexhaustible resources, was destined to become a great manufacturing nation, Hamilton delivered in the purest Marxian style this astonishing prediction: "Let it be remembered that in this suffering class will be practically deposited the whole political power of the state; that there can be no military force to maintain civil order, and protect property; and to what quarter, I should be glad to know, is the rich man to look for security, either of person or fortune? . . . Democracy necessarily leads to anarchy and spoliation, it does not seem that the mere length of the road to be travelled is a point of much importance."[28]

Marx needed merely to substitute the word "communism" for Hamilton's "anarchy and spoliation"; later, in the chapter

[28] *Men and Manners in America* (Edinburgh/London: 1833); reprint, 2 vols. in one (New York: Augustus Kelley, 1968), vol. 1, pp. 299–308.

in *Capital* on "The Historical Tendency of the Accumulation of Capital," he was to provide theoretical reinforcement to the warnings voiced by the Scottish writer.[29]

The encounter with socialism

In Kreuznach Marx was no less distrustful and skeptical toward socialist and communist propaganda than he had been during his earlier tenure with the *Rheinische Zeitung*. What did Marx know at this time of socialist literature apart from the philosophical exposition of it in some of Moses Hess's contributions to that newspaper? His study notebooks provide no answer, and because his library was dispersed following his death we are deprived of an important source of information; we do know that during the months he spent in Paris and Brussels, in 1844–5, he acquired a series of utopian and socialist writings.[30]

Here we shall treat only briefly Marx's initial hesitancy. He read the articles by Hess, who is called the "father of German communism," in the *Rheinische Zeitung* and the *Einundzwanzig Bogen aus der Schweiz*.[31] In his *Rheinische Zeitung* articles Hess had boldly exposed the idea of a proletarian revolution as the inevitable result of growing pauperism in industrial countries.[32] This caused the newspaper to be suspected of "communist" tendencies, an accusation that Marx,

[29]Cf. M. Rubel, "Notes on Marx's Conception of Democracy," *New Politics* I, no. 2 (1962), esp. 83–6.

[30]Cf. *MEGA* I, 1/2, xvii ff.; also *Ex libris Karl Marx und Friederich Engels. Schicksal und Verzeichnis einer Bibliothek*, ed. B. Kaiser and I. Werchan (Berlin [East]: Dietz Verlag, 1967), publication of which has revealed the interest Marx showed in utopian literature beginning in 1843–4.

[31]Regarding Hess's contributions to the *Rheinische Zeitung* and the *Einundzwanzig Bogen*, the latter a collection of articles edited by Georg Herwegh and published in Switzerland in 1843, see August Cornu, *Karl Marx et Friedrich Engels*, vol. 2 (Paris: 1958), pp. 71 ff., 136 ff; also Cornu and Wolfgang Mönke, eds., *Moses Hess, Philosophische und sozialistische Schriften, 1837–1850* (Berlin [East]: 1961); and Edmund Silberner, ed., *Moses Hess Briefwechsel* (The Hague: 1969).

[32]Hess coupled his philosophic and visionary speculations on humanity's future with an investigation of the material conditions that accompany social and political changes. He foresaw an imminent revolution, an "effective revolution... which, in contrast to earlier revolutions, will exert not a certain relative influence on social life, but an *absolute* influence." (Cornu and Mönke, *Moses Hess*, p. 120) It will be the work of England, which unites Germany's speculative spirit with France's will to action. Because of the growing concentration of industry and commerce in the hands of a reduced number of capitalists, "it is only in England that the opposition between pauperism and the aristocracy of money will attain that degree of acuity necessary to engender a revolution." M. Hess, *Die europäische Triarchie* (1841); in Ibid., p. 160.

then editor-in-chief, felt obliged, if not to refute, to at least comment on. Feigning a certain skepticism, his response nevertheless betrayed the seriousness with which he himself raised the question of the "class that possesses nothing" and wants – in analogy to the *Tiers Etat* characterized by Sieyès – "to be everything."[33] At this point, still some months before the suppression of the *Rheinische Zeitung*, Marx was thinking of doing a "serious criticism" of communist ideas and mentioned for the first time authors whose ideas if not writings were apparently familiar enough to him. The *Augsburger Zeitung*, he wrote,

> would have to admit . . . that writings like those of Leroux, Considerant, and above all the penetrating work of Proudhon should be criticized not through superficial intuitions, but after long and intensive study . . .We are firmly convinced that the true danger lies not in the practical existence, but rather in the theoretical exposition of communist ideas; for indeed, practical attempts, even those made *en masse,* can be answered with cannons when they become threatening; but ideas that win over our intelligence and conquer our spirit, ideas which reason has imposed on our conscience, are chains from which we cannot tear ourselves away without breaking our hearts, demons which we can overcome only by submitting to them.[34]

Marx was irked with wasting his efforts in a vain struggle against the ill-tempered interference of Prussian censorship. Apparently he was already thinking about the choice of his future study program and had, as early as September 1842, envisaged moving to Paris. Communism as a "dogmatic abstraction" provoked in him the same irritation as Hegel's political philosophy had earlier, and the list of communist authors who intrigued him grew longer: Cabet, Dézamy, Weitling. He even began a first critique: "This communism is itself but a particular manifestation of the humanist principle infected by its contrary, the essence of private property [*Privatwesen*]. The suppression of private property and communism are, therefore, in no way identical. It is not by accident but rather by necessity that communism saw socialist doctrines such as those of Fourier, Proudhon, etc. develop in

[33]"Der Kommunismus und die Augsburger *Allgemeine Zeitung*" (Oct. 16, 1842); *MEW* 1, p. 106.
[34]*MEW* 1, p. 108.

opposition to itself, for communism is itself only a particular, partial realization of the socialist principle."[35]

Careful note should be made of the first doctrinal distinctions found in this text, which appeared some months later at the beginning of the *Deutsch-Französische Jahrbücher:* The same distinctions reappear in Marx's first economic writings, where communism is conceived of as a new humanism. For the moment he preferred socialism to communism; but neither the one nor the other satisfied him as yet because both neglected aspects of man's "theoretical existence" such as religion, science, and politics; these real phenomena are also subject to that radical and pitiless critique of the existing order that, for Marx, must be the vocation of the new type of philosophy. But critical interest alone does not sufficiently explain his distrust of the socialist and communist schools he became acquainted with prior to his departure for France. He must have had some acquaintance with the writings of authors such as Weitling and Lorenz Stein. True, he only spoke of them later; but when he did his words show how much their writings had taught him.[36] As for their influence on his decision to align himself with the working-class movement, without for all that lessening his distrust of the organized schools, it may be said that Marx discovered the modern proletariat in the works of Weitling, Hess, and Stein, and undoubtedly in other authors as well, before coming into direct contact with it in Paris. Weitling personified the proletarian as described by the German intellectual, Stein, who had been sent by his government to Paris to study the "socialism and communism of contemporary France" and to inform the Minister of Police about the political agitation of the German artisans in that city. Marx's reading of Stein and his encounter with the proletarian thinker Weitling would of themselves have sufficed to gain his adherence to the worker's cause without necessarily adopting any socialist or communist doctrine whatsoever. More precisely, it was the vision of the proletariat as executor of a "historic mission" that allowed Marx to

[35]Letter to Arnold Ruge, dated "Kreuznach, in September 1843" and published in the *Deutsch-Französische Jahrbücher* (Feb. 1844); *MEW* 1, p. 344.

[36]Cf. his praise of Weitling's *Garantien der Harmonie und Freiheit* (1842) in "Kritische Randglossen zu dem Artikel 'Der König von Preussen und die Sozialreform.' Von einem Preussen." (*Vorwärts*, Paris, Aug. 1844); *MEW* 1, pp. 392–409. He commented on Lorenz Stein's *Sozialismus und Kommunismus des heutigen Frankreichs* (1842) in an article devoted principally to Karl Grün's book, *Die soziale Bewegung in Frankreich und Belgien* (1845); cf. *MEW* 1, pp. 404–5, and *MEW* 3, pp. 473 ff.

propose a new meaning to socialism and communism, as he attempted a theoretical synthesis, at once scientific and ethical, analytic and normative, of the different doctrines with which he was acquainted. This "development of socialism from utopia to science" – or the transformation of utopian socialism into scientific socialism, as Engels later termed this evolution – was in fact only an unflagging effort to synthesize the multiple schools of thought based on socialist and communist ethics, and to give this synthesis a scientific foundation.[37]

Marx's hesitancy in his first contacts with socialist literature may be interpreted in different ways. What cannot be denied, however, is that the encounter was marked from the beginning by a profound ambiguity. The thirst for realization that carried Marx toward the working-class movement characterized an entire generation of German intellectuals, disciples of Hegel who had, so to speak, dialectically liberated themselves from their master by transforming his speculative philosophy into a "philosophy of action" (*Philosophie der Tat*).[38] Thus, one might readily expect them to produce a program of political action, for example, within the framework of a liberal party. Marx, however, could not be satisfied with such expedients; the empty spiritualism that suffices for the philosopher, even the "critical" philosopher, seemed to him to be a denial of human miseries. After all, did not Hegel's greatness consist in his having abolished (*aufgehoben*) philosophy by perfecting it, that is, by raising it to the heights of a dialectic that itself exposed the vanity of all speculative thought? After a long inner struggle, Marx renounced what he held to be the sterile glory of founding a new philosophy that he knew would be fatally destined to become a new ideology. He bared something of this personal drama to Arnold Ruge when, on the

[37]From among the serious studies of the influences to which Marx was susceptible during his conversion to socialism, we call attention to the following: David Koigen, *Zur Vorgeschichte des modernen philosophischen Sozialismus in Deutschland* (Berne: 1901); Charles Andler, *Introduction historique et commentaire au Manifeste Communiste* (Paris: 1901); and Gustav Adler, *Die Geschichte der ersten sozialpolitischen Arbeiterbewegung in Deutschland* (Breslau: 1885). Although they are outdated in certain respects, these works clarify in an admirable way the intellectual climate that brought Marx's thought to fruition. All of them ascribe much importance to the work of Lorenz Stein in forming Marx's socialist thought. Marx found in Stein the distinction between socialism and communism that was current above all in the writing of French social reformers.

[38]See Horst Stuke, *Philosophie der Tat: Studien Zur "Verwirklichung der Philosophie" bei den Junghegelianern und den Wahren Sozialisten* (Stuttgart: 1963).

verge of quitting his country, he dreamed of a "new rallying point for the truly independent thinking spirits." Then he spoke of "inner difficulties" that seemed more serious than the external obstacles:

For though there is no doubt about the point of departure, there is all the greater confusion about the destination. Not only has general anarchy erupted among the reformers, but each one will have to admit to himself that he has no precise view of what is to come. Nevertheless, this is precisely the advantage of the new trend of thought: far from wanting to anticipate the world dogmatically, we want instead to discover the new world through criticism of the old. Until now the philosophers had the solutions to all enigmas in their desk drawer, and the idiotic world of the uninitiated had simply to open its mouth in order to swallow on the fly the precooked morsels of absolute science. Philosophy has been secularized, and the irrefutable proof of this is the fact that philosophic consciousness has been caught up in the torment of the struggle, outwardly as well as inwardly. If our concern is not to construct the future and achieve it for all times, it is all the more certain that our present task must be *the ruthless criticism of the entire existing order,* a criticism that fears neither its own conclusions nor the conflicts with the powers that be.[39]

We spoke earlier of a certain ambiguity in this attitude. Ambitious to "overcome" Hegelian philosophy, Marx renounced all means of doing so other than through a radical critique of the institutions behind the social order. But is not this critique itself a form of political participation, an access to the arena of real struggles? In other words, in denouncing political emancipation and the political state as hybrid and contradictory phenomena, Marx became convinced, not without some reticence, that his role as a social reformer and educator had to be exercized from within a "large political party."[40] The radical critique of institutions must clarify, through a supremely eminent mental effort, the finality of the social upheaval to be accomplished by the action of a party—and *therefore* of a class. To organize oneself within and according to the rules of the established order is to risk moral perversion; to speculate philosophically outside the

---

[39]Letter to Ruge (Sept. 1843); *MEW* 1, p. 344.

[40]*MEW* 1, 345. This "great party," according to Marx, would have the task of promoting the representative system. The critical thinker would thus oblige this party to "transcend itself" because "its victory is at the same time its defeat." This recourse to dialectics, in our opinion, only aggravates the ambiguity of what Marx, in the same text, defines as "political participation."

reality of the social struggles is to pass directly into a state of sterility. The sole protection against these ills is to remain conscious of the ambiguity of the choice. The new party, Engels was to say, must be "a philosophical party." Indeed, its animators believed in the spiritual vocation of Germany, which had "realized" in the domain of philosophy the revolutionary gains accomplished in the political domain by France and in the social domain by England.[41] To unify these three advances, to achieve an "alliance of suffering humanity which thinks and thinking humanity which is oppressed," it is necessary to abandon the metaphysical fiction of an identity between the rational and the real and to demonstrate instead the existence of a material determinism capable of orienting human consciousness along the lines of spontaneously grasped and accepted rationality, the presupposition of any revolutionary political action. Later, a school was to appear that would appeal to the authority of Marx's teaching while replacing its ambiguity with a quasi-mathematical certitude. Simultaneously it would thus eliminate that element of spontaneity that, in Marx's "new materialism," always remained the absolute condition for the revolutionary transformation of men and their relations. That school transformed into a scientifically demonstrated law what could only be, and was intended to be, a norm of ethical conduct: "We do not approach the world in a doctrinaire fashion, armed with a new principle: Here is the truth, kneel here! We propose to the world new principles derived from the world's principles. We do not tell it: Cease your struggles, for they are folly; we want to call out to you the real battle slogan. We merely show the world the true motive of its struggle; consciousness is something it *must* acquire for itself, whether it wishes to or not!"[42]

This text summarizes the program of the *Deutsch-Französische Jahrbücher* (of which only a single issue appeared, in February 1844, in Paris), and it is completed by the motto chosen by the editors, Ruge and Marx: "The reform of consciousness, not through dogmas, but through analysis of

[41]Cf. F. Engels, "Progress of Social Reform on the Continent: Germany and Switzerland." Published in Nov. 1843 in the Owenite daily, *The New Moral World*, and in the Chartist paper, *The Northern Star*, this study aims to prove the necessity of founding a "communist party" in Germany "among the educated classes." According to Engels, German philosophy from Kant to Hegel must inevitably culminate in communism. See Engels's article in the appendix to Shlomo Avineri, "The Hegelian Origins of Marx's Political Thought," *The Review of Metaphysics* 21, no. 1 (Sept. 1967), 50–6.
[42]Letter to Ruge (Sept. 1843); *MEW* 1, p. 345.

that mystical consciousness, whether religious or political, which is obscure even to itself."[43]

Nothing in Marx's Kreuznach writings indicates that this program, with an ambitious plan of application and no less wide-ranging critical aims, would soon give way to a project apparently far more modest, and even narrow, a project that supplanted the initial plan for a total critique of the "world." Political economy became the fatal trap for Marx from the moment he realized that the evil corroding modern society and threatening it with irreparable catastrophe was rooted in money and the state. Official legend attributes the origin of these two institutions to the people's instinct for self-preservation; but in fact they derive from the imperious need of the possessing and dominant elites to preserve their power and wealth. Other authors had long asserted this, but it was Marx's task to provide the scientific demonstration and to change those authors' intuition into theoretical understanding: Political economy would provide the justification *more geometrico* of a death sentence that is destined to be executed before the end of time.

An anarchist and proletarian manifesto

The Jewish Question and the *Introduction to a Contribution to the Critique of Hegel's Philosophy of Right* were elaborated on the basis of a single ethical conviction, and, as such, they constitute together an inseparable whole: first, the diagnosis of the ill symbolized by the state and money, then the prescription of the remedy – proletarian revolution. In these essays literary polemic, directed on the one hand at two of Bruno Bauer's studies on the Jewish question and on the other hand at Hegel's political philosophy, is but a pretext. Their real intent corresponded to that of the *Deutsch-Französische Jahrbücher*, which Marx defined when he wrote that there must be general mutual agreement about humanity's struggles and its aspirations. "It is a task for the world and for us. It can only be the work of united forces. It is a question of a confession and nothing else. To have its sins forgiven, humanity has only to recognize them for what they are."[44]

---

[43]Ibid., p. 346.

[44]Ibid. In what follows we quote from Marx's articles, *Zur Judenfrage* and *Zur Kritik der Hegelschen Rechtsphilosophie. Einleitung*, according to the German in *MEW* 1, pp. 347–77, 378–91.

In these two essays, religious paraphrasing cloaks a profession of ethical faith that can be summarized in two words: human emancipation. *The Jewish Question* paradoxically defends the religious rights of believers, whether Jews or Christians, whom Bauer had exhorted to abandon their religion in order to be deserving of political emancipation. The state in turn, according to Bauer, must emancipate itself from religion in order to become true and real. In Germany, it must cease to be Christian; the Christian must renounce being Christian, the Jew being Jew, and both must think "scientifically" and recognize their respective religions as stages in the development of the human spirit, "different snake skins shed by history; *man* must appear then as the snake on the way to emancipation."

Bauer's error, according to Marx, was that he criticized the Christian state and not the state as such; in other words, he mistook political emancipation for human emancipation. The former, while an advance, is not the condition of the latter, because although the politically emancipated state can lead to human emancipation, it nonetheless favors the flowering of religion. Thus in the United States of America, where political emancipation is the most fully advanced, religion is the basis of private life and flourishes in all its splendor. "But since the existence of religion is the existence of a defect [*Mangel*], its source can only be sought in the *nature [Wesen]* of the state itself. We no longer consider religion to be the *cause* of secular defects, but merely the *phenomenon* of those defects." The state can be free without man himself also being free. Moreover, freedom by grace of the state is freedom by proxy, by a detour, by a mediator. In a godless state, the atheist himself remains under the sway of religion: To recognize himself as human he must have recourse to a mediator. "The state is the mediator between man and man's freedom. Just as Christ is the mediator whom man endows with all of his divinity, all of his *religious constraint*, so the state is the mediator to which man transfers all of his non-divinity, all of his *human spontaneity*."

Here Marx terminates the analysis begun at Kreuznach to clarify the relationship of the political state to civil society. Writing in a style at once epigrammatic and aphoristic, he condemns in turn the democratic state as the realization of religious spirit in its profane form: "Political democracy is Christian in the sense that within it man, not just one man but every human being, is regarded as a *sovereign*, supreme being;

in fact, however, this is man in his uncultivated and asocial manifestation, man in his fortuitous existence, common man ruined by the whole organization of our society, who, lost to and alienated from himself, is subjected to the rule of inhuman conditions and elements; in a word, man who is not yet a real species-being [*Gattungswesen*].[45] In democracy, man's sovereignty – the chimera, dream and postulate of Christianity – has become a perceptible reality, a concrete presence, a profane maxim; but this being is alienated and distinct from real man." The "Rights of Man and of the Citizen" are those of the egoistic man who belongs to bourgeois society; his freedom is that of a solitary monad, his right is that of enjoying his property or fortune according to his own desires, without concern for others, and society is for him only a means of assuring his person, rights, and property. The French Revolution, which as the model of political emancipation and the perfection of the idealism of the state, suppressed the political character of bourgeois society and broke it down into its simple elements. In so doing it liberated the egoistic spirit and the materialism of bourgeois society, and man was thereby condemned to a double existence, that of an independent egoistic individual on the one hand, and citizen or moral person on the other. Human emancipation will be realized when the individual has recovered in his life, work, and individual relations that social force of which, according to Rousseau, he had to be deprived in favor of the state.

What is said of religion in general applies necessarily to Judaism as well. The secret of the Jew does not lie in his religion; rather the secret of his religion lies in the secular Jew. Like a number of socialists of his time, Marx entertained a common prejudice: The "Jew" is the man of the money cult; and "Judeophobia" was born of the phobia of money, which was considered to be both the symbol and incarnation of social evil. The religion of the Jew – not as a profound belief, but as an everyday, practical morality – is the religion of egoism and practical need, the two vital principles of bourgeois society. Marx reproaches this "Jew" not for his religion but for his cult of money, for seeking to emancipate himself

[45]*MEW* 1, p. 360. Marx also speaks of the *Gemeinwesen*, which may be translated as "social being"; its usage is soon to become exclusive. See Marx's explication of it in a letter to his teacher Feuerbach; cf. Marx to Feuerbach (Aug. 11, 1844); *MEW* 27, p. 425.

"in the Jewish manner," that is, by appropriating for himself
the "power of money." One passage in *The Jewish Question*
suggests a possible mode of emancipation: "A social organization that would eliminate the conditions for usury
[*Schacher*], thus barring the possibility of his existence, would
render the Jew impossible. His religious consciousness would
dissipate like thin vapor in the real vital atmosphere of society. On the other hand, if the Jew recognizes the nullity of his
practical being [i.e. the practice of usury] and works for its
abolition, he actively works for genuine *human emancipation*
from the standpoint of his own previous development, and
turns against the highest *practical* expression of human self-
alienation." One might suppose that in describing this emancipatory struggle, Marx, whose Jewish consciousness seems to
have been in a latent state, was in fact depicting his own
effort.

There is some justification for the comparison that has been
made between Marx's Judeophobia and the attitude of the
Jewish prophets who invoked a curse on their coreligionists for
prostrating themselves before idols. The style of Marx's essays
invites the comparison: "Money is the jealous god of Israel
before whom no other god may exist. Money humbles all of
man's gods – and changes them into commodities . . . Money is
the alienated substance of man's work and existence; and this
alien substance dominates him, and he adores it." But this
biblical tone, which will reappear later in *Capital*, is inseparable from Marx's sociological explanation; and his objective
analysis is based on an empirical phenomenon of general significance: With or without the "Jew," money is the universal
power, and "the practical spirit of the Jews is identical with
the practical spirit of Christian peoples; the Jews have been
emancipated to the extent that the Christians have become
Jews." This law of historical development makes of Judaism,
Christianity, and every religion an antisocial element with a
single essence, engendered unendingly by society. Christianity,
which issued from religious Judaism, has been dissolved into
practical Judaism and through this reversion matured into the
perfected religion of man alienated from himself and from
nature. In *Capital*, Marx was to retain this initial conception
while transcending the Judeophobic tendency of *The Jewish
Question*, which was written almost twenty-five years earlier.
In *Capital*, it is Christianity, particularly in its Protestant ver-

sion, that figures as the most adequate religious form for the cult of abstract man.[46]

The *Introduction to a Contribution to the Critique of Hegel's Philosophy of Right* is the necessary sequel and logical conclusion to *The Jewish Question.* Written in a more sober style, this second part of the manifesto has gained in sociological clarity what has been lost, relative to the other essay, in prophetic emotion. The *Introduction* provides an analysis of the social origin of religion in which the paradoxical moral justification of religious belief assumes the character of an apology: Deprived of real happiness, man takes refuge in a religion that imparts illusory happiness; and the reality of the illusion procured by this "opium" is preferable to the absence of all consolation and dreams. "Religious misery is at once the expression of real misery and the protest against it." Humanity, tormented and destroyed, rediscovers in religion the heart and spirit that have fled from the world and must be restored to it, to this vale of tears, which must be transformed so that its religious nimbus vanishes forever. A philosophy that serves history must abandon the critique of religion and theology and devote its attention to the profane forms of human alienation; it will become the *critic* of law and politics. Germany did not appear to offer fertile ground for such criticism because of its economic backwardness and its anachronistic political regime. But insofar as Germany had attained, through its philosophy, the level of the historically most advanced peoples, the realization of this philosophy would put an end to all speculative philosophy and restore man to his integral humanity. Luther

[46]Cf. M. Rubel, *Karl Marx. Essai de biographie intellectuelle,* new edition (Paris: 1971), pp. 80 ff. We are not partisans of Edmund Silberner's views on Marx's anti-Semitism in *Sozialisten zur Judenfrage. Ein Beitrag zur Geschichte des Sozialismus von Anfang des 19. Jahrhunderts bis 1914* (Berlin: 1962). For a more elaborate and nuanced judgment, see Helmut Hirsch, "Marxiana judaica," *Cahiers de l'Institute de Science Economique Appliquée,* no. 147 (Aug. 1963), 5–52; Roman Rosdolsky, "La *Neue Rheinische Zeitung* et les juifs," Ibid., 53–71; and by the same author "Friedrich Engels und das Problem der 'geschichtslosen Völker'," *Archiv für Sozialgeschichte* 4 (1964). On *The Jewish Question* as a "youthful sin" that Marx "never publicly disavowed," see S. M. Dubnow, *Die neueste Geschichte des jüdischen Volkes,* vol. 2 (Berlin: 1920), pp. 113 ff. This historian of the Jewish people terms Marx a "renegade" and even ventures the following comparison: "Like the biblical Jeroboam, Marx identified the God of Israel with the golden calf" (p. 115). If Marx perhaps erred in taking account of only the "everyday Jew," i.e. the financier, Dubnow goes astray at the other extreme in equating the history of the "Jewish people" with a history of the "spiritual and cultural content of Judaism," while neglecting a sociological analysis of the phenomenon of anti-Semitism.

and Protestantism pointed the way to a solution of the problem. What the Reformation left unfinished is incumbent on
philosophy, or more precisely on a radical theory capable of
becoming a material force; in other words a radical theory
capable of seizing the masses and impelling them to revolution,
thus putting an end to religious alienation. Marx substitutes
Feuerbach's humanist anthropology for Kant's ethics of the
abstract individual, while retaining the rigor of the latter's
universal maxim: "The criticism of religion concludes with the
thesis that man is the supreme being for man, thus with the
categorical imperative to overthrow all the conditions in which
man is a degraded, enslaved, abandoned, contemptible being."
In Marx's mind, this revolutionary teaching could still be the
philosopher's; and thus he speaks indiscriminately of "theory"
or of "philosophy." Herein we find the proof of his attachment to that discipline that demanded of Marx a long inner
struggle before he could detach himself from it. At this point
he abandoned philosophical speculation in favor of an ethical
credo. This ethic underlies all social criticism that Marx will
undertake in his political and literary tasks. The *Introduction*
definitively formulates the principles of proletarian ethics that
(regardless of the views held by the political church that has
taken possession of Marx's teaching) will remain indissolubly
linked to his name.

Marx is credited with having made the first attempt to relate
"Socialism," a movement of ideas, to the movement of proletarian political and social emancipation. This *Introduction*, styled
in the manner of a manifesto, indeed exalts the proletarian
mission and human emancipation. But in this text Marx was
thinking of the German proletariat and the emancipation of
Germany. Neither socialism nor communism are mentioned.
Yet the text does speak of the "negation of private property" as
the demand of a proletariat that changes into a social principle
what society itself executes in practice. Marx expects the German proletariat to develop a consciousness that will surpass
that principle and hence that demand as well. He exhorts the
proletariat to an *inner* revolution, to a "philosophical transformation," to become conscious of its universal vocation. Neither
the French nor the English proletariat can attain this consciousness because neither France nor England can experience the
need for it: Having both experienced a normal historical evolution, these countries will be able to achieve total emancipation

through political emancipation. A similar development, which would result from "partial" and purely political revolutions, is inconceivable for Germany. The reason: Only in philosophy, and thus abstractly, has Germany passed through the intermediate stages of political emancipation that the other modern nations have undergone in practice. Its historical backwardness forces Germany, the country of theoretical emancipation, to clear the way toward practical emancipation before the modern peoples in turn actually attain this goal.

Why is this so? Both sociological analysis and ethical paradox are implicated in Marx's reply; as such, it prefigures the more exact arguments presented in *Capital,* which is the developed theory of modern economic misery and of the need for its abolition through revolution. What predestined Germany to this exceptional role is that, having shared in all the sufferings inherent to the development of modern nations, it had been unable to enjoy any of the partial satisfactions resulting from that development: "This is why Germany will one day find itself at the level of European decline without ever having attained the level of European emancipation. We shall be able to compare it to a fetishist wasting away from the ills of Christianity."[47] Deprived of all the advantages of the modern political state, the German governments have all of its views together with the barbarous defects of the *ancien régime.* The historical secret of Germany is hidden within its hybrid political structure. Unlike France, Germany does not have a social class capable of demanding general power in the name of the general rights of society in order to begin the work of social emancipation from the standpoint of its own particular class situation. The German bourgeoisie is the prototype of the philistine mediocrity of all the other classes. It lacks revolutionary audacity and that largeness of soul and moral enthusiasm that are indispensable if it is to become the class *par excellence* of social emancipation. No more than the other existing classes does it aspire to a special historical role. If such is the character of the German bourgeoisie, it results from the fact that Germany as yet has failed to produce that class that embodies all the defects of society; in other words, a numerically large industrial proletariat. What Marx entertains here is the ideal vision of the *future* proletariat, a vision that, above all sociological analysis, vividly illustrates the ethical credo mentioned earlier.

[47]*MEW* i, p. 387.

Where is therefore the *positive* possibility of German emancipation? *Answer:* in the formation of a class with *radical chains,* a class in bourgeois society which is not a bourgeois social class, an estate [*Stand*] which is the dissolution of all estates, a sphere whose universal sufferings lend it a universal character, and which claims no *particular* right because it suffers not a *particular wrong,* but *absolute wrong;* a sphere which can no longer invoke an *historical* title but only a *human* title . . . ; finally, a sphere which cannot emancipate itself without emancipating itself from all the other spheres of society, thereby emancipating all other spheres as well; in short, a sphere which is the *total loss* of man and which therefore cannot redeem itself except by the *total redemption of man.* This dissolution of society embodied by a particular class is the *proletariat.*[48]

Here, Marx is not describing an existing state of affairs, but rather anticipating a process when, namely, the German proletariat will be formed in the wake of a flourishing "industrial movement." Moreover, he does not speak of the "historical necessity" but rather of the "positive possibility" of that total emancipation; he recognizes that material bonds are of themselves insufficient to arouse in the German proletariat the desire to "dissolve the old universal order," which is the "secret of its [the proletariat's] own existence." And so, in conclusion, Marx speaks of the role that devolves upon "philosophy" – whose inevitable "negation" he has just proclaimed – in the human emancipation of the Germans:

For Germany, the only emancipation that is *practically* possible is a liberation based on *the* theory which proclaims that man is the supreme being for man . . . In Germany, no kind of servitude can be destroyed without destroying *all* kinds of servitude . . . The *emancipation of the German* is the *emancipation of man.* The *head* of this emancipation is philosophy, its *heart* the *proletariat.* Philosophy cannot be realized without the abolition of the proletariat, the proletariat cannot abolish itself without philosophy being realized. When all the internal conditions are fulfilled, the *German day of resurrection* will be announced by the *crowing of the Gallic cock.*[49]

---

[48]Ibid., p. 390.

[49]Ibid., p. 391. Just a few months after the publication of this premonitory text the revolt of the Silesian weavers broke out. Marx saw in this event the material proof – furnished in the realm of theory by the artisan tailor Wilhelm Weitling – of Germany's "classical vocation" to social revolution and of the German proletariat to socialism; it also demonstrated that country's inability to accomplish a purely political revolution. Cf. Marx's article, "Kritische Randglossen zu dem Artikel 'Der König von Preussen und die Sozialreform.' Von einem Preussen," a retort against Ruge published in *Vorwärts; MEW* 1, pp. 392–409.

First readings in economics, or the beginning of a traumatism

The Introduction published in the *Deutsch-Französische Jahrbücher* was not followed by any sequel, and Marx never again took up the anti-Hegelian manuscript dating from Kreuznach. At first, he considered doing a historical study on the history of the Convention, before turning to readings in economics. The historical work, however, was left unwritten. Marx left a testimony that reveals how, in the end, he was obliged to make the study of political economy his life's task and unwittingly a living "nightmare." He thought, however, that he had exhausted this subject matter only a few months after promising in the *Jahrbücher* to deliver a critique of Hegelian philosophy. In the preface to this new work, known today as the *Economic and Philosophic Manuscripts,* he explained that the plan for a critique of Hegel's speculative philosophy would not harmonize with the critique of law, morals, politics, and so forth; therefore he had decided to break down his material according to its various "rubrics" or headings to avoid the impression of pseudosystematization. Each of these topics would thus be treated in a separate "brochure," and finally he could, at will, coordinate them in a comprehensive critical work that would attack speculative philosophy. The section on political economy must have seemed to be nearing completion, for he referred, in the same preface, to a "serious critical study" of the economists made before beginning his own research and reporting its results.[50]

Thanks to these *Economic and Philosophic Manuscripts* and a series of reading notebooks that date from the same period, the spring and summer of 1844, we know why Marx undertook this first study of economics. He intended that study to be the final one, or at least considered it to be the most important. His first commentaries on the political economists and the elaboration that followed form an entity whose style betrays a single, preconceived purpose: indictment. More than any other document, Marx's reading notes enlighten us about his turn of mind at that time: When first tackling the science of political economy he had no idea that it was to become the obsession of his intellectual career.[51] *Capital* was the eventual

[50] K. Marx, *Zur Kritik der Nationalökonomie* ("Economic and Philosophic Manuscripts"), Paris 1844; *MEGA* I, 3, pp. 33 ff.
[51] Cf. *Aus den Exzerptheften,* Paris, early 1844 to early 1845; *MEGA* I, 3, pp. 411–16, 437–583.

fruit of that permanent obsession, which began with the traumatic shock that Marx experienced during his first contacts with political economy.

From Manchester, Friedrich Engels sent his *Outlines of a Critique of Political Economy* to Marx for inclusion in the *Jahrbücher*. There can be no doubt that this work produced a decisive impression on Marx that his subsequent studies only served to reinforce.[52] In his friend's work Marx found the theme of *Capital,* which shows the extent to which he was struck by Engels's severity in denouncing political economy as the "accomplished system of legitimate swindling" and the "complete science of enrichment." Engels's essay can hardly be termed an objective analysis; it is marked more by the violence of the pamphleteering moralist than by the rigor of a critic dissecting a system of production and exchange. The psychological motives of the merchant and the financier provide the subject matter for this indictment along with the "categories" of the scientific economist. The essay is a riot of invective in which the word "immorality" occupies a central place and in which terms of moral stigma alternate with economic concepts and a vocabulary familiar to the economist. (Some examples of his vocabulary: egoism, cupidity, envy, avarice, theft, pillage, violence, trickery, deceit, extortion, terror, barbarity, crime, distrust, sordid traffic, hypocrisy; Malthus's doctrine is described as infamous and odious; commerce is said to have its crusades and its inquisitions, etc.) In his historical précis of economic systems and doctrines, Engels reviews mercantilism and the theory of the commercial balance, Adam Smith's system of commercial liberty, the Malthusian theory of population, the doctrinal quarrels over the "category" of value, the determination of price, the origin of rent in land, and so forth. He rapidly outlines the separation of capital and labor, the antagonism of competition and monopoly, the contradictions of private property, the crises of overproduction, and the consequences of unemployment. This diatribe is highlighted by the perspective of a humanity that, freed from this monstrous conspiracy, will have no material worry beyond that of enjoying scientific and technological progress. "The productive force at the disposal of humanity is infinite." The irrefutable proof of this truth has been furnished by industrial development. Engels

---

[52]F. Engels, *Umrisse zu einer Kritik der Nationalökonomie; MEW* 1, pp. 499–524.

then addresses to his contemporaries an exhortative, presage-
ful word of caution:

Produce with consciousness, like men, and not like fragmented atoms
lacking generic consciousness; in this way you will have overcome all
of your artificial and untenable contradictions. But so long as you
continue to produce as you do now, unconsciously, unreflectively,
and exposing yourself to chance, commercial crises will not disappear; they will become more universal and increasingly violent; an
increasingly large mass of small capitalists will fall into poverty, and
the class of those who live by their labor alone will increase in
growing proportion; in consequence, the mass of unemployed
workers, already the chief problem for our economists, will visibly
increase; all of this will end in a social revolution which our economists in their pedantic wisdom cannot even conceive.[53]

In this verbal agitation, in which the naiveté and profound
intuition of the observer vie with the indignation of the moralist, one can easily discern major themes of Marx's future "Economics." Not only did Marx adopt certain ideas from Engels's
Outlines; we sometimes hear its tone as well echoed in the
commentaries of Marx's Parisian notebooks. In later years Engels set no great store by his *Outlines,* although Marx, fifteen
years later, called it "a work of genius" and cited it several
times in *Capital.* This was Marx's homage to the first author
who, although he may not have revealed to him any new
theoretical truth, at least shared his own hatred for a morality
disguised as science in order to justify the scandal of mass
poverty and human degradation.[54]

We must emphasize Marx's constant habit, acquired during
his university years, of reading and making extensive notes from
his sources. He selected his authors in keeping with the spirit of
an age that was anxious to confer scientific recognition according to preestablished standards, a practice that Marx too seemed
to approve of. In addition to Engels, whose *Outlines* Marx summarized in half a page, the following economists appear in the
two hundred or so pages of his nine notebooks of excerpts and
notes: Pierre Boisguillebert, A. L. C. Destutt de Tracy, James
Lauderdale, John Law, Friedrich List, J. R. MacCulloch, James
Mill, David Ricardo, J. B. Say, C. W. C. Schüz, Frédéric Skar-

[53]*MEW* 1, p. 515.
[54]K. Marx, *Zur Kritik der politischen Oekonomie* (1859); *MEW* 13, p. 10; *Das
Kapital* (1867); *MEW* 23, pp. 89, 166, 168.

bek, and Adam Smith. Special mention must be made of Eugène Buret, whose then well-known work on the *Misère des classes laborieuses en Angleterre et en France* is represented in these notebooks by more than twenty-four pages of excerpts. Buret's discerning testimony undoubtedly had influenced Engels, and consequently Marx, who methodically extracted from Buret's work the notions of absolute and relative poverty, the analysis of poverty as a phenomenon of civilization, the concept of labor as a commodity, and the notion of industry as perpetual war. Buret, a Christian and an admirer of Fourier, arouses our interest for the seriousness of his inquiries, his talent for observation, and his noble spirit. He denounced political economy as an "ontology of wealth," a science of poverty that views man only as a commodity destined to produce and consume. We encounter a number of his unequivocal views in Marx. Capital, Buret declared, is a power that commands labor and thus engenders a relationship of domination and servitude; the concentration of capital threatens to divide society into two classes of individuals with opposed interests – the class of possessors of the instruments of labor, and the class of individuals "who possess nothing but their life"; the modern epoch is a feudalism, an industrial Middle Age whose brutalizing pauperism threatens society with appalling upheavals. In his description of the present state of the world, Buret challenged corruption with its arms of science, an exploit that Marx and Engels could rightly admire. But as for the remedy offered, Marx ceased to follow Buret, who did not want "capital to lose the smallest part of its security and its guarantees." As a Christian, Buret held that man is unable to emancipate himself truly and that an equitable distribution of wealth would lead to universal poverty. He believed in "redemption through work"; the economic system should be organized so as to allow labor to appropriate a part of the instruments that serve to exploit it. At that point Marx must have sensed the dilemma: reform or destruction? There is a "price to be paid" for the development of production and its techniques, and capital has decided that it shall be paid – by the workers. This is the first insight that Marx gained from his early readings in economics, in contrast to the conclusions that Buret drew from his critique of the economists.[55]

[55]Cf. M. M. Cottier, "Une source de K. Marx et de F. Engels: *De la misère...* d'E. Buret," *Nova et Vetera* 2 (1956), 132–52.

Marx's reading notebooks do not cover all of the literature in economics that he studied during his stay in Paris. For one thing, it is not certain that all of the notebooks have been preserved; for another, we have to allow for books in his personal reference library and for the practical impossibility of his copying out everything that interested him. Accordingly, we have to complete our list by adding those authors mentioned in his works that date from the Parisian period – the *Economic and Philosophic Manuscripts* and *The Holy Family* – omitting those whose writings are not directly related to political economy but deal rather with the history of the French Revolution and philosophy (English and French materialism). Marx cited successively Proudhon, Wilhelm Schulz-Bodmer, Constantin Pecqueur, Charles Loudon, Sismondi, Charles Ganilh, Michel Chevalier, Saint-Simon, Charles Fourier, Robert Owen, Lorenz Stein, and others. In the preface to the *Economic and Philosophic Manuscripts* he acknowledged his debt to the German socialists, Hess, Weitling, and Engels, and the "French and English socialists," whose names he does not mention. He undoubtedly had in mind J. P. Proudhon, who might be said to represent for Marx in political economy what Hegel represented in philosophy. Despite the limits of his method of analysis, which remained a captive of its object, Proudhon had opened the way to criticism. Like Hegel, he exercised on Marx a constant influence both of attraction and repulsion; and notwithstanding Marx's later thoughts and remarks, it was as a disciple and continuator of Proudhon that he undertook in 1844 what was to become his exclusive life task. Proudhon marks a transition and a new point of departure in Marx's work. He never ceased to haunt Marx, and it is no exaggeration to say that an important part of what Marx published was "in answer" to Proudhon. Their confrontation in 1846–7 was not to be the last: Marx returned to work on his "Economics" in 1857 following the appearance of a Proudhonian work, *De la Réforme des banques,* by Darimon. Earlier, Marx was ready to reopen the polemic at the appearance of Proudhon's *Idée générale de la révolution au XIXe siècle* (1851). There are numerous examples of this kind of reaction on Marx's part. Thus it seems altogether appropriate to conclude this sketch of the route that lead Marx from philosophy to political economy by quoting his tribute to Proudhon, which is all the more remarkable in that its critical note in no way reduces its spontaneity and warmth:

Just as the first critique of every science necessarily bears the mark of the science it opposes, so Proudhon's *Qu'est-ce que la propriété?* is the critique of political economy from the viewpoint of this science itself. . .Proudhon's work must, therefore, be superceded scientifically by the critique of political economy, even political economy as it stands in Proudhon. It is Proudhon himself who has made this work possible, just as the critique undertaken by Proudhon presupposes the critique of mercantilism by the physiocrats, that of the physiocrats by Adam Smith, that of Adam Smith by Ricardo along with the works of Fourier and Saint Simon. All progress in political economy has presupposed *private property*. This fundamental presupposition appears to political economy as an unshakeable fact subject to no further examination . . . Now, Proudhon submits the basis of political economy, *private property*, to a critical examination, the first that is decisive, pitiless and at the same time scientific. This is the great scientific advance he realized, an advance that revolutionizes political economy and finally renders a true science of political economy possible. Proudhon's *Qu'est-ce que la propriété?* has for political economy the same importance as Sieyès's *Qu'est-ce que le Tiers Etat?* has for modern politics.[56]

The "Economics": the critique of a civilization

One day, while visiting Marx, the young Karl Kautsky asked if the time had not finally come to edit his complete works. "They would have to be written first," Marx responded. Kautsky assured him that his young followers fervently hoped to see the second volume of *Capital* finished. "I do too," declared the master.[57] This conversation, which took place two years before Marx's death and fourteen years after the publication of the first volume of *Capital*, characterizes in a few words the unfinished state of his work. Toward the end of his life, beginning in 1875, Marx, the eternal student, undertook an ambitious program of readings, as if everything he had done until then had been merely preparatory essays, as if he considered nothing, published or unpublished, as finished. "It is self-evident that if an author continues his work, he cannot

---

[56]*Die heilige Familie* (1845); MEW 2, p. 33.
[57]Karl Kautsky, *Aus der Frühzeit des Marxismus* (Prague: 1935), p. 53.

publish *literally* what he wrote six months earlier."[58] When *Capital* was published, he was pleased with Engels's favorable judgment of the volume for "I am very dissatisfied with my things once I see them in print."[59] Marx's reply to Kautsky, however, reveals something else. Marx, the "bourgeois" pariah who was rejected by the academic establishment and deprived of all official support, condemned to waste his time with journalism in order to earn his daily living, finally questioned the usefulness of his political activity and set himself a goal that was above all scientific: "Since 1852 I have had no connection whatever with any association, and I have held the firm conviction that my theoretical endeavours were of greater utility for the working class than my participation in any of the organizations whose days were now over on the Continent."[60] Distinguishing between the "ephemeral" political formations he had known and the proletarian party "in the eminently historical sense of the term," he resolved not to participate in the congress of the International. He thought it better to finish the "Economics."

Having deserted his class, Marx the man of science thought, first of all, that for him the best form of revolutionary praxis would be to elaborate a theory of the proletariat. He was nonetheless aware that one mind alone would be unable to accomplish that immense task. Finally, he resolved not to lose sight of the ethical finality of that movement that the theory would both express and animate. The desire for political engagement can be interpreted as stemming from a concern to join action to thought, conduct to ethical norm. However, this was not Marx's notion of action. Marx the communist was not a "party" man in the ordinary sense of the word; living and thinking on the fringe of the dominant classes, he became the conscious witness of poverty and the denunciator of the institutions that consecrate and perpetuate it: His "party" was the whole of the working class.

Just after the interruption of the *Deutsch-Französische Jahr-*

[58]In a letter to the publisher Leske, Aug. 1, 1846. He addressed the same remarks to Lassalle (Apr. 28, 1862): "... I find a work finished four weeks ago insufficient and rewrite it completely. In any case, the writing is no worse for that"; *MEW* 27, p. 449; *MEW* 30, p. 622.
[59]Letter to Kugelmann, June 10, 1867; *MEW* 31, p. 551
[60]Letter to Freiligrath, Feb. 29, 1860 (during the Vogt Affair), alluding to a reconstitution of the old Communist League, proposed in 1857 by friends who had emigrated to the United States; *MEW* 30, p. 489.

bücher[61] Marx drafted a plea *pro domo* that was simultaneously an account of his studies in economics and a condemnation of their subject matter, the bourgeois system for the exploitation of labor: This was the first draft of his critique of economics.[62] He now had to transcend the stage of private confession, of borrowing from his masters, whether Feuerbach, Proudhon, or the utopians. Still, one idea formulated at this stage was his own: the need to abolish philosophy by "realizing" it. This he had announced in his published critique of Hegel when declaring philosophy to be the "head" of that "emancipation" whose "heart" is the proletariat. Here then, in the manuscripts of 1844, Marx ousted philosophy once and for all.[63]

Although Marx was not satisfied with that first negative essay in economics, Engels urged him to finish his "book on

[61]Arnold Ruge, a convinced liberal, left surprisingly penetrating observations about Marx: He was a "very particular personality, most suitable for a scholarly and litereary vocation, but completely lost for journalism. He reads quite a lot; he works with uncommon intensity and possesses a critical gift which at times degenerates into arrogant dialectics; yet he never finishes anything, completely breaks off and precipitates himself time and again into a fathomless ocean of books." Ruge to Ludwig Feuerbach, May 15, 1844; cf. Arnold Ruge, *Briefwechsel und Tagebuchblätter aus den Jahren 1825–1880*, vol. 1–2. Edited by Paul Nerrlich. (Berlin: 1866), p. 344.

[62]*The Economic and Philosophic Manuscripts*, written in Paris between March and August 1844.

[63]This is an important point to keep in mind today, at a time when Marx's exegetes invent the most extraordinary jargons in order to disguise him in the costume of a philosopher. A good example is the following avatar of Marxism, which Marx himself would never have dreamed possible: "Such is the second reading of Marx: a reading which we shall venture to call *symptomal*, to the extent that in one and the same movement it discloses what is undisclosed in the very text it reads, and refers it to another text that is present, with a necessary absence, in the first, present with an absence that is nevertheless produced as a symptom by the first as its own *invisible*. As with the first reading, the second reading of Marx rightly supposes the existence of *two* texts, and the standard of the first is the second." Louis Althusser, *Lire le capital* vol. 1 (Paris: 1965), pp. 31–2. The author of this feat of verbal prowess was nevertheless inspired to choose as an epigraph Marx's letter to his French publisher that begins: "I applaud your idea of publishing the translation of *Das Kapital* in periodic installments. In this form the work will be more accessible to the working class, and for me this consideration outweighs all others." A "better reading of the early works" of Marx has helped the strange exegete quoted above to discover a half-truth: "It absolutely cannot be said that Marx's youth pertains to Marxism." *Pour Marx* (Paris: 1965), p. 81. However, a good reading of Marx's mature works yields the whole truth: Never, at any moment of his career, did Marx pertain to Marxism, i.e. submit to an ideological system, whether constructed by others or by himself – which, moreover, was never his intention. And we ought to retain the warnings Engels directed at the first French disciples (who were infinitely more comprehensible than their modern successors!): "The so-called Marxism in France is indeed a most peculiar product, the proof being that Marx said to Lafargue: What is certain is that I am not a Marxist" (Engels to Bernstein, Nov. 3, 1882; *MEW* 35, p. 388).

political economy" despite its containing "many things [that] might dissatisfy you": It should be finished "before April" for "feelings are ripe, and we should strike while the iron is hot" (Engels to Marx, January 20, 1845).[64] Ten days later Marx signed a contract with the publisher Leske, of Darmstadt, for the publication of a two-volume work entitled "Critique of Politics and Political Economy."[65] Shortly thereafter, he was expelled from France for having attacked Prussia in the Parisian journal *Vorwärts*, and in February 1845 he moved to Brussels. Two years later the contract with Leske would be annulled because Marx had failed to fulfill it: Not that his exile in Belgium had prevented him from working, but he had found it absolutely essential to write another work first. The purpose of this latter work, *The Holy Family*, was to settle accounts with the neo-Hegelian philosophers grouped around Bruno Bauer, not with a view to creating a new philosophy, but rather to show the impotence of all philosophy, to show it to be an illusory solution to human problems. In place of all metaphysical speculation Marx asserted a "humanism" that he would later call "materialism": "Like Feuerbach in the realm of theory, French and English socialism and communism represent in the practical realm a materialism which coincides with humanism."[66]

In Brussels Marx again submerged himself in readings in economics; between February and June 1845 he compiled notes on some sixty books.[67] The legitimate impatience of his

[64] *MEW* 27, p. 16.
[65] Engels announced the forthcoming publication of this work in the Owenite paper, *The New Moral World* (Mar. 8, and May 10, 1845); cf. *MEW* 2, pp. 514. 519.
[66] *Die heilige Familie*; *MEW* 2, p. 132. See also the *Theses on Feuerbach*; *MEW* 3, pp. 5–7. On "positive humanism," see the *Economic and Philosophic Manuscripts*; *MEW* Suppl. vol. I, pp. 467–588. In a recently discovered letter to Feuerbach Marx exposed his plans for a pamphlet against Bauer; he affirmed warm admiration for Feuerbach and declared: "In these writings you have given – whether intentionally I do not know – a philosophical basis to socialism, and the communists have immediately understood your work in this way as well. The unity of man with man, founded on the real differences between men, the notion of the human species transferred from the heaven of abstraction to the real earth, what is this but the concept of society! . . . Man is completely defined by his passions." Letter to Feuerbach, Aug. 11, 1844; *MEW* 27, p. 425.
[67] He filled a dozen notebooks with excerpts, more than four hundred pages in all; but unlike the excerpts from his Paris readings, these pages contain few commentaries. He also composed a number of notebooks in Manchester, where he spent July–August of 1845 with Engels. The authors represented in these excerpt notebooks are: Aikin, Anderson, Atkinson, Avenant, Babbage, Bray, Browning, Buret, Carlyle, Chamborant,

publisher was of little importance to him for there was still much to learn before he could draw the balance. Moreover, in order to criticize political economy, it had to be considered in its relationship to the whole of society. This level of observation radically distinguishes Marx's analysis from that of his predecessors, and especially that of the pioneer critic of political economy, Proudhon.

The project for a "Critique of Politics and Political Economy"

There are, therefore, profound reasons behind Marx's momentary abandonment of his "Economics." As early as the preface to the *Economic and Philosophic Manuscripts* of 1844, he had declared that his intention was to present "the critique of law, morals, politics, etc." in a series of separate booklets, then "to present in a special work the *unity* of the whole, the relations between the various parts, and finally the critique of the speculative manner in which these subjects have been dealt with until now." And apparently desirous of reserving himself time for another plan he alluded to a *more general* project that would examine the "relationship between political economy and the state, law, morals, civil life, etc."[68] In addition he touched on the question of method, a natural consequence of his critique of Hegelian dialectics. These passages were the

Cobbett, Cooper, Defoe, Eden, Edmonds, Ferrier, Fix, Ganilh, Gilbart, Girardin, Gisborne, Greg, Hilditch, Hope, Jarrold, Laborde, MacCulloch, Mill, Misselden, Moreau de Jonnès, Morse, Owen, Parkinson, Pecchio, I. Pereire, Petty, Quesnay, Rossi, Sadler, Sagra, L. Say, Senior, Sismondi, Storch, Thompson, Tooke, Trioen, Ure, Villegardelle, Villeneuve-Bargemont, Wade, Watts. Special mention should be made of the work by Georg von Gülich, *Geschichtliche Darstellung des Handels, der Gewerbe und des Ackerbaus der bedeutendsten handeltreibenden Staaten unsrer Zeit* (Jena, 1830–45), which Marx apparently read around 1847 and from which he excerpted numerous passages filling two notebooks of two hundred pages in-folio; cf. M. Rubel, "Les Cahiers d'étude de Marx," in *Marx Critique du marxisme*, pp. 307–12. We can add to this list a number of titles that appear in an inventory of his personal library, which was prepared in 1850, after Marx's departure from Cologne, by his friend, Roland Daniels; see *Ex libris Karl Marx und Friedrich Engels. Schicksal und Verzeichnis einer Bibliothek* (Berlin: 1967), pp. 211–28. In addition to a number of historical works (among them the *Mémoires* of the Cardinal de Retz, the Duke de Saint-Simon, the Princess de Lamballe, Levasseur, Peuchet, Grégoire, Caussidière, the Duke de Gramont, and Bertrand de Molleville) the inventory includes the names of economists and economic historians; in particular two volumes of writings by economists from the collection edited by Eugène Daire deserve mention: *Les Economistes financiers du XVIIIe siècle* (Paris: 1843), and *Les Physiocrates* (Paris: 1846).
[68]Cf. *MEGA* I, 3, p. 33.

beginning of that analytical view that Marx was soon to call "materialist." Speculation about spirit and matter, subject and object, the ideal and the real is sterile; what matters is only "men's practical energy"; resolving such antinomies is not the task of knowledge alone; rather, it is a "real task of human life."[69] Here we see the first sketch of the relationship between the natural sciences and industry, which is the conception of history as the "act of genesis of human society." Political economy expresses man's economic alienation, and Marx wanted to subject it to a sociological critique; witness the following passage that, already in 1844, sets forth the materialist method: "Religion, the family, the state, law, morals, science, art, etc. are only particular modes of production and fall under its universal law."[70] A similar statement is found again, more clearly expressed, at the beginning of *The Holy Family*. While energetically defending Proudhon, that revolutionary author of the *Mémoire sur la propriété* who has "done everything the critique of political economy is capable of doing from the point of view of political economy," Marx reproaches him on the same basis for having remained imprisoned in the bourgeois system: "Proudhon abolishes economic alienation from within that alienation"; he abandons neither the institution of private property nor that of wage labor; his dream is the equality of property and wages.[71]

When Leske canceled his contract, Marx (who had in the meantime composed *The German Ideology* with Engels, Hess, and Weydemeyer) wrote him a letter full of excuses and explanations that convincingly demonstrate his concern to acquaint his reader with the premises of his "Economics" as based on his fundamental opposition to both German philosophy and German socialism. "Since I have had the manuscript – which is almost finished – of volume one in hand for so long, I cannot let it be printed without one more revision of its contents and style." Accordingly, Marx did further readings in

---

[69]Ibid., p. 121. If it is at all possible to qualify Marx as "existential," then it is only in the sense that can be drawn from this rejection of the speculative mode of thought. As we have seen in Essay 2, another thinker of Hegelian formation, Søren Kierkegaard, developed a similar critique on different grounds.

[70]*MEGA* I, 3, p. 115.

[71]*Die heilige Familie; MEW* 2, pp. 34, 44 ff. Pierre Naville has given a pertinent analysis of the opposition between Marx and Proudhon in his work *De l'aliénation à la jouissance* (Paris: 1957), pp. 291 ff; he fails, however, to stress the central point of the alienation of the producer in the wage system.

England; two volumes in-folio of the works of the Physiocrats had just appeared (the Daire edition already noted), and Marx was obliged to take account of them. "The revised first volume will be ready for printing *at the end of November*. The second volume, which is more historical, can then be rapidly finished . . . I already wrote you that because of new material accumulated in England, on one hand, and of requirements that have arisen during elaboration, on the other, the manuscript will run to more than twenty printer's sheets . . ." (August 1, 1846).[72]

In short, then, Marx wanted to compose, prior to his "Economics," a work at once polemical (in the spirit of *The Holy Family*) and theoretical, that would illustrate the position he called "materialist" as derived from his sociological method. He actually accomplished this task, in particular in the first part of *The German Ideology*. In mentioning the almost finished first volume of his "Economics," he forcibly alluded to the 1844 manuscripts drafted in Paris; he had, therefore, no intention of abandoning that first work to the "gnawing criticism of the mice," as he and Engels would subsequently do with *The German Ideology*.[73] It would be difficult to explain the abandonment of those manuscripts because in them Marx advanced, in a style he would no doubt later judge too intimate, his fundmental demand: the abolition of wage labor, and therefore of private property, the state, and capital. What is more, Marx thought he was close to finishing his "Economics," with three hundred pages remaining to be done: in all, nine hundred pages in-octavo, deliverable in three months. The manuscripts of 1844 would have accounted for two hundred of these; the rest of the notebooks, as we have seen, were filled with excerpts from the works of other authors, together with Marx's critical comments. It appears, then, that at the time Marx believed he had exhausted the subject. The title of the work in preparation ("Critique of Politics and Political Economy") leads us to believe tht Marx would have included his 1843 reflections, and particularly the anti-Hegelian manuscript from Kreuznach, which was a critique of politics, or in other words, *of the state*. This is how, in mid-1846, he conceived of the structure of his "Economics."

[72]MEW 27, pp. 448–50.
[73]Cf. *Zur Kritik der politischen Ökonomie. Vorwort* (1859); MEW 13, p. 10.

The method and themes of the "Economics"

In Marx, the man of science and the social critic were one and the same. When in 1846 he joined the secret society known as the "League of the Just" and also allied himself with the leaders of English Chartism, he moved into a "new system of propaganda." While continuing work on his "Economics," he wanted to participate in the working-class activity of that tense period prior to the 1848 revolution. He did not think he was abandoning in the least his role as educator when writing *The German Ideology, The Poverty of Philosophy,* and the *Communist Manifesto.* On the contrary, these texts were, broadly speaking, part of the "Economics"–in the three-fold historical, sociological, and economic sense of the term. The same can be said of the talks he gave at the Brussels Association of German workers, where for the first time he publicly lectured on capital and wage labor.[74] All of these efforts constitute the "investigations" that he mentioned later, in the preface to *A Contribution to the Critique of Political Economy* (1859). Their summary takes up some thirty lines in the same preface and is rightly considered to be the resumé of his social theory.[75] Marx did not want to restrict himself to in-group dueling: Setting aside their circumstantial aspects, the settling of personal accounts and the phobias reflected in them, the polemical works of 1845–51 contain a complete account of Marx's sociological principles. When in 1857 he finally undertook the first draft of his "Economics" and set forth the method and plan of the work in six "rubrics," he made these principles the basis of his work.

The title of the manuscript promised to Leske in 1845 and a good many other references found in Marx's writings of the same period clearly show that the "critique of politics," one of the two facets of the projected work, was to be centered on the problem of the state. A noteook from the Paris-Brussels period, for example, clearly shows this.[76] In addition to the eleven *Theses on Feuerbach,* the notebook contains the scheme for a study on the state that proposes the following eleven themes:

[74]*MEGA* I, 6, pp. 451–72.

[75]*MEW* 13, pp. 8–9.

[76]See the description of this notebook given in *Die deutsche Ideologie,* Volksausgabe (Berlin: 1932), pp. 547 ff. There we also find a list of thirty-seven books "to be bought or procured otherwise," including titles by Buonarotti, Sismondi, List, Owen, and Considérant.

1. The history of the genesis of the modern state or the French
Revolution. The presumptuous exaggeration of the political element,
confounded with the state in antiquity. The revolutionaries opposed
to bourgeois society. Bisection of each individual into a bourgeois
and a political being. 2. The proclamation of the rights of man and
the state constitution. Individual freedom and public power. Liberty,
civil equality and unity. Popular sovereignty. 3. The state and bourgeois society. 4. The representative state and the Charter. The representative constitutional state; the representative democratic state. 5.
Separation of powers. Legislative power and executive power. 6.
Legislative power and legislative bodies. Political clubs. 7. Executive
power. Centralization and hierarchy. Centralization and political civilization. Federalism and industrialism. State administration and local
administration. 8. Judicial power and law. 9. The Nation and the
people. 10. Political parties. 11. Suffrage, the struggle for the abolition of the state and bourgeois society.[77]

We have already noted these points, and others, in Marx's
critique of Hegel. Everything he wrote subsequently on history
or on politics confirms our assumption that the "critique of
politics" was to follow this plan.

The method defined in *The German Ideology* obliged Marx
to make a crucial choice: either abandon the "Economics" as
originally conceived, that is, as but one work among others, or
devote his entire life to it. His decision was influenced by
external factors and brought to a head by the failure of the
1848 revolutions, whereupon the "Economics" received its definitive plan. How did Marx come to reverse the elements of
the problem, putting the critique of political economy (of capital) before the critique of politics (of the state)? The answer is
found in the first part of *The German Ideology:*

This conception of history is based on the analysis of the real
process of production departing from the material production of
simple elemental life; it considers the form of commerce corresponding to and engendered by the mode of production, in other
words bourgeois society in its different stages, to be the foundation
of all history. It must demonstrate the activity of this society as
state and from it explain the different theoretical creations and
forms of consciousness, religion, philosophy, morals, etc., and also
derive the process of the genesis of society on the basis of these
elements. It will then be of course possible to expose the question in

[77]Cf. *MEW* 3, p. 537. In the original, Marx numbered points 8–11: 8', 8", 9', 9".

its totality (and therefore at the same time, show the reciprocal action of these diverse aspects).[78]

Further on in the same text Marx raises the question of the relations between the social structure and industry and commerce, production and exchange. He then passes to the problem of dominant ideas as a function of the classes in power; the division of labor; the opposition between town and country; the birth of the commercial class and the bourgeoisie and subsequently that of the proletariat; the extension of productive forces and means of communication; the origin of manufacturing and of mechanization; questions of population and vagrancy in relation to the development of factories; the political importance of commerce; the discovery of gold in America; colonial expansion and its repercussions on the extension of the world market and monetary commerce; the genesis of large-scale industry and industrial capital; the appearance of competition; the evolution of the forms of property and the modern forms of the state, of the fiscal system, the stockmarket, and private rights; the transformation of the relations between the mode of production and the mode of distribution; the historical conflicts that result from the antagonism between productive forces and the modes of distribution; class conflicts and the new forms of the revolutionary process; the prospects of proletarian communism. This introduction to *The German Ideology* concludes on the following note: "The proletarians are . . . in direct opposition to the form in which the individual members of society have hitherto expressed their collective being, that is in opposition to the state; and in order to assert their personality, they must overthrow the state."[79]

All of these themes are to reappear later, in *Capital*, with the exception of the last one mentioned – the state; Marx had reserved for it a special treatise in the 1857 plan, that of the "Economics," the groundwork of which was laid in *The German Ideology*.

Not only does this text present Marx's method, it also gives a justification of his activity from the Brussels period, which continued in 1848, first in Paris, then in Cologne. "The development of productive forces has given birth to a class which is the majority in society, *and from which emanates the con-*

[78]*Die deutsche Ideologie; MEW* 3, pp. 37–8.
[79]Ibid., p. 77 (and not, as some would translate it: "overthrow *this* state" (Paris: Editions Sociales, 1966), p. 135).

sciousness of the imperative need for a radical revolution, in other words, communist consciousness." For this conscious-ness to become the consciousness of everyone, a "massive transformation of man. . .in the *revolution"* is required.[80] Here is a key to Marx's intellectual life during the pre-revolutionary period that closed with the *Communist Manifesto:* For this "party" man, writing is action.

Capital cannot be adequately discussed from the standpoint of capital, nor poverty from the standpoint of poverty. This maxim is repeated in *The Poverty of Philosophy.* Nevertheless, it was on the grounds of classical and post-Ricardian theory that Marx combated Proudhon's theses on value. Proudhon had essentially adopted the economists' own reform plan while rejecting their social tendencies; Marx, the disciple of Ricardo, answers him. Proudhon had parodied Hegel's metaphysical method; Marx, the disciple of Hegel, chides him. Proudhon had erected by means of economic concepts and categories the "edifice of an ideological system";[81] Marx interprets those concepts and cate-gories sociologically and masters the "materialist" criticism of the classical economists.[82] Most of these reproaches and meth-odological views are to be found later on in *Capital,* frequently in direct reference to *The Poverty of Philosophy.* As a "theorist of the proletariat," Marx excludes himself from the category of the professional economists; he also takes his distance from the constructors of utopias, those who seek a regenerative science and "see in misery only misery, without remarking its revolu-tionary, subversive side which will overthrow the old society."[83] What in 1847 is simply a hypothesis, the idea of the "accumula-tion of misery," will later be the central thesis of the theory of capitalist accumulation. Indeed, all of the great theses of *Capital* were originally postulates or hypotheses: Beginning in 1847, Marx recognized that the critique of *money* had to precede the critique of the state; but he had long since proclaimed as a "historical" necessity the abolition of both. It is, therefore, un-derstandable that he was later to recommend the reading of *The Poverty of Philosophy* as an introduction to *Capital.*[84]

[80]*Die deutsche Ideologie; MEW* 3, pp. 59 ff.

[81]*Misère de la philosophie; Oeuvres,* vol. 1, p. 80.

[82]*Misère de la philosophie,* Ch. 2. See for example, the "seventh and final observa-tion"; *Oeuvres,* vol. 1, pp. 88–93.

[83]Ibid., p. 93.

[84]Cf. "Lettres et documents de Karl Marx 1856–1883. Avant-propos à *Misère de la philosophie* dans *Egalité* n. 12, 1880," in *Annali,* Instituto Giangiacomo Feltrinelli, Milan, I (1958), 204.

In *Capital*, Marx treats the Hegelian dialectic with as little regard as he had earlier treated Proudhon's parody of it; and when he eventually qualifies his own method as "dialectical" he is careful to present it as the "exact opposite" of Hegel's: He calls it "critical and revolutionary."[85] At first glance, this definition hardly appears theoretical, but the conclusion to *The Poverty of Philosophy* provides us with the key. There, Marx introduces the idea of a "revolutionary class" – a "productive power" *par excellence* – and at the same time the vision of a historical finality, "the abolition of all classes" and of all "political power . . . the official *résumé* of the antagonism at the heart of civil society."[86] This theme, too, recurred later: Marx thought of using it for the conclusion of *Capital*, Book III, as suggested in the plan communicated to Engels[87]; and it resounds already in the conclusion of Book I, which ends with a citation of the *Communist Manifesto* announcing the ruin of the bourgeoisie and the triumph of the proletariat.[88]

There can be no doubt that the events of 1848 caused Marx to abandon momentarily the "Economics." On the eve of the revolutionary days of February, Marx was preparing to publish the talks on *Wages* that he had delivered to an audience of workers in Brussels.[89] In these talks he summarized the doctrines of certain English economists and adopted the thesis of Cherbuliez: that the growth of productive capital relative to wages is detrimental to the workers. This is his first statement of what he later called the "organic composition of capital."[90] When reworking this text for the *Neue Rheinische Zeitung*, Marx defines capital as a set of social relations of production. Following Bray and Cherbuliez, he takes up the theme of relative pauperization as an effect of competition and mechanization: Already the concept of the industrial reserve army, a major theme of *Capital*, is outlined there.[91] However, Marx was forced to leave Germany before completing this work.

Established in London, and before returning to work on the "Economics," he set about drawing the historical and political

[85]*MEW* 23, pp. 27, 28.
[86]*Oeuvres*, vol. 1, p. 136.
[87]*MEW* 32, pp. 74–8.
[88]*Capital*, ch. 32; *MEW* 23, p. 791.
[89]Cf. *Zur Kritik der politischen Ökonomie. Vorwort; MEW* 13, p. 10.
[90]Cf. *MEW* 6, pp. 550 ff.; *Capital*, Book I; *MEW* 23, pp. 640 ff.; *Capital*, Book III; *MEW* 25, pp. 151 ff.
[91]*Lohnarbeit und Kapital; MEW*, 6, pp. 416, 421.

lesson to be won from the abortive revolution.[92] He discovered the "real basis" of the revolutionary events, that is to say their economic causes: the overproduction and overspeculation of the years 1843–5, then the financial panic of 1846–7. He broadened his inquiry to embrace the Continent, England, and the United States. Then he moved on to study the industrial and commercial recovery that occurred in France and England from 1848 to 1850, giving for the first time a sociological outline of cyclical crises and defining the conditions of social upheaval: "In the face of the general prosperity in which the productive forces of bourgeois society develop to profusion . . . there can be no question of a real revolution. Such a revolution is possible only in those periods in which these *two factors*, the *modern productive forces* and the *bourgeois forms of production*, enter into *conflict* . . . *A new revolution is possible only following a new crisis. But it is to occur just as certainly as is the latter.*"[93]

This analysis is focused on England, a fact that indicates the future orientation of Marx's economic studies. "Just as the period of crisis begins on the Continent later than in England, so too the period of prosperity. The initial process always takes place in England: this country is the demiurge of the bourgeois cosmos. On the Continent, the different phases of the cycle through which bourgeois society continually passes arise in secondary and tertiary forms."[94]

Renewed studies in economics (1850–1851)

The new reader at the British Museum was particularly interested in financial questions.[95] He read the *Economist* regularly and followed the vicissitudes of market speculation. He had already discovered that in France the chief victor of the 1848 revolution had been the financial aristocracy. Precious metals were amassed in the coffers of the Bank of France; paper money could thus be created continually, leading to the "con-

[92]"Die Klassenkämpfe in Frankreich," *Neue Rheinische Zeitung Revue*, 1850; *MEW* 7, pp. 11–107.

[93]"Monthly Review for May to October 1850", *MEW* 7, p. 440. Engels inserted this part of the article into *The Class Struggles in France, 1848–1850*.

[94]*MEW* 7, p. 97.

[95]Among his first readings: John Fullarton, *Regulation of Currencies* 2d ed. (London: 1845); Robert Torrens, *Principles of R. Peel's Bill* (London: 1848); Thomas Tooke, *A History of Prices* (London: 1848).

centration of all of French credit in the hands of the Bank." Proudhon had taken this sign as a confirmation of the reform plan (metamorphosis of the Bank of France into a popular bank) that he was defending against Bastiat,[96] and Marx did not tire of mocking his monetary utopianism: "[Proudhon] does not even need to know the history of the restrictive banking measures of 1787–1819; he need only look across the Channel to see that this phenomenon, which he believes to be so extraordinary in the history of bourgeois society, is no more than an ordinary bourgeois phenomenon, although it has just occurred in France for the first time. It is clear that the so-called revolutionary theoreticians who were authorities in France after the advent of the provisional government, were as ignorant of the measures taken and of their results as were the men in the provisional government themselves."[97] Another work by Proudhon would soon preoccupy Marx. For the moment, however, he studies problems of money and ground rent.[98] At the time, England was witnessing the struggle between the industrial bourgeoisie and the landed aristocracy. Even before he reached London Marx had realized the importance of this conflict: "This economic campaign against feudalism...will have incalculable consequences" (letter to Engels, August 17, 1849).[99] He undertook his first critique of the Ricardian theory.[100] Science and advanced industry must be shown to outweigh the arguments of Ricardo – and the Malthusian law of decreasing returns of the soil and of capital investments.[101] He also tackled for the first time the theory of

[96]He published his polemic in 1850 under the title, *Gratuité du crédit*.

[97]"Monthly Review for May to October 1850"; *MEW* 7, p. 439.

[98]We have access to three study notebooks dating from the last months of 1850 and containing excerpts from works later cited in *Capital*. One of the authors Marx read was Ricardo, whose *Principles of Political Economy* he reread in English, translating and annotating a series of passages on monetary problems.

[99]*MEW* 27, p. 141.

[100]See his letter to Engels, Jan. 7, 1851; *MEW* 27, pp. 157–62.

[101]Engels, who had himself used these arguments in his *Outlines* of 1844, congratulated his friend: "If there were still any fairness and justice on earth, you would now have the right to all ground-rent for at least one year." And Engels suggested that he publish an article on ground rent, and emphasized the importance of finishing the "Economics" as rapidly as possible (Jan. 29, 1851; *MEW* 27, pp. 170 ff.). It was a sadly ironic response he received from Marx, whose wife was expecting their fourth child: "The fact that the earth's fertility is in inverse proportion to that of man was bound to have a profound effect on a family father as prolific as I am, all the more since *mon mariage est plus productif que mon industrie* [my marriage is more productive than my work]" (Feb. 3, 1851; *MEW* 27, p. 173).

currency, and his comments about it to Engels prefigured his later treatments in *A Contribution to the Critique of Political Economy* and *Capital*.

In the course of 1851 Marx consumed an enormous amount of literature and filled nearly fifteen notebooks with excerpts. Although desperately short of money, calumniated by certain German émigrés, and disrupted in his studies, he nevertheless believed that in five weeks he would be able "to finish with all the economic muck . . . *Cela fait,* I will write the Economics at home and at the Museum plunge into another science. *Ça commence à m'ennuyer* [It's beginning to bore me]. *Au fond,* since Smith and Ricardo, this science has made no progress, despite the importance of the specialized studies, which are often hyperdelicate" (letter to Engels, April 2, 1851).[102] Nevertheless, we cannot be certain that Marx was actually determined to write the projected work. On the contrary his notebooks of 1851 show that he continued to be an insatiable and eclectic reader: He read studies on monetary questions, agriculture, the application of electricity in agriculture, industry and technology, economic history, the history of civilization and of colonialism, political economy, and population.[103]

Marx's friends were waiting for the work to be published. A letter from Lassalle appears to reflect accurately the impatience of the "party": "I have heard that your *Political Economy* will finally see the light of day! Three big volumes at one stroke! I am consumed by curiosity . . . Besides, your brochure against Proudhon is enough to provoke the desire to know your positive contribution. Indeed, it attests to a truly astonishing historico-literary erudition and a most penetrating comprehension of economic categories! But it is limited—as it had to be—to a refutation of Proudhon without developing the problem in a positive sense . . . That is precisely why I am burning with desire to see on my desk the three-volume monster by Ricardo turned socialist, Hegel turned economist, for you surely will be both of them." Ricardo is "our direct forefather"; his theory of rent is "the most formidable communist act" (Lassalle to Marx, May 12, 1851).[104] Having decided to compose and publish his work, Marx, who now gave himself "six to eight

[102]*MEW* 27, p. 228.
[103]Cf. M. Rubel, *Bibliographie des oeuvres de Karl Marx* (Paris: 1956), pp. 225–6.
[104]Franz Mehring, ed., *Aus dem literarischen Nachlass von Karl Marx, Friedrich Engels und Ferdinand Lassalle,* vol. 4 (Stuttgart: 1902), pp. 30–1.

weeks," discovered the multiple "ramifications" of his subject: "It must be finished once and for all, at all costs. Naturally, the democratic imbeciles who receive their illumination from above have no need of such efforts. Why should they, infants born with silver spoons in their mouths, tire themselves with economic and historical material?"[105] Somewhat earlier he had told Engels that it would take him "five weeks"; his friend had exhorted him to finish quickly and had asked about the chances of finding a publisher "for those two volumes of sixty notebooks" (Engels to Marx, April 3, 1851).[106] In fact, a publisher still had to be found. Marx hoped to interest the publishing house of Cotta in Stuttgart and sent them the plan of the "Economics." But his resources were at an end, and he was obliged to abandon his writing and even his readings at the British Museum: "I feel sorry for my wife. She has to carry the entire burden. . .*Il faut que l'industrie soit plus productive que le mariage* [Work should be more productive than marriage]" (letter to Engels, July 31, 1851).[107]

A new critique of Proudhon

In the midst of these difficulties, Marx learned of Proudhon's latest book, the *Idée générale de la révolution au XIXe siècle;* reading this convinced him that his critique of Proudhon in 1847 had been well-founded; although Proudhon criticizes certain "evils," he does not attack capital itself; he is against interest, for example, judging that its conversion into an annuity paid to the capitalists would suffice to abolish it.

Marx's remarks in this connection forecast one of the fundamental theses of *Capital:* Society automatically observes the "laws of progressive devaluation of captial . . . without worrying about the advice of Proudhon," who would like to make it into a social norm and proposes a panacea, namely the bank. There is nothing more typically "French" than Proudhon's polemic against the communists: "The French peasant and the French shoemaker, tailor and merchant are for him *données éternelles et qu'il faut accepter* [things eternally given, and which must be accepted]. The longer I deal with this rubbish

---

[105]Marx to J. Weydemeyer, June 27, 1851; *MEW* 27, p. 560. Here Marx is attacking the German refugees in London.

[106]*MEW* 27, pp. 233–4.

[107]Ibid., p. 293.

the more I am persuaded that agricultural reform – and therefore the property right based on it as well – will be the alpha and the omega of the coming upheaval. Otherwise Father Malthus is right" (Marx to Engels, August 14, 1851).[108]

A week earlier, Marx had made a brief résumé of Proudhon's book for Engels's benefit (August 8, 1851).[109] This outline is instructive on several counts for its objectivity; Marx was possibly thinking of the plan of his own "Economics." Let us consider, for example, his résumé of the "Second Study of the *Idée générale*":

Y a-t-il raison suffisant de la Révolution au XIXe siècle [Is there sufficient reason for the Revolution in the 19th century]? The revolution of 1789 overthrew the *Ancien Régime,* but passed up an opportunity to found the new society or to renovate the old. It had *politics* alone, instead of *political economy,* in view. The contemporary condition is the reign of the "anarchy of economic forces," whence society's "tendency toward poverty." This condition is evidenced in the division of labor, in the mechanization of industry, competition, the credit system. There follows the growth of pauperism and of crime. Then: the *state* has become more and more extensive, has been vested with all the attributes of the absolute and has continually gained in autonomy and power. Enlargement of the public debt. The state defends wealth against poverty. Corruption. The state subjugates society. A new revolution is necessary. The task of the revolution consists "in changing, rectifying society's adverse tendency." Society itself need not be touched. There can be no question of an "arbitrary reconstitution."[110]

The subsequent "studies" concern association, then authority: "More government!" follows a condemnation of universal suffrage. In the latter Marx sees the notion of the state taken to its extreme and revealed in "all its absurdity." He devoted particular attention to Proudhon's fifth and sixth studies, which concern "Social Liquidation" and "Organization of the Economic Forces." He copied a series of passages dealing with the following topics: the Bank of France, officially declared an "establishment of public utility"; the public debt, to be reimbursed by "annuities"; mortgage debts; real estate; landed property (the commune as substitute for the proprietor in re-

[108]Ibid., pp. 313, 314.
[109]Ibid., pp. 297–304.
[110]Ibid., p. 297.

deeming rents and reimbursing properties; abolition of the land tax, equalization of differences in quality of the lands, etc.); the progressive withdrawal of precious metals from circulation and their replacement by paper money; the association of workers in large-scale industry from which arise societies in which each worker has the right to serve successively in all capacities and must do his share of the arduous labor while benefiting from a comprehensive aptitude and an adequate income, with wages proportional to the nature of the function, the importance of talent, and the extent of responsibility. "Here," notes Marx, "is the solution to two problems: collective force and the division of labor; in the transition period, those who produce are the directors of the workshops." Marx then broaches the problem of the "constitution of value" (a Proudhonian idea he had already criticized in *The Poverty of Philosophy*) that must lead to "the organization of the cheap price" by establishment of the "just price"; as for foreign commerce, the reforms proposed by Proudhon tend ultimately to suppress custom duties. From the seventh and last study, on "The Dissolution of Government within the Economic Organism," Marx copies out these propositions: "The society without authority. Elimination of cults, law, administration, police, public education, war, navy, etc." And he adds: "All of this embellished with phrases *à la* Stirner."[111]

Both in this letter and in one he was to write six days later, Marx showed his sympathy for Proudhon's anti-Jacobinism: "Above all, the book contains very well-written attacks on Rousseau, Robespierre, *la Montagne*, etc."[112] When Marx asked him what he thought about this "recipe," Engels attempted an answer on three occasions.[113] He admitted that Proudhon "seems to be making progress." "*Au bout du compte*, Proudhon has finally come to recognize that the true meaning of the property right consists in the disguised confiscation of all property by a more or less disguised state, and that the true meaning of the abolition of the state lies in the enforced centralization of the state." Engels considered this

[111]Ibid., pp. 297–304.

[112]Ibid., p. 297.

[113]Two letters written before having read the *Idée générale*, on Aug. 10 and 11, 1851; one letter after reading it, on Aug. 21, 1851; *MEW* 27, pp. 305–11, 317–19. Moreover, Engels intended to write for Marx a detailed critique on Proudhon; only a fragmentary first draft of this unfinished work has been preserved. Cf. *Arkhiv Marksa i Engelsa* (1948), 5 ff.

work to be "much more wordly than [Proudhon's] earlier books": Since 1847 there had been an "advance," a "complete transition from Hegel to Stirner." It can no longer be said that he understands nothing of German philosophy, "since he has passed through all of its phases right up to the last, that of rigor mortis."[114] An interesting detail in Engels's reply is that he suspects Proudhon of having borrowed from the *Communist Manifesto* and the *Neue Rheinische Zeitung* of 1850: "A number of points have no doubt been stolen from there, for example the idea that the government, as the power of one class for oppressing the other classes, disappears along with class antagonism. Moreover, numerous points concerning the movement in France since 1848. I do not think he found all that in the book you wrote against him." Engels agreed with Marx's judgment:

His appeal to the bourgeoisie, his reference to Saint Simon and a hundred other tales . . . show that he identifies industrial class, bourgeoisie and proletariat . . . His pseudo-philosophical construction of history leaves not a shadow of a doubt: before the revolution, the industrial class existed virtually; in the period 1789–1848, as antithesis: it is the negation; then a Proudhonian synthesis to wind up the entire thing with a flourish. All of this strikes me as a final attempt to give the bourgeoisie a theoretical justification; our premises of the decisive historical initiative of material production, the class struggle, etc., are largely adopted, deformed more often than not and used as the basis of an experiment to seemingly recover the proletariat within the bourgeoisie by means of a pseudo-Hegelian sleight-of-hand . . . The attacks on Louis Blanc, Robespierre and Rousseau include at times some pretty strokes, but on the whole, nothing is more pretentiously superficial than his critique of politics, for example, of democracy. . .And what a great idea, his assertion that power and freedom are irreconcilable antinomies, and that no government could give him a sufficiently moral reason to make *him* (Proudhon) decide to obey it! *Par dieu,* what then would be the good of power?" (Engels to Marx, August 21, 1851).[115]

[114]Aug. 10 and 11, 1851; *MEW* 27, pp. 306, 310–11. This letter also refers to a "plan" that Marx appears to have exposed to him during their discussion of the reduction in interest rate – through the intermediary of a "privileged national bank, having a monopoly on the issuance of bills, with precious metals having been withdrawn from circulation." Engels made the same objections to Marx that he had to Proudhon.

[115]*MEW* 27, pp. 317–18.

Our reason for having dwelt on this exchange of views was two-fold: First, the 1857 plan of the "Economics" was to include most of the themes raised by Proudhon in his *Idée générale;* and second, Marx was later to be stimulated in a sense by the reform project advanced by Proudhon's disciple, Darimon. After reading the *Idée générale,* Marx read Proudhon's *Gratuité du crédit,*[116] and here he lost his temper: "charlatanism, poltroonery, a lot of noise and weakness . . . If you could see how this old fellow swaggers before Bastiat with the *Hegelian dialectic*" (Marx to Engels, November 24, 1851).[117] He could not resist doing battle with Proudhon once again. For a while he thought of publishing his criticisms together with Engels's glosses in a single brochure. Engels felt that his contribution would be rather inadequate. But Marx persisted with the project and proposed to Weydemeyer a series of articles: "New Revelations on Socialism, or the *Idée générale* of P. J. Proudhon. A Critique by Karl Marx" (Marx to Weydemeyer, December 19, 1851).[118] Like Hegel in philosophy, so Proudhon in political economy had the singular privilege of provoking Marx to energetic refutations. Although the teacher had been a disappointment, he remained nonetheless an instigator.[119]

Hopes of publication

There were the quarrels among the German émigrés, the trial of the Cologne communists, the essay on *The 18th Brumaire of Louis Bonaparte,* and the journalism that devoured hours and days. But a publisher for the "Economics" was found as well. The three-volume plan submitted to the publisher contained the following titles: "Critique of Political Economy," "Socialism," "History of Political Economy." The publisher would have preferred beginning with the last-named volume, reversing the initial plan. Nevertheless, Marx considered accepting, provided he receive a satisfactory author's fee.[120] Engels suggested that Marx prescribe two volumes for the "History,"

[116]Published in Paris, 1850.

[117]*MEW* 27, p. 371.

[118]Ibid., p. 595.

[119]See the article on Proudhon, which is a cross between a funeral elegy and censure; *MEW* 16, pp. 25–32.

[120]Letter to Engels, Nov. 24, 1851; *MEW* 27, p. 370. It was the journalist Hermann Ebner (Marx was unaware of the fact that he also served as an agent for the Austrian secret police), who undertook to interest the publisher, Löwenthal, of the Frankfurt company of Rütten and Lüning.

which would make the affair "lucrative" and also gain space for material that would anticipate some of his critical views. "Socialism" would follow; then the "Critique" – "*what would remain of it*"; – and finally the statement of his positive ideas, "which is what you really want." The reader would await until the end the "mystery so greatly anticipated," that is, that Marx had no miraculous panacea to offer. "The indications in the first volumes together with the Anti-Proudhon [i.e. *The Poverty of Philosophy*] and the *Manifesto* will suffice to lead normally intelligent readers in the right direction; the great majority of the buying and reading public would lose all interest in the History if the great mystery were to be revealed to them in the first volume; they would say, as with Hegel's *Phenomenology:* I have read the 'Preface,' and the general idea is to be found there." Engels's letter is full of persuasion: "For each *Louis d'or* less that he pays you for a printer's sheet [*Bogen*] you must impose enough additional sheets to compensate for your loss, and you can fill these up with citations, etc., which will cost you nothing." He stressed the importance of producing something substantial after such a long absence from the book market. The "History" could only be written in London; the rest elsewhere. Marx must act rapidly because new revolutionary movements could occur, above all in France, and destroy the chances of finding a publisher. "*Sois donc un peu commerçant, cette fois* [So this time act like a businessman!]" (Engels to Marx, November 27, 1851).[121]

These steps miscarried. Lassalle proposed setting up a joint-stock company to publish the "Economics," but Marx refused: After Bonaparte's coup d'état the bourgeoisie had other risks to run; and he personally had no desire to let the public know of his financial distress. He turned to Weydemeyer and the United States: "In view of the setback in Germany, wouldn't it be possible for me to find a publisher there for my 'Economics'?" (January 30, 1852)[122] But all hopes faded. During the summer of 1852 Marx tried, once again, to resume his studies; his research was historical, concerned in particular with the history of institutions, of civilization, and the condition of women. Many of his articles in the *New York Tribune*, which analyzed the major economic events of the 1850s, benefited from these readings. But his reporting dealt mainly with politi-

[121]*MEW* 27, pp. 373–5.
[122]*MEW* 28, p. 486.

cal events, which necessitated extensive reading. In August 1852 he made a last try, offering the editor Brockhaus, for his review *Die Gegenwart,* a work on "modern economic literature in England from 1830 to 1852"; it was to treat general works and writings on the great controversies of that era such as population, colonies, banking problems, protectionism, and free trade. The offer was quickly refused.

The balance sheet for 1844–1853

Except for the unlikely possibility that manuscripts from this period have been lost, it is surprising that Marx expected to compose several large volumes of the "Economics" in a relatively short time. We may reasonably suppose that Marx felt certain he could finish his research on schedule and therefore thought he would be able to draft the work in a few months. This was perhaps his way of deceiving himself and allaying the impatience of his friends during those years of material want and calumnious suspicions.

In 1853, nine years had passed since the Paris manuscripts, and the "Economics" had not yet been published. Despite this failure, the balance of those years of reflection was, in a sense, positive. Whatever one might think of the theoretical results, it must be conceded that Marx considered them to be useful gains. He nevertheless continued tirelessly to educate himself and thus excluded any possibility of conserving textually even a recently written work. Must we therefore conclude that he was continually modifying his schema of values? Were this true, Marx would have been nothing more than a man of purely theoretical learning, whereas in fact – and herein lies his glory – he was concerned with contemporary *realities* as much as, and more than, any writings; and the face of poverty and oppression did not change in the space of ten, or even twenty, years.

Marx, the communist of 1851, who had already elaborated the sociological foundations of his revolutionary theory, republished the *Anekdota* and the *Rheinische Zeitung* articles from his liberal and precommunist days, repudiating none of them.[123] Nor did his mature works render null and void that

---

[123]*Gesammelte Aufsätze von Karl Marx,* edited by Hermann Becker, 1851. It should be added that Engels, a few months before his death, tried to promote a reedition. He wanted to provide the introduction and annotations himself and even suggested as a title, "Karl Marx: Early Writings. Three Essays from the *Rheinische Zeitung* 1842"; cf. Engels's letter to Fischer, Apr. 15, 1895: MEW 39, p. 467.

first sketch of a critique of political economy, attempted in Paris in 1844. The Paris writings, together with those early articles collected and republished by Hermann Becker, contain the ethical inspiration of Marx's works: Their central theme, the concept of the alienation of labor and the working man, is also the pivot of the proletarian political economy that animates the whole of *Capital*. When rereading his early works, including *The Holy Family*, Marx no doubt experienced a measure of embarrassed surprise; but this was certainly the case whenever he reread any of his works. Admittedly he spoke less of alienation in *Capital* than in the *Manuscripts* of 1844, but he did in fact speak of it.[124] His critique of political economy is and remains the critique of the alienation of men by capital and the state.

Although the Young Hegelians had abused the term "alienation" to the point of arousing Marx's sarcasm, this did not lead him to repudiate his debt to Hegel and Feuerbach. He was also concerned that his language not lend itself to confusion; so, for example, he no longer spoke of communism as a "humanism." But we need only eliminate *words* such as "alienation," "humanism," and "naturalism" from the 1844 *Manuscripts* to discover behind them the same *facts* that are described and analyzed in *Capital*. In the draft of his preface to the *Manuscripts*, Marx declared that his analysis was "based on a detailed, critical study of political economy," on the works of the English, French, and German socialists and the "discoveries" of Feuerbach.[125] This is what gave his analysis from the outset its ultimate direction. In fact, most of the major themes of the "Economics" are present in the *Manuscripts*: capital, interest, landed property, wages, profits, rent, wage labor considered as a commodity, overproduction, joint-stock companies, labor productivity, the accumulation of capital, competition, private property, division of labor, crises, the revolution, the separation of the worker from the means and objects of his labor, the "reification" of labor (the same definition of alienation as is found in *Capital*), the slavery of wage labor, pauperization, monopoly, money fetishism, communism, socialism, human needs and their historical evolution, overpopulation, and so on. In the preface, Marx was careful to point out that in the *Manuscripts* he would only treat in passing the "connection with the

[124]For example, *MEW* 23, pp. 86–7, 122, 381–2, 445–6, 455, 596, 603, 635.
[125]*MEGA* I, 3, pp. 33–4.

state, law, morality, civil life, etc." At that time the plan of the "Economics" was still vague in his mind, because it was then projected as but one "brochure" among others.

Little by little Marx's horizon grew, entailing on his part a more profound examination of his principles. In order to write the "Critique" promised to Leske, he first had to clear the terrain encumbered by ideology. His method, applicable to every scientific discipline whose field of inquiry is man and his society, was precisely that "materialism," that antispeculative criticism, that "active" idealism (as opposed to the contemplative idealism of the materialist Feuerbach) that links our comprehension of realities to a revolutionary praxis – to ethics, if like Spinoza, we understand by that term the unity of knowledge and action. Beginning with the first part of *The German Ideology*, this line of reasoning, whatever we call it, provides the clue to the future plan of the "Economics." Marx's critique of the state, the "illusory community," shows us why a rubric necessarily had to be reserved for the state in the 1857–9 plan. By the same token, the final rubric of this plan was to be devoted to the problem of the world market, which merits substantial treatment in *The German Ideology:* As a historical process, alienation finds in the world market both its most brutal expression and the situation that will produce its end.[126] Not only did these themes remain unchanged after fifteen years, but they were articulated in a similar manner: It is possible neither to eliminate any of them from the general scheme, nor to subsume one theme "dialectically" under another in the context of a modified plan. Later, Engels was to ask Marx constantly for clarification about their "dialectical connections," and he always paid careful attention to them.

It goes without saying that Marx did not exhaust his topic in the fragmentary writings of the pre-1857 period. Most of his scientific "discoveries" date mainly from the second period, when, having elaborated the plan of the "Economics," he went to work on the individual "rubrics."[127] But his writing was frustrated by poverty, and he was often disgusted by political economy, refusing to become its victim altogether. Thus, he

[126]Cf. *MEW* 3, p. 37. On the development of the world market and alienation, see *Grundrisse*, pp. 78–9. Marx envisaged this process as a condition of its own "transcendence."

[127]See the précis of Marx's discoveries in economics, given in the appendix to the present essay.

persisted in the self-imposed task of extensive reading that was
to absorb him until his death.

The plan and significance of the "Economics"

Between 1853 and 1856 Marx consulted his study notebooks
on rare occasions: At Lassalle's request, for example, he
looked up statistics on English agriculture, the importations of
grain (1847–50), land left fallow (1853–4), the effects of free
trade on the price of raw materials, wages, and so on (Marx to
Lassalle, January 23, 1855).[128] Still, he continued to manifest
interest in monetary problems, as we can deduce from the
existence of a study notebook composed circa 1854–5. There
is a second notebook that consists of more than forty pages of
excerpts from some twenty-four books and entitled *Das vol-
lendete Geldsystem* ("The Perfected Monetary System"). Here
Marx makes frequent references to the numbers affixed to his
earlier notebooks. Journalism "disgusted" him and, during the
second half of 1857, a pending financial crisis fanned his revolutionary hopes. "The revolution will have a hard time finding
as beautiful a *tabula rasa* as the present one. All of the socialist
dodges [of Napoleon III] have been exhausted"; this was Engels's opinion (Engels to Marx, November 17, 1856),[129] and it
induced Marx to resume the "Economics" once again. What is
more, he felt the publication of Proudhon's *Manuel du
spéculateur à la Bourse* (5th ed., Paris, 1857) and the Proudhonian, Darimon's, writing on the *Réforme des banques* (Paris,
1856) to be new provocations.

Immediately following the Crimean War a widespread wave
of speculation in banking, commerce, industry, and agriculture
broke over France, then spread rapidly over all Europe and the
United States. As early as June 1856, in the *New York Daily
Tribune,* Marx began investigating the activities of the French
Crédit mobilier; in absence of such an analysis "one could not
understand the prospects of the French Empire nor the symptoms of social depression" in Europe.[130]

[128]*MEW* 28, pp. 612–15.

[129]*MEW* 29, p. 86.

[130]In three articles, beginning June 21, 1856. The ambition of the *Crédit mobilier*
was apparently to buy up, by means of its own shares, all of the stocks and assets of
all the enterprises. The government had accorded it the privilege of executing public
works. "Napoleon le Petit" thus appeared as the manager of French industry; this is
what Marx ironically referred to as "imperial socialism." CF. M. Rubel, *Karl Marx
devant le bonapartisme* (Paris/The Hague: 1960), pp. 31 ff.

A few months later he predicted a crisis and its probable consequences. He probably profited from his most recent study notebooks in writing for the American newspaper articles that dealt largely with speculation and monetary questions.[131] In these correspondent's reports from the years 1856–8 we note a wealth of materials later incorporated in the theoretical explications of *Capital*, especially in Books I and III. Commenting on the crisis of 1857–8, Marx attributed a great deal of importance to the role played by the joint-stock companies; in *Capital* he would consider their operation as fundamental to the theory of accumulation, which is at the same time a theory of social evolution. In fact, although the foundations of the system remain intact, the capitalist mode of production is in the process of abolishing itself: This is the destructive or negative aspect of the "transition" from capitalism to socialism.[132]

There is more than journalism in the words of the journalist as he clarifies the relationship between the enormous development of the system of credit and the phenomenon he christened "imperial socialism":

All of the varied past experience of Bonaparte pointed to the one great resource that had carried him over the most difficult economical situations – Credit. And there happened to be in France the school of Saint-Simon, which in its beginning as in its decay deluded itself with the dream that all the antagonism of classes must disappear before the creation of universal wealth by some newfangled scheme of public credit. And Saint-Simonism in this form had not yet died out at the epoch of the coup d'état. There was Michel Chevalier, the economist of the *Journal des Débats;* there was Proudhon, who tried to disguise the worst portion of the Saint-Simonist doctrine under the appearance of eccentric originality; and there were two Portuguese Jews, practically connected with stockjobbing and Rothschild, who had sat at the feet of Père Enfantin, and who with their practical experience had the boldness to suspect stockjobbing behind Socialism, Law behind Saint-Simon.

[131]He announced to Engels his intention to examine the relationship between exchange rates and precious metals and drew his attention to the importance of two recently published volumes of Tooke's *History of Prices* (letters of Apr. 9 and 23, 1857; *MEW* 29, pp. 123, 130). At this time Marx probably composed a twenty-page notebook entitled "The Monetary System; Credit; Crises," which contains excerpts and various statistical materials.

[132]Cf. *Capital*, Book III; *MEW* 25, pp. 451 ff. Its "positive" abolition is the workers' production cooperative.

These men – Emile and Isaac Pereire – are the founders of the *Crédit Mobilier,* and the instigators of Bonapartist Socialism.[133]

Marx discovered that joint-stock companies have a historical function as heralds of a new era in the economic life of modern nations. To designate this development he used – as did Proudhon (whom he nevertheless criticizes) – the expression "industrial feudalism" borrowed from Fourier. At the same time, however, he recognized its positive virtues, for the "productive powers of association" are incomparably more fertile than the efforts of individual capitalists.

The concentration of capital has been accelerated, and, as a natural corollary, the downfall of the small middle class. A sort of industrial king have been created, whose power stands in inverse ratio to their responsibility – they being responsible only to the amount of their shares, while disposing of the whole capital of society. . .Beneath this oligarchic Board of Directors is placed a bureaucratic body of the practical managers and agents of the society, and beneath them, without any transition, an enormous and daily-swelling mass of mere wage laborers – whose dependence and helplessness increase with the dimensions of the capital that employs them, but who also become more dangerous in direct ratio to the decreasing number of its representatives.[134]

Marx's numerous newspaper articles that analyze political events throughout the years 1851–6 are filled with insights about classes, parties, and the power of the state. Thus, they give us some indication of what would have been the general study of the modern state, which he had thought of doing ever since 1845. His thoughts repeatedly returned to that project, inspired not only by moments of economic crisis, but also by political events such as the fourth bourgeois revolution in Spain, which was defeated by the reaction, with Espartero leaving the field to O'Donnell (*New York Tribune,* August 8 and 18, 1856). Politics and political economy were inseparable in Marx's thinking; no less cohesive were his praxis and understanding of history since his departure from philosophy. In 1857, as in 1845, his explicit intention was to treat the contradictions of both capitalist production and the state. In 1859 he

[133]*New York Daily Tribune,* June 24, 1856. Cf. *Capital,* Book III; MEW 25, pp. 457, 619.
[134]*New York Daily Tribune,* July 11, 1856.

was to reaffirm this intention in his preface to *A Contribution to the Critique of Political Economy.*

A new start on the "Economics"

Ill, without resources and yet often unable to write for the *Tribune,* Marx also had to put his pen in the service of an American encyclopedia from July 1857 to October 1860.[135] In the midst of these subaltern intellectual tasks his thoughts returned to the "Economics." This wonder was produced by the American and international crisis of 1857, which he had been awaiting for the last seven years. Engels and he, tireless watchmen of sociopolitical upheaval, feverishly kept abreast of the latest events: "Although personally in financial difficulties, I have never since 1849 felt so well-off as I do facing this crisis" (letter to Engels, November 13, 1857).[136] "I work like mad during the night preparing a synthesis of my economic studies in order to have at least the outlines [*Grundrisse*] clear before the deluge."[137] "I work as if I were possessed, often until four in the morning. My work is two-fold: 1. elaboration of the basic features [*Grundzüge*] of the Economics (for the public it is absolutely necessary to get to the bottom of things, and for me personally, to get rid of this nightmare); 2. the present crisis. All I've done is to keep the books on it – apart from the articles for the *Tribune* – but even that took a lot of time. In the spring we might be able *together* to write a pamphlet on this history, as a sort of come-back before the German public, in order to let it know that we are, as always, still here. I have put together three large notebooks, for England, Germany, France . . ." (letter to Engels, December 18, 1857).[138] "The present commercial crisis has prompted me to begin seriously the elaboration of my outlines on economics and also to prepare something on the present crisis. I am obliged to sacrifice

---

[135]Cf. M. Rubel, *Bibliographie des oeuvres de Karl Marx,* p. 137; and *Supplément,* p. 46.

[136]*MEW* 29, p. 207.

[137]Marx to Engels, Dec. 8, 1857; *MEW* 29, p. 225. Statistical material was compiled in a notebook dated December 1857 and entitled *Book of the crisis 1857* (bankruptcies; rates of exchange; commodity markets, etc.; clippings from the *Economist* and other newspapers). A second notebook, from January 1858, bears the title *Book of the commerical crisis* (fluctuations of the financial market; commodity market, industrial market, etc.).

[138]*MEW* 29, p. 232.

the day with work to earn our daily living. For the *real* work I am left only the night, and I am often upset by illness. I have not yet set about finding a publisher . . . I have no news to report because I am living like a hermit."[139]

Such were his sufferings and hopes as he drafted in some ten months the beginning of the "Economics," known otherwise as the *Grundrisse,* the most important first draft of a future part of *Capital.*[140]

The plan of the "Economics"

When he spoke of a "synthesis" of his studies, Marx was probably thinking of the heap of various writings that he had been accumulating since 1843. It was, therefore, logical to begin with an introduction that would establish the direction and the plan of that synthesis. He started a draft of this, then thought better of it: It not only demanded a considerable intellectual effort, but also tended "to anticipate results not yet verified."[141]

The first part of the *General Introduction* was to treat the following topics: "Production, consumption, distribution, exchange (circulation)."[142] It is subdivided into four parts entitled: "1. Production. 2. The General Relation of Production to Distribution, Exchange and Consumption. 3. The Method of Political Economy. 4. Production: Means of Production and Relations of Production. Relations of Production and Social Institutions. Forms of the state and of consciousness corresponding to Production Relations and Social Institutions. Law. The Family." This first part, or first chapter, with its four subdivisions, was never finished. Marx hardly touched the

---

[139]Letter to Lassalle, Dec. 21, 1857; *MEW* 29, p. 548. In this letter Marx also mentions his wife's state of health following a stillbirth.

[140]It was David Riazanov who first announced the discovery of the *Grundrisse* during a conference of the Socialist Academy in Moscow, Nov. 20, 1923; see D. Riazanov, "Neueste Mitteilungen über den literarischen Nachlass von K. Marx und F. Engels," *Archiv für die Geschichte des Sozialismus und der Arbeiterbewegung,* vol. 11 (1925), 385–400. Riazanov said that Engels had either forgotten this manuscript or was unaware of its existence. It was published in Moscow in 1939 and 1941 and republished in Berlin in 1953.

[141]*Zur Kritik der politischen Ökonomie. Vorwort; MEW* 13, p. 7. For the fragment of that *General Introduction* that has been preserved, see *Grundrisse,* pp. 3–31. Two recent English translations of the *General Introduction* are in: Karl Marx, *The Grundrisse,* ed. and trans. David McLellan (New York: 1971), pp. 16–46; and Karl Marx, *Grundrisse,* trans. with foreword by Martin Nicolaus (Harmondsworth, 1973), pp. 83–111.

[142]*Grundrisse,* p. 5.

fourth of the subdivisions.[143] Stylistically this writing can be likened to an intense meditative effort interrupted by moments of criticism or sarcasm directed at contemporaries whom Marx particularly disdained: Bastiat, Carey, Proudhon. Also characteristic is the fact that it incorporates a direct confrontation with Hegel's method and sporadic use of Hegelian formulas.[144] At times, Marx's sentences appear to be merely aids for his memory, which he no doubt intended to develop subsequently. He opens the chapter on "method in political economy" on a note of hesitant questioning, first reviewing the two successive schools whose task had been to define a method for analyzing economic phenomena. The school of the seventeenth century chose an apparently empirical method that starts with the "living whole," such as the population, the nation, the state, and so on and then deals with the simpler elements such as the division of labor, money, and value. Marx contested the pretended empiricism of this school and passed on to the second. The latter, proceeding from the "particular moments" that the first school had attained by abstraction, became the parent of those "systems" that departed from the simpler elements, such as labor, division of labor, need, exchange value, and proceeded to the state, international exchange, and the world market.[145] Marx considered this second method to be "scientifically exact" and therefore gave it his unconditional adherence. He compared the first method to that of Hegel, according to whom the "concrete," as the synthesis and unity of empirical data, evaporates into abstract determinations that create reality.

We shall not dwell here on the somewhat hazy explanation that Marx attempts to give of his "method of proceeding from the abstract to the concrete," which he identifies as a "manner of appropriating the concrete and of reproducing it as the concrete in thought." In the preface and in the afterword to

[143]*Grundrisse*, p. 29–30.

[144]From a letter to Engels we learn that a coincidence drew Marx's attention to Hegel's *Logic* in 1857: "For my method of elaboration I have profited greatly by perusing once more, by pure chance, the *Logic* of Hegel. Freiligrath found some volumes of Hegel that had belonged to Bakunin and sent them to me as a gift. If there is ever time for such work again, I should quite like to write two or three printers sheets which would enable the ordinary mind to understand the *rational* element in the method discovered but at the same time mystified by Hegel" (Jan. 16, 1858; *MEW* 29, p. 260). Marx never got to this project.

[145]*Grundrisse*, p. 21.

Capital he will again bring up the subject of his method of abstraction, comparing it with the methods employed in the natural sciences.[146] It should be emphasized here that when Marx defines the methodological principle to be followed in constructing his "Economics," he systematically links the genesis of the "economic categories" to social structures, to historically modified "relations of domination and servitude," to constantly evolving juridical and economic institutions. At the outset, he conceived of his "Economics" as an analysis of concepts no less than as a history of institutions. The order of thematic exposition in this analysis was to be determined by the degree of historical maturity of the "categories" and not by their chronological order. Thus, the simplest and most universal category—labor, for example—is not necessarily, despite its high degree of abstractness and "neutrality," the most decisive in a sociological sense and therefore must not forcibly be taken as the point of departure in the analysis.

"Bourgeois society," Marx declared, "is the most developed and the most differentiated of all the historical organizations of production. The categories that express its conditions and the comprehension of its structure permit us at the same time to understand the structure and the production relations of all earlier forms of society, whose ruins and elements provide its foundations; it continues to drag with it certain elements of the old which have not yet become obsolete, while some of their latent features have assumed mature form, etc. The anatomy of man provides the key to the anatomy of the ape."[147] To illustrate this thesis, which we believe contains the secret to both the method of exposition and the plan of the "Economics," Marx cites the example of ground rent and landed property. Although the latter is linked to agriculture, the "source of all production and of all existence," it would nevertheless be wrong to begin with it, because ground rent is incomprehensible without capital: "Capital is the all-dominating economic force of bourgeois society. It must be both the point of departure as well as the terminus, and its analysis must precede that of landed property."[148] The categories and the economic institutions should not succeed one another in the "natural" order of their historical evolution, but instead

[146]*MEW* 23, pp. 12, 25–6.
[147]*Grundrisse*, pp. 25–6.
[148]Ibid., p. 27.

must correspond with the role and the functions they fulfill relative to one another in modern society.

Marx now recapitulates the foregoing methodological reflections, presenting in the form of a plan the logical outcome of his research. Somewhat hesitantly he writes:

> Clearly, the division will have to be as follows:
> 1. The definitions which, in their abstract generality, are applicable more or less to all types of society . . .
> 2. The categories that constitute the internal structure of bourgeois society and the basis for the fundamental classes. Capital, wage-labor, landed property. Their reciprocal relations. The city- and rural-regions. The three great social classes. Exchange among these. Circulation. The institution of credit (private).
> 3. Synthesis of bourgeois society in the form of the state. The state considered in itself. The "unproductive" classes. Taxes. Public debt. Public credit. Population. Colonies. Emigration.
> 4. Production in its international relations. International division of labor. International exchange. Exportation and importation. Rates of exchange.
> 5. The world market and crises.[149]

The legendary "change" in the plan of the "Economics"

Some of the foremost Marx specialists have adopted the interpretation according to which the plan of the "Economics" in six rubrics, as given in the 1859 preface to *A Contribution to the Critique of Political Economy*: that is, *capital, landed property, wage labor; state, foreign commerce, world market*, is held to have been abandoned.[150] Karl Kautsky seems to have been the first to have advanced this opinion.[151] In fact, however, Kautsky only asserted that the 1859 plan did not coincide with the plan of *Capital* (1867); but he did not investigate the reasons behind this discrepancy. Thirty years later, Henryk Grossmann elevated Kautsky's simple remark to the stature of a methodological principle. According to Grossmann, Marx, in

---

[149]Ibid., pp. 28–9.
[150]*MEW* 13, p. 7.
[151]In his preface to the 1897 reedition of *Zur Kritik der politischen Ökonomie*.

1862, replaced the six-rubric plan of 1859 with the plan of *Capital* outlined in the preface to Book I, dated July 25, 1867.[152] On the basis of Marx's letters to Kugelmann and Engels, Grossmann situated the date of this change in July–August 1863; and he termed "whimsical" the interpretation advanced by R. Wilbrandt,[153] according to whom the four books of *Capital* represent the *first* part of the plan of 1859, which left five parts still to be written. Unlike Kautsky, Grossmann did not distinguish between the "Economics" and *Capital*, despite the fact that Marx in his 1859 preface spoke *expressis verbis* of the "system of bourgeois economy" that he intended to examine in six divisions, "capital" being the first one of them. In other words, according to Grossmann's thesis, *Capital* (Book I, plus Books II, III, and IV published by Engels and Kautsky) is nothing other than the "Economics," which has, therefore, been "essentially completed."[154]

What reasons are advanced for this supposed change of plan? Grossmann asserted that for methodological reasons Marx established the six-part plan of 1859 "from the viewpoint of the material [*Stoff*]," while that of 1863, the "definitive" plan, was organized "from the viewpoint of knowledge [*Erkenntnis*]." However, it should be noted that Marx already considered his subject from the "viewpoint of knowledge" as early as 1857–8: The manuscript of the *Grundrisse*, which is based on the six-rubric plan, contains the same plan for *Capital* that we shall later discover in it in 1867–that is, three "books" (called "chapters" in the *Grundrisse*). Although in 1929 Grossmann was surely unaware of the existence of the *Grundrisse*, the correspondence between Marx and Lassalle was known.[155] Marx in fact disclosed to Lassalle the plan of the "first installment" on March 11, 1858, that is, one year before the publication of the preface to *A Contribution to the Critique of Political Economy*. Here is that plan:

1. *Value; 2. Money; 3. Capital in general (the process of production of capital, the process of circulation of capital, unity of the two processes or capital and profit, interest).*[156]

[152]Henryk Grossmann, "Die Änderung des ursprünglischen Aufbauplans des Marxschen 'Kapitals' und ihre Ursachen," *Archiv für die Geschichte des Sozialismus und der Arbeiterbewegung*, vol. 14 (1929), 305–38.

[153]*Karl Marx* (Leipzig: 1913), pp. 97, 307.

[154]Grossman, "Die Änderung des. . . Aufbauplans. . .," p. 308.

[155]Published by Gustav Mayer in 1922.

[156]*MEW* 29, p. 554. In sum, Marx thought he could fit the whole "rubric" on capital into one "part" (later "notebook") of about one hundred pages!

Obviously the "viewpoint of the material," rather than opposing the "viewpoint of knowledge," on the contrary implied it. Three weeks earlier, even before informing Engels, Marx had also communicated to Lassalle the plan for the "Economics" in six books. The importance of this letter warrants our quoting its essential passages:

I want to let you know how I am doing with the economic work. For the past several months I have in fact been in the process of elaborating the final draft. However, the thing is advancing only very slowly, because matters that have for years been the principal object of my studies reveal new aspects and invite new reflections every time I want to wind them up. Besides, I am not the master of my time, but rather its slave. Only the night is left me, and frequent recurrences of a liver ailment disrupt these nocturnal labors. Under these circumstances, it would be most convenient for me if I were able to publish the whole work in consecutive brochures . . . This procedure would perhaps also have the advantage of allowing me to find a publisher more easily, since it would not be necessary to invest much financial capital in the enterprise . . .

The work is primarily a *critique of economic categories* or, if you like, a critical presentation of the system of bourgeois economy. It is both an analysis of the system and as such a critique of it. I am not at all sure how many notebooks the whole will consist of. If I have the time, the tranquility and the means really to finish all of it before presenting it to the public, I will condense it considerably, for I have always liked condensation as a method . . .

The exposition—I mean the manner of presentation—is utterly scientific, thus lawful in the ordinary sense of the term. The whole is divided into six books: 1. On Capital (containing some preliminary chapters). 2. On Landed Property. 3. On Wage-Labor. 4. On the State. 5. International Commerce. 6. World Market . . . Generally speaking, however, the critique and the history of political economy and socialism will be the object of another work. A third will be devoted to a brief *historical sketch* of the development of the economic categories or relations. After all, I have the feeling that now, after fifteen years of study, at the very moment when I have reached the point of actually tackling the work, tumultuous external factors are probably going to interfere. Never mind. If I finish too late to find the world receptive to works of this kind, the fault will no doubt be my own. There are stormy times in store for us in the near future. Were I to listen to my personal feelings, I would wish for the calm to continue in the outside world for several more years. It is, in any event, the best time for scientific investigations, and in the end, after the experience of the past ten years, every thinking being must have developed such mistrust of the masses and of individuals that the *odi profanum vulgus et arceo* becomes an almost obligatory insight. But all that is merely the momentary whim of a philistine and will be swept away by the first tempest!"[157]

In his subsequent letter of March 11, 1858, Marx, without the slightest allusion to any "change of plan," informed Lassalle of the plan for the "first part" with its three subparts (value, money, capital); the last, "capital in general," was subdivided into three sections, which were to provide the material for the future three books of *Capital*. Thus, the plan of 1863 that Grossmann takes as his reference is absolutely identical to that of 1858–9, with a single modification, given in the 1867 preface to *Capital:* the addition of a fourth book on the "History of the Theory."[158]

All the errors committed regarding the plan of the "Economics" have previously obscured this one fact, that Marx failed to publish the "Economics" in accordance with the plan given in the 1859 preface (six rubrics) not due to "methodological" reasons, such as Grossmann speaks of, that would have lead him to change the *Aufbauplan* (plan of composition) of the work; but rather because, instead of writing "booklets," he found himself obliged to compose "large volumes."[159]

[157]Marx to Lassalle, Feb. 22, 1858; *MEW* 29, pp. 550–2.
[158]*MEW* 29, pp. 553–4.
[159]For a more fully documented treatment of the question examined here, see Otto Morf, *Das Verhältnis von Wissenschaftstheorie und Wirtschaftsgeschichte bei Karl Marx* (Bern: 1951), pp. 75 ff. (A second edition of this work was published in Frankfurt and Vienna in 1970 under the title *Geschichte und Dialektik in der politischen Ökonomie. Zum Verhältnis von Wissenschaftstheorie und Wirtschaftsgeschichte bei Karl Marx.*) Not until after the original French version of the present text had been sent to press in 1968 was our attention called to Roman Rosdolsky's *Zur Entstehungsgeschichte des Marxschen "Kapital"* vol. 1 (Frankfurt: 1968), pp. 24–85, in which the author comments on the changes in Marx's original outline for his "Economics." In contrast to Grossmann, Rosdolsky believes that in the "altered" (?) plan, Books IV, V, and VI (on the state, foreign commerce, and the world market) were dropped but "never really abandoned"; rather, they were retained for the purpose of an "eventual continuation" of this work (p. 29). Rosdolsky's arguments for the inclusion of Books I–III in *Capital,* although interesting, are nonetheless untenable. First of all, he overlooks Marx's letter of Mar. 11, 1858 to Lassalle and, what is even more serious, in his treatment of the "methodological meaning," etc. of Marx's work, he fails to recognize the significance attached to the division of the economic topics into two sets of three topics each, as set down by Marx in his preface of 1859 (to *Zur Kritik. . .*). If Hegel's "triadic" method was ever instrumental for Marx in his work, then most certainly it

Capital *as part of the "Economics"*

Once he had outlined the contents of the "first installment," its size estimated at "five or six printer's sheets" (nearly 100 pages), Marx immediately added: "This will make one separate booklet." Thus, we see that Marx counted on treating the whole of *Capital*, with its "preliminaries" on value and money and its three "processes" (production, circulation, unity of the two), in *one hundred pages*.[160]

Nevertheless, Marx himself did not rule out the possibility of an error in his calculation. "As for the total number of sheets," he wrote to Lassalle, who had offered to find him a publisher, "I haven't in fact a very clear idea since the material for this book has been accumulated in my notebooks only in the form of monographs; they often go into great detail, but that will vanish in the process of composition. I do not intend to develop uniformly the six books that constitute the whole; in the last three, I will give only the rudiments [*Grundstriche*], whereas in the first three, which contain the fundamental economic analysis, it will not always be possible to avoid going into detail. I hardly think that the whole can be less than 30 to 40 sheets. . .If the publisher accepts the thing, the first installment could be sent towards the end of May."[161]

In the 1859 preface as well, Marx spoke of a "whole batch of material" that he had prepared "in the form of monographs written at great intervals, not for publication, but for my personal clarification."[162] He was undoubtedly referring not only to the large manuscript of the *Grundrisse*, which was drafted from October 1857 to the end of February 1858, but also to the Paris and Brussels manuscripts of 1844–5 and to his research from the first years in London, 1851–4. When speaking of the "first installment," however, he could only have

was in his conception of the two-part division of the six topics for the "Economics." A fuller treatment of this point is given in Essay 4 of the present volume on the plan and method of the "Economics."

[160]The following part of the letter shows what, in the eyes of its author, the originality of his research consisted in: "You will have noted, in your economic studies, that in analyzing profit, Ricardo came to contradict his own definition of value, which was nevertheless correct. These contradictions have led the Ricardian school either to abandon completely the basis of the theory or to fall into a repugnant eclecticism. I believe I have resolved the problem (it is true that, in regarding the matter closely, the economists will realize that altogether it is a dirty business)."

[161]Marx to Lassalle, Mar. 11, 1858: *MEW* 29, p. 554.

[162]*Zur Kritik der politischen Ökonomie. Vorwort; MEW* 13, p. 7.

been thinking of the *Grundrisse,* from which he intended to draw the substance of the "first book," to be titled *On Capital.* To reduce to one hundred pages that material, which represented close to fifty printer's sheets (of sixteen pages each, that is, eight hundred pages in all), and to do this in the space of three months, would be a difficult enterprise even for someone masterfully gifted in the art of condensation. This first booklet was to constitute "from all points of view an articulate whole [*ein relatives Ganzes*]" and was to serve as the basis of the work that was to be developed subsequently. If we keep in mind the fact that reference here is to the *whole* of *Capital* and not merely the future first book, we can appreciate Marx's insistence on the decisive character of that "first installment" and also his later, almost fierce refusal, voiced to Engels, to have the first book printed alone. Meanwhile, he informed his friend of Lassalle's steps and provided him with the entire plan of the "Economics" in six books.[163] This was the first time he divulged the principal traits of what he then considered to be the "preliminaries" of *Capital.* Here are the essential passages of this outline, many of whose elements resemble the schema given in the *Grundrisse:*

I. *Capital* is divided into four sections [*Abschnitte*]. a) Capital *en général. (This is the material of the first notebook).* b) *Competition,* or the interaction of the many capitals. c) *Credit,* where capital appears opposed to the different capitals as the general element. d) *Share-capital,* the most developed form (passing over into communism), pregnant with all of its contradictions. The transition from capital to landed property is at the same time historical, since the modern form of landed property is produced by the action of capital on feudal etc. landed property. Likewise, the transition from landed property to wage labor is not only dialectical but historical, since the final product of modern landed property is the generalization of wage-labor, which then appears as the basis of the whole scheme.[164]

Marx then returns to "capital in general," the content of the "first section" and subject of the "first installment." We learn

---

[163]Letter to Engels, Apr. 2, 1858; *MEW* 29, p. 312.

[164]Replying in advance to allegations of a "change of plan," Marx clearly indicates that the method adopted obliges him to treat, after capital, landed property and wage labor.

once more that wage labor and landed property will not be treated systematically in this "section":

I. *Capital. First section. Capital in general.* (Throughout this section we assume wages as always equal to their minimum. The movement of wages themselves and the rise or fall of the minimum will be analyzed in the study on wage labor. Moreover, landed property is given as = 0; in other words, landed property as a particular economic relation does not yet concern us here. Only by employing this procedure can we avoid constantly speaking of the entire set of relations when treating one of them.)

1. *Value.* Reduced entirely to the quantum of labor . . . Value as such has no other "substance" than labor itself. This definition of value . . . is merely the most abstract expression of bourgeois wealth. It presupposes: 1. the abolition of primitive communism (India, etc.), 2. of all undeveloped, pre-bourgeois modes of production . . . Although an abstraction, it is a historical abstraction which in fact could be made only on the basis of a particular economic development of society . . .

The second chapter of the first section – on money – is a condensation of the material destined for the first notebook (or installment) of the *Contribution to the Critique of Political Economy,* including the attacks against the Saint-Simonians, the "harmonists" (Bastiat and Carey), the Proudhonians. As for the third chapter, on "Capital," momentary illness prevented Marx from continuing with its description.[165] Hence this letter contains nothing regarding the three divisions of "capital in general," which Marx had indicated in his letter to Lassalle.[166] However, in an "Index" that he composed toward

[165]"This subject is in fact the central theme of the first notebook, and I need your opinion on this point. But I cannot write any more today. My *Gallendreck* keeps me from holding the pen and I get dizzy when I lean my head forward. So I'll talk about that next time." (To Engels, Apr. 2, 1858; *MEW* 29, pp. 312–18.)

In his reply of April 9, Engels said that he found the "first half-notebook" quite abstract and had trouble finding the "dialectical transitions," and he concluded: "The arrangement of the whole in six books seems excellent and I like it very much, even though I cannot as yet clearly distinguish the dialectical transition from landed property to wage-labor. . ."(*MEW* 29, p. 219.) Then, for several weeks Marx was unfit to work. At the end of May 1858, he could finally resume writing and began the definitive text of the first brochure for the *Contribution to the Critique of Political Economy.* (Cf. his letters to Engels and Lassalle written on May 31, 1858; *MEW* 29, pp. 329, 560.)

[166]He probably discussed it with Engels, whom he visited in Manchester during most of May 1858.

the end of May 1858 in order to coordinate the material in the *Grundrisse* manuscript, he nevertheless proceeded according to the plan communicated to Lassalle and Engels.[167]

The following outline is the first of two versions of Marx's "Index" appended to the seven notebooks of the *Grundrisse*, the "first part" of the "Economics."[168]

I. Value

Ricardo, Malthus, A. Smith. Use-value and Exchange-value. Steuart, Torrens. Unskilled and skilled labor.

II. Money

In general. Transition from value into money. Product of the exchange itself.

The three definitions of money (Bailey).

1. Money as a measure.

That paper-money is attributed denominations in gold or silver, whether legally convertible or not, means that it is necessarily exchangeable for the quantity of gold or silver that it represents. As soon as it ceases to be convertible, it is depreciated, with or without legal convertibility. Gold and silver as money of account express no value, but only the aliquot parts of their own matter. They cannot claim to represent a value: they constitute nominal values. (As a consequence they cannot be nominally depreciated.) Fall and rise in the value of gold and silver. On the denomination of values expressed directly in labor time.

Mental conversion of commodities into money. Money as money of account, as a means of exchange (Steuart, Gouge, Bailey, Müller, *Economist.*) Assignates. Account books in France (Garnier).

[167]Cf. *Grundrisse*, pp. 855 ff. Title: "Index for the seven notebooks of the first part." Marx drafted two versions of the index. He mentioned it to Engels: "... The manuscript (which, when printed, will make a big volume), is in total disorder, and I have included in it a good many things that are intended for other parts" (May 31, 1858; *MEW* 29, p. 330).

[168]Marx's references to the numbers and pages of the notebooks have been omitted here.

Money as a measure needs no constant value, but only quantity. (Bailey, Urquhart, Gray, Fullarton.)

2. Money as a medium of exchange or simple circulation (Steuart). Coins . . . Privilege of money in circulation . . .

Value of money . . .

Contradiction between money as medium of circulation and as an equivalent . . . M - C easier than C - M . . .

3. Money as money . . . Disintegrating effect of money (free trade).

4. Precious metals as backing for money. Montanari. Enthusiasm for the "invention" of money . . .

5. The law of appropriation as manifested in simple circulation.

6. Transition of money into capital.

III. Capital in general

Transition of money into capital.

1. The process of production of capital.
   a) Exchange of capital for labor power.
   b) Absolute surplus value (Ricardo. Surplus labor. Steuart).
   c) Relative surplus value.
   d) Primitive accumulation (preconditions of the relation between capital and wage labor).
   e) Conversion [Umschlag] of the law of appropriation (Ricardo).
2. The process of the circulation of capital.[169]

We have no trouble in discovering, in this first Index, the important themes, money and simple circulation, developed first in the 1859 Contribution to the Critique of Political Economy, then in Capital, Book I. The entry entitled the "process of the circulation of capital," however, is not followed by any reference to the seven notebooks of the Grundrisse, although this subject was extensively treated there. It seems,

---

[169]Grundrisse, pp. 855–9. The second version (Grundrisse, pp. 860–7) is a summary, more detailed than the first, of the theme of money.

therefore, that Marx interrupted this draft of the Index to begin the second version. As we shall see, he was to resume the task of arranging and focusing his materials in 1859.

This index, more than any other document, amply proves that *Capital* represents only the "first part" of the "Economics" and that Marx could not have renounced his initial plan without simultaneously effacing his studies of the previous fifteen years and the methodological principles he had drawn from them. In other plans for the book on "Capital," the first part of the "Economics," Marx continually improved the logical and thematic structure of this work, which approached its definitive form — except for one detail: Instead of a chapter or a section, *Capital* would become a book.

The first brochure

Marx set the end of May 1858 as the deadline for delivery of his first brochure, but material obstacles prevented him from finishing anywhere near that date. It was August before he seriously began writing *A Contribution to the Critique of Political Economy*. This new text was no more definitive than the *Grundrisse* that preceded it, and Marx began the work again without, however, being able to develop the three themes reserved for the first brochure of the "Economics."[170] For although he wanted to "condense" the material that was amassed in the first manuscript, his field of observation had widened. Acquaintance with new sources induced him to give many more references, and his need for confrontation and criticism caused him to digress and to anticipate subjects that would have to be treated later and in a different context. Most importantly, in composing his treatise he discovered unforeseen aspects of the problem.[171] Thus his entire work was, as he was fond of saying, a sort of *Selbstverständigung*: at once self-

---

[170] See the fragment that has been preserved of the primitive version of the *Contribution to the Critique of Political Economy*, in the *Grundrisse*, pp. 871–947.

[171] One can follow Marx's reasoning as he developed, from his analysis of the concept of "labor" (*Arbeit*), the concept of "labor force" (*Arbeitskraft*), and from the concept of "productive labor" that of "surplus labor," culminating with the concept of "surplus value." (See for example, *Grundrisse*, pp. 170–5, 212–13, 201–2, 734–6.) In these preparatory works of 1857–8 he often returned directly to his unedited papers of 1844–5, and thus the years that separate the two periods appear insignificant. *It is a case of maturation, not of "rupture"* ("*coupure*").

examination and self-education. His correspondence alone provides clear evidence of the extent to which poverty kept him at the level of a student.[172]

Surprisingly, the published text of the *Contribution to the Critique of Political Economy* begins with a chapter that is not forecast in the plan of the *Grundrisse:* "The Commodity," instead of "Value."[173] Moreover, Marx's correspondence with Lassalle reveals, in addition to his endless frustrations, a concern for the form and an uncertainty about the contents of the "first installment." In November 1858 he hoped to finish in about "four weeks," and he announced that his manuscript would consist of "two notebooks," which together would equal the "first section" dealing with "capital in general." This, he wrote, is "the most abstract part of political economy" and would therefore be difficult for the general public to understand should he condense it excessively. "Furthermore, the second section should appear *simultaneously.* This is essential to the coherence of the content and will determine its whole effect."[174] These were serious reasons; nevertheless, Marx was going to be forced to submit only a fragment of the whole. "The manuscript amounts to about twelve printer's sheets (three *notebooks*),"[175] he wrote to Engels, "and – don't lose your balance – despite the title, 'Capital in general,' these *notebooks* as yet contain *nothing* about capital, but only the two chapters: 1. *The Commodity;* 2. *Money or simple circulation.* So you see that the part devel-

[172]This is the principle reason why, in our French edition of Marx (*Oeuvres*, vol. 2), we have arranged our selection of pieces of the *Grundrisse* manuscript so as to give it the appearance of a "condensation"; were this not done, it would be difficult to insert these preparatory writings into the thematic organization of the "Economics," in accordance with the plan of 1857.

[173]It is true that the *Grundrisse* manuscript ends with an unfinished chapter entitled "Value," which begins as follows: "The first category under which bourgeois wealth is presented is that of *commodity.* This itself appears as the unity of two determinations. It is *use-value,* that is to say, means of satisfaction of a determined system of human needs. . . " (*Grundrisse*, p. 763). This is very similar to the beginning of the *Contribution to the Critique of Political Economy.*

[174]Marx to Lassalle, Nov. 12, 1858; *MEW* 29, p. 567. The style of the manuscript betrays the author's attacks of hepatitis, and for a dual reason Marx could not tolerate this state of affairs: "1°, [my writing] is the result of 15 years' research, therefore of the best period of my life; 2°, it presents scientifically for the first time an important conception of the social conditions." This concern for form was, in Marx's eyes, a duty to the "party." (*MEW* 29, p. 566.)

[175]That is, 192 printed pages.

oped in detail (in May, when I was at your place) will not yet be published."[176]

The preface to A Contribution to the Critique of Political Economy is dated "January 1859." The work that Marx had previously referred to simply as his "Economics" now became "A Contribution to the Critique of Political Economy" (Zur Kritik der politischen Ökonomie). However, this title appeared nowhere in his correspondence with Engels nor in the letters to Lassalle, although the latter had served as "literary agent" in negotiating with the Berlin publisher Franz Duncker. The title page bearing the words "First Brochure" (Erstes Heft), is followed by the preface, then by a new title page that reads "First Book. On Capital" (Erstes Buch. Vom Kapital). The two chapters of the brochure ("The Commodity" and "Money or Simple Circulation") are preceded by the indication: "First Section (Abschnitt I): Capital in General." Consequently, the first section, first brochure of the First Book was to have been followed by other sections. Which ones? The plan in the Grundrisse tells us: After "Capital in General," Marx was to present three other "sections," namely, "Competition among the Many Capitals," Capital as Credit," and "Capital as Share Capital."[177]

The publisher seemed to be in no hurry to publish the "second brochure"; not only did the Contribution to the Critique of Political Economy sell poorly, but Marx failed to submit the new manuscript by the promised deadline.[178] He thought he would be able to submit the "second brochure" before the end of December 1859, even though it would have to be "reworked entirely, for the manuscript of the second brochure is already a year old."[179] Although the first brochure was larger

[176]Jan. 15, 1859; MEW 29, p. 383. A few days later, he found himself without enough money to pay the postage and send off the manuscript: "I do not think that anyone has ever written about money under such conditions of financial destitution. Most of the authors on the subject were in utmost harmony with the topic of their research." (Jan. 21, 1859; MEW 29, p. 385.)

[177]Grundrisse, p. 175.

[178]The task of gathering evidence to defend the "honor of the party" against the defamations launched by the naturalist, Karl Vogt, was to make the year 1860 one of the darkest periods in Marx's life. Yet, his Herr Vogt turned out to be more than merely an incidental pamphlet for in it he summarized his political sociology, emphasizing that in countries where the feudal aristocracy had not yet been ousted from power "the primary condition for a proletarian revolution is lacking, namely an industrial proletariat on a national scale." Herr Vogt (London: 1860), p. 43.

[179]Letter to Lassalle, Oct. 2, 1859; MEW 29, p. 613.

than provided for in the original plan, that first section was not supposed to be limited to the two chapters on the commodity and money. But Marx had changed his mind for "political" reasons; accordingly, he held back the third chapter, the one that would finally deal with capital.[180]

Neither before nor after the publication of the 1859 preface did Marx ever betray even the slightest intention of changing the plan of the "Economics." However, journalism and political quarrels devoured his time, and although he continually returned to his studies, he found it most difficult to condense his writing. Nevertheless, in the preface of 1859 he succeeded in presenting, in some twenty lines of text, "the guideline" of his fifteen years of study.[181] What is stated there confirms from every point of view Marx's intention to develop the "Economics" dialectically in six parts. He repeated himself on this in a letter informing Joseph Weydemeyer of the forthcoming publication of the *Contribution to the Critique of Political Economy:*

I divide the whole of political economy into six Books: Capital; Landed Property; Wage-Labor; State; Foreign Commerce; World Market. Book I on capital is composed of four sections. *Section I: Capital in General,* is divided into three chapters: *1. The Commodity; 2. Money or Simple Circulation; 3. Capital.* Chapters 1 and 2, about ten sheets in all, represent the contents of the first parts to be published . . . In these two chapters I likewise demolish the foundations of that Proudhonian socialism now fashionable in France, which proposes to maintain private production *but* wants to *organize* the exchange of private products, and wants *commodities* but not *money.* First and foremost communism must rid itself of this "false brother." But regardless of any polemical designs, you will agree that the analysis of the elementary forms of money is the most difficult, because the most abstract, part of political economy.[182]

---

[180]Letter to Engels, Jan. 15, 1859; to Weydemeyer, Feb. 1, 1859; to Lassalle, Mar. 28, 1859: "For the real battle begins with chapter 3, and I thought it would be advisable not to frighten people *de prime abord* [at the very outset]." (*MEW,* vol. 29, pp. 383, 572, 586.)

[181]*MEW* 13, p. 8.

[182]Marx to Weydemeyer, Feb. 1, 1859; *MEW* 29, p. 572–3. In the passage omitted, Marx reproduced the table of contents for chapters I and III of the *Contribution to the Critique of Political Economy.* In another passage Marx recalled having refused "very remunerative offers" in order to be able to devote his time to studies, and remarked: "I must pursue my goal against wind and tide, without permitting bourgeois society to turn me into a money-making machine." (*MEW* 29, p. 570.)

In October 1859 Marx thought that he could finish the "second brochure" before the end of the year, while concurrently revising the manuscript for the chapter on "Capital" already elaborated in the *Grundrisse*—a total of over 250 pages of his small handwriting, or nearly six hundred printed pages. In actuality, he was to need more than six years to finish just one part of that chapter. This part was to be the first book of *Capital*, which figured in the different plans of 1857–8 as the first section (*Abschnitt*) of the first book (or first rubric) of the "Economics." And as for the third chapter, that was destined to grow into three books, the first of which contained almost eight hundred printed pages. The miscalculation that Marx had feared obviously began to assume catastrophic dimensions. The only "change" in Marx's plan consonant with his method was in fact that he executed only a small part of his vast program and that this part gradually assumed unforeseen dimensions! Engels's silence concerning the 1859 plan has favored the development of certain "Marxist" myths, but in no way proves that Marx ever abandoned his project in six books. The same can be said of Engels's declaration that, despite the unfinished character of Books II and III, Marx had "said all that he wanted to say in one way or another" (preface to *Capital*, Book II).[183] Engels's ignorance seems instead to be proof of the contrary. Grossmann discovered, for his part, an "interconnection" between the "change of plan" and the "methodological structure of the schema of reproduction." Under the presumption that Marx "nowhere expressed himself about the way in which he arrived at his genial conception of the schema of reproduction,"[184]

---

[183]Cf. *MEW* 24, p. 12.

[184]Grossmann, "Die Änderung des. . .Aufbauplans. . .," p. 313. On July 6, 1863, Marx sent Engels the first outline of the schema of reproduction that he substituted for Quesnay's *Tableau économique* (*MEW* 30, pp. 361–7). When looking through the manuscript on Aug. 15, 1863, he realized that he had "to overturn everything" (*MEW* 30, p. 368). Grossmann comments on this: "The change of plan appears here to be a *fait accompli*." For one familiar with Marx nothing, alas, is more common than writings "overturned." On this occasion in particular, Marx specified what he had done: he had to rewrite the "historical" part (the two supplements to the *Contribution to the Critique of Political Economy*) in the light of new, "entirely unknown material." We shall see what that material was. In passing, it should be noted that Grossmann, when speaking of the "articulation of the empirical matter," omits the two rubrics on the state and the world market from his enumeration of the themes of the "Economics"!

Grossmann decided to fill that lacuna and in so doing attacked Rosa Luxemburg for contending that Book III had never been finished. It is not our objective here to follow Grossmann's arguments in trying to "reconstruct" certain missing links in Marx's reasoning and thus prove that the latter succeeded in completing his project. In affirming that "economic Marxism, as it has been bequeathed to us, is neither a *fragment* nor a *torso*, but represents in the main a fully elaborated system, that is, one without flaws,"[185] Grossmann could not have more perfectly expressed the very contrary of what we have discovered bit by bit.

The plan of "Capital"

In August 1861, after the commercial failure of the *Contribution to the Critique of Political Economy* and subsequent to the Vogt Affair, Marx continued his journalism and set to work on the third chapter dealing with the transformation of money into capital. Before beginning he composed several new summaries and plans, included in the *Grundrisse*, that demonstrate his desire to avoid any discrepancies in executing the 1857–9 plan.[186] The material to be treated expanded in fact to the point where the third chapter became a separate work, while the first two chapters (on the commodity and money) were turning into a kind of introduction. In composing *Referate* (summaries) for the notebooks that constitute the *Grundrisse*, Marx simply noted pell-mell the essential ideas, heedless of their logical order or any precise plan.[187]

Once these *Referate* were finished, Marx finally established a concrete plan for the third chapter. Here we discover the first clear mention of the three "sections" of "capital in general," referred to earlier in the letter to Lassalle of March 11, 1858. The plan, drawn up in February or March 1859, thus after Marx had submitted to the publisher the manuscript of the first brochure for the *Contribution to the Critique of Political Economy*, reads:

[185]"Die Änderung des. . .Aufbauplans. . .," p. 337.
[186]See these summaries in the *Grundrisse*, pp. 951–80.
[187]*Grundrisse*, p. 950. Marx indexed the notebooks marked M, I to VII, B' and B".
All the major themes of the three books of *Capital*, except for ground rent, are dealt with there not in order but with an apparent concern that nothing be forgotten.

I. The process of the production of Capital

1. Transformation of money into capital:
   a) Transition[188];
   b) Exchange between commodity[189] and labor power;
   c) The process of labor;
   d) The process of valorization.
2. Absolute surplus value.
3. Relative surplus value.
   a) The cooperation of the masses;
   b) Division of Labor;
   c) Machinery.
4. Primitive accumulation.
5. Wage-labor and capital.[190]

II. The process of the circulation of capital[191]

III. Capital and Profit[192]

A new beginning (1861–1863)

As he set to work according to the outlined plan, Marx suddenly realized that further research was necessary. He had added three historical appendixes (on the commodity, unit of measure and of money, means of circulation and money) to the *Contribution to the Critique of Political Economy* of 1859. Likewise, it now seemed appropriate to add to the third chapter a historical treatment of the theory of surplus value. This research, however, was to cost him at least three years of study. Later, as he recognized that the third chapter had grown into three books, he thought to use these materials on surplus value for a "Book IV" of *Capital*.

Marx never changed his plan; instead, it constantly ex-

[188]We omit the list of themes and the references to the notebooks and pages that follow each title.

[189]*Grundrisse* gives *Kapital;* in the manuscript, we read *Ware.*

[190]*Grundrisse*, pp. 969–73.

[191]Unlike the first section, the second contains no subdivisions but rather a list of themes; cf. *Grundrisse*, pp. 974 ff.

[192]No subdivisions, but a list of themes: rate of profit and surplus value, capital and profit, growth of capital. . .,risks. Production costs. Salary and profit as forms of production, therefore of distribution, etc. Interest and profit.

panded under his very eyes as he discovered new aspects to problems and gained new insights concerning, for example, absolute ground rent and amortization of fixed capital (letters to Engels, August 2 and 20, 1862).[193] Again, he hoped to finish in "two months" (letter to Lassalle, April 28, 1862);[194] and then he finally realized that it would be impossible to finish his "Economics." However, he decided that he could provide at least the "principles" in *three books* and was determined not to publish anything before these were completed.

Writing to Kugelmann, a reader full of admiration for the *Contribution to the Critique of Political Economy*, Marx disclosed:

The second part is finally finished now, that is, except for the final recopying and stylistic polishing for publication. It will make approximately 30 printer's sheets. This is the sequel to the first brochure but will be published separately under the title "Capital," with Critique of Political Economy as its subtitle. It contains in fact only the material for what was to have been the third chapter of the first part, i.e. "Capital in general." It therefore omits the competition of the many capitals and the credit system. This volume will contain what the English call the "principles of political economy." Together with the first part it forms the quintessence, and its continuation would be easy for others to develop on the basis of what I have provided (except perhaps for the relationship between the various forms of the state and the different economic structures of society) (December 28, 1862).[195]

In other words, Marx had retained in its entirety his six-rubric plan of 1859.[196]

By May 1863 he again thought that his new studies were nearing completion. He had filled twenty-three notebooks (1472 pages) with preliminary drafts of the three books.[197] He

[193]*MEW* 30, pp. 267, 281.

[194]Ibid., p. 622.

[195]Ibid., p. 639.

[196]Marx could not at that moment have been thinking of publishing only section I, on the process of production, as Marxist orthodoxy would have it. In fact he was not yet thinking of three books, but rather of a second part in three sections, and was convinced that he could provide at the very least the whole of the "Principles" bearing on the two "processes" – of production and of circulation – and on the "unity of the two." And it was only with extreme reluctance that he later yielded to Engels's prodding and delivered Book I by itself to his publisher.

[197]They included as well excerpts from authors prior to Marx who had discovered surplus value. Engels wanted to publish this part as "book IV" of *Capital*, but it finally had to be left to Bernstein and Kautsky. See Engels's description of these manuscripts in his preface to *Capital*, Book II; *MEW* 24, pp. 8–11.

began the rewriting of what was to be merely a preliminary version.[198] As his financial problems began to diminish, Marx devoted considerable effort to the International Working Men's Association, founded in 1864. He lectured to a working-class audience on *Value, Price and Profit*.[199] Engels believed that, once again, Marx was diverted from his central task. But Marx was working:

Three chapters still have to be written to finish the theoretical part (the first three books). This will leave the fourth book, the historico-literary part, which will be, relatively speaking, the easiest for me since all the questions are settled in the first three books and the last is therefore more of a repetition in historical form. However, I cannot make up my mind to send off what has been finished before I have the whole thing in front of me. Whatever shortcomings they may have, the merit of my writings is that they constitute an artistic whole, and this can be attained only with my method of never letting them be printed until I have them *in their entirety* in front of me. This is impossible using Jakob Grimm's method [publication in installments] which is altogether more practicable for writings that do not form a dialectically organized whole.[200]

Henceforth Marx was aware that he would be able to provide only the "principles" as described to Kugelmann, that he had enough material to fill "three books" and, should there be time, a "fourth," and that the work would accord with his real intentions only if it were to be published as an integral whole.

In March 1865 he signed the contract with the publisher Otto Meissner of Hamburg, agreeing to deliver by the end of May the complete manuscript of *Capital* in two volumes, a total of sixty printer's sheets (about nine hundred pages). At that time he apparently did not imagine the possibility of publishing only one book because the rough draft of Book III dates for the most part from 1865. In the two volumes prom-

[198]Marx to Engels, May 29, June 22, and Apr. 15, 1863; cf. *MEW* 30, pp. 350, 359, 368. A number of manuscripts are lost or inaccessible. (In particular, we have no information on the precise state of the archives in the possession of the Moscow Institute for Marxism-Leninism; the holdings in the archives of the International Institute of Social History in Amsterdam appear to be incomplete for this period). Our only information is derived from Engels's Prefaces to Books II and III of *Capital*.

[199]The lectures remained unpublished until 1898, when they appeared under that title in an edition prepared by Marx's daughter Eleanor (London: Swann Sonnenschein and Co.).

[200]Marx to Engels, July 31, 1865; *MEW* 31, p. 132.

ised to Meissner he intended to unite the three books of *Capital*. He also envisaged finishing the fourth book, on the "History of the Theory," in the near future.

As he began the definitive manuscript of *Capital*, Marx was forced to lengthen rather than "condense" the text. In January 1866 he became seriously ill and, temporarily incapable of theoretical reflection, could only "expand" on what he had already written. Uneasy about his friend's state of health, Engels advised him to take a rest and to come spend a fortnight in Manchester. He suggested that Marx bring enough "notebooks" to work there, and then dispassionately proposed: "In any event the sixty printer's sheets will certainly make two big volumes. Couldn't you manage it so that at least the initial volume be sent to the printer first, and the second some months later? This way both the publisher and the public will be satisfied, and in fact no time will be lost" (February 10, 1866).[201] Marx's reply:

Yesterday I was again out of action. . . If I had enough money, that is to say >-o for my family, and if my book were finished, it would be all the same to me if today or tomorrow I were tossed onto the garbage-heap, *alias* if I were to kick the bucket. Under the given circumstances, however, this is not yet possible. As for the "cursed" book, here is where I am: it was ready at the end of December. In the present version, the next-to-last chapter dealing with ground rent alone constitutes almost a book.[202] I went to the Museum during the day and wrote at night. I had to sweat through the new literature on agricultural chemistry in Germany, especially Liebig and Schönbein, who are more important in this matter than all the economists put together, and also the tremendous material which the French have produced since I began studying this problem. I finished my theoretical research on ground rent two years ago; and in the meantime much has been done which, by the way, precisely confirms my theory . . . *Although finished, the manuscript, gigantic in its present form, cannot be edited by anyone other than me, not even by you.*[203] On January 1st I began the work of recopying it and improving the style and the work advanced very rapidly since I naturally took pleasure in licking the baby clean after such violent labor pains. But the carbuncle again interfered so that I have not yet gotten back to work;

[201]*MEW* 31, p. 176.
[202]We should keep in mind that ground rent forms a section of Book III.
[203]Emphasis added.

all that I have done is to add to the part already finished in accordance with the plan. In any event, I agree with your view and shall take the first volume to Meissner as soon as it is finished.[204]

The publisher's deadline passed and Marx was still working on the early chapters of Book I. Remarkably enough, although he was actually elaborating the final version of the text of the first volume, he did not succeed in finishing even the first book of *Capital* in accordance with the definitive plan established in 1863. The plan for that first section (at the time Marx was unaware that it would become a book) that dealt with the "process of production of capital," envisaged eleven subdivisions![205] The situation was fatal for Marx, who in the end was never able to exhaust even the subject matter of the first book: While expanding the first section to make a book and working at the same time on the other sections, which he would likewise have to transform into books, he found himself constantly under pressure and forced to deliver the manuscript prematurely or risk breaking his contract with Meissner. Consequently, Marx was unable to treat the following topics in that book, although they had been provided for according to the 1863 plan and although he had accumulated material for them in several notebooks dating from the period 1863–5:

1. Productive and unproductive labor
2. Results of the process of production
3. Theories of surplus value
4. Theories of productive and unproductive labor[206]

If we take account of Marx's physical weakness and material hardships in 1866, not to mention his militant activity in

[204]Feb. 13, 1866; *MEW* 31, p. 178. Marx was then working on the chapter on machinery in Book I.

[205]The plan is given in *MEW* 26/1, p. 389.

[206]Theme 1 figures in the fifth division of the first section. Moreover, we can consider the whole of this division to have been only partially dealt with in Book I. See *MEW* 26/1, pp. 365 ff. A selection of texts on productive labor, etc. is in *Oeuvres* vol. 2, pp. 383 ff. The "Result of the process of production," probably edited around 1864, was doubtless to have been the real theoretical conclusion of Book I; cf. *MEW* 26/1, p. 389. In the manuscript published in 1933 (*Arkhiv Marksa i Engelsa* II (VII), 4–266) Marx wrote "Results of the immediate process of production." This text has been reprinted in Frankfurt in 1969: *Archiv sozialistischer Literatur* 17, Verlag Neue Kritik. The theories of surplus value and productive labor constitute respectively the eighth and ninth divisions of the plan of 1863. Marx followed this plan when he composed the greater part of the twenty-three notebooks of 1861–3 and the 1864–5 draft of *Capital*, only fragments of which appear to have been preserved.

the International, it is evident why he was never able to finish what he really wanted to write. In July he hoped that the "first volume," which he had agreed to have published separately, would soon be ready.[207]

In October 1866, one year before that volume appeared, Marx was still uncertain about its contents, or in other words, he still thought that he could include in it both Book I and Book II of *Capital*. Once he had resigned himself to finishing just the first rubric containing the "principles," he obviously ceased mentioning the "Economics" with its six rubrics. Experience had taught him not to have any illusions about an improvement in his material conditions, and because he was in fact responsible for the affairs of the International, to which he attributed a great future, he knew that *Capital* would probably be *the* book of his life, if indeed he actually succeeded in finishing it.

Kugelmann was the first to learn of his decision to begin with a first volume containing Books I and II:

My circumstances (permanent physical and bourgeois disturbances) make it necessary for the *first volume* to appear right away, rather than the two volumes at once, as I had intended. Moreover, there will probably be three volumes. The work as a whole can be divided into the following parts, namely:
Book I. The Process of the production of capital;
Book II. The Process of the circulation of capital;
Book III. Modes [*Gestaltungen*] of the process as a whole;
Book IV. On the history of the theory.
The first volume contains the first two books. Book III, I think, will take up the second volume and book IV the third.[208]

Marx then adds a detail that implicitly confirms the validity of the 1859 plan for the *Contribution to the Critique of Political Economy:* "I thought it necessary to begin *ab novo* in the first book, that is, to summarize my text published by Duncker in one chapter on commodity and money. I felt this had to be done not only for the sake of completeness, but because even intelligent readers have not quite grasped the matter correctly; thus something must have been missing in that first presentation, especially in the *analysis of the commodity.*"[209]

[207]Letter to Engels, July 7, 1866; *MEW* 31, p. 232.
[208]Marx to Kugelmann, Oct. 13, 1866; *MEW* 31, p. 534.
[209]*MEW* 31, p. 534.

In mid-November 1866 Marx sent the first pages of his book to the publisher. He expected to receive the proofs without much delay, but Meissner informed him that no printing would be done until he had in his possession both volumes at the same time, completely finished.[210] However, Marx already knew that he would be able to provide only one volume, containing Book I alone. He decided, therefore, to take the last part of the manuscript to Germany himself in order to pressure the publisher to have it printed without waiting for the manuscript of the second volume.[211] He submitted indeed only the copy of Book I. Despite this, Meissner remained agreeable to the idea of publishing three volumes provided that the last one would be complete enough to interest a large public.[212] He insisted that the manuscript for volume II be delivered in the autumn of 1867 and volume III in the winter of 1867.[213] During the years that were left to him until his death, Marx continually worked on the two books, which he thought could both be included in volume II. Book II had to be entirely rewritten, but he never succeeded in giving it a definitive form. The financial failure of the first volume, illness, and his increasingly intense participation in the affairs of the Interna-

[210]Marx to Engels, Jan. 19, 1867; MEW 31, p. 273. The publisher refused to print piecemeal and offered to correct the galleys himself, leaving to Marx just the final revision.

[211]To Engels Apr. 2, 1867; MEW 31, p. 281. This brought an outburst of joy from Engels, who sent his friend the money necessary for the voyage.

[212]To Engels, Apr. 13, 1867, from Hamburg; MEW 31, p. 288. From Hanover, on Apr. 17, 1867, Marx wrote to J. P. Becker: "The first volume encompasses book I: 'the Process of Capitalist Production.' It is assuredly the most terrible missile ever launched at the heads of the bourgeois (the landowners included)!" MEW 31, p. 541. To Siegfried Mayer, Apr. 30, 1867, from Hanover: "Why haven't I answered you? Because I have been hovering constantly at the edge of my grave. I had therefore to take advantage of every moment when I was able to work to finish my book, to which I have sacrificed health, happiness and family. . . I laugh at the so-called practical men and their wisdom. If one wished to be a brute, one could naturally turn one's back on the sufferings of humanity and look after one's own skin. But I would really have considered myself an impractical man had I died without having finished my book, be it only in manuscript form. . . I hope that between now and next year the entire work will have appeared. Volume II will be the continuation and the conclusion of the theories, volume III the history of political economy since the mid-17th century." (MEW 31, pp. 542–3.)

[213]Marx to Engels, May 7, 1867; MEW 31, pp. 296–9. This "pressure" from the publisher seems to have pleased Marx, who thought that he would advance his work more quickly as the proofs came back to him. But he was already thinking of new studies, of new material on credit and landed property. He hoped that Capital, once finished, would bring him a substantial income. Engels, who dreamed of quitting "abject commerce," thought the same.

tional, with no means of assuring his family's subsistence except through Engel's generous contributions, all weighed heavily on his spirit.

The last studies

The first book of *Capital*, Marx remarked, is a "consummate whole" or, in other words, it was theoretically justifiable to publish it separately from Books II and III that were to follow. Yet, some years earlier he had refused to deliver one part of the work alone, as Engels had advised him to do, because he intended to give the whole an "artistic" composition. But in view of the sort of life he led, we can easily understand why he resigned himself to the inevitable. Nevertheless, he did what he could to include the last book, the conclusion, in the "first," both potentially and substantially. This solution imposed itself by virtue of the basic method, the originality of which can be considered to be the choice of an introductory subject – necessarily, the *process of production*. It is evident from a second reading of the 1857 *General Introduction* that the central idea that dominates the whole of Marx's "Economics," unfinished works as well as published texts, is to unveil the secret of human social life and its various manifestations as deriving from the system of men's labor, from their "relations of production." This is both the point of departure and the conclusion of Marx's work. Formulated in the preface to *A Critique of Political Economy*, it is at once the argument and the object of demonstration in Book I and in fact is what makes Book I a "consummate whole." The conclusion of this first volume is also the conclusion of the entire "Economics," and Marx did not try to conceal its "subjective tendency":[214] the triumph of labor over capital.

He never stopped improving this first book himself. The second German edition (1873) and the French translation (1875) occasioned these revisions; he even said that the French edition "possesses a scientific value independent of the original," and he therefore recommended it to the German reader.[215] He also thought he would himself prepare the third edition, reworking it in its entirety.

When Book I left the press, Book II was, of all the remaining

[214]Cf. Marx to Engels, Dec. 7, 1867; *MEW* 31, p. 404.
[215]See Marx's *"Avis au lecteur"* in the French translation; *Oeuvres*, vol. 1, p. 546.

manuscripts, the farthest from completion. Marx's correspondence with Engels reveals how much was still to be done. Undoubtedly, the quasifailure of Book I hardly encouraged Marx to work on it;[216] but theoretical difficulties, and above all the inadequacy of his documentary sources, also played a role. He noted that in economics interesting facts are very different from theoretical postulates: He therefore had to amass the necessary materials (letter to Engels, May 16, 1868).[217] He appealed to friends abroad to find him "anti-bourgeois" material on agricultural conditions in the United States[218] for his work on Books II and III (which, as we have noted, he always planned to publish in a single volume). He also made his own discoveries: One day in an antiquary shop[219] he found a statistical report on agriculture in Ireland, a crucial problem for the propaganda of the English working-class movement. This prompted him to write to Engels: "In order to transform political economy into a positive science, conflicting dogmas must be replaced by conflicting facts and the real antagonisms which constitute the unseen background of these dogmas."[220] This is a most accurate description of Marx's "materialist" method.

He exploited every opportunity for self-instruction and for observing the most typical events of the day. Accordingly, he interrogated Engels: "Since praxis is better than any theory, I am asking you to describe to me *most exactly* (using examples) the way in which you conduct your business *quant à banquier* etc. [as concerns the banker]. Since for the most part volume III is much too theoretical, I shall use the chapter on credit for *actual denunciation* of fraud and *commercial morals*" [*Eng.*

---

[216]Marx wanted someone to "beat the drum" in order to oblige the "enemies" to talk about *Capital*. Engels published several anonymous articles in different German periodicals, but in vain. Marx wrote to Kugelmann that completion of the second volume would depend on the success of the first (Oct. 11, 1867; *MEW* 31, p. 562) but that it might never appear if the author's material situation did not improve (Mar. 6, 1868; *MEW* 32, p. 38).

[217]*MEW* 32, p. 88.

[218]Letter to Siegfried Meyer, July 4, 1868: " . . . since in volume II, I am treating ground rent." (*MEW* 32, p. 551.) It was also a matter of demolishing Henry Carey's *Harmony of Interests*.

[219]We emphasize in passing, for the benefit of those clever people who smirk at Marx's tedious labors, that both his means of investigation and the possibilities of preparing the results obtained were far different from the conveniences presently afforded even the lowliest academic worker.

[220]Letter to Engels, Oct. 10, 1868; *MEW* 32, p. 181.

in text].[221] Engels was a marvelous interlocutor, and Marx, who admired his practical knowledge and a certain detachment from pure theory, was most willing to learn from his friend. Moreover, Engels was also an avid reader, and Marx profited from this habit as well.[222]

Although in fact Marx's plan and his working method had reserved the treatment of landed property for the second rubric – following *capital* and preceding *wage labor,* he apparently decided to devote a section of Book III to it and began a study of agriculture that was to fill his remaining years. Land reform was for him "the alpha and the omega of the future revolution."[223] He learned Russian in order to compare the agricultural situation in Russia with that in the United States[224] – and above all in order to read Flerovsky's work on *The Situation of the Laboring Class in Russia* (1869), which reminded him of Engels's book on England.[225] He was preparing himself to read Chernyshevsky, for he rather suspected that in Russia the intellectual movement was the product of a fermentation that emanated from the "lower strata" of the society.[226] Finally, he studied official publications on Prussian agriculture. The Paris Commune again turned his attention toward the problem of the state, the fourth of the plan's six rubrics, and obliged him to assume additional, substantial responsibilities.[227] He thought of "completely reworking the manuscript,"[228] but was hindered in doing so by his involve-

[221]Letter to Engels, Nov. 14, 1868; *MEW* 32, p. 204. It is the least coherent and most poorly written chapter of Book III; it was to be the despair of Engels.

[222]See Engels's critique of Marx's analysis of the value form: It is so abstract that its revolutionary consequences are not apparent, and the reader may fail to grasp them. Marx then composed an appendix. (Engels to Marx, June 24, 1867; Marx to Engels, June 27, 1867; *MEW* 31, pp. 308–9, 314–16.)
Their discussions have not yet been analyzed sufficiently. See for example, the letters exchanged between them on Carey and differential rent; Engels to Marx, Nov. 19, 1869; Marx to Engels, Nov. 26, 1869; Engels to Marx, Nov. 29, 1869; *MEW* 32, pp. 396–400, 401–4, 406.

[223]Cf. Marx to Engels, Aug. 14, 1851; *MEW* 28, p. 314.

[224]He obtained numerous documents from his Russian correspondent and translator, Nicolai Danielson. See his letters to Danielson, Dec. 12, 1872 and Jan. 17, 1873; to Petr Lavrov, Feb. 11, 1875; to F. A. Sorge, Apr. 4, 1876; *MEW* 33, pp. 549, 559; and *MEW* 34, pp. 122, 179.

[225]Letter to Kugelmann, Nov. 29, 1869; to Engels, Feb. 10, and Apr. 14, 1870; Engels to Marx, Apr. 19, 1870; *MEW* 32, pp. 637, 437, 475, 481.

[226]Letter to S. Meyer, Jan. 21, 1871; *MEW* 33, p. 173.

[227]See, from among the different texts of this period, the *Address on the Civil War in France, 1871.*

[228]Letter to Danielson, June 13, 1871; *MEW* 33, p. 231.

ment in the International, now seriously beset by internal problems.

From 1874 until his death Marx tried in vain to finish Books II and III. He wrote little, while studying and copying an astounding amount of material. *Capital* was actually written in the inverse order, with the historical part preceding Books III and II—which, he wrote, "remained in that rough state typical of all research at the outset" (letter to S. Schott, November 3, 1877)[229]—and finally Book I. His last letters to Danielson show that he was satisfied to have a "pretext for continuing my studies, instead of winding them up finally for the public"; and he found this pretext in the innumerable documents he had received, notably on Russia and on the American crisis of 1873–8. He also found it necessary to follow the industrial crisis in England, a premonitory symptom of an agricultural crisis, before "theoretically consuming" the facts he had registered. Moreover, how would he ever be able to publish his book in Germany with the Bismarck government hounding the Social Democrats? (letters to Danielson, November 15, 1878, April 10, 1879)[230] "The second part of Capital cannot appear in Germany under the present circumstances. This is good news for me inasfar as certain economic phenomena have at this very moment entered a new phase of development and consequently necessitate further analysis in my work" (letter to F. Domela-Nieuwenhuis, June 27, 1880).[231] A year and a half later, when asked by Meissner to prepare a third edition of the first volume, Marx, as noted, replied that he would have to rework the whole of it.[232]

Although his last years were spent chiefly in study and excerpting, Marx was still able to concentrate his energy on a final denunciation of that sort of "state idolatry" that characterized the "socialist panaceas" of Henry George, Adolph Wagner, J. G. Collins. His hopes for a social "regeneration" of Russia centered on the peasant commune.[233] These two themes, among others, would have been treated under the fourth rubric of the plan, the one that we perhaps most sorely miss today: the *state*.

[229]*MEW* 34, p. 307.
[230]Ibid., pp. 359, 370–2.
[231]Ibid., p. 447.
[232]Letter to Danielson, Dec. 13, 1881; *MEW* 35, p. 247.
[233]See Marx and Engels, *Die russische Kommune. Kritik eines Mythos*, ed. M. Rubel (Munich: 1972).

Engels as the editor of Capital

Marx did not leave a written testament. It appears that as the end neared he gave oral instructions to his youngest daughter, Eleanor, naming her and Engels his "literary executors."[234] We have already observed how Engels could exert considerable intellectual stimulus on his friend; what is more, Marx appreciated him as a literary critic as well. It was Engels who, when reading the proofs of Book I, had called for more historical examples to support the dialectical results and had severely criticized the makeup of the volume, its divisions and subdivisions, the disproportion of the chapters, and so on.[235] Marx had every reason, therefore, to rely on him.

Everything Engels said about Marx's unedited papers confirms that he was forced to change his estimate of their state of completion. Since the publication of Book I, Engels probably imagined that the following books would pose only problems of form. Therefore, when he examined Marx's provisional manuscripts, outlines, rough drafts, and the "two cubic meters" of American and Russian statistics,[236] his surprise and disappointment must have been extreme. "You ask how it happened that even I was kept in the dark about how far advanced the thing was? Very simple: had I known, I would not have given him a moment's peace until the work was completely finished and printed" (Engels to August Bebel, August 30, 1883).[237] Did Engels seriously think that Marx would have accepted such goading? Could he have been so ignorant of his friend's character? When writing these lines to Bebel, Engels did not yet have a complete picture of the condition in which Marx had left the material for Books II and III. As his letters and prefaces confirm, he finally ceded to the obvious impossibility of finishing an often neglected style and form altogether. From the beginning, his attitude was ambiguous. It became even more so in another respect. Having delayed publishing the results of his own efforts, Marx knew that Engels could assume this task continuing in the spirit of social criticism that was common to

[234]Engels to P. Lavrov, Apr. 2, 1883; to Ferdinand Domela-Nieuwenhuis, Apr. 11, 1883; to August Bebel, Aug. 30, 1883; MEW 36, pp. 3, 7, 56.

[235]Marx to Engels, June 27, 1867; MEW 31, pp. 312–13.

[236]Engels to F. Sorge, June 29, 1883; MEW 36, p. 46. "These detailed studies detained him for years."

[237]MEW 36, p. 56.

them.[238] Engels, however, did not venture to put himself in his friend's place and said that he was incapable of doing so. Instead, he decided on a procedure whereby Marx would remain "the sole author" of the posthumous works, and Engels would limit his own efforts to their presentation and only those stylistic improvements that he felt Marx himself would have made. Engels neither produced the material for a work yet to be constructed, nor did he construct this work from the materials; instead, he simply gave it a facade. This intermediary formula had certain exceptional merits and shows with what remarkable care, prudence, and concern the editor distinguished his own work from that of the author. But it also had drawbacks, because it let writings that were never more than drafts and, at times, unpromising attempts, pass for finished "books." Three volumes, four "books," an "artistic whole": this had been Marx's vow as he imagined the possibility of presenting at the very least the "principles" of his "Economics." However, despite his friend's moral and material support, that vow was never fulfilled. Engels was presumably conscious of this. Immediately after taking stock of the unedited material, he remarked that Book II was nothing more than a number of rough drafts, some of which had several versions. Recopying and rendering them legible became a severe test for his eyes.[239]

It took him only two years to publish Book II. "The second volume [probably book II] of *Capital* will cause me a good deal more work. The greater part of the manuscript dates from *before 1868* [this is the case for Book III, because the manuscript of Book II dates from the years 1875–8] and in part is pure *brouillon* [draft material]. The second book will greatly disappoint the vulgar socialists; it is almost exclusively concerned with very subtle and rigorously scientific research on things happening within the capitalist class itself; hence, nothing from which aphorisms and declamations could be fabricated . . ."[240] "The second book is purely scientific and deals only with questions of the relations between the bourgeois; but the third will contain passages that make me doubt the very possibility of publishing it in Germany under the anti-socialist

[238]It was through Eleanor that Engels received this final message from his friend; see Engels's letter to Bebel, Aug. 30, 1883; *MEW* 36, p. 56.

[239]Before his death he taught Bernstein and Kautsky the techniques of deciphering Marx's "hieroglyphics" in view of publishing the *Theories of Surplus Value*.

[240]To Kautsky, Sept. 18, 1883; *MEW* 36, p. 61.

laws."[241] There is a trace of disappointment in these lines; they might also be characterized as a kind of self-consolation. Engels was careful to tell his reader "that it is indeed a work of Marx"[242] that he was publishing, and that he was doing it because he was the sole living person able "to decipher that writing and those abbreviations of words and style."[243] While dictating the manuscript of Book II he noticed the "large gaps" in the second section; "naturally, this composing is only provisional"; but he knew where he was going, and "that suffices."[244] He protected his weakening vision by dictating only during the daytime.[245]

The third book, he thought, would be less disappointing; it would bring "concluding results," "revolutionize all economics and make an enormous noise."[246] It "will work like a lightning bolt, because it treats the entire capitalist production for the first time in its internal coherence and jettisons official bourgeois economics altogether." However, he admitted with some reluctance that in fact at the middle of Book III "the most important chapters are in rather great disorder – as far as form is concerned."[247] Was this rhetorical precaution or genuine conviction? In any case, the work of arranging the text was to take not "four months," as he had imagined, but nine years that were made all the more arid by the total silence with which both "German science" and the various socialist groups received Book II. Book III, he hoped, "will compel" the German economists to speak out (letter to Danielson, November 13, 1885).[248] At that time he had already realized that important parts of the "draft" of Book III were nothing but raw material, the product of "empirical investigation" and not "abstract exposition": These two procedures, we recall, although formally distinct, are complementary aspects of Marx's method.[249] So, for example, we would expect to find a treatment of the central theme of Book III – namely the problem of

[241]To Lavrov, Feb. 5, 1884; Ibid., p. 99.
[242]To Lavrov, Jan. 28, 1884; Ibid., p. 95.
[243]To Lavrov, Feb. 5, 1884; Ibid., p. 99.
[244]To Kautsky, June 26, 1884; Ibid., p. 168.
[245]To Kautsky, May 23, 1884; Ibid., p. 149.
[246]To J. P. Becker, Apr. 2, 1885; Ibid., p. 290. See also the preface to Book II; MEW 24, p. 26.
[247]To Sorge, June 3, 1885; MEW 36, p. 324.
[248]Ibid., pp. 384–5.
[249]Afterword to Capital; MEW 23, p. 27.

financial capital, of interest and credit – in section V. However Engels uncovered what was neither a rough draft nor even an outline, but simply an accumulation of notes and excerpts.[250] Nevertheless, he wanted to present this *material* as a "work of Marx." Answering the reproach of a serious critic, he gave a very significant explanation. At issue was the process of equalization of different rates of profit converging objectively (but unknown to the "historical participants") in the general and average rate of profit:

How was this process of equalization realized, however? It is a very interesting point, but Marx did not say much about it either.[251] Marx's whole manner of conceiving things is not a doctrine, but a method. It offers no finished dogmas, but rather points of reference for further research and the method for that research. Thus we have a bit of work to do which Marx himself did not elaborate in this first draft . . . Finally, I must thank you for your good opinion of me in thinking that I could have made of book III a better work than it is. I cannot share that opinion and believe I have done my duty by allowing Marx to express himself in his own words, at the risk of exacting from the reader a greater effort of personal reflection.[252]

There is nevertheless an element of contradiction in Engels's invocation of his duty to respect literally Marx's manuscripts. Logically this respect for the preparatory material should have led Engels to concern himself with Marx's pre-1861 manuscripts, such as the writings of 1844–5 or the *Grundrisse* of 1857–8. Their originality in both style and contents makes these works often superior to the unpublished material of the later period. Engels's attitude induces us to ask why he never tried to clarify in any way the plan of the "Economics," even though he had witnessed its gradual crystallization. A moot question – all we can ascertain is that he preferred reediting Marx's works rather than spending all of his time and efforts on the drafts and manuscripts of *Capital* alone. And although

---

[250]"Many new things, and even more things to finish." (Engels to C. Schmidt, July 1, 1891; *MEW* 38, p. 128.)

[251]Further on, Engels affirms that a "serious historical description of this process . . . would be a most valuable complement to *Capital*."

[252]The man whom Engels thanked with this remarkable letter was Werner Sombart, author of an article published in 1894 on Book III. Engels's letter, dated Mar. 11, 1895, is in *MEW* 39, pp. 427–9. See also Engels's *Complement and Supplement to book III of "Capital"*; *MEW* 25, pp. 903–5; he avoided answering the criticisms voiced against his work as editor.

he never mentioned the plan of the "Economics," he did indicate that he considered Marx's works to be intrinsically related, and that the earlier works already provided considerable material to be found in the later, unedited writings. He resolved, consequently, to provide the reading public with new or first editions of *Wage Labor and Capital, The Class Struggles in France, Revelations Concerning the Communist Trial in Cologne, The Civil War in France,* and *The Critique of the Gotha Program;* furthermore, he revised two German reeditions and an English translation of the first book of *Capital,* a task he judged to be no less important than the preparation of the other books.

All things considered, his work as Marx's first posthumous editor is indeed remarkable. The greatest homage that we can pay him is to continue along the path he had trod and, as far as possible, work as he did on the original texts and on the unformed material. But this also means that we acknowledge the fragmentary state of the "Economics"; that, even finished, it would not have represented a *system;* that we do not have before us a Marxist bible of eternally codified canons. We engage ourselves, therefore, to substitute an examination of Marx's writings for their recitation. The earlier conspiracy of silence against Marx has now given way to a conspiracy of quasireligious mutterings: We must interrupt these seances and desecrate the rosary — especially to honor Marx on the approaching centenary of his death. The works he produced, as great as they may be, only fulfill a fragment of the whole project. Myths must be destroyed before we can begin to create today, just as was the case in Marx's time. And the foremost myth is that of the *state,* one that he counted on personally demolishing one day, after providing its key back in the period of the Paris *Vorwärts!:* "the existence of the state and the existence of slavery are inseparable" (1844).[253] Through his writings Marx continues to call for revolution against all the established orders, including those established in his name:

In our days everything seems pregnant with its contrary. Machinery, gifted with the wonderful power of shortening and fructifying human labor, we behold starving and overworking it. The new-fangled sources of wealth, by some strange weird spell, are turned into sources of want. The victories of art seem bought by the loss of character. At

---

[253]"Kritische Randglossen. . ."; *MEW* 1, pp. 401–2.

the same pace that mankind masters nature man seems to become enslaved to other men or to his own infamy. Even the pure light of science seems unable to shine but on the dark background of ignorance. All our inventions and progress seem to result in endowing material forces with intellectual life, and in stultifying human life into a material force. This antagonism between modern industry and science on the one hand, modern misery and dissolution on the other hand; this antagonism between the productive powers, and the social relations of our epoch is a fact, palpable, overwhelming, and not to be controverted. Some parties may wail over it; others may wish to get rid of modern arts, in order to get rid of modern conflicts. Or they may imagine that so signal a progress in industry wants to be completed by as signal a regress in politics. On our part, we do not mistake the shape of the shrewd spirit that continues to mark all these contradictions. We know that to work well the new-fangled forces of society, they only want to be mastered by new-fangled men – and such are the working men. They are as much the invention of modern time as machinery itself. In the signs that bewilder the middle class, the aristocracy and the poor prophets of regression, we do recognize our brave friend, Robin Goodfellow, the old mole that can work in the earth so fast, that worthy pioneer – the Revolution.[254]

Appendix: A précis of Marx's discoveries in economics

Marx had no part in the creation of Marxism; on the contrary, he formally repudiated it at the first signs of its appearance. Engels, for his part, thought it advisable to lend his authority to this term which was used by their adversaries as an expression of contempt, and was provoked to change it into a title of glory. He preferred, nonetheless, to speak of "scientific socialism," attributing its foundations to Marx as author of "two great discoveries, the materialist conception of history and the revelation of the secret of capitalist production through surplus value" (Anti-Dühring).

[254]Speech given in London, Apr. 14, 1856, at a meeting commemorating the fourth anniversary of the Chartist *People's Paper*. The speech concludes with an appeal to the English workers, "the first born sons of modern industry," who are called to aid "the social revolution produced by that industry, a revolution which means the emancipation of . . .wages-slavery." Marx concludes: "There existed in the middle ages in Germany, a secret tribunal called the '*Vehmgericht*.' If a red cross was seen marked on a house, people knew that its owner was doomed by the '*Vehm*.' All the houses of Europe are now marked with the mysterious red cross. History is the judge–its executioner, the proletarian."

As to the first "discovery": What Marx modestly referred to as the "guideline" of his studies he termed simply the "materialist method." Engels's second formula seems no more than the first to express satisfactorily his friend's actual conviction. Marx was occasionally obliged to indicate his relationship to "scientific economics." More often than not, he did so in unedited writings or in letters to close friends. What follows is a set of eighteen passages, offered as an aid to the reader's memory, consisting of Marx's principal statements regarding his innovations in the field of political economy.

Engels should have mentioned another "discovery" that Marx did actually claim as his own, namely, the postulate of a "phase of transition" between capitalism and socialism, which he called the "dictatorship of the proletariat":

As far as I am concerned, I deserve no credit for having discovered either the existence of classes in modern society or the struggle among them. Long before me, bourgeois historians pointed out the historical development of this class struggle and bourgeois economists exposed its economic anatomy. What I did for the first time was show (1) that the *existence of classes* is simply linked to *particular historic phases of the development of production;* (2) that the class struggle necessarily leads to the *dictatorship of the proletariat;* (3) that this dictatorship itself is merely the transition to the *abolition of all classes* and to a *classless society.* (Marx to Weydemeyer; March 5, 1852; MEW 28, pp. 507–8)

I

Even when a society has hit upon *the natural law that governs its movement* – and the final aim of this work is to expose the economic law of movement of modern society – it can neither skip over any phases of its natural development nor abolish them by decrees. But it can shorten and ease the birth-pangs (Preface to the first German edition, *Capital,* vol. I; MEW 23, pp. 15–16).

2

The *value form,* which finds its perfect expression in the *money form,* is a very simple thing that lacks inherent meaning. Yet the human mind has sought in vain for more than 2000 years to penetrate its secret, while forms that are much

more significant and more complex have been successfully
analyzed, at least approximately. Why? Because the fully developed body is easier to study than the *cell* of that body...
However, for bourgeois society the *commodity form* of the
product of labor or the *value form* of the commodity is the
economic cell-form (*Capital*, vol. I; *MEW* 23, pp. 11–12).

3

It is strange that [Eugen Dühring] has not detected the three
fundamentally new elements in my book [*Capital*]:
   1. That in opposition to *all* earlier economics which assume
as the basis of their analysis the particular elements of surplus-
value, in their fixed forms of rent, profit and interest, I start by
analyzing the general form of surplus-value in which all these
elements are found still in their undifferentiated state, as it
were.
   2. That the following simple fact has escaped the attention
of all the economists without exception: if the commodity is
simultaneously use-value and exchange-value, then the labor
represented in that commodity must itself also have this
double character; on the other hand, the analysis based on
labor alone, such as found in Smith, Ricardo, etc., must necessarily encounter inexplicable phenomena at every turn. This, in
fact, is the whole secret of the critical conception.
   3. That wages are shown for the first time to be the irrational
outward form of a hidden relation, and this is demonstrated
specifically in respect to the two forms of wages: hourly wages
and piecework wages. (My analysis was facilitated by the fact
that such formulas occur frequently in higher mathematics.)
(Marx to Engels, January 8, 1868; *MEW* 32, pp. 11–12)

4

The progressive tendency of the general rate of profit to fall is
therefore simply *one way, proper to the capitalist mode of production,* of expressing the progressive development of the social
productivity of labor... As simple as this law appears... political economy has had up till now little success in discovering
it. The economists perceived the phenomenon and exhausted
their brains in contradictory attempts to interpret it. Since this
law is of great importance for capitalist production, we may say

that it represents the mystery whose solution has preoccupied all of political economy since Adam Smith, and that the successive schools are distinguished by their different approaches to its solution (*Capital,* vol. III; *MEW* 25, p. 223; see also *Grundrisse,* pp. 271–2).

5

What is better about my book is (1) that the double character of *labor* was brought out in the *first* chapter, showing how it manifests itself either as use-value or exchange-value (the *whole* understanding of the facts depends on this thesis); (2) that *surplus-value is analyzed independently of its particular* forms, profit, interest, ground rent, etc. This will be demonstrated especially in the second volume (Marx to Engels, August 24, 1867; *MEW* 31, p. 326).

6

However, I demonstrate that precisely *because* the value of the commodity is determined by the *labor time,* the average price of the commodities *can never* be equal to its value (except for the *one* case when the individual profit rate, so to speak, within a particular sector of production, i.e. the profit determined by the surplus-value produced within that sector, is equal to the average profit rate of the total capital (*Theories of Surplus Value; MEW* 26/2, p. 28; on the difference between the value of commodities and the cost of production, see *Oeuvres,* vol. 2, pp. 1369 ff.).

7

If we take Rodbertus's explanation of ground rent and divest it of its nonsense . . . the following core proposition remains: . . . Agriculture belongs to the category of industrial production sectors in which the proportion of variable capital compared to constant capital is higher than the average for the industrial sectors in general. Consequently, agricultural surplus-value calculated in relation to costs of production must be superior to the average for the industrial sectors. This in turn means that its *specific* rate of profit is higher than the *average profit rate* or the *general profit rate.* In other words, within any sector of production, the particular rate of profit varies according to the relation between variable capital and constant capital within the particular sectors, provided the rate of surplus-value remains constant and the surplus-value itself is given. This would then be the *general* law which I have developed, applied only to a particular industrial sector (*Theories of Surplus Value; MEW* 26/2, pp. 85–6).

8

May I remind . . . the reader that I was the first to employ the categories *variable capital* and *constant capital*. Political economy, since Adam Smith, has confused the connotations expressed by these categories with the formal distinction between *fixed* capital and *circulating* capital, derived from the *process of circulation* (*Capital*, vol. I; *MEW* 23, p. 638).

9

The unfortunate [Faucher] does not see that, even if my book had no chapter on "value," the analysis of real conditions which I furnish would contain both the proof and the demonstration of the real relation of value. . . The vulgar economist hasn't the slightest inkling that real, day-to-day relations of exchange *cannot directly coincide* with the magnitudes of value. The whole point of bourgeois society is just that *a priori* it does not admit any conscious social organization of production. What is rational and necessary from the standpoint of nature operates blindly and prevails only in the long run (Marx to Kugelmann, July 11, 1868; *MEW* 32, pp. 552–3).

10

The actual difference in magnitude that exists between profit and surplus-value – and not merely between their rates – in the various sectors of production completely conceals the real nature and the origin of profit, not only from the capitalist, who has every interest in deceiving himself on this score, but also from the worker. The transformation of values into prices of production helps to obscure the basis for determining value itself. . . This intrinsic connection is revealed here for the first time . . . Political economy has, up to the present, deliberately ignored the differences between surplus-value and profit, as well as between their rates, so as to retain value determination as a basis; or else it has abandoned value determination and with it all vestige of scientific method in order to cling to purely apparent differences (*Capital*, vol. III; *MEW* 25, pp. 177–8).

11

The individual capitalist (or even all the capitalists in each particular sector of production), whose horizon is limited, rightly thinks that his profit does not stem solely from the labor exploited by him or in his branch of industry. This is quite true as far as his average profit is concerned. The extent to which that profit derives from the global exploitation of labor by the total social capital, i.e. by all his capitalist colleagues – this interrelation is a complete mystery to him; all the more so since thus far no political economists, those bourgeois theorists, have taken the trouble to reveal it (*Capital*, vol. III; *MEW* 25, pp. 179–80).

12

I want to tell you briefly about a "detail" that *occurred* to me spontaneously as I was just glancing over the part of my manuscript on the profit rate. It gives a simple solution to one of the most difficult questions – i.e. to explain why the *rate of profit* increases when the value of money – or of gold – declines, and declines when the latter increases. . . The whole difficulty lies in the confusion between the *rate of surplus-value* and the *rate of profit* (Marx to Engels, April 22, 1868; *MEW* 32, p. 65).

13

Economists have not distinguished the different relations of the turnover of capital to its cycles any more than they have distinguished between these cycles. They generally consider the formula M...M', because it dominates the individual capitalist and serves for a basis of his calculations, even if money is the starting point of this cycle only in the form of calculating money. Others start out from the outlay of capital in the form of elements of production and follow the cycle to its point of return, without alluding to the form of the returns, be they commodities or money! (*Capital,* vol. II; *MEW* 24, pp. 155–6).

14

All that I have to demonstrate *theoretically* is the *possibility* of absolute rent without a violation of the law of value. The *theoretical* quarrel from the physiocrats up to today has hinged on this quarrel. Ricardo denied that possibility; I affirm it. At the same time I affirm that its denial is based on a theoretically false dogma adopted from Adam Smith: the supposed identity between cost prices and values of commodities (Marx to Engels, August 9, 1862; *MEW* 30, p. 274).

15

Messieurs the economists have hitherto overlooked this extremely simple thing, namely that the form *20 yards of linen = 1 coat* is only the undeveloped basis of the formula *20 yards of linen = 2£,* in other words, that the *simplest commodity form* – in which its value is not yet expressed as a relation to all other commodities, but simply as *something distinct* from its own natural form – contains the *whole secret of the money form,* and therefore, *in nuce,* the secret of *all bourgeois forms of the product of labor* (Marx to Engels, June 22, 1867; *MEW* 31, p. 306).

16

In *Misère de la Philosophie*. . . I showed . . . for the first time that division of labor as practised in manufacturing is a *specific form of the capitalist mode of production* (*Capital,* vol. I; *MEW* 23, pp. 383–4, n. 70).

17

At the Museum – by and by – I studied, among other things, old Maurer's most recent writings . . . on the constitution of the Germanic *Mark,* village, etc. He gives detailed proof that private property arose at a late date, etc. . . . This confirms (although Maurer has no idea of doing so) my proposition which says that the Asiatic or, respectively, the Indian forms of property constitute the origin of all property forms in Europe (Marx to Engels, March 14, 1868; *MEW* 32, p. 42).

18

The only other case where, with the number of workers remaining constant, more capital is applied per worker, and so surplus capital used or dispensed for the increased exploitation of the same number of workers, occurs when there is *increase in the productivity of labor, change in the manner of production.* This implies change in the organic relationship between constant and variable capital. In other words, the increase of capital relative to labor is here identical with the increase of constant capital as compared with variable capital and, in general, with the amount of living labor employed.

This is where Hodgskin's view, therefore, reduces to the general law which I have developed.

The surplus value, i.e. the exploitation of the worker, increases, but at the same time the rate of profit falls because the variable capital declines as against the constant capital, because in general the amount of living labor falls relatively in comparison with the amount of capital which sets it in motion. A larger part of the annual product of labor is appropriated by the capitalist under the heading of profit! (*Theories of Surplus Value; MEW* 26/3, pp. 304–5).

4

The plan and method of the "Economics"

Relation of plan and method

London, January 1859: Marx completes the preface to his forthcoming *Critique of Political Economy,* a comprehensive critical undertaking planned as a series of consecutive, separate brochures. According to a plan Marx had developed in 1844, political economy was the first of the topics to be investigated, and critical treatment of that theme was to be followed by the "critique of law, morality, politics, etc." The project was to be wound up with a "special work" that would demonstrate the unity of the whole, show the relation between the various parts and finally end with a "critique of the speculative manner in which these subjects have been dealt with until now." In other words, Marx had at that early date envisaged the critique of political economy as being but one brochure among several, all designed as prolegomena to a fundamental work whose thematic construction was to be the systematic critique of bourgeois social institutions and ideologies.

In the 1859 preface Marx explained to his readers how he came to conceive of his project for a critique of bourgeois economy and gave a brief resume of his intellectual career. After a long period of study and reflection and numerous personal difficulties, he now felt himself capable of executing definitively the enterprise that dated back fifteen years, that is, to the time when he decided to abandon the project of a "critique of jurisprudence and political science in the form of a critique of the Hegelian *Philosophy of Right.*" The precise plan for the treatise on economics was developed in this preface and consisted of two sets or triads of rubrics, the first devoted to the economic conditions of life of the three modern social classes – peasantry, capitalists, and industrial workers. As for the second triad, Marx simply enumerated the topics, adding enigmatically that the "relation between the other three headings is self-evident." He apparently considered his readers all – without exception – capable of grasping the logical relation between these three concepts, the state, foreign trade, world market, and dispensed with further explanation. However, we may well ask ourselves how Marx arrived at this certitude about his readers' unconditional acceptance of a particular schema of concepts that represented neither a simple "catalogue of themes" nor a "provisional" classification.[1]

Although the connection between the first three themes may at once appear evident, the same can by no means be said of the second triad. And if Marx was absolutely certain of the self-evidence of their relation, his conviction must have derived from the choice of a method of exposition that precluded his adopting at random any order of succession for his topics or inverting the stated order. Nevertheless, Marx was oddly discreet about his choice of method. He referred vaguely to a "general introduction" that apparently anticipated "results which still have to be substantiated" and recommended to the reader "who really wishes to follow me . . . to advance from the particular to the general."[2]

Despite his seemingly enigmatic discretion Marx made no attempt to conceal from his readers that the plan in two triads derived from a specific *methodological rule* and that he would therefore be obliged to proceed according to an established conceptual order. The exposition of the concepts would allow the reader to form his own judgment of the validity of Marx's method by following the process of elaboration step by step and discovering the methodological rule through the text itself. As if he were deliberately taking the reader into his confidence, Marx gave a most succinct account of the vicissitudes of his professional and literary career. He underlined in particular the importance of the "guideline" in his studies that was the result of research into the "anatomy of civil society." This description of Marx's "materialist conception of history," concise though it may be – and Engels was later prompted to call it a "scientific discovery" no less important than Darwin's the-

---

[1]Cf. Rudolf Hickel, afterword to Book III of *Kapital* (Frankfurt a.M/Berlin/Vienna: Ullstein: 1971), pp. 880 ff. The author, to all appearances "Marxist," can be reproached for wearing the same blinders for which he criticizes his "bourgeois" rivals. What Marx first presented as a conceptual construction, maturely deliberated and logically convincing, Hickel terms a "catalogue of themes" and a "first provisional plan." In so doing, he breaks the faith that Marx, in ignorance of the possibility of such "Marxist" followers, invested in his readers.

[2]*A Contribution to the Critique of Political Economy* (Moscow: 1970), p. 19.

ory of evolution in the field of biology – nevertheless demonstrates why the plan of the "Economics" is inseparable from the method developed fifteen years earlier and the research executed during the intervening years. To avoid any confusion about the extent of his engagement in this methodological procedure, Marx declared, probably exaggerating the actual state of advancement of his work, that all the necessary material for his project had already been compiled in the form of monographs, composed irregularly over a long period of time for his personal ends rather than for publication: " . . . their reshaping into a coherent whole *in accordance with the plan* indicated above will depend on circumstances" (italics added).[3]

These declarations in clear and frank language should leave no doubts whatsoever as to the definitive and compelling validity of the 1859 plan. Marx intentionally placed this plan at the beginning of the brochure designated as the first installment of his work, thereby giving the whole of the work a logical structure and at the same time committing himself to follow the given methodological path. It is, consequently, difficult to imagine that he would decide to separate the plan and the "guideline" – in other words to change this plan, without informing his readers and providing an explanation of the methodological grounds that necessitated such a change. The plan and the method, both selected and announced at the same time, were related to one another in a way that would have required a new method of exposition had the schema of two triads been abandoned. It seems doubtful that Marx would have effected such a blow to his project without some clear explanation of his motives.

More than eight years passed before the sequel to the 1859 *Critique* appeared in the form of Book I of *Capital*. The material destined for a third chapter (on "capital in general"), which taken together with the two preceding chapters (on "the commodity" and on "money") was to complete the first book, developed into an enormous mass of manuscripts, all devoted to the same theme. In the end the author was obliged to leave them, in an unfinished state, to his friend Engels whose task it became to compose three of the four final books. The second brochure thus furnished the material for three or four books!

The reader can hardly escape astonishment at these remarks and might therefore be led to adopt a quick and easy answer:

[3]*MEW* 13, p. 7.

When setting about constructing his "Economics," Marx decided to change the plan originally conceived of in six rubrics, with "capital" as the first; the new plan would incorporate all six rubrics into one, entitled "Capital"; hence it is quite natural and logical that this new brochure assumed such vast dimensions because it now had to include all of the material of the six books announced in the 1859 preface. Moreover, Marx was in no way obliged to comment explicitly on this change of plan: A simple change of title would suffice to indicate that the 1859 plan had been given up! And indeed the fact that Marx entitled his "Economics" *Capital* with the earlier title "critique of political economy" as the subtitle seems to indicate clearly the rejection of the first plan. Henceforth *Capital* alone would incorporate the five rubrics or books dealing with landed property, wage labor, the state, foreign trade, and the world market.

However, any reader acquainted with the three books in which *Capital* is considered in its various "processes" will not hesitate to object: The titles of the sections (*Abschnitte*) of *Capital* bear no resemblance whatever to the rubrics of the 1859 plan! The more attentive reader will even remark that Marx was explicit in this regard, formally declaring that *Capital* was to treat neither "wage labor" nor "landed property." In *Capital* he deliberately called attention to these rubrics, the first time at the beginning of a discussion of wages in their diverse forms, where he states: "An exposition of all these forms, however, belongs to the special study of wage-labor, and not therefore to this book."[4] Similarly, at the beginning of part six of Book III he makes the general remark regarding the rubric on "landed property": "The analysis of landed property in its various historical forms is beyond the scope of this work."[5]

These statements should in fact suffice to end all debate about a "change of plan" for they attest to the author's will and resolution to respect the initial plan at least concerning the first triad of rubrics. When treating the subjects of wages and ground rent, Marx was obliged to make such specifications in order to prevent his readers' confounding these economic categories with the concepts of "wage labor" and "landed property" as derived from the sociology of classes. *Capital* was conceived of as the book in economics by a sociologist that would analyze the role of the capitalist class in the process of

[4] *MEW* 23, p. 565.
[5] *MEW* 25, p. 627.

material production. The subsequent two books were to study from the same point of view the respective roles of landowners and wage laborers. Although Marx was less formal in his statements about the second triad of rubrics, they nonetheless continued to be part of his theoretical concerns.

When, eight years after the publication of the 1859 *Critique,* Marx composed the preface to *Capital,* he specified that the present volume represented the continuation of the earlier work. There is little likelihood that he would have deliberately neglected mentioning any renunciation of the six-rubric plan. Yet why did he not incorporate the 1859 preface into the later one? Why did he limit himself to recapitulating briefly the 1859 publication in the first section of *Capital* without any indications about his choice of intellectual orientation and his resulting discovery of the "materialist basis" of his research method (as he would later, in his afterword to the 1873 second German edition of *Capital*)? Despite the many unanswerable questions pertaining to Marx's project, we can acknowledge one evident fact: In 1867 he recognized that it would be impossible for him to realize the plan of the "Economics" as announced in 1859. He therefore chose to keep silent about this irredeemable promise, and he refrained from commenting on his own intellectual biography, giving no more than a brief account of his conflict with Hegel's political philosophy and its outcome.

For the rest, there is no need to introduce the idea of a change in plan to explain the dimensions attained by the manuscripts for the "Economics"; the cause is to be found in Marx's working habits, for he was indeed afflicted with a kind of literary gluttony. "I am a machine condemned to devour books and then throw them, in a changed form, on the dung-hill of history."[6] What he first calculated in chapters was redefined in sections and finally elaborated in books. The way he used his time, once the first brochure of the *Critique* had been published, amply demonstrates his insatiable desire to include every important economist in his study. His primary concern, however, when he returned in 1857 to his study notebooks and to the various drafts accumulated since 1844, was to reexamine the subject matter itself. His hopes mounted as the international economic crisis of 1856–7 seemed to threaten

[6] Letter to Laura Lafargue, Apr. 11, 1868; in *Annali,* Instituto Giangiacomo Feltrinelli, Milan, I (1958), 167.

the very foundations of bourgeois society and its capital in the industrially developed countries. Moreover, the "historic party" was awaiting his long-promised work.

The quintessence of the "Economics"

The "general introduction" to which Marx referred somewhat vaguely in his 1859 preface, and that he had composed in August–September 1857, was published for the first time by Karl Kautsky in 1903. This posthumous document confronted the followers of "scientific socialism" with a serious theoretical problem: On the one hand, it gave evidence of Marx's methodological choice just prior to his undertaking the critique of the capitalist system; on the other, it shed light for the first time on the intimate relationship between the method he had chosen and the plan of the work in six rubrics or "books," a relationship that Marx left unclarified in the 1859 preface. Given publication of the Introduction, Marx's later silence on the subject of the plan for the "Economics" as presented in the 1859 preface—a silence that Engels never attempted to explain—could be interpreted either as a tacit admission of an involuntary abandonment of the plan or as an indirect proof of a new choice of method.

In fact, however, Kautsky's publication of the Introduction incited no noticeable reaction whatever on the part of the various tendencies in the Marxist school. It stirred up no doubts or debates regarding this "Marxism," which seemed to have already been codified *in aeternam* and therefore to be beyond touch. In lieu of discussion there were vague allusions to a change in Marx's plan, which seemed natural since Engels had left no trace of any other explanation. Had the question been raised, whether in Marxist circles or elsewhere, prior to his death, Engels would not have hesitated to give his opinion as an authority on Marx's works. However his silence, coming in the wake of Marx's own discretion, served as a kind of guarantee and rendered superfluous any critical evaluation of Marx's writings. When editing *Capital,* Engels devoted not a single word to explaining either Marx's lack of references to the 1859 plan in the prefaces and afterwords of Book I or the absence from the mass of Marx's unedited papers of materials for the five rubrics that were to follow "Capital." All things considered, Engels was probably pleased to have fulfilled to some extent his dead friend's desire that he "do something" with the unedited manuscripts that were intended for the first rubric on capital.

Strangely enough, when Engels took charge of Marx's literary remains he made no effort to sort out the material earmarked for the five other enumerated rubrics, although Marx had maintained, when establishing the plan of the *Critique,* that everything was already at hand. It seems we must conclude either that this was a fiction of Marx's intellectual vanity or that these papers have disappeared, either accidentally or because at some point Marx judged them to be of no further use. Although it is not our intention here to examine the manner in which Engels fulfilled his tasks as heir to and editor of Marx's literary remains, we should note with regret that he remained unacquainted with the "general introduction" of 1857 and the enormous *Grundrisse* manuscript, for these texts might well have stimulated him to reconsider seriously the nature of Hegel's influence on Marx. In any case, Engels was the best placed of all Marx's friends to recognize the gravity of his "bourgeois misery" together with the profundity of his scientific interest. We may conjecture, therefore, that after taking stock of the impressive number of manuscripts dating from 1861–75, he simply set aside those written prior to the publication of the first "brochure" in 1859, thus assuming an attitude of disinterest toward what would seem to be the outdated and consequently useless material in the mass of papers that Marx had left him.

What Engels himself added to the Marxian legacy lies more in the domain of exegesis than of creativity. Albeit involuntarily, he was the chief codifier of the "Marxist" *Weltanschauung* and fixed the guidelines for the thinking of the future generations of adepts. He molded into the rigid form of a system what was actually an incomplete theory open to extensions and fertile deductions.

Marx believed he had provided the "quintessence" of his projected critique and left to his disciples the task of its elaboration. This quintessence consisted primarily, but not exclusively, in the three processes of *Capital* together with the material of the *Grundrisse*—which he had imagined he could condense into a single "brochure." He had calculated that the work as a whole would require thirty to forty printer's sheets (each totaling sixteen printed pages) or a maximum of about six hundred pages. At the moment, he based his figures on the volume of the "monographs" that he had already prepared and that contained the essence of Book I. He still hoped to be able to condense this material and in fact had no concrete notion of the size of the five other projected books. Conscious, moreover, of his habitual manner of working, he prudently wrote to Ferdinand Lassalle, who had found him an editor for his "Economics" in Germany, that six hundred pages was an approximate figure. He added: "Moreover, I do not intend to develop uniformly the six books that constitute the whole; in the last three, I will give only the rudiments [*Grundstriche*] whereas in the first three, which contain the fundamental economic analysis, it will not always be possible to avoid going into detail."[7]

The "quintessence" consists essentially of the first three rubrics—the triad of capital, landed property, and wage labor. Marx had accumulated much material for these three rubrics but was actually able to elaborate only the first of the three into what he termed a "monograph." It is also possible to justify inclusion of the 1844 Paris manuscripts in this concept because they contain chapters that relate to the second and third rubrics.[8]

[7]Marx to Lassalle, Mar. 11, 1858; *MEW* 29, p. 554. Here Marx exposed not only the plan of the "Economics" in six books but also that of the three parts of "capital," i.e. the "process of the production of capital, the process of the circulation of capital, the synthesis of the two, or capital and profit, interest." As noted in our preceding essay, Henryk Grossman neglected this information, which led to his inventing the legend of a "change in plan." Had he taken it into consideration, he would never have maintained that as late as 1863 Marx adopted a new method of elaboration based on the principle of knowledge [*Erkenntnis*] in place of the earlier method presumably inspired by the principle of the matter [*Stoff*]. In fact the "principle of knowledge" is the basis of the plan of the "Economics" and the principle according to which Marx composed the *Grundrisse*.

Although in 1929 Grossman presumably could not know of the existence of the *Grundrisse*, he must have been aware of Marx's letter to Lassalle that gave the definitive plan for the "Economics," and that had been published since 1922. The same criticism can be made of the work of Roman Rosdolsky, who in his desire to "save at least half of the Marxist system" readily imitated Grossman's error: Not only did he neglect this important letter in his discussion, but he even omitted it from a "register of annotated outlines for the plans . . . relative to the organization of the Marxian work." Rosdolsky, *Zur Entstehungsgeschichte des Marxschen "Kapital"* (Frankfurt, Vienna: 1968), p. 78. Yet at the beginning of his book, this same author reminds us that the *Grundrisse* manuscript "must be regarded as an important reference to Hegel and necessarily reveals an essential filiation, more specifically to Hegel's *Logic*" (Ibid., p. 10).

[8]We may also add to this enumeration the 1847 unpublished manuscript on "Wages," as well as "Wage Labor and Capital," published in 1849 in the *Neue Rheinische Zeitung*.

Four years passed after Marx wrote to Lassalle informing him of his plan before he was to write anew to a friend regarding the actual state of advancement of his work. He had little to add to his earlier report: "The second part is finally finished now . . . It will make approx. 30 printer's sheets [480 pages]. This is the sequel to the first brochure but will be published separately under the title 'Capital,' with 'Critique of Political Economy' as its subtitle. It contains in fact only the material for what was to have been the third chapter of the first part, i.e. 'Capital in general.' It therefore omits the competition of the many capitals and the credit system. This volume will contain what the English call the 'principles of political economy.' Together with the first part it forms the quintessence, and its continuation would be easy for others to develop on the basis of what I have provided (except perhaps for the relationship between the various forms of the state and the different economic structures of society)."[9]

Here Marx has clearly betrayed his intention to leave to his successors the task of elaborating a critical theory of landed property and wage labor, namely, the last two books in the first triad of rubrics. However, he reserved for himself the whole of the second triad; in other words, the rubrics on the state, foreign commerce, and the world market! This decision again attests to Marx's fidelity to the plan decided upon eighteen years earlier when signing the contract with the editor Leske for a two-volume work on the "Critique of Politics and Political Economy."[10] In other words, in 1862 Marx was convinced that he would still be able to produce the "quintessence" of the "Economics" and was willing to leave an important part to "others." Once *Capital* was sent to the printer's, he hoped for his part to be able to resume a subject that he considered fundamental: a critique of the state. His

[9]Marx to Ludwig Kugelmann (Dec. 28, 1862); *MEW* 30, p. 639. This document is extremely important for two reasons: (1) it contradicts any notion of a change in plan and (2) it shows that Marx continued to respect in every sense the original plan of *Capital* in its "three processes and four sections." The plan as elaborated beginning in 1858 in fact foresaw that after capital in general the author would treat the competition of the many capitals, credit and finally share capital (cf. *Grundrisse*, p. 175; and Marx's letter to Engels, Apr. 1, 1858; *MEW* 29, p. 312). Although he did treat certain aspects of competition, credit and share capital in the manuscripts prepared for the third book of *Capital*, he instructed his readers that these inquiries were only preliminary. See for example, *Capital*, Book III; *MEW* 25, p. 413 (at the beginning of the chapter entitled "Credit and Fictitious Capital").

[10]See "The project for a 'Critique of politics and political economy' " in Essay 3.

optimism indeed proved to be in vain. Five more years passed before he was able to publish not the "quintessence" of the "Economics" but merely a part of *Capital*—the first book, devoted to the process of the production of capital, which appeared in 1867. During the last decade and a half of his life, Marx's health continued to deteriorate; he was able neither to finish Book II nor to complete the final version of Book III on the basis of the rough draft dating from 1865. For Book IV, which was to treat the "history of the theory," Marx had accumulated during the years 1862–3 a dozen notebooks with material under the heading "Theories of Surplus Value."[11] Apparently, Marx thought that he had given the "quintessence" of a critique of political economy in these various writings, the finished as well as the fragmentary ones. Yet it is obvious that he was able to realize only a sixth of the plan announced in 1859 and never had the chance to work on the critique of the state that he had reserved exclusively for his own pen. He nevertheless did leave us with a small number of writings, chiefly on historical topics, which taken as a whole provide the groundwork for a theory of anarchism.[12]

As we see, there is in fact no need for astonishment that Marx was unable to fulfill his plan, so overwhelmed was he by "misère bourgeoise." Yet this failure suggests another conclusion, pregnant with consequences: If Marx was convinced, and explicitly stated, that he had left to his disciples the quintessence of his teachings, then he must have assumed that they also had the key to his method of thought—an instrument for

[11] The twenty-three notebooks that Marx wrote between August 1861 and May 1863 probably constitute, together with the 1857–8 manuscripts of the *Grundrisse*, the first version of *Capital* in its four books. In contrast to Engels, we consider the bulk of Marx's posthumous manuscripts to be simply the raw, and often amorphous, material of *Capital*. Only the first book, which Marx also revised thoroughly for the French edition, represents a completed whole. The following remark pertaining to Book I, written in a letter to Engels a year before publication, is an even more apt characterization of the subsequent books; "Although finished, the manuscript in its present mammoth proportions cannot be edited by anyone but myself, not even you" (letter to Engels, Feb. 13, 1866; *MEW* 31, p. 478).

[12] Few of Marx's writings lack a description of or a critical attack on the state as such. Although these remarks are incomplete or fragmentary, they suffice to reveal his thought to have been essentially anarchist. On the basis of these fragments we may even claim for Marx, from among the avowed defenders of a stateless, moneyless, Godless society, the title of anarchism's only veritable theorist. Cf. "Marx théoricien de l'anarchisme," in M. Rubel, *Marx critique du marxisme* (Paris: Payot, 1974), pp. 42–59.

comprehension no less than a means for representation, a rational method with a double attribute – analytical and mandative – for judging the past and projecting the future. Once he had shaken off the influence of his teacher Hegel and discovered the "guideline" for his own thought and studies, Marx's task was to construct a theoretical work in strict conformity with the principles of the method he had discovered and adopted. The plan for the critique of political economy in two triads and six rubrics was conceived according to this method that, for Marx, had the same significance as the dialectic had for Hegel, who defined his method as the "construction of everything in its pure essentiality."[13]

Methodological foundations

For Marx, there is neither essentiality in ideas nor movement in concepts; rather there is human thinking about things either concretely or abstractly, and there is the "rational kernel" of the Hegelian dialectic, which he disengaged in establishing the

---

[13]*Phänomenologie des Geistes* (1807), preface, p. lvii. Our use of the expression "the same significance" is deliberate because Marx himself maintained that he had "put back on its feet" and demystified the Hegelian dialectic. Equally important is the manner in which Marx demonstrated the contrast between Hegel and himself – Hegel his former teacher whom he had virtually forgotten for a number of years and then rediscovered as a stimulating impulse in his development: "My dialectical method is not utterly different from the Hegelian, it is its direct opposite. For Hegel, the movement of thought which he personifies under the name of the Idea is the demiurge of reality, and the real world is merely the phenomenal form of the Idea. For me, by contrast, the movement of thought is only the reflection of real movement, transposed into and translated in the human mind" (*Capital*, Book I, afterword to the 2d German edition 1873). We note with interest the dissimilarity between the original of this text and the first French translation prepared by Joseph Roy and revised by Marx. The original speaks not of the "réflexion du mouvement réel" (reflection of real movement) but of the "Ideale" (the ideal), which is for Marx "nothing more than material being transposed into and translated in the human mind" ("nichts anderes als das im Menschenkopf umgesetzte und übersetzte Materielle," *MEW* 23, p. 27). Our interest in these two published versions is heightened by the fact that the epistemological dualism negated in the original is reconstituted in the translation. To affirm that reality is "transposed and translated" by the human mind as thought contents signifies that the "real" is subjective. From Marx's *Theses on Feuerbach* we know that he defined his "new materialism" in contrast to the "old" and conceived of the world and society as the creations of an active, "critical and practical" subject. The theory of "reflected reality" accords much better with the epistemological views of Engels and his fervent and equally naïve emulator Lenin than with those of Marx. In a sense, Marx replaced Hegel's demiurge of reality – the "Idea" or "Concept" – with another demiurge: the critical, active, and revolutionary subject.

plan for the whole of his "Economics," and whose rational aspect he hoped to spell out someday in a special treatise on methodology.[14]

The choice of plan was therefore tantamount to an intellectual responsibility. Were this plan to be changed after the "guideline" of future research had been explicitly defined, the results of fifteen years of study in a series of scientific fields would necessarily be annulled. Moreover, Marx would have been obliged to recommence *ab ovo* the whole project, beginning with an exposition of the scientific premises for this radical change in methodology. There is, however, no trace of any such doubts about his methodological choice either in his published papers or in the posthumous manuscripts. Therefore, those who really want to study Marx should be less concerned with protecting at any price the apparent systematic structure of his thought and be willing to undertake an investigation into the nature of the uncompleted plan, which reveals a system of thought open to rectification and continuation. The concept of Marxism, if at all admissable as the designation for research along the Marxian lines of thought, should be conceived of in the sense of scientific continuity, that is, of achieving the work Marx was unable to complete. In place of continuity and amelioration, however, the Marxists, with a few rare exceptions, have remained intractable in what is either apologetic dogmatism or ideological demagogy serving not science but dissimulated political goals.

It is possible for us to follow step by step Marx's process of intellectual maturation as he began examining the plan and method for the work originally designated as an "elaboration

[14]Marx to Engels (Jan. 16, 1858): "By mere chance, I once again perused the *Logic* of Hegel, which has helped me greatly in regard to the *method* of elaboration" (*MEW* 29, p. 260). Marx's friend Freiligrath had made him a gift of several volumes of Hegel that had belonged to Bakunin; this occasioned Marx's renewed dialogue with the "master" whom he had broken with fifteen years earlier in criticizing and denouncing his political philosophy as a dangerous "mystification." Eighteen years later Marx would again speak of writing a treatise on the dialectic; cf. the letter from Joseph Dietzgen to Marx, Jan. 16, 1876 (Archives of the International Institute of Social History, Amsterdam; D II, 23). Marx must have regretted being unable to realize this project not only because he recognized its intrinsic importance, but even more because he must have himself sensed the ambiguity of his attachment to Hegel. And in view of the continual quarrels about this subject within the Marxist school, any such feelings of regret have certainly proved to be justified: "Marx and Hegel" is still the most controversial subject in Marxist scholastics.

of the basic features [*Grundzüge*]¹⁵ of the Economics." From 1844 to 1852–3 he multiplied the number of his study note-books, filling them in part with original critical reflections, in part with simple extracts from his readings in political econ-omy, early as well as modern authors. The fruits of his re-search are evident in *The Holy Family* (1845), in his articles on *Wage Labor and Capital* (1849) and in *The Poverty of Phi-losophy* (1847) no less than in the numerous correspondent's reports he sent to the *NYDT* in the years between 1852 and 1857 on questions of finance, commerce, and industry. These papers are not, strictly speaking, monographs but rather mate-rials to be used for what Marx called the *Grundrisse* or *Princi-ples of Political Economy*.

The problem of method arose even before he began tackling this work itself, when he decided to compose a general intro-duction, which in the end he preferred not to publish. In a notebook marked with the letter "M" and begun on August 23, 1857, he outlined this introduction in four parts: production in general; the general relation between production, distribution, exchange, and consumption; the method of political economy; means of production, production relations, and commerce. These chapters are unequally elaborated, but their theoretical orientation is quite evident. Indeed, here Marx takes up again his earlier theses in confronting the views of economists from older and contemporary schools regarding these concepts. Moreover, in his confrontation he by no means renounced polemics, whether attacking Proudhon or Carey, John S. Mill or J. B. Say, the "socialist men of letters" or the "Hegelians."

Once admitted that production, distribution, exchange, and consumption, without being identical, nevertheless constitute an "organic whole" and influence one another reciprocally, with production as the primordial and determining factor, the choice of a method of exposition becomes inseparably linked to the problem of order in this exposition. Marx, in fact, re-cognized this necessity.¹⁶

¹⁵Marx used this term almost simultaneously in letters to Engels (Dec. 18, 1857) and to Lassalle (Dec. 21, 1857) specifying that he had been working "most colossally" and "seriously" under the stimulating effect of the current business crisis. He hoped to finish "before the deluge" (Marx to Engels, Dec. 8, 1857) and break loose from the "night-mare" (to Engels, Dec. 18, 1857) that weighed on him, because he was obliged to work by day at journalism, with only the nights for his own scientific research, and was frequently plagued and handicapped by ill health. Cf. *MEW* 29, pp. 225, 232, 548.
¹⁶*Grundrisse*, p. 22.

Seventeenth-century political economists traditionally began their analyses with a discussion of the "living whole," that is, the population, nation, state, or national groupings—all comprehensive and complex concepts—from which they deduced abstract denominations, such as division of labor, money, and value. They proceeded, in other words, from a rather obscure image of the whole to develop at the end a progressively more subtle abstraction. According to Marx, this procedure was discarded by eighteenth-century political economists in favor of the truly scientific method, that of "economic systems which ascend from the simple elements such as division of labor, needs, exchange value, to the state, international exchange and the world market."[17] The necessity of culminating the analysis of political economy with the world market is explained conceptually and methodologically in the "Theories of Surplus Value":

However, only foreign trade, the development of the market to a world market, transforms money into world money and *abstract labor* into social labor. Abstract wealth, value, money—hence *abstract labor* develops in proportion to the development of concrete labor into a totality of different modes of labor which encompasses the world market. Capitalist production is founded on the *value* or the development of the labor contained in the product as social labor. But this is only [possible] on the basis of foreign trade and the world market. It is therefore both a condition and a result of capitalist production.[18]

For a better understanding of the "ascent" from the abstract to the concrete, Marx refers to Hegel, apparently adopting Hegel's epistemological theory relative to "sense certainty" at the beginning of the *Phänomenologie des Geistes*. However, Marx carefully draws his reader's attention to the error committed by his teacher Hegel: Namely, the latter conceived of

---

[17]Marx identified none of the representatives of these two systems by name. For the seventeenth century he undoubtedly had in mind the defenders of the mercantile system during the formative period of large nation-states directed by strong governments, governments that favored rapid population growth, the accumulation of precious metals, the extension of urban manufacturing, and foreign commerce. From among the modern scientific economists Marx considered the physiocrats to be the "fathers of modern economics," a title merited by their original analysis of capital "within the limits of the bourgeois horizon", (*Theories of Surplus Value; MEW* 26/1 p. 12).

[18]*MEW* 26/3, p. 252.

reality "as the result of thought that is reabsorbed in itself, deepens in itself, moves itself." For Marx, however, "the method of ascending from the abstract to the concrete in thought is simply the manner in which thought masters the concrete and reproduces it mentally as something concrete," a procedure that should not be confused with the "process of the genesis of the concrete itself."[19]

These methodological reflections preceded Marx's rereading of Hegel and may be compared with certain paragraphs in the *Rechtsphilosophie*, which Marx mentioned in this essay, and above all to the critical remarks in *The Holy Family* regarding Hegel's speculative constructions in the *Phänomenologie des Geistes*. In writing his general introduction Marx takes pains to situate his contribution in political economy relative to the classical economists of recognized scientific reputation. The confrontation with Hegel's method bears significance only as concerns the selection of certain epistemological principles for a reversal of this method. Hegel is indeed the teacher – but only on the condition that the student is allowed to follow the master's dialectic in the reverse sense. The most highly abstract economic categories are inconceivable without the background of a social whole composed of explicitly defined human relations – such as the type of family, state, or community. This holds true as well for exchange value; in other words, money that also has an "antediluvian existence" prior to capital and wage labor, and for labor, an apparently simple general category that is in fact as old as humanity.

Such "concrete totalities" are of course products of our thought, of the reflective mind exploiting its experience of the world scientifically, in a manner different from that of the artist or the religious believer who knows nothing of theoretical speculation. A long historical experience is necessary if primitive institutions are to be retained in more highly evolved societies without an evident terminological similarity that would betray the secret of the mutational process that gave rise to social forms and relations of an entirely new character. Concerning money, for example, "one might affirm that the

---

[19]*Grundrisse*, p. 22. In the original we read ". . . es als ein geistig Konkretes zu reproduzieren," which may also be translated as "to reproduce the concrete in the mind." For further discussion of Hegel's manner of conceiving this step from the abstract to the concrete, see J. Hyppolite, *Genèse et structure de la Phénoménologie de l'esprit de Hegel* (Paris: 1946), pp. 66–7.

simplest category can express the dominant relations in a less developed whole or the subordinate relations in a more developed whole which existed historically prior to the development of the whole which is expressed by a more concrete category. In this perspective, therefore, the process of abstract thought ascending from the simplest to the most complex may correspond to the real historical process."[20] "Simple," "concrete," "abstract," "complex," "developed," "less developed": These terms are all part of the methodological vocabulary that Marx employed in order to provide an instrument of scientific knowledge for the critical analysis of economic systems. With this instrument it should be possible to determine scientifically the direction in which mankind, individuals as well as the species (society), is developing. In 1857 he decided not to publish the first results of his reflections on methodology, waiting a decade before revealing them in more concise terms that, however, cannot be truly understood except in light of the earlier and fuller statement. In the preface to Book I of *Capital* Marx comments on the difficulties that the reader might encounter at the beginning of the work, in the section concerning commodities and their value form. Here Marx reminds us that "for the analysis of economic forms, neither the microscope nor chemical reagents are of any use; the force of abstraction is the only possible substitute for both."[21]

Since the general introduction of 1857 had been discarded and the explications furnished in the 1867 preface proved insufficient, Marx felt justified in returning to the subject of his methodology in the 1873 afterword, without giving all the details found in the *Grundrisse*, however. In the latter work historical illustrations are paired with theoretical expositions, and consequently we can follow Marx's mental process that led him to choose as his point of departure, not landed property, the issue of agriculture, which is the "first form of production in every more or less stable society," but rather capital, which is the "economic force of bourgeois society that dominates everything."[22] According to the methodological principle adopted, the scientist investigating earlier social systems must look for the key to their economic organization in the more complex system that succeeded it. "Human anatomy

[20]*Grundrisse*, p. 23.
[21]*MEW* 23, p. 12.
[22]*Grundrisse*, p. 27.

provides the key to the anatomy of the ape," Marx wrote in
1857, three years before declaring that the Darwinian theory
on the origin of species contained "the foundation of our conception in the domain of natural history."[23] However, to understand earlier evolutionary phases in this manner the researcher must manifest a certain critical spirit that prohibits
him from considering the last level of civilization attained as
being the result of providential evolution. Sociological understanding of institutions and their conceptual formulation calls
for a choice of historical perspective in contrast to simple
chronological succession. "In every historical and social science in general it must never be forgotten that the subject—
here modern bourgeois society—exists both in reality and in
the human mind; that categories express forms and modes of
existence, which are often simple aspects of this society, of this
subject; and that, consequently, this society does not begin to
exist scientifically speaking, only at the moment when it is
spoken of *as such*. The same thing is true for the development
of economic categories. This rule is essential for it aids deci-
sively in establishing the definitive study plan [*Einteilung*]."[24]

Once he had finished the first stage of his studies in economics, Marx adopted the following methodological norms for the
continuation: Proceed from the simple to the complex, from
the abstract to the concrete, from the present for an understanding of the past, from the imaginary future in order to live
and act in the present. Unless we recognize that this was
Marx's mode of procedure, the dual character of his teachings—analytical and mandative—*must* appear as self-contra-
dictory. He closely held to this schema when establishing the
plan of the work that in 1857 he still thought he would be able
to finish relatively quickly. However, his calculations proved
erroneous in evaluating both the level of his acquired knowledge in economics and the dimensions of the various sections
of the "Economics" projected in the plan. After the first brochure (*Heft*) was published he therefore took up his studies of
the various economists once again. He now filled whole
"books" rather than "chapters" with the results of his investigations. But this quantitative change in no way influenced the
methodological structure of the initial plan. Having opted for
the structural model furnished by the classical economists, he

[23]Ibid., p. 26; and Marx to Engels (Dec. 19, 1860); *MEW* 30, p. 131.
[24]*Grundrisse*, p. 27.

was obliged to present the economic categories not in the order of their historical importance but according to their importance for modern bourgeois society. Marx's original contribution to the classical model was two-fold: 1) his effort to give a dialectical interpretation of the relations between the economic categories and the institutions found in the society characterized by the bourgeois mode of production; 2) his derivation of analyses of capitalist economy from an abstract model, which functioned as though in an ideal vacuum, into and out of which he would alternately add or remove perturbing factors. It is essential to keep this two-fold approach in mind when examining the first draft of the plan for the "Economics," found in the general introduction at the end of the chapter on method:

1. The general abstract determinations which can be applied to all types of societies.
2. The categories which constitute the internal structure of bourgeois society and which serve as the basis for the fundamental classes. Capital, wage-labor, landed property. Their reciprocal relations. Town and Country. The three major social classes. Exchange among these. Circulation, Credit (private).
3. The synthesis of bourgeois society in the form of the state. The state considered in itself. "Unproductive" classes. Taxes. The public debt. Public credit. The population. Colonies. Emigration.
4. The international relations of production. International division of labor. International exchange. Exportation and importation. Exchange rates.
5. The world market and crises.[25]

Here we have the logical and dialectical structure of a plan that was never subjected to further modification except in several points of detail and was ultimately fixed as a double triad of rubrics with a rigorous and definitive order. Marx was, consequently, committed both morally and scientifically to fulfill the established schema; and it was in this spirit that he described his plan when informing his closest friends of its concretization. An attentive reading of the *Grundrisse* and of

[25]*Grundrisse*, pp. 28–9.

the indexes Marx established for his study notebooks reveals an author perfectly conscious of both the objective and the direction of his research. The seven notebooks of this manuscript contain just two chapters, the first on money, the second on capital; but it is clear from the outset that Marx scrupulously respected the plan of the whole, yet at the same time did not foresee that, in developing the theses, he would encounter problems with the chapters which would surpass their projected dimensions as their analytical and critical arguments multiplied. Finally, he constructed the following plan for the "chapter on capital":

    I. The process of the production of capital.
    II. The process of the circulation of capital.
    III. Capital and Profit.[26]

Although he continued filling notebooks with material for the first of the six rubrics, he never succeeded in exhausting his topic. Despite this, he never lost sight of the original schema established in the 1857 general introduction; indeed, it seems that he placed special emphasis on this choice of method, tested its solidity, and thus assured himself of his fidelity to it. For once the general introduction and the first draft of the work were finished, Marx permitted himself a rereading of Hegel's *Logic* and could not resist the temptation of "flirting" with the style of his erstwhile teacher. In the chapter on money, where he refutes the monetary utopia of Proudhon's disciple Darimon, he hesitantly begins using expressions borrowed from the "objective logic," gradually becoming more and more confident and even daring in his use of them. In his analysis of the relation between the market value and real value of goods and its equalization, he uses the magic dialectical formula of the "negation of the negation";[27] and to indicate the latent dualism implied by the existence of the commodity as both concrete product and exchange value, he has recourse to the logical concept of "contradiction" — itself not free of ambiguity: The "particular nature" of the commodity-product is judged to be incompatible with its "general nature

[26]Marx established this plan in early 1859 on the basis of the seven notebooks of the *Grundrisse*. The three parts correspond to the themes of the future books of *Capital*. But Marx was able to publish only the first of these books — the most extensively elaborated, whose structure is also most intimately related to its contents — as *Capital*, Book I. Cf. *Grundrisse*, pp. 969–74.

[27]*Grundrisse*, p. 56.

as exchange value."[28] Finally, after a long description of the role of money in its various functions as a representation of universal wealth, as "God among commodities" and creator of the world market,[29] Marx interjects a parenthesis, apparently with the objective of recalling the revolutionary perspectives of the plan of his "Economics":

In the first section, where we investigate exchange value, money, price, commodities always appear as given entities. The determination of the form is simple. We know that they represent particular aspects of social production, itself given in advance. But they *are not given* in this determination. And thus, the first exchange only appears really as an exchange of superfluous objects without encompassing or determining production as a whole. It is the *existing* surplus of total production which is found outside the realm of exchange values. And even in evolved society this phenomenon appears as the immediately perceptible universe of existing goods. In any event, it refers us beyond its own limits to the economic relations established as *production relations*. Consequently, the internal structure of production constitutes the second section and the synthesis [*Zusammenfassung*] in the form of the state the third, international relations the fourth and world market the final section where production is given as a totality along with all of its elements, but where, simultaneously, all contradictions are activated [*zum Prozess kommen*]. The world market thus represents both the essential condition and the foundation of the whole. Crises, in turn, are the general sign that the existing situation is to be surpassed and they are also the impulsion towards a new historical form.[30]

Here, again, we find the five-point plan of the general introduction, dressed up with some Hegelian ornaments. For the first time the author manifests his desire to divide the work into sections [*Abschnitte*], which he will later rebaptize as books when he perceives that the first two of the five planned sections are far from completion and that years of work would be needed before he could begin elaborating the themes of the later sections. He therefore preferred to keep silent on the subject of the five additional books announced in the preface to the *Critique* of 1859. It is chiefly the extant unpublished manuscripts that shed light on this matter.

[28]Ibid., p. 65.
[29]Ibid., pp. 132, 138.
[30]*Grundrisse*, pp. 138–9.

As in the chapter on money, so too in the chapter on capital Marx returns repeatedly to the problem of the plan and the method of his "Economics," each time explaining at greater length the manner of proceeding from the abstract to the concrete, from the logical to the historical, from the dialectical to the empirical, in passages that often assume the tone of a *pro domo* discourse. In the following, for example, we note his justification of the methodological priority given to capital before landed property:

Within the system of bourgeois society, therefore, capital derives immediately from value. *Historically other systems arise* which serve as the material basis for a less perfect development of value. Since in the latter exchange value plays only a secondary role, subordinate to use value, not capital but the landed property relationship appears as their real basis. Modern landed property, by contrast, cannot be understood without capital as its prerequisite because it cannot exist without capital; and historically it indeed appears as an adequate form, produced by capital for its own ends, of the earlier historical manifestation of landed property.[31]

Marx had accumulated a considerable amount of historical material for the rubric on landed property both in his study notebooks and in writings dating from disparate periods. Thus he probably would have written this section following that on capital. In the *Grundrisse* he again repeated the historical sketch of the different types of landed property first presented in another unedited work, *The German Ideology*, only now supplemented by the readings in pertinent literature that he had done in the intervening years.[32] When he finally realized that the section on capital alone was going to require more than three books, each hundreds of pages in length, he presumably discontinued this research pending his completion of Book I. With the help of Hegel's *Logic* Marx then developed a more and more precise plan for the section on capital, as we can see from the following outline, which he placed between brackets in the last part of the second notebook of the *Grundrisse*:

[31]*Grundrisse*, pp. 163–4. For a lucid explanation of Marx's view of use value and exchange value in their historical perspective, see R. Rosdolsky, "Der Gebrauchswert bei Karl Marx. Eine Kritik der bisherigen Marx-Interpretation," *Kyklos* XII, no. 1 (1959), 27–53.

[32]*Grundrisse*, pp. 375–413 (Formen, die der kapitalistischen Produktion vorhergehen. . .); and *The German Ideology*, in *MEW* 3, pp. 61–5 and 333–60 passim.

[(A) Capital]

I. 1. The general concept of capital.
2. The particularity of capital: *capital circulant, capital fixe* [Fr. in the orig.]. (Capital as a means of subsistence, as raw material, as an instrument of labor.)
3. Capital as money.
II. 1. *The quantity of capital. Accumulation.*
2. *Capital in proportion to itself. Profit. Interest. The value of capital:* i.e. capital distinct from itself as interest and profit.
3. *The circulation of capitals.*
a) Exchange of capital for capital. Exchange of capital for revenue. Capital and *prices.*
b) *Competition among capitals.*
c) *Concentration of capitals.*
III. Capital as credit.
IV. Capital as share capital.
V. Capital as the money market.
VI. Capital as a source of wealth. The capitalist.

[B] Landed Property[33]

[C] Wage Labor[34]

With these three categories as given, there would be the movement of prices, i.e. circulation determined henceforth in its internal totality. Further, the three classes both as the three fundamental forms and as conditions for circulation.

[D] The State[35]

State and bourgeois society. – Taxes or the existence of unproductive classes. – The public debt. – The population.

[33]Literally, in the original: "After capital landed property should be treated" (*Grundrisse*, p. 175).
[34]Literally: "After this, wage labor" (Ibid.).
[35]The original reads: "Then the state" (Ibid.). The topics that follow are put in parentheses as if to indicate that they are all to be treated within the rubric on the "state."

[E]

The state towards the exterior: Colonies. External commerce. Exchange rates. Money as international currency.

[F] World Market[36]

The encroachment of bourgeois society on the state. Crises. Dissolution of the mode of production and type of society founded on exchange value. Individual labor becomes identical with social labor and vice-versa.[37]

Here we find for the first time a clear presentation of the plan of this work in its six parts, called sections throughout the *Grundrisse,* in a general outline of the author's chosen methodological itinerary. At the same time we note that the rubric with the most complex structure, the rubric on capital, conspicuously 'flirts' with both the style and method of Hegel's 'subjective logic': Marx constructed this rubric using Roman and Arabic numerals followed by Greek letters to produce the triads for which Hegel had a particular fondness. We might even imagine that Marx deliberately chose the most difficult of Hegel's triads, the logic of the concept, as an example to illustrate his 'reversal' of the master's dialectic. Imitating the three moments of the Hegelian triad – generality, particularity, individuality – Marx pursued this game of dialectics with increasing bravado until he finally developed a new scheme for the rubric on capital:

Capital

I. *Generality:*
    1. a) Formation of capital from money.
       b) Capital and labor (mediated by the work
         of others).

[36]In the original: "Finally, the world market" (Ibid.).

[37]*Grundrisse,* p. 175. We have ordered these entries in outline form and added the letters A–F in order to facilitate the reader's recognition of the six rubrics.

    c) The elements of capital taken separately in
       function of their relationship to labor (Prod-
       uct. Raw material. Instrument of labor).
  2. *Particularization of capital:*
    a) *Capital circulant, capital fixe* [In Fr.]. Cir-
       culation of capital.
  3. *Singularity of capital:* capital and profit. Capi-
     tal and interest. Capital as value, distinct from
     itself in the form of interest and profit.
II. *Particularity:*
  1. Accumulation of capitals.
  2. Competition among capitals.
  3. Concentration of capitals (the quantitative dif-
    ference of capital being simultaneously quali-
    tative as a *measure* of both its size and its ac-
    tion).
III. *Singularity:*
  1. Capital as credit.
  2. Capital as share capital.
  3. Capital as money market.[38]

Whatever reservations we might have concerning this construction in triads, one fact remains: The plan's logical rigor
derives less from a formal arrangement of conceptual "moments" than from its conformity to a dialectic of the social
totality, each element of which must be treated separately and
in a fixed order. The "Hegel parody" was soon to become
superfluous, however. While elaborating his ideas, Marx discovered a means for methodological simplification that allowed him to group all the problems of capital around the
three "processes" as initially conceived: production, circulation and what appears to be "distribution." The 1859 *Critique*
and *Capital* of 1867 still "flirt" with the Hegelian style, yet
their use of it bears little resemblance to the almost unnatural
manipulation of dialectical artifices that marks the style of the
Grundrisse. Marx had, moreover, taken steps to avoid the
pitfalls of purely formal dialectics from the very beginning of
his work in methodology. He jotted down the following note —
and retrospectively it sounds as if it were meant as a warning —
in a list of "points not to be forgotten":

[38]Ibid., p. 186.

Dialectic of the concepts of productive force (means of production) and production relations, a dialectic whose limits must be defined and which does not eliminate the real distinction.[39]

Capital and systematic Marxism

None of Marx's outlines for the section – sometimes called rubric or book – on capital contains any confirmation whatsoever of the notion that Marx intended to change the initial plan of the "Economics" elaborated in 1857. Confronted with the choice between two methods in political economy – the ancient and the modern – he opted for the second and added to its scientific conclusions a kind of dialectical epistemology, the theory of which he proposed to explain some day in a work that would take as its point of departure the "rational" core of the method "mystified" by Hegel.[40] And rather than produce a modified version of the basic plan, he organized, for example, the material of Book I – or what was destined to be so entitled – according to the fundamental scheme: the process of the production of capital: 1) transformation of money into capital; 2) absolute surplus value; 3) relative surplus value; 4) primitive accumulation; 5) wage labor and capital. Each of these five parts is in turn divided into chapters whose themes correspond to those of the future Book I.[41] The structure of this book was definitively established more than four years before its publication, when Marx, constantly respectful of the outline given in the first brochure (the 1859 *Critique*), was preparing the material for the third chapter on capital, which became in fact Book I:

> The first section, "*The process of the production of capital,*" will be divided up as follows:
> 1. Introduction. Commodities. Money.
> 2. The transformation of money into capital.
> 3. Absolute surplus value. a) The labor process and the process of producing value. b) Constant capi-

[39]"General Introduction," 1857; *Grundrisse*, p. 29.

[40]Marx to Engels (Jan. 16, 1858) and Marx to Kugelmann (Mar. 6, 1868); *MEW* 29, p. 260, and 32, p. 538.

[41]Plan drafted in 1859, cf. *Grundrisse*, pp. 969–74. Point 5 evidently marks the transition from capital to its negation, wage labor, via the stage of landed property. In the numerous references to the *Grundrisse* notebooks elsewhere in Marx's writings there is no evidence of his including the rubric on wage labor in that on capital.

tal and variable capital. c) Absolute surplus value. d) The struggle for the normal working-day. e) Simultaneous working-days (number of working-men employed simultaneously). Amount and rate of surplus value (quantity and level).
4. Relative surplus value. a) Simple cooperation. b) Division of labor. c) Machinery, etc.
5. Absolute and relative surplus value combined. Relation (proportion) between wage labor and surplus value. Formal and real subsumption of labor under capital. Productivity of capital. Productive and unproductive labor.
6. Reconversion of surplus value into capital. Primitive accumulation. Wakefield's theory of colonization.
7. Results of the process of production. [...]
8. Theories of surplus value.
9. Theories of productive and unproductive labor.[42]

Several important facts can be gleaned from this outline: first and foremost, that Marx strictly respected the original plan for the "Economics." Indeed, the process of the production of capital, described here as a single section of one work, encompasses the same material as Book I except for a few chapters that Marx left out because of their length.[43] As for the "flirtation" with Hegel and his triads, Marx held it in abeyance until elaborating the labor theory of value in the first chapters of *Capital*. Finally, we surmise that the dimensions soon attained by this, the first of the work's six rubrics, made it impossible for Marx to finish composing the second and third sections and obliged him to leave them to Engels. The single rubric on capital was soon to become his exclusive preoccupation; in the end, the material he accumulated for it furnished not one but *three* books! His silence on the subject of an eventual continuation of the "Economics" is therefore comprehensible. He obviously preferred giving his friends a maximum of details on

[42]This outline is to be found in notebook XVIII of the 1861–3 manuscript and dates from January 1863; cf. *MEW* 26/1, pp. 389–90. Here we find as well the plan of "section" III, in fact, Book III of *Capital*. However, the composition of the future Book II is missing.

[43]In other words, Marx did not finish even Book I of *Capital*, leaving among his papers a manuscript for the theme indicated under number 7 and fifteen notebooks for themes 8 and 9, intended as Book IV of *Capital*.

the projected contents of the first and only rubric for which he already had material at hand.

Lassalle and not Engels was the first to receive relatively precise information about the work in six parts–by now already called books–that Marx was undertaking.[44] Yet, at this moment in late February 1858, Marx was able only to describe the basic outline and to approximate the length of the whole.[45] Engels did not learn of the plan until April 1858; this time Marx provided more than just an enumeration of the six books that were to compose the "whole mess": his friend received a veritable analysis of both contents and method, primarily for the first book entitled *Capital:*

1. *Capital* is divided into four sections. a) Capital en général [in Fr.]. (*This is the material of the first brochure.*) b) *Competition* or the reciprocal action of the many capitals. c) *Credit,* where capital appears as the general element in opposition to the many capitals. d) *Share capital* as the most perfect form (assuming the character of communism), together with all its contradictions. At the same time the transition from capital to landed property is historical since the modern form of landed property is a product of the action of capital on feudal etc. landed property. Similarly, the transition from landed property to wage labor is not only dialectical but also historical, because the last product of modern landed property is the universalization of wage labor which then appears as the basis of the whole mess.[46]

In this passage Marx could hardly have been more explicit about the relationship between the six-part plan and the

[44]Marx to Lassalle (Feb. 22, 1858); *MEW* 29, pp. 550–1. Marx wrote that he was unable to estimate the dimensions of the "whole," that he wanted to publish it in "consecutive brochures," and that conciseness would therefore be sacrificed for the sake of its general comprehensibility. Yet he planned this work as just the first in a series, namely as the "Critique of Economic Categories" or "a critical analysis of the bourgeois economic system." The second in the series was to deal with the "Critique and History of Political Economy and Socialism" and a third "a short *historic sketch* of the development of economic categories or relations." In declaring such ambitious scientific intentions, Marx probably wanted to impress his vainglorious friend Lassalle who had just published an enormous volume on *The Philosophy of Heraclitus the Obscure* and in it announced his intention to devote himself, as a disciple of Hegel, to political economy. Marx remarked ironically to Engels: "[Lassalle] will learn to his own detriment that it's one thing to apply an abstract, perfected system of logic to vague notions of such a[n economic] system and something entirely different to develop a science through criticism to the point where it can be presented dialectically" (letter to Engels, Feb. 1, 1858; *MEW* 29, p. 275).

[45]Marx to Lassalle (Mar. 11, 1858); *MEW* 29, pp. 550–1.

[46]Marx to Engels (Apr. 2, 1858); *MEW* 29, p. 312.

historico-dialectic method that inspired its structure. Whereas the future Marxist school was to confound dialectics with history, abstraction with empirical reality, Marx clearly distinguishes here between the two research plans in view of underlining the scientific nature of the method used in uncovering the material determinism of social "transitions." Engels fully approved of "this arrangement of the whole in six books," but was forced to admit that he had not quite grasped "the dialectical transition from landed property to wage labor." He, of course, had no knowledge of the arguments Marx developed in the *Grundrisse* on "transitions," exemplified by the following passage:

Both through its very nature and historically as well, capital is the *creator* of modern landed property, of land rent; its action therefore appears as the dissolution of the old form of landed property. The new is created by the action of capital on the old form. Capital acts thusly as the creator of modern agriculture . . . The question is then how does the transition from landed property into wage labor take place? (The transition from wage labor to capital is automatic, for here the latter has returned to its active cause.) Considered historically, the transition is unquestionable.[47]

The entire analysis could be quoted in support of our central thesis, for here Marx gives what may be termed a methodological synopsis of the construction of the "Economics" according to historical stages. He emphasizes the necessity of treating each rubric separately in order to respect scrupulously the transitions. It is possible, therefore, to imagine what Marx would have produced out of the rubrics on landed property and wage labor where historical illustrations would have probably predominated. In any event, Marx was clearly concerned with pointing up above all the evolutionary nature of the capitalist mode of production, and this necessarily and irrevocably committed him to his basic methodological principle, namely, the organic nature of the "bourgeois system." The statement of this principle in the following passage assumes the form of a theoretical postulate:

If in the fully developed bourgeois system each economic relation presupposes every other relation in its bourgeois-economic form, each given factor thus being at the same time the condition of

[47]*Grundrisse*, p. 187.

another, this also holds for every organic system. The organic system as a totality itself has its premises, and its development into a totality consists in its subordinating all elements of society or creating from society all organs which this system yet lacks. It therefore historically becomes a totality. The coming into being of the totality thus forms a moment of its process, of its development . . . Capital as the creator of land rent thus goes back to the production of wage labor as the general source of its creativity. Capital results from circulation and establishes labor as wage labor; it is formed in this way and when developed as a whole it establishes landed property both as its condition and as its antithesis. But in so doing it has evidently just created wage labor as its general premise. The latter must therefore be examined separately.[48]

When Engels examined the summary of the first brochure sent him by his friend, he of course knew nothing of the lines just quoted nor of the rest of the pages in the *Grundrisse* where Marx quite rationally employs the dialectic of "positive" and "negative" transitions. He therefore found the exposition "very abstract indeed" and had difficulty discovering the "dialectical transitions." He must have found difficult particularly the concise methodological preamble with which Marx introduced the resumé on "capital in general":

In this whole section wages will always be taken to be at their minimum. The movements of wages themselves and the rise or fall of the minimum will be examined in the study of wage labor. Furthermore, here we take landed property = o, i.e. we are not concerned with landed property as a particular economic relation. This procedure alone enables us to avoid speaking of everything when dealing with each relationship.[49]

This statement, dating from April 1858, again denies the possibility of any change in plan. Yet neither it nor a whole series of similar remarks and expositions has been able to shake the convictions of Marxism's "true believers" who, to protect their faith in the integrity of the "system," persistently main-

---

[48]*Grundrisse*, pp. 189–90.

[49]Letter to Engels (Apr. 2, 1858); *MEW* 29, pp. 314–15. Writing to Weydemeyer on Feb. 2, 1859, Marx specified that he divided "all political economy into six books" and for the first time communicated the exact contents of the "first notebook." He added: "You understand the *political* reasons that have persuaded me to hold back the third chapter on 'Capital' until I have re-established my position" (*MEW* 29, p. 572).

tain that Marx "abandoned the triple structure" and included the books on landed property and wage labor in Book I of *Capital*.[50] Glorification of the two "founders" of Marxism has a very special function in the thought and behavior of those who refuse to take up the problem where Marx was forced to abandon it: It exempts them from reconsidering, and therefore entertaining doubts about, the supposedly philosophical bases of a socialism christened "scientific." Consequently, Marx's wish — to find "readers willing to learn something new and therefore to think for themselves" — has thus fallen on deaf ears.[51] For several generations his disciples have upheld a quasireligious belief in the fiction of a "Marxist system," so that a real dialogue with Marx, the author of an unfinished and amendable work entitled *Capital*, has never taken place, neither during his lifetime nor beyond the grave, as he had wanted.

[50] Cf. Rosdolsky, *Zur Entstehungsgeschichte des Marxschen "Kapital"* vol. 1 (Frankfurt: 1968), p. 59. Although he rejects the motivation for the change of plan given by Grossmann, Otto Morf nevertheless accepts the thesis of a change and with it Rosdolsky's arguments. Thus, Marx is said to have given the analysis of landed property together with ground rent in Book III of *Capital*. Morf, *Geschichte und Dialektik in der politischen Ökonomie. Zum Verhältnis von Wissenschaftstheorie und Wirtschaftsgeschichte bei Karl Marx* (Frankfurt a.M./Vienna: 1970), pp. 105, 173–4. This concession to the traditional dogmatism of the Marxist school is all the more astonishing in view of the author's knowledge of Marx's formal statements affirming that the systematic study of landed property was not part of the plan of *Capital* (*MEW* 26, p. 632)! Moreover, Morf is acquainted with Marx's methodological views on the double — i.e. dialectical and historical — nature of transitions (cf. Morf, *Geschichte und Dialektik*, pp. 195–215). Although the texts of the *Grundrisse* do clearly betray Marx's heritage from Hegel, we must nevertheless recognize the full significance of his abandonment of Hegelian formalization.

Another recent author, Winfried Schwarz ("Das 'Kapital im allgemeinen' und die 'konkurrenz' im ökonomischen Werk von Karl Marx. Zu Rosdolskys Fehlinterpretation der Gliederung des 'Kapital,' " in *Gesellschaft: Beiträge zur Marxschen Theorie* I (Frankfurt a.M.: 1974, pp. 222–47), has understood Rosdolsky's error regarding Marx's methodology and regarding the place due to the discussion of "competition" in *Capital*. However, he has utterly ignored the consequences of this reasoning for the question of the plan for the whole work. In his own words, "The question of the structural plan and systematization in the Marxian work is . . . a problem not of philology but of methodology" (Ibid., p. 222).

[51] *Capital*, Book I, preface; *MEW* 23, p. 12. In an unpublished manuscript of 1920 Karl Korsch takes issue with the negligence of Marx's followers who show no concern for the extension of the "principles furnished by Marx into a complete, critical system of Marxism" ("Einige Grundbegriffe der politischen Oekonomie von Karl Marx." Manuscript of five pages conserved in the archives of the International Institute of Social History, Amsterdam, p. 2).

The physiology of utopia

Marx abandoned the scheme of triads in the exposition on capital, although he had made systematic use of it in the *Grundrisse*. Nevertheless, he retained it when constructing the overall plan of the "Economics" in its six rubrics or books and, consequently, it became impossible for him to modify it in any way without simultaneously altering the dialectical nature of the mode of analysis whose objective was to "lay bare the economic law of motion of modern society."[52] Essentially, this plan predates Marx's unforeseen rediscovery of Hegel's *Logic;* however, once Marx was again caught up in the throes of the master's long forgotten dialectic, he could free himself only by substituting for the *Logic*'s conceptual triads, the rubrics of the "Economics" organized in categories of three in a double scheme centered on capital, for the first part, and on the state, for the other. For Marx dialectics were not what Hegel termed "the moving principle of the concept," nor was method "the essence and the concept of the contents."[53] And if Marx accepted Hegel's definition of "negativity" as "the internal source of all activity, of all spontaneous living and animated movement, the dialectial soul,"[54] he in fact interpreted this definition in an entirely different manner: For Marx, negativity assumed the significance of antagonisms and emancipatory struggles of masses on the terrain of history, which was to be understood as the memory of past generations and as the creative and spontaneous activity of the future.

Marx's use of the Hegelian dialectic therefore amounted to a transmutation, or even sublimation, of the conceptual contents of nearly all of Hegel's logical "categories." It was Hegel who had written that "all things are inherently contradictory," a proposition that "in contrast to others, expresses the truth and the essence of things," or even of "institutions."[55] Marx in

---

[52]*Capital,* Book I, preface; *MEW* 23, pp. 15–16.

[53]*Enzyklopädie der philosophischen Wissenschaften,* §243. Cf. *Rechtsphilosophie,* §31 (Bemerkung): "This activity is not the *external* activity of subjective thought, but the *very essence* of its contents which causes it to bud and flower."

[54]*Logik,* part II, section III, chapter 3; in the Lasson ed. (Leipzig: 1951), p. 496.

[55]*Logik,* part II, section I, chapter 2, C, note 3; Lasson ed., p. 58. Lenin expressed enthusiastic admiration for this note dealing with the principle of contradiction and of all spontaneous movement. "Who would have believed," he asked, "that there we find the heart of the 'Hegel business,' of the abstract, ponderous and absurd Hegel business? It was necessary to discover, grasp, extract, purify this essence, and that is

turn applied this principle of objective negativity to the relationship between capital and labor, between the bourgeoisie
and the working class. The first triad of the plan for the "Economics" is easily adaptable to this rational use of "negativity."
We need only compare Marx's procedure in the *Grundrisse*
with that in *Capital* to appreciate the true dimensions of that
conceptual transmutation. Had he introduced the rubric on
wage labor into that of capital, he would have consequently
been obliged to abandon the methodological premise of his
work, namely, negativity "put back on its feet." In other
words, he would have had to renounce the "materialist" foundation of the dialectical method.

The two-fold transition from capital to wage labor—in its
positive aspect through the transformation of agricultural laborers into wage laborers (clearing of estates), and in its negative aspect through the dissolution of landed property as private property and its transfer to the hands of the state (ground
rent being converted into public rent)—finally leads to the "negation" of capital by wage labor. "The negation [of landed
property] effected by wage labor is only the hidden negation of
capital and thus of itself as well. It must therefore be examined
now as an independent element in relation to capital."[56] The
relation between plan and method is clearly perceptible as an
obligatory order of priority for the economic categories determined by their level of abstraction—in the specific sense of a
maximum of concretion and complexity—on the one hand,
and as the degree of historic evolution of the three social
classes on the other.

The evident recourse to the virtues of Hegel's dialectic, often
perceptible in the pages of the *Grundrisse*, becomes in *Capital*

---

precisely what Marx and Engels did. The notion of universal movement and transformation [*Logik*, 1813] was discovered intuitively before it was applied to life and
society. It was proclaimed relative to society (1847) before it was illustrated in its
application to man (1859)." *Philosophic Notebooks*, Sept.–Dec. 1914. Cf. R. Dunay-
evskaya, *Marxism and Freedom* (New York: 1958), p. 331. Lenin was obviously
referring to the *Communist Manifesto* (1847) and to Darwin's *The Origin of Species*
(1859). In pursuit of traces of "materialism" in Hegel's dialectic, Lenin was apparently
uninterested in the problem we are dealing with here; he probably even ignored its
existence. But what are we to say of his disciples who discuss at length such aspects of
the dialectic without breathing a word about the plan of the "Economics"? See for
example, M. Rosental, *The Problems of the Dialectic in Marx's Capital* (Moscow:
1959); E. V. Ilienkov, *The Dialectic of the Abstract and the Concrete in Marx's
Capital* (Moscow: 1960) (in Russian).
   [56]*Grundrisse*, p. 190.

a procedure resembling parody. And we note this desire to "flirt" with the Hegelian style of exposition not only in the first chapters of *Capital* on the theory of value, but in the last chapter as well, a chapter that might also be taken as the natural conclusion of the work in its entirety, that is, of the sixth and last rubric of the "Economics." It would appear that Marx began to doubt his chances of finishing the first triad and therefore wanted to anticipate its dialectical conclusion. He first sketches briefly the "prehistory" of capital – the brutal expropriation of the individual independent peasant and craftsman, "free" and private owners of their means of production – then describes the second phase, the actual history of capital or the expropriation of the capitalist who is "the head of an army or troop of wage laborers." The process is accomplished "by the action of the immanent laws of capitalist production itself." As capital grows more and more concentrated in the hands of an ever smaller number of monopoly capitalists, science and technology progress and there is a growing "entanglement of all peoples in the net of the world-market, and with this, the international character of the capitalist regime." Finally, in introducing onto the historic scene new slaves transformed into new individuals and into new expropriators, Marx gives an unexpected illustration of the principle of contradiction borrowed from Hegel:

The capitalist mode of appropriation, consequence of the capitalist mode of production, and therefore capitalist private property, is the first negation of individual private property founded on individual labor. But capitalist production engenders with the necessity of a law of nature its own proper negation. It is the negation of the negation. It does not reestablish private property for the laborer but does institute individual property based on the acquisitions of the capitalist era: on cooperation and common ownership of the soil and the means of production produced themselves by labor.[57]

[57]*Capital*, Book I; *MEW* 23, p. 791. When rereading his text Marx may well have thought of readers less familiar with the dialectic of the Master whose seductive charm had influenced him once again, for he decided to go back to a more concrete and direct language. In fact, he ended the last chapter of *Capital* with two quotations from the *Communist Manifesto*, added in a footnote. Here the "negating agents" of capital appear as capital's "gravediggers."

We have deliberately referred to this chapter on the "Historical Tendency of Capitalist Accumulation" as the "final" chapter although it preceded rather than followed the chapter on "The Modern Theory of Colonialization" in the original edition of *Capital*: At the time the volume appeared, Marx was concerned with avoiding the

Dialectical formulas such as this must have naturally occurred to Marx when he was thinking ahead to the book on wage labor destined to reveal in detail the historical and dialectical process of the "negation" of capital. But it would be wrong to conclude that the absence of this work leaves an irremediable gap in Marx's writings.[58] This holds for the other books of the "Economics" as well: For example, we can piece together the outline of the book on the state from numerous expositions in his published and unpublished writings. As noted earlier, Marx established with some precision the conceptual limits of the theoretical field to be examined for the rubric on the state when first systematically arranging the various economic themes and categories. The state, the "synthesis" of society, the political institution *par exellence*, the fatal con-

censors' watchfulness and followed his political instinct rather than the dictates of logical reasoning. We therefore maintain that Marx consciously reversed the order of these two final chapters so that the work ended not on the triumphant note of the expropriation of the expropriators by the proletariat but with the "first negation of private property," the expropriation of the worker. He thus hoped to pass the censor in Prussia, where article 100 of the penal code branded as "high treason" "excitation to reciprocal hatred or disdain." This is why Engels thought that "prohibition of the book in Prussia would be possible in any event" (letter to Marx, Sept. 1, 1867; *MEW* 31, p. 334).

[58] Marx was not only the scientific theorist of the working-class movement but also the author of an implicit theory of ethical values. The ethical principle of working-class self-emancipation has been rightly taken up in the works of certain "Marxists" such as Anton Pannekoek, Rosa Luxemburg, and Paul Mattick. Especially in France during the early 1900s, the working-class movement was marked by a revolutionary syndicalism that in the eyes of Georges Sorel, its theoretician and protagonist, inaugurated the most "Marxian" in spirit of all social and revolutionary experiences; cf. Neil McInnes, "Georges Sorel: Aperçu sur les Utopies, les Soviets et le Droit nouveau," in *Cahiers de l'I.S.E.A.*, Series S, *Etudes de marxologie*, no. 5 (Jan. 1962), 81–112.

The first scientific effort executed truly in the spirit of Marx was uncontestably Rosa Luxemburg's *Akkumulation des Kapitals* (1913). Although she disregarded the problem of the plan for the "Economics," she did recognize that the manuscript of Book II of *Capital* was left unfinished. Exploiting the possibilities of Marx's method of abstraction, moreover, in fulfilling the promise held in her work's subtitle: to furnish "a contribution to the economic explication of imperialism." Despite the insufficiencies of her demonstration, the basic inspiration of the writing was certainly genial. That her "contribution" incited debates and controversies within the ranks of the Marxist school was due to her courageous, independent thinking, while her tragic personal destiny symbolized the fate of the working-class movement under the stifling aegis of political parties. This independence of spirit can be found in a small handful of authors whose "Marxism" reduces essentially to an ethic of working-class self-emancipation; see Serge Bricianer, *Pannekoek et les Conseils ouvriers* (Paris: 1969). Paul Mattick, whose affinities with the Dutch Marxist Pannekoek are evident, has kept alive Marx's critical approach in the field of contemporary economic theory; see his *Marx and Keynes* (Boston: P. Sargent, 1969).

sequence of the division of labor, is open to analysis and criticism as a complex of apparently strange factors and institutions such as the unproductive classes, taxation, public debt, credit, population, colonies, emigration.

When preparing his "Critique of Politics and Political Economy" twelve years earlier, Marx elaborated in one of his notebooks the following plan, which, in covering only political and juridical topics, seems rather rudimentary in comparison to the later scheme:

1. The *history of the genesis of the modern state* or the *French Revolution.*
   The *presumptuous exaggeration of the political element,* confounded with the state in antiquity. The revolutionaries opposed to bourgeois society. Bisection of each individual into a bourgeois and a political being.

2. *Proclamation of the rights of man* and the *state constitution.* Individual freedom and public power.
   Liberty, civil equality and unity. Popular sovereignty.

3. The *state* and *bourgeois society.*

4. The *representative state* and the *Charter.* The representative constitutional state; the representative democratic state.

5. *Separation of powers.* Legislative power and executive power.

6. *Legislative power* and legislative bodies. Political clubs.

7. *Executive power.* Centralization and hierarchy. Centralization and political civilization. Federalism and industrialism. *State administration* and *local administration.*

8. *Judicial power* and *law.*

9. The *nation* and the *people.*

10. *Political parties.*

11. *Suffrage,* the struggle for the *abolition* of the state and bourgeois society.[59]

This outline constitutes an extensive program of research and exposition to be realized within the framework of the

---

[59]*MEW* 3, p. 537 (Marx's numbering for the last four rubrics was originally 8', 8", 9', 9").

"Economics." And let us insist on this point once again, it was not by reason of any change in plan that Marx never wrote the book on the state! If we examine with great care the extant plans and schemes of the "Economics" and of *Capital* in particular, along with the thoughts on methodology to be extracted from various unfinished and finished works, we may conjecture – if 'understand' is too strong a word – the nature of the logical relation between the three last rubrics of the plan: the state, foreign trade, and world market. We are led to this realization by the notion of the "transgression" or encroachment of civil society on the state and, moreover, by the notion of the state as an "emanation" of civil society, the former being merely the corollary of the latter.[60] Marx committed himself to treating the problems of foreign trade and the world market in separate works by his choice of a principle of abstraction. With this principle as his basis he developed a method of research similar to that of the physicist observing "physical phenomena where they occur in their most typical form and most free from disturbing influence."[61] Thus, in order to account for the formation of capital, Marx supposed a perfect equality between the price and value of a commodity "in order that the phenomena may be observed in their purity and our observations not interfered with by disturbing circumstances that have nothing to do with the process in question."[62] Furthermore, to explain accumulation through the transformation of surplus value into capital, Marx's method demands that foreign trade be excluded from the analysis:

In order to examine the object of our investigation in its integrity, free from all disturbing subsidiary circumstances, we must treat the whole commercial world as one nation and assume that the capitalist mode of production has been established everywhere and become dominant in all branches of production.[63]

[60]It has been suggested recently that the relationship of the last three rubrics of the "Economics," and indeed the relationship of all six rubrics as falling into two triads, parallels the logical and thematic development in the latter part of Hegel's *Rechtsphilosophie*. Cf. J. O'Malley, "Marx, Marxism and Method," in *Varieties of Marxism*, ed. S. Avineri (The Hague: Nijhoff, 1977), pp. 7–41, esp. pp. 22–5.

[61]*Capital*, Book I; *MEW* 23, p. 12.

[62]*Capital*, Book I; *MEW* 23, p. 180. That Marx consistently respected this principle may be seen in remarks such as the following: "The category of wages does not yet really exist at this stage in our exposition" (Ibid., p. 59).

[63]*Capital*, Book I; *MEW* 23, p. 607.

And although there can be no capitalist production without foreign trade, this heuristic fiction must be employed for the sake of the method of abstraction:

It can therefore only create confusion to include foreign commerce into the analysis of the value of products produced annually without bringing in any new elements of the problem or of its solution. For this reason we must disregard it entirely.[64]

Of course, these remarks are by no means exhaustive enough to permit an adequate notion of what the form of the book dealing with foreign trade would have been; nor do they add substantially to the initial plan of 1857, although Marx's later writings suggest that he would have oriented his study toward the international division of labor and international exchanges. It is equally difficult to conjecture about the probable structure of the final book of the "Economics" that, according to the first plan, was to have treated crises as well as the world market. Still, Marx did leave a few statements, notably in unpublished manuscripts, from which we can glean an impression of what he would have made out of this rubric. Had he finished the "Economics," he would have used these remarks in constructing the conclusion to this rubric, the last of the six, destined to highlight the "contradictions" of capitalism as a universal phenomenon, of capitalist production as a "totality" supported and nurtured by the world market. In the final analysis, the "historic task" of the capitalist mode of production is to create this world market and to develop the productive forces, the material bases, for a new mode of production.[65]

The germs of crisis inherent in the credit system are themselves signs of a future renewal that is also presaged by two forms of capitalism's sublimation (*Aufhebung*) within that very system of production: the joint-stock companies and the working men's cooperatives. This is what Marx calls, using once again the language of the Hegelian dialectic, the "negation" (or

[64]*Capital*, Book II; *MEW* 24, p. 466. Here Marx is following the example of his teacher Sismondi. H. Grossmann, who certainly knew of this methodological principle, nevertheless dared to speak of Marx's "completed system" and in this respect opposed Georg Lukács who defended the thesis of Rosa Luxemburg; cf. Grossmann, *Die Änderung* ... , p. 336; and G. Lukács, *Geschichte und Klassenbewusstsein.* (Berlin: 1923), p. 336. Lukács nonetheless elevated his favored "category of the totality" into a "principle of the revolution" whose abandonment would, in his view, be tantamount to the collapse of "the entire system of Marxism" (Ibid.).

[65]*Capital*, Book III; *MEW* 25, p. 457.

sublimation: *Aufhebung*) of the capitalist mode of production within the capitalist mode of production itself.[66] It represents the limit of an economic process that, from the standpoint of capital, succeeds in transforming the active agent of capital into a simple manager in charge of capital belonging to another, that is, in separating ownership of the means of production and surplus labor from the function exercised in the real process of reproducing capital. From the standpoint of labor, it represents the first break in the old system because the working men as associates in an enterprise become themselves the masters of their means of production. Freed from the personal authority of the capitalist within the very framework of this system, they prefigure the men who will live in that future time when associated labor will have been extended over entire nations and a new mode of production will have been instituted:

The capitalist joint-stock companies no less than the production co-operatives are to be considered forms of transition from the capitalist mode of production into the associative mode, with the sole difference that in the first the antagonism has been overcome negatively, and in the second positively.[67]

As an economist in the tradition of Adam Smith and David Ricardo, Marx's ambition was not to construct any scientific or philosophical system of thought but simply to study the "physiology of bourgeois society,"[68] although — in contrast to his teachers — from the viewpoint of a critique of the capitalist system and bourgeois mode of existence. If he was ultimately unable to provide the integral scientific proof that man-become-human and society-become-social are historic necessities, he nevertheless did succeed in demonstrating, with eloquent emphasis provided by the story of his own life, the ethical necessity of a human emancipation, the dream of all utopians before him.

The critique of the bourgeois mode of production and its economic categories did not alone suffice for Marx's vision: In the societies dominated by capital and the state he saw as well the germ of constructive elements and factors for a new system. His refusal to concoct and prescribe recipes for the cook-pots of the future, that is, to imitate his utopian precursors and

[66]Ibid., p. 454.
[67]Ibid., p. 456.
[68]*Theories of Surplus-Value; MEW* 26/2, pp. 162–3.

teachers, in no way signified the negation of utopia, but rather its sublimation. His projected critique, outlined beginning in 1844, was to be followed by a series of writings exposing the "positive conception."[69] Marx wanted to begin this second project in preparing, together with Moses Hess and Engels, a "History of Socialism and Communism Since the 17th Century."[70] In a notebook dated 1844–7 we find the following scheme, most probably elaborated in view of the new, but never developed, historical project:

Morelly	Cercle social	Bentham
Mably	Hébert	Godwin
Babeuf	Leroux	
Buonarotti	Leclerc	
Holbach		Helvetius
Fourier		*Saint-Simon*
	Owen	
	(Lalande)	
		The writings
Considerant	*Producteur, Globe*	of the school
Cabet		*Dezamy. Gay.*

Fraternité, l'Egalitaire, etc., l'Humanitaire, etc. Proudhon[71]

This arrangement evidently represents more than an inventory of names distributed at random across the paper; rather, it corresponds to a carefully determined chronological and logical order of succession, to a personal study program and publication project that were to lead Marx in his research to discover the revolutionary access to utopia's historical realization.

[69]*The Holy Family*, Preface; *MEW* 2, p. 8.

[70]Engels to Marx (Mar. 7, 1845): "Here we propose to translate Fourier and in general bring out a 'Library of the Best Socialist Writers'. . . . You can suggest to us the writings of the Frenchmen you think best suited for translation in the Library." A few days later, Engels spoke again of this project, emphasizing that the choice of texts should be made according to their "positive contents" for the present day and, preferably, with attention to their chronological order: "Because we two have gotten this idea in our heads, it must be realized at any price – I mean the 'Library.' Hess will be pleased to join us, and I shall as well, as soon as I have some free time" (Mar. 17, 1845). The authors mentioned included Fourier, Owen, the Saint-Simonians, Morelly. Cf. *MEW* 27, pp. 22, 24–5. The project was discontinued after the publisher Leske turned it down.

[71]*MEGA* I, 5, p. 549. A list of those books in Marx's possession at the time he left Cologne in 1849 is to be found in *Ex Libris Karl Marx und Friedrich Engels*, ed. B. Kaiser and I. Werchan (Berlin: Dietz Verlag, 1967), pp. 212–20. Here we note among others the presence of works by: Campanella, Louis Blanc, Bakunin, Weitling, Thomas Paine, Lorenz Stein, Reybaud, Pecqueur, etc.

To the rigorous methodological plan for the "Economics" as the scientific critique of capital and the state, he added another project no less methodical in its form and portentous in its significance for today's world: to reveal the "rational core" of utopia as the model of a human environment that is to be constructed by a species now at the crossroads of its destiny.

5

A visionary legacy to Russia

Europe or Asia?

Such is Russian propaganda, infinitely diversified, in keeping with the peoples and the countries. Yesterday she was telling us: "I am Christianity." Tomorrow she will say to us: "I am socialism . . . "

Jules Michelet, *Légendes démocratiques du nord*, Paris, 1854

Historians of the past century saw Russia as a sphinx whose riddles were contained in the simple yet significant question: Europe or Asia? Even as late as the eve of World War I the spiritual and cultural allegiance of this gigantic country still seemed uncertain.[1] Her wartime participation on the side of the Entente and the revolution that broke out two and a half years later finally revealed the long-concealed secret of Russia's historical decision by irrevocably linking her fate to that of Western Europe, one of Peter the Great's own aspirations. The revolution, and especially the overthrow of czarism, had had its prologue in 1905 and was long overdue. It therefore came as no surprise outside Russia, and certainly it was no surprise to Western Europe. What attentive observers had not expected, however, was that the leaders of a victorious political party that professed its adherence to "scientific socialism" would, in November 1917, proclaim the revolution to be a "step towards socialism," mediated and assured by the dicta-

---

[1]Dieter Groh has provided a very useful treatment of the points at issue, drawing from the pertinent literature in his *Russland und das Selbstverständnis Europas. Ein Beitrag zur europäischen Geistesgeschichte* (Neuwied: 1961). Earlier works on this same topic include: Thomas G. Masaryk, *Russland und Europa. Studien über die geistigen Strömungen in Russland* (Jena: 1913) (cf. Alexander Brückner, "Russland und Europa" in *Archiv für die Geschichte des Sozialismus und der Arbeiterbewegung* VI (1916), 84 ff.); K. Nötzel, *Die Grundlagen des geistigen Russlands* (Jena: 1917). On Russia's philosophical interpretation of its own history see Alexander von Schelting, *Russland und Europa im russischen Geschichtsdenken* (Bern: 1948).

torship of the proletariat.[2] As recently as February of that
same year the members of all Russian social classes, and in
particular the immediate participants themselves, had recognized the bourgeois-democratic nature of this revolution.
Now, the politico-military general staff resolved that the rule
of the elite would be regarded as a manifestation of the social
will and, what is more, as a mandate for social reorganization.
It is highly probable that neither the overwhelming majority of
peasants nor the numerically weak industrial working class
understood this decision as the expression of their own conscious aims. More important to the Russian peasants than any
political ideology was their legal right to seize land; the
workers inevitably saw the Bolshevist prospect of constituting
a state power based on soviets of worker, soldier, and peasant
deputies as the only way to bring the economic structure of
their war-torn country under their own control. Thus Lenin
and Trotsky could have had no illusions about the peasant and
worker masses possessing enough intellectual maturity to comprehend and accept as the confirmation of their own will the
Bolshevist postulate of a "social revolution led by the working
class."[3] It was therefore clear from the outset that the future
development of all facets of Russian society, material as well
as intellectual, would be subject to the prescriptions of the
party elite that had now become the supreme power. The peasant masses had been the mainstay of the Russian revolution
that began, as we read in the *Communist Manifesto*, with
reference to the Western European proletariat, as the "independent movement of the overwhelming majority in the interests of the overwhelming majority."[4] However, it was transformed into a type of revolution not anticipated by the
founders of materialist sociology: It became the independent
movement of a politically mature minority in the interests – no
doubt honorably understood – of the immense majority. That
Marx and Engels did not foresee such a development is no
evidence of a defect in their theory; rather, it indicates the
incompatibility of the dictatorial Bolshevist ideology with the

[2]V. I. Lenin, "From the Central Committee . . . ," *Pravda* 182, Nov. 7, 1917; CW
26, p. 307.
[3]V. I. Lenin, "Theses on the question of Immediate Conclusion of a Separate and
Annexationist Peace," *Pravda* 34, Feb. 24, 1918; CW 26, p. 447.
[4]*MEW* 4, p. 473.

notion of the proletarian dictatorship that Marx had conceived for the industrially developed countries that obeyed the laws of the capitalist economic system. Only a thorough examination of the circumstances that led the Soviet Union – irrespective of Stalin – to proclaim itself the first "socialist state" and to be recognized as such, can explain why its domestic and foreign policies can at the same time contradict the value judgments of Marx's proletarian-socialist ethics and yet be scientifically interpreted in terms of Marx's materialist theory of history. This theory demonstrates, on the one hand, the impossibility of a socialist way of life under the historical conditions of the 1917 Russian Revolution; on the other hand, it explains why a ruling elite found it necessary to use "socialist" ideology as an *ersatz* doctrine or religion: With the state power in its hands this elite was bent on making its minority rule credible and thus acceptable under the guise of a "dictatorship of the proletariat." The subtle dialectic maneuver could be accomplished only by inverting the materialist theory of revolution and then contrasting this inversion as "genuine" Marxism to "vulgar" and "scholastic" Marxism. Incredible as it may seem, the "Marxist" thesis used to justify the ideology of this elite can be reduced to the following theorem: Precisely because in October 1917 Russia fulfilled none of the economic, social, and intellectual conditions that in Marxian revolutionary theory are the prerequisites for a proletarian dictatorship and for a socialist upheaval, it succeeded in realizing the "first stage of the world revolution," "the first proletarian state," the "first step towards socialism"![5]

This theorem is the single logical conclusion that can be drawn from the Bolshevist theory of "unequal historical development" and its corollary of the "weakest link in the chain of capitalism."[6] In Marxist terms, these propositions "dialecti-

[5]Trotsky's "theory of permanent revolution" provides a characteristic example of his perfidious manipulation of dialectics later empirically refuted. As late as 1928 – in exile – he quoted with pride the following passage from an article of 1906: "In an economically backward country the proletariat can come to power more easily than in the advanced capitalist countries. The notion of some automatic dependence of the proletarian dictatorship on the country's technical forces and capacities is a prejudice of an 'economic' materialism which has been simplified to the utmost. This viewpoint has nothing to do with Marxism." *The Permanent Revolution* (New York: Pioneer Publishers, 1965), p. 57.

[6]Basically this "theory" is limited to apodictic assertions or meaningless trivialities that simply decree the fait accompli of the party victory as the indubitable guarantee of conformity to any arbitrary formulation of social or historical laws. See on this

cally" cancel the "founders' " critical, materialist sociology of revolution; they represent an emotionally founded reversion to the beliefs of many nineteenth-century Russian intellectuals that there is an essential difference between Russian man and European man and that Russia's vocation is to achieve the socialist or religious salvation of the world. The notion of Russia's historical mission, defined either in social, political, or religious terms, that is, the "Russian Idea," is found, not in Marx, but in Chaadayev, Herzen, and the Slavophiles; in Chernyshevsky, Tkachov, and Bakunin; in Dostoyevsky and Berdyaev – to name just a few important representatives of the multiple forms of Russian messianism.[7]

The historical mission of the bourgeoisie

Whether interpreted as socioethical, pragmatic political, or pseudoreligious, the notion of a historical mission, not only of the modern working class, but also of the bourgeoisie in the process of freeing itself from feudal modes of production and life, is the pillar of Marx's conception – or model – of history.[8] To be sure, Marx sought to establish the "materialist" nature of that consciousness of great revolutionary tasks that he ascribed to both the exploiters and the exploited, deriving it from the pressure of the economic conditions of existence. But this did not prevent him – or his student Engels – from playing

"dialectics of retrogression" Alfred G. Meyer, *Leninism* (Cambridge, Mass.: Harvard University Press, 1957), pp. 257 ff. In the introductory chapter of his *History of the Russian Revolution* Trotsky appeals to the so-called law of combined development, according to which the "revolution" had in a few months brought the proletariat to power, with the communist party at the head!

[7]Cf. Nicolai Berdyaev, *L'Idée russe. Problèmes essentiels de la pensée russe au XIXe et début du XXe siècle* (Tours: 1969; the original Russian edition appeared in Paris in 1946). According to Berdyaev, 1917 proved that in keeping with Russia's special religious mission the Russian revolution could only be socialist, not in the sense of Marx and Engels, but in the spirit of the specific Russian tradition that was represented by Tkachov (Lenin's predecessor!) rather than Plekhanov. Berdyaev's mystical view of history can reasonably be rejected even if it is true that Russia's revolutionary vocation is a main component of Bolshevik ideology. Cf. Lenin, who saw in the backwardness of his country one of the historical causes for the fact that the revolution broke out earlier there than in other countries and "that as regards its *political* system Russia had overtaken the advanced countries in a few months." *The Impending Catastrophe and How to Combat it*, written in Sept. 1917; CW 25, p. 364.

[8]Cf. especially the description of the revolutionary role of the bourgeoisie in *The Manifesto of the Communist Party; SW* 1, pp. 33 ff.

the role of moralizing mentor throughout his political career, and accordingly from exhorting now the bourgeoisie now the proletariat to fulfill its historical tasks. The first imperative was to channel toward new revolutionary outbreaks the liberal and national forces that had been restrained by the restoration policy of the Holy Alliance, forces that had been accumulating in the Western European bourgeoisie since the French Revolution. It was equally important to prepare as favorably as possible the terrain in which the fledgling workers' movement could act and develop, by making impossible, once and for all, any reversion to absolutism.[9] A few months before the February revolution Marx circumscribed unambiguously and with uncommon precision the historical relations between the two main classes of modern society, justifying "materialistically" his and Engels's abiding interest in liberalism and bourgeois democracy:

Why should they [the German workers] . . . prefer the brutal oppression of the absolute regime with its semi-feudal consequences to direct *bourgeois control?* The workers know very well not only that the bourgeoisie must make them broader political concessions than does the absolute monarchy, but also that in serving business and industry the bourgeoisie involuntarily creates the conditions for the unification of the working class, and the workers' unification is the primary prerequisite for their victory. They know that the withering away of *bourgeois* property relations is not achieved by preserving *feudal* relations. They know that the revolutionary movement of the bourgeoisie against the feudal estates and the absolute monarchy can only hasten their own revolutionary movement. They know that their own battle with the bourgeoisie can erupt only on the day when the bourgeoisie is victorious . . . They can and must assume the *bourgeois revolution* as a condition of the *workers'* revolution. But at no time can they consider it their goal.[10]

The fervor of this statement reveals the profound meaning of Marx's lifelong, vehement indictments of the political ideals of the Western European bourgeoisie. These accusations showed Marx to be one of the most consistent revolutionary democrats of his time; what is more he considered himself duty

[9]Cf. Heinrich Scharp, *Abschied von Europa?* (Frankfurt am Main: 1953), p. 166.
[10]Marx, "Die moralisierende Kritik . . . ," *Deutsche Brüsseler Zeitung,* Nov. 18, 1847; *MEW* 4, p. 352. Marx and Engels referred to this article eighteen years later when attacking the "socialism of the Royal Prussian Government" represented by Johann Schweitzer in the *Sozial-Democrat; MEW* 16; p. 79.

bound to act as the political educator of the bourgeoisie and, after the March revolution, of the German bourgeoisie in particular. In this quasipermanent attitude of a liberal attacking a bourgeoisie that clings to reactionary conservatism we note the evident *ethical* tendency of his "scientific" socialism. If it may be rightly said of Edmund Burke that he "incorporated the genuine political concerns of liberalism into the conservative world view,"[11] then it can be affirmed with even greater justification that Marx incorporated these same genuine political concerns into his socialist theory of history.

Only in this context can we understand why Marx and Engels occasionally—and not only in the revolutionary year 1848—used "Jacobin slogans": Their Jacobinism was not (as Karl Korsch held during his period of critical reevaluation of latter-day Marxist mythology) proof that their revolutionary theory was historically qualified and limited;[12] rather, Jacobinism appears as a political necessity for a particular historical phase of development to be borne actively by the bourgeoisie as long as the social terrain of class struggle was obstructed by the overgrowth of feudal absolutism. In a word, it was a bourgeois-moral weapon against a bourgeoisie that was betraying its *historical* task in favor of *momentary* interests, against a bourgeoisie that had the responsibility of the *revolution* yet had formed a treacherous alliance with the *counterrevolution*.[13] How deeply the bourgeois Jacobinist element was rooted in the whole perspective of Marx's and Engels's theory of proletarian revolution is revealed in the following passage quoted from a series of articles in which Marx critically evaluated the German bourgeoisie in the light of revolutionary history after the dispersion of the Prussian national assembly:

[11]Cf. Scharp, *Abschied von Europa?*, p. 164.

[12]Cf. Siegfried Bahne, "Zwischen 'Luxemburgismus' und 'Stalinismus.' Die 'ultralinke' Opposition in der KPD," *Vierteljahrshefte für Zeitgeschichte*, no. 4 (Oct. 1961), pp. 378 ff. Bahne deals with the view developed by Karl Korsch in various essays that not only "Trotskyism" and "Stalinism" are founded "on the 'neo-narodnik' negation of the possibility of normal capitalist development in Russia," but that even Lenin himself propounded "with full consciousness and in contradiction to all his earlier explanations the new Marxist myth of the essentially socialist character of the soviet state in Winter 1920–21" (quoted from *Der Gegner* no. 3, p. 11). Bahne, "Zwischen Luxemburgismus und Stalinismus," p. 377. See by the same author "Der 'Trotzkismus' in Geschichte und Gegenwart," *Vierteljahrshefte für Zeitgeschichte*, I (1967), pp. 56 ff.

[13]Cf. for example Marx, "Sieg der Kontrerevolution in Wien," *Neue Rheinische Zeitung*, Nov. 7, 1848; *MEW* 5, pp. 455 ff.

Unlike the French bourgeoisie of 1789 the Prussian bourgeoisie was not the class that represented the *whole of* modern society against the representatives of the old society, the monarchy and the nobility. It had sunk to a kind of *estate,* as markedly opposed to the crown as to the people . . . from the beginning it was apt to betray the people and to compromise with the crowned representative of the old society, for it itself belonged to the old society; it represented, not the interests of a new society against the old, but the renewal of interests within an obsolete society; it found itself at the helm of the revolution not because the people stood behind it, but because they pushed it ahead of them; it was in the forefront because it represented not the initiative of a new society, but only the rancor of an old society . . . slogans instead of ideas, intimidated by the world tumult, exploiting the world tumult – directionless energy, plagiarism in all directions, commonplace, because not original, original in its commonness, haggling with its own wishes, without initiative, lacking confidence in itself, and in the people, without an historical vocation – a cursed old man who saw himself damned to lead and mislead a robust people's first torrent of youth in his own decrepit interests – sans eyes, sans ears, sans teeth, sans everything – thus the *Prussian bourgeoisie* found itself at the helm of the Prussian state after the March revolution.[14]

The collapse of the revolution proved not only that the bourgeoisie did not want to play the "utmost revolutionary role" proclaimed for it in the *Communist Manifesto* but, further, that it was far from wanting to create the world in its own image as the *Manifesto* had announced in dithyrambic tones.[15] Not until Marx resumed his studies in revolutionary history and in political economy in London was he better able to understand the causes and course of the past events and to estimate more accurately the prospects of the European workers' movement. He realized that, because of the discovery of gold in California and Australia and the very gradual formation of a European colonial empire, the historical role of the bourgeoisie and its capital was far from its conclusion. However, this insight did not prevent him from continuing to act as the nagging conscience of a bourgeoisie that was selling itself out to the reaction, and two decades of

[14]Marx, "Die Bourgeoisie und die Kontrerevolution," in *Neue Rheinische Zeitung,* Dec. 15, 1848; *MEW* 6, pp. 108 ff.
[15]*MEW* 4, p. 464.

the Bonapartist regime in France. The German bourgeoisie and petty bourgeoisie, both of whom sold out to the monarchy and to junkerdom,[16] offered him ample occasion to fulfill the same role.

To the problem of the barely developing bourgeois democracy was added the crisis produced by nationalist aspirations, a crisis that could be resolved ultimately only by destroying the system established by the great powers in 1815.

The irony of history, so often celebrated by Marx and Engels, willed that the adherents to revolutionary communism who founded modern labor politics were necessarily advocates of bourgeois revolutionary liberalism. By positing the overthrow of bourgeois democracy by the proletariat as the first goal of the incipient workers' movement they committed themselves to support the realization of this democracy. Democracy was the price the capital-accumulating bourgeoisie had to pay the exploited producers – moral compensation, as it were, for their material oppression.

The mission of the proletariat

In order to fulfill the mandate of the French Revolution, bourgeois liberalism in the nineteenth century was obliged to center its European struggle on the formation of democratic constitutional nation-states. In view of this it is understandable why Marx and Engels directed their political and educational activity within the workers' movement chiefly toward spurring on "the organization of the proletariat into a class, and thus into a political party."[17] Here both the goal and the limits of their activity were sharply circumscribed by the central axiom of their theory of revolution, according to which the "historical spontaneous action" of the proletariat needs no alien so-called socialist or communist systems, no social plans concocted by systematizers, to develop into a world-liberating power.[18] The materialist conception of history that Marx and Engels elaborated in the mid-1840s was understood simply as a theoretical expression of the existing social movement, not as a "primer

---

[16] Cf. M. Rubel, *Marx devant de bonapartisme* (Paris/The Hague: 1960).
[17] *Manifesto of the Communist Party; SW* 1, p. 37.
[18] Ibid., p. 55.

for action" – let alone a "credo."[19] Their attempts to influence
the embryonic European workers' movement, first through the
Communist Correspondence Committees and then through the
Communist League, were designed mainly to add "elements of
education" to the working class.[20] When through the failure of
the revolution of 1848–9 the workers were deprived of "legal
means of party organization" – press, freedom of speech, and
the right of assembly – and secrecy was the only course left open
to the League, Marx felt he had to make clear to the representatives of bourgeois-reactionary legality that the League's goal
was "the formation, not of the future ruling party, but of the
future opposition party," and that its task was not to "prepare"
a revolution whose principal agents would be the bourgeoisie
and the middle classes.[21] Members of the League could and
must leave this preparation "to the general economic situation
and the classes directly participating in it," because otherwise
they "would have to relinquish their own party position and the
historical tasks which proceed from the general conditions of
existence of the proletariat itself."[22]

During the 1850s and at the beginning of the 1860s the
"Marx party" – a derogatory term that, if not invented by secret agents of the Prussian police, was popularized by them,
and that gained a certain public notoriety in Germany during
the Cologne communist trial – had no substantial contact with
the abating European workers' movement. High-quality jour-

[19]"Our theory is not a dogma but the exposition of an evolutionary process, a
process involving successive phases. To expect that the Americans will begin with the
full consciousness of the theory elaborated in the older industrial countries is to expect
the impossible." Engels to Florence Kelley-Wischnevetzky, Dec. 28, 1886; MEW 36,
p. 589. See also Engels to Florence Kelley-Wischnevetzky, Jan. 27, 1887; MEW 36,
pp. 597–8. "Our conception of history . . . is above all a guide for learning, no lever
for constructions à la Hegelian" (Engels to C. Schmidt, Aug. 5, 1890; MEW 37, p.
436). See Note 102.
[20]Cf. Manifesto of the Communist Party; SW 1, p. 37. Also Marx, Engels to Bebel,
Liebknecht, Bracke et al., Sept. 17/18, 1879; MEW 34, p. 406.
[21]Cf. Marx, Enthüllungen über den Kommunisten-Prozess zu Köln, 1853; MEW 8,
pp. 458 ff.
[22]Ibid., p. 458. Even the March 1850 address of the League's central committee to
the members, which was composed in a decidedly "Jacobin" spirit, authorizes no –
"Leninist" – party fetishism. The postulate of the "permanent revolution" presented
there stresses the progressive nature of the proletarian seizure of power as contrasted
to a sudden upheaval; hence the thesis that the foundation of a new society presupposed the previous rule of "petty bourgeois democracy," "the association of the proletarians not in one country alone but in all the ruling countries of the world," as well as
the concentration of the "decisive productive forces in the hands of the proletarians"
(MEW 7, pp. 244–54 passim).

nalism, an intensive study of economic theory and practice, and work on his "Economics" were Marx's main concerns during a period of personal financial difficulties, which Engels did his best to alleviate. This interim lasted almost fifteen years, and of necessity not the proletariat but the world bourgeoisie stands in the foreground of all the writings that stem from it. Expanding in a feverish drive for power, this bourgeoisie knew, despite financial and trade crises, how to enforce the economic law of capital upon the masses of workers who had apparently fallen into lethargy. Even after capitalism had withstood the international economic crisis of 1857, which Marx and Engels had foreseen as the beginning of its end, Marx continued to express his revolutionary optimism, yet in a way that suggests that henceforth, given the growing worldwide domination of the bourgeoisie and capitalism, he reckoned in longer periods of time when gauging the chances of socialism in Western Europe:

The real task of bourgeois society is to establish the world market, at least its contours, and the production based upon it. Since the world is round, it appears this has been achieved with the colonization of California and Australia and with the opening up of China and Japan. The difficult question for us is this: on the Continent the revolution is imminent and it will immediately assume a socialist character. Will it not necessarily be crushed in this small corner, since the new movement of bourgeois society is still ascendant in a much larger area?[23]

When Marx wrote these lines he was convinced that in spite of Austria's defeat in the Italian war the days of the Bonapartist empire were numbered and that a new European crisis would result in violent social and national upheavals whose revolutionary hearths would be Germany and France.[24] The "Marx party" had strongly condemned Lassalle's animosity toward Austria, which amounted to a justification of the politics of Napoleon III, while Karl Vogt's slander campaign gave Marx a welcome opportunity to settle polemically historical accounts with "imperial socialism" and its ally, the Russian czar, "liberator of peoples."[25] Reflecting on his post-1846 political ca-

[23]Marx to Engels, Oct. 8, 1858; MEW 29, p. 359.
[24]Cf. for example, Marx's article "A Prussian View of the War," New York Daily Tribune, June 10, 1859.
[25]Cf. Marx, Herr Vogt, 1860; MEW 14, pp. 385 ff., especially chapter 8, pp. 490 ff.

reer, Marx felt he had to return to the problem of the historically conditioned relation between the communist working-
class movement and the bourgeois-liberal movement: His concern was to break a lance for the moral purity of the party,
understood "in the eminently historical sense"[26] of the term,
and to make clear that his own revolutionary role was neither
that of the founder of a system nor that of a party dictator – as
his opponents insisted. He characterized his scientific task as
that of "critical insight into the conditions, course, and general
results of the actual social movement."[27] There remained the
accusation that in the *Communist Manifesto* he had elaborated
a "proletarian's catechism" expressing disdain for the bourgeoisie and esteem for the aristocracy.

Marx's reply is of decisive importance for the understanding
he and Engels had of their own activity as propagandists at a
time when political parties were first forming as part of the
nineteenth-century Western European workers' movement;
moreover, it may also be seen as an anticipatory criticism of
those twentieth-century socialist and communist party movements that have developed in the name of Marxism and in the
spirit of Lassalleanism. In *Herr Vogt* (1860) Marx presents,
with reference to earlier writings, his "way of conceiving the
relationship between the aristocracy, the bourgeoisie and the
proletariat":

The first section of the *Manifesto,* entitled "Bourgeois and Proletarians" . . . develops in detail the position that the economic and, therefore, in one form or another, the political *rule of the bourgeoisie* is
the basic condition both for the existence of the modern proletariat
and for the creation of the material conditions of its liberation. The
"development of the modern proletariat (see the *Revue der Neuen
Rheinischen Zeitung,* January 1850, p. 15) is conditioned through
and through by the development of the industrial bourgeoisie. Only
under the rule of the bourgeoisie does the proletariat rise to an
extended national level which enables its revolution to become national and itself create the modern means of production which become so many means for its revolutionary liberation. Only *the rule of
the bourgeoisie* materially uproots feudal society and levels the terrain *on which alone a proletarian revolution is possible.*" Therefore,
in that same *Revue* I declare that any proletarian movement in which

[26]Marx to Freiligrath, Feb. 29, 1860; *MEW* 30, p. 495.
[27]Marx, *Herr Vogt; MEW* 14, p. 449.

England does not participate is a "tempest in a teapot." Engels developed the same notion in 1845. Thus, in countries where the aristocracy in the continental sense . . . is still to be ousted there is lacking, in my view, the first condition of a proletarian revolution, namely, an *industrial proletariat* on a national scale.[28]

Concerning the relationship of the German workers to the bourgeois movement Marx likewise appealed to the *Communist Manifesto,* raising the fundamental validity of the theses presented there to the highest norm of a rationally founded theory of labor politics:

As soon as the bourgeois revolutionary appears in Germany the communist party will battle in common with the bourgeoisie against the absolute monarchy, feudal landed property, and the petty bourgeoisie. However, it will not neglect for an instant to develop in the working man as clear a consciousness as possible of the inimical opposition between bourgeoisie and proletariat.[29]

During the 1860s, which may be seen as probably the most decisive period both for the development of Marx's political theory and for the elaboration of his "Economics," Marx found himself for the first time in the position of defending his highest ethical norm, the principle of proletarian self-liberation, before a wider European forum. Two events—Lassalle's agitation, so important for the revitalization of the German labor movement, and the founding of the International Workingmen's Association, which represented a first attempt to surpass the limits of national efforts toward independence as the condition for the united action of the working classes in the economically developed countries—provided Marx with the long-desired opportunity of imparting those "elements of education" that he had acquired through painstaking, incessant study, to men whose actions he expected would radically revolutionize social conditions. In his battle against the charismatic antiliberal party politics of Lassalle and his heirs, on the one hand, and against the romantic-histrionic conspiratorial activity of Bakunin and the Western European and Russian versions of that activity on the other, Marx fought two tendencies within the labor movement that were diametrically opposed to the creative principle of proletarian self-emancipation. These tendencies would finally

[28]Ibid., pp. 449 ff.
[29]Ibid., p. 450.

flower only in the twentieth century under the guise of Marx-ism in its multiple variants.[30] It must not be forgotten that both Lassalle and Bakunin considered themselves to be Marx's disciples with respect to their rationally founded understand-ing of history. However, led by their own idiosyncrasies and charisma, they misused the master's social theory, using pla-giarism and propagandistic subterfuge as expedients to legiti-mate their unprincipled action. Lassalle was unacquainted with the term Marxism, which was probably invented by Bakunin in order to avenge himself on Marx by intentionally confusing the master and his disciples, as he did with all Marx's contemporary followers.[31] Bakunin, who believed the Russian peasantry would save the world, could have had no inkling that, scarcely four decades after his death, a party would come to power in his native land that would unite the contrasting tendencies of an elitist Lassallean Association and a disciplined anarchist sect of true believers.[32] When the Bol-shevist version of twentieth-century Marxism made political capital chiefly out of the intellectual heritage left by Lassalle and Bakunin, the cunning of history triumphed once again.

Asiatic despotism

Throughout their political careers, first as radical democrats, then as revolutionary communists, Marx and Engels fought Russian absolutism with a passion that could justly be called

[30]On Marx's relation to Lassalle see especially Marx's letter to Ludwig Kugelmann, Feb. 23, 1865; MEW 31, pp. 451 ff. He detested the dictatorial, imperious style of the "Realpolitiker" who shook Bismarck's hand "in the interest of the proletariat." See also Marx to Engels, Apr. 9, 1863, Jan. 30, 1865, and Feb. 18, 1865; MEW 30, pp. 340-1 and MEW 31, pp. 47-8, 76-7. Hans Mommsen gives a concise general description of Lassalle in his article "Lassalle" in Marxism, Communism and Western Society, vol. 5, C. D. Kernig ed. (New York: Herder and Herder, 1973), pp. 107-27. Cf. the latest, most detailed political biography of the founder of the Allgemeines deutscher Arbeiter-Verein by Shlomo Na'aman, Lassalle (Hannover: 1970). On Baku-nin's aristocratic anarchism see Ein Komplott gegen die Internationale Arbeiter-Assoziation; MEW 18, pp. 331-471. See also Marx's letter to Paul and Laura La-fargue, Apr. 19, 1870; MEW 32, pp. 673 ff.

[31]Cf. M. Rubel, "La Charte de la Première Internationale. Essai sur le marxisme dans l'A.I.T." Mouvement social, no. 51 (1965), 3 ff.; also M. Manale, "Aux Ori-gines du concept de 'Marxisme'," Cahiers de l'I.S.E.A., Série S, no. 17 (Oct. 1974), 1397-1430.

[32]On Lenin's positive assessment of Lassalle's political efficacy and conception of didactic dictatorship, see H. Mommsen, "Lassalle," pp. 125-6.

Russophobia.[33] That their theoretical justification for this anti-Russian attitude amounted to a condemnation is not so surprising when we consider that their conception of history was ruled from the beginning by ethical impulses; their development from bourgeois liberalism to anarchical communism thus seemed quite natural. In passing from apologetics for the democratic representative state in the period of the *Rheinische Zeitung* (1842) to an identification with the cause of the working class, Marx was led not by his critical study of political economy but by his break with Hegel's philosophy of the state in 1843 and his awakened interest in the history of the bourgeois revolution in its English, North American, and French manifestations.[34] The results of these historical studies are clearly evident in his unfinished *Critique of the Hegelian Philosophy of Right:* We find here both the beginnings of his "materialist" interpretation of the relation between the state and economics and an effort to define a concept of democracy that far exceeds the limits of right as understood in bourgeois law. At this time Marx recognized that Hegel's concept of the state as "the reality of the moral idea" was upon closer scrutiny "a religion of private property."[35] Undoubtedly the profound reflections of Alexis de Tocqueville and Thomas Hamilton on the inherently revolutionary consequences of North American democracy inspired in Marx the conviction that communism would prove to be a "historical necessity" under liberal bourgeois economic and legal conditions. To Hegel's mystical, metaphysical conception of the state, which ultimately demonstrated that the monarch is the subjectivization of the state and the self-embodiment of popular sovereignty, Marx opposed the ethical, humanist concept of creative, multi-form democracy. This concept permitted him shortly thereafter to take the logically consistent step toward communism as the ideal of a stateless and classless social order. The following

[33]On the anti-Russianism of the German radicals produced by the left-Hegelian school, see Helmut Krause, *Marx und Engels und das zeitgenössische Russland* (Giessen: 1958), pp. 12 ff. Much less instructive is the short work by W. N. Kotow, *Karl Marx und Friedrich Engels über das russische Volk* (East Berlin: 1953).

[34]A survey of Marx's historical studies in Kreuznach in 1843 is given in *MEGA* I, 1/2, pp. 118–36.

[35]Cf. *Kritik des hegelschen Staatsrechts, MEW* 1, pp. 203–331. Cf. Joseph O'Malley's "Introduction" to Karl Marx, *Critique of Hegel's Philosophy of Right* (Cambridge: 1970), pp. ix ff.

quotation helps us grasp why Marx at times waged his battle against French, German, and especially Russian absolutism with a hatred that betrays the fundamentally idealist impulse behind his "materialist" understanding of history:

Democracy is the *resolved enigma* of all constitutions. Here the constitution, not only *in itself,* with respect to its essence, but with respect to *existence,* to actuality, always goes back to its real basis, the *actual man,* the *actual people* and is established as their *own* work. The constitution appears as what it is, the free product of men . . . Just as religion does not create man, but man religion, so the constitution does not create the people, but the people the constitution. In a certain sense democracy is to all other forms of the state what Christianity is to all other religions. Christianity is religion *par excellence,* the *essence of religion,* deified man as a *particular religion.* So also, democracy is the *essence of every state constitution,* socialized man as a *particular* state constitution . . . All other forms of state are related to democracy as its Old Testament. Man does not exist for the sake of the law, but the law for the sake of man; democracy is *human existence,* whereas in the other forms man has only *legal existence.* This is the specific character of democracy.[36]

A few months later Marx undertook a critique of political emancipation that brought him logically very close to anarchism: "The existence of the state and the existence of slavery are inseparable,"[37] he concluded.

We may assume with near certitude that when writing this sentence Marx was thinking not only of Prussia but also of its "protector," Russia, because *Vorwärts!* from its first appearance to its demise, was constantly concerned with Russian internal affairs insofar as they had become known through the sensational revelations of the Marquis de Custine.[38] In many of Marx's later anti-Russian writings there are thoughts and stylistic usages that recall de Custine's formulations. The French aristocrat had traveled to Russia in search of arguments against representative forms of government and in support of his monarchist convictions; he returned committed to the constitutional state. Passages from de Custine's report of his trav-

[36]*MEW* I, p. 231.
[37]"Kritische Randglossen . . .", in *Vorwärts!,* Aug. 7, 1844; *MEW* I, p. 347.
[38]Beginning with the fourth number of the Paris *Vorwärts!* (Jan. 13, 1844) many articles appeared dealing with de Custine's book together with refutations of it prompted and paid for by the Russian czar. See D. Groh, *Russland . . . ,* pp. 184 ff.

els may well have been deeply inscribed in Marx's memory. De Custine first lets an old Russian prince speak:

The barbarians invaded Russia scarcely 400 years ago; while the West was subjected to this crisis 1400 years ago. A thousand years of civilization makes an immeasurable difference in the culture of nations.[39]

The complete despotism which prevailed among us was established when serfdom was being abolished in the rest of Europe. Since the invasion of the Mongols, the Slavs, who until then were one of the freest peoples in the world, have become slaves, first of the victors, then of their own princes. Serfdom arose among them at that time not just *de facto* but as the constitutive law of the society. In Russia it has devalued a man's word to the point where it is seen only as a snare. Our government lives on lies, for like the slave the tyrant too fears the truth.[40]

Not only does Russian despotism count feelings and ideas for nothing, it alters the facts, battles the evident and wins the battle because among us the evident has as few advocates as does honor when opposing power.[41]

De Custine's first letters, dated from St. Petersburg, contain diplomatic testimony and remarks by historians familiar to Marx, including the Russian author Karamsin. De Custine quotes the description of Czar Vassily III Ivanovich taken from the correspondence, mentioned by Karamsin, of von Herberstein, the German ambassador to the court, and then adds:

This letter, written more than three hundred years ago, describes the Russians of that time just as I see them now. Like the envoy of Maximilian, I ask myself whether the character of this nation created the autocracy or whether the autocracy created the Russian character, and I am as much at a loss to answer the question as was the German diplomat.[42]

With a feeling of horror de Custine reports on the unanimity between the people and the government. What amazes him is not the fact that the czar does not discourage this idolization

[39] A. de Custine, *Russland im 1839*, trans. A. Dietmann (Leipzig: 1843), Vol. I, p. 106 [37]. Bracketed page numbers in this and subsequent references refer to *Journey for our Time. The Russian Journals of the Marquis De Custine*, ed. and trans. Phyllis Penn Kohler (Chicago: Henry Regnery, 1951).
[40] Ibid., p. 108f [37–8].
[41] Ibid., p. 138 [44].
[42] Ibid., p. 178 [77].

but that in a giant country like Russia no voice is raised to protest against this idolatry of absolute sovereignty:

Among the voices which recount these accomplishments to the glory of this one man, not one separates itself from the chorus to protest for the sake of truth against the amazing deeds of autocracy. One can describe the Russians, great and small, as drunk with slavery.[43]

Nor did the condition of the Russian peasantry escape the Marquis:

Only with great effort can we form an accurate idea of the true situation of this class of men who have no acknowledged rights but nonetheless are the nation. Deprived of everything by law, they are not so much morally degraded as socially debased; they have intelligence, occasionally pride, but cunning is the dominant element in their character and in their whole mode of life. No one has the right to reproach them for this only too natural consequence of their situation. These people are always on guard against their masters, whose shameless treachery they must feel at every moment, and with great craftiness they get even for the masters' dishonesty towards their serfs.[44]

The contrast between Western civilization and Russian barbarism, which was current among the important bourgeois historians of the nineteenth century and which Marx and Engels unhesitatingly appropriated, is expressed in a "Marxist" fashion by de Custine:

It is all too easy here in Petersburg to be fooled by the appearance of civilization. When you see the Court and the people connected with it, you believe you are in a country much advanced in culture and political economy; however, when you consider the relations that exist between the various classes of society; when you realize how few in number these classes are, and finally when you observe in detail the customs and conditions, then you perceive beneath the revolting magnificence what it scarcely conceals, genuine barbarism.[45]

The cowardly obsequiousness of the Russian nobility and of all higher levels of Russian society prompted the aristocratic observer to a general reflection that reminds us of Marx:

[43]Ibid., p. 180 [78].
[44]Ibid., p. 217f [93].
[45]Ibid., p. 223 [97].

An oppressed people always deserves its suffering; tyranny is the work of nations. Within fifty years either the civilized world will fall once again under the yoke of barbarism, or Russia will undergo a revolution more terrible than that whose effects are still felt in Western Europe.[46]

Today even Marxist thinkers are beginning to realize what that Russian revolution has led to, less than a hundred years after it had been so strikingly predicted. But what Marx was able to read in de Custine definitely did not lead him to imagine that the Russian abuses denounced by the Marquis could be institutionalized in "socialist" dress and in the name of his teaching:

The more I see of Russia the more I agree with the emperor's policy of forbidding the Russians to travel and of preventing aliens from entering his country. The political system of Russia could not withstand twenty years of free communication with Western Europe.[47]

Before his trip to Russia de Custine had studied despotism by observing Austria and Prussia. By virtue of his Russian experience he became convinced that these states were despotic in name only; only now did it become clear to him what it meant to conjoin an absolute system of rule and a nation of slaves. In Russia he saw clearly what results when the European mind and its science are united with Asiatic genius. This "mixture" appeared to him all the more frightening because potentially eternal. In Russia, unlike other countries, ambition and fear produced not general outcry but universal, apathetic silence. In the course of these reflections the "reactionary" Marquis was struck by a comparison whose significance will escape no reader schooled in Marxism:

With what right, after all, do we censure the Russian emperor for his lust for power? Wasn't the revolution in Paris just as tyrannical as the despotism in Petersburg? However, we ought to introduce a certain qualification in order to establish the difference between the social situations of the two countries: in France revolutionary tyranny is a temporary evil; in Russia the tyranny of despotism is a permanent revolution.[48]

[46]Ibid., p. 227 [101].
[47]Ibid., p. 236 [105].
[48]Ibid., Vol. II, p. 28 [139–40].

This concept of "permanent revolution" has found its way in an altered form into the materialist conception of history inspired by Marx; to a still greater extent this is also the case with respect to de Custine's notion of "oriental despotism," based upon what he had personally witnessed:

Imagine the skill of our governments, tested over centuries of practice, placed at the service of a state still young and crude; imagine how, in this totally new experience, the rubrics of the Western administrations would lend support to oriental despotism, how European discipline would support Asiatic tyranny, how culture would be used to conceal barbarism for the sake of perpetuating rather than suppressing it; imagine how the disciplined brutality and cruelty, the tactics of Europe's armies, would reinforce the politics of the Orient. Imagine a half-savage people, regimented but uncivilized, and you will understand the spiritual and social condition of the Russian people.[49]

After his five-month trip through Russia, de Custine looked back on what he had experienced, and in a final report he summarized his overall view in a series of aphorisms. Here, as it were, he passed judgment on that system of government on which he had modeled his personal aristocratic expectations. Let us examine in his last letter some of those verdicts whose traces are discernible in Marx's and Engels's anti-Russian writings:

In Russia the government dominates everything but quickens nothing.[50]

Russia, civilized late, was the only country robbed by the impatience of its rulers of a deep fermentation and of the blessing of a slow and natural development. Russia lacked that interior leavening which forms great peoples and prepares a nation to rule over, that is, to form, others.[51]

Peter I and Catherine II gave the world a great and useful lesson for which Russia has paid: they showed us that despotism is never to be feared more than when it wants to do good, for then it believes that its goals justify its most outrageous actions, and evil which poses as a remedy knows no bounds.[52]

[49]Ibid., p. 64 [155–6].
[50]Ibid., Vol. III, p. 339 [352]. De Custine's last remarks are dated, "Ems, October 22, 1839."
[51]Ibid., p. 347 [356].
[52]Ibid., p. 352 [359].

... I do not believe I exaggerate when I assure you that the Russian empire is that one country on earth where men are unhappiest, for they suffer simultaneously from the disadvantages of barbarism and the disadvantages of civilization.[53]

Measureless, monstrous ambition, an ambition which can take root only in the souls of the oppressed, which can feed only on the unhappiness of a whole nation, ferments in the hearts of the Russian people. This essentially acquisitive nation, greedy as a consequence of deprivation, has to pay in advance at home with degrading submissiveness for the hope of exerting tyranny over others; the fame and wealth she anticipates let her forget the disgrace she bears, and to cleanse herself of that blasphemous sacrifice of social and personal freedom, the kneeling slave dreams of world domination.[54]

A call to arms against czarism!

The idea that the bourgeoisie and capitalism are agents of civilization is a main pillar of the materialist conception of history. Marx and Engels worked out this theory together in Brussels in 1845–6, but were unable to persuade any German editor to publish the manuscript entitled *The German Ideology*. Instead, they had to leave it to the "gnawing criticism of the mice,"[55] not altogether unwillingly because its polemics by far outweighed the genuinely theoretical part, that is, the introductory excursus containing a clear presentation of what was mainly Marx's theory of history. They were satisfied to have settled accounts with their "former philosophical consciences" through this effort in "self-clarification."[56] The most important part of this methodological key to their analysis of society and history, what Marx later termed the "guideline" of his studies, is summarized in just a few pages of the *Communist Manifesto,* where Marx and Engels relate most of their theses to the revolutionary roles of the modern bourgeoisie and proletariat. What is striking about these assertions, which were presented as a description of existing social relations and social conflicts, is their note of expectancy. The *Manifesto* seems to assume that the bourgeoisie has virtually fulfilled its historical function. The various levels of development of the bourgeoisie

[53]Ibid., p. 365 [362].
[54]Ibid., p. 373 [363].
[55]Marx, *Zur Kritik der politischen Ökonomie. Vorwort;* MEW 13, p. 10.
[56]Ibid.

and the corresponding levels of political progress are described step by step with respect to the formation of the world market, which results from the development of industry and the means of transportation. It is conceded as a historically accomplished fact that the bourgeoisie has gained exclusive political control over the modern representative state and will draw "all, even the most barbarian nations, into civilization" by improving the means of production and commerce.[57]

In the light of world events since the publication of the *Communist Manifesto* and especially in view of the new historical era that began with the world wars of the twentieth century, one cannot help but think of Friedrich Nietzsche's distinction between three different kinds of historical investigation: monumental, antiquarian, and critical.[58] Marx viewed his own historical thinking as "critical" and as "in the service of life"; and thus he would have subscribed to Nietzsche's remarks about "history as understood in the Hegelian fashion" and about the "priests of the mythology of ideas." The sketch in the *Manifesto* that presents the developmental schema of the historically necessary domination of the world by the bourgeoisie should therefore be understood not as an acquiescence to the "power of history" but as a wishful image born of the passion for freedom and the belief in a historic mission.

> Just as it [the bourgeoisie] has made the country dependent upon the city, it has made barbarian and semi-barbarian countries dependent upon civilized countries, peasant peoples upon bourgeois peoples, the Orient upon the Occident.[59]

Although it may appear that Marx is stating a given fact here, he is actually anticipating a historical process of development whose beginnings coincide with the more or less rapid expansion of large-scale industry in Western Europe and especially England. Upon closer inspection the hymn of praise to the bourgeoisie proves to be a task with binding goals both for those who are to accomplish it and for the gravediggers they

---

[57]*Manifesto of the Communist Party; SW* 1, p. 36.

[58]Friedrich Nietzsche, *Vom Nutzen und Nachteil der Historie für das Leben; Werke* I (Munich: 1966), pp. 219 ff. "History understood in the Hegelian way" is dealt with on pp. 263 ff. It should be stressed, however, that Neitzsche's contemptuous treatment of "history from the standpoint of the masses" (pp. 272 ff.) is diametrically opposed to Marx's conception.

[59]*Manifesto of the Communist Party; SW* 1, p. 37.

produce, namely, the proletariat that is abandoned to capitalist exploitation. The double-edged character of capitalist production corresponds to a dramatic conflict: Upon the stage of history a drama is taking place that will be decisive for the destiny of mankind; the two antagonistic classes of modern society must play their roles in the service of a worldwide cultural revolution.

This historical model, outlined in the *Manifesto*, served as the theoretical basis for Marx's and Engels's politico-journalistic activity in Cologne during the revolutionary year of 1848. At that time they were expecting a proletarian revolution in France and a bourgeois democratic revolution in Germany. Their *Demands of the Communist Party in Germany* contains no mention of communism, but there is talk of abolishing all feudal oppression, of introducing universal suffrage, of transferring the ownership of feudal estates to the state, and of creating a state bank "to regulate credit in the interest of *all* the people" and to undermine the "rule of the big money-men"; the latter measure was intended "to relate the interests of the conservative bourgeoisie to the revolution."[60]

Nationalization of the means of transportation, separation of church and state, limitation of the right of inheritance, establishment of national workshops, universal free education — although this program envisioned goals more radical than those whose legal foundations were established by the French Revolution, its chief concern was nevertheless identical with that of the French bourgeoisie: the destruction of feudal property and "establishment of the free, landed peasant class."[61]

The manner in which, twenty-six years later, Engels discussed the domestic and foreign policies of the *Neue Rheinische Zeitung* is of great importance for the theme we are treating here. In 1884 he was able to write that the program of principles and tactics laid down in the *Communist Manifesto* in 1848 and adopted immediately thereafter by the "party" in Germany was still "completely valid."[62]

With respect to the domestic policy of the *Neue Rheinische Zeitung* he wrote:

---

[60]*Forderungen der Kommunistischen Partei in Deutschland; MEW* 5, pp. 3 ff.

[61]Marx, "Der Gesetzentwurf über die Aufhebung der Feudallasten," *Neue Rheinische Zeitung,* July 30, 1848; *MEW* 5, p. 283.

[62]"Marx und die 'Neue Rheinische Zeitung' 1848–1849," *Der Sozialdemokrat,* Mar. 13, 1884; *MEW* 21, p. 16.

The German bourgeoisie, which had only just begun to establish large-scale industry, had neither the strength nor the courage nor the pressing need to fight absolute rule in the state; the proletariat, undeveloped to the same degree, having grown up in complete mental servitude, disorganized and even incapable of independent organization, felt only vaguely its natural opposition to the bourgeoisie. Thus, although it was by nature a threat to the bourgeoisie, the proletariat remained its political dependant. Frightened, not by what the German proletariat was but by what it threatened to become and by what the French proletariat had already become, the bourgeoisie saw its salvation in every and any sort of compromise with the monarchy and the nobility, even the most cowardly; the huge mass of the proletariat, still unfamiliar with its own historical role, had at first to assume the role played by the progressive extreme left-wing of the bourgeoisie. Above all, the German workers had to fight for those rights which were indispensible to their independent organization as a class party: freedom of the press, freedom to organize and to assemble – rights which the bourgeoisie had had to fight for in the interest of its own supremacy, but which, in its anxiety it now wanted to deny the workers. The few hundred isolated members of the League were swallowed up by the huge mass which was suddenly catapulted into the movement. Thus at the outset the German proletariat entered the political stage as a most radically democratic party.[63]

Engels further summed up the political program of the *Neue Rheinische Zeitung* in two main points: "a united, indivisible, democratic German Republic and war with Russia, together with the re-establishment of Poland."[64] Recalling the *Zeitung*'s foreign policy he wrote:

Support for every revolutionary people, a call to arms for the war of revolutionary Europe against the great mainstay of European reaction – Russia. From February 24th on it was clear to us that the revolution had only *one* really fearsome enemy, Russia, and that this enemy would be increasingly compelled to enter the fight the more the movement took on European dimensions. The events of Vienna, Milan, Berlin postponed the Russian attack, but its inevitability was all the more certain the closer the revolution came to Russia. But if we could bring Germany to war against Russia, then Hapsburg and

[63]*MEW* 21, pp. 17 ff.
[64]Ibid., p. 19.

Hohenzollern would be done for, and the revolution would be victorious all along the line.[65]

The crisis that broke out in the Orient in 1853 and the Crimean war that followed gave Marx and Engels the opportunity to defend in print, mainly in the American and English press, their theory of civilization and progress that they had conceived thoroughly in the spirit of the French Revolution.[66] What they defended in their numerous articles were "bourgeois" values: civilization, European revolution, and democracy. Commitment to these values determined their point of view and their judgments about the destiny of Turkey, the future of the Southern Slavs, and the unavoidable military confrontation between the Western European powers and Russia. In defending these values they did not hesitate to remind the politically ineffective French and English bourgeoisie – that is, the "class enemy" – of its historical task and duty; its mission was, as it were, to become the spokesman for a philosophy of history that stressed the heroic military virtues of the progressive European peoples in the face of "semi-Asiatic" Russia and its aspiration for "world domination." Hence, Marx and Engels rebuked the "foolishness, indolence, perpetual inconstancy and cowardliness of the West European governments" in the face of Russia's policies of expansion and annexation;[67] hence

[65]Ibid., p. 22. Twelve years later Marx commented on the anti-Russian attitude of the *Neue Rheinische Zeitung* in a letter to Lassalle: "Concerning our relation to Russia, I think you are mistaken. Engels and I developed our viewpoint quite independently and, I may say, laboriously, through many years of study of Russian diplomacy. At any rate, Russia is hated in Germany and even in the first issue of the *N. Rh. Z.* we presented the war against Russia as Germany's revolutionary mission. But hate and understanding are two entirely different things" (*MEW* 30, p. 565). Lassalle had written to Marx that "war against Russia" would be the "most popular, universally compelling battle cry that has ever been raised in Germany" and that he saw this war as Germany's "best and necessary heritage." Cf. F. Lassalle, *Nachgelassene Briefe und Schriften,* vol. 3 (Berlin: 1922), pp. 324 ff.

[66]Pronouncements such as the following are characteristic of the tendency of those newpaper reports: "Russia is decidedly a nation bent on conquest and was for a whole century long, until the great movement of 1789 created a fearsome, energetic opponent. We mean the European revolution, the explosive force of democratic ideas and innate human drive to freedom" (F. Engels, "The Real Issue in Turkey," *New York Daily Tribune,* Apr. 12, 1853). "In judging the foreign policy of the ruling classes and the cabinet [England is meant] we must not lose sight of a war with Russia, which would kindle a universal revolutionary blaze on the continent and would, today probably, call forth a portentous echo in the masses of Great Britain." K. Marx, "Affairs Continental and English," *New York Daily Tribune,* Sept. 5, 1853.

[67]Thus Engels, "The Turkish Question," *New York Daily Tribune,* Apr. 19, 1853.

Marx's "cartel-relationship" with the Russophobe David Urquhart. Marx admitted that the Scottish diplomat was "subjective-reactionary (romantic)," but assessed his tendency in foreign politics as "objectively revolutionary."[68]

In the fight against Russian absolutism Marx and Engels felt that above all they had to advocate the "great movement of 1789."[69] They did so throughout their political careers and never deviated from this approach, even when it became clear that the disintegration of Russian society had already begun and that therefore internal revolutionary forces were in play. The historical priority of the West in the social and cultural transformation of mankind was the primary ethical axiom of their materialistically founded social theory.

A consideration of Russian messianism

In Marx's and Engels's materialist interpretation of history the notion of a historic mission is ambiguously interwoven with the notion of a socioeconomically conditioned revolutionary mandate that classes as well as peoples are called to fulfill when their historic hour strikes. The geographical and historical realm in which the modern development and upheaval takes place is Western Europe and its natural offshoot, Europeanized North America. The instruments of power that the bourgeoisie employs to shape the world in its own image are the formation and accumulation of capital—both goal and purpose of the capitalist mode of production. The bourgeoisie, as it were, enjoys that famous "royal right of culture to oppress and enslave the barbarians," extolled by Jacob Burckhardt.[70] This point of view was defended consistently in 1848–9 in the *Neue Rheinische Zeitung,* the "organ of democracy" established by the "Marx party." In the struggle against the Pan-Slavic tendencies that had surfaced since the Slavic Congress at Prague, the role of agitator now fell to Friedrich Engels.[71] To a certain extent, the

[68]Marx to Lassalle, ca. June 2, 1860; *MEW* 30, pp. 547 ff. Marx praised the Urquhartists for pursuing a great cause, namely the struggle against Russia, and he made the "diplomatic" observation: "We revolutionaries have to use them as long as they are necessary. This is no obstacle to our hitting them right on the head when they try to check us in domestic politics." Ibid., p. 549.

[69]See Note 66.

[70]Jacob Burckhardt, *Weltgeschichtliche Betrachtungen* (Leipzig: n.d.), p. 37.

[71]See F. Engels, "Der magyarische Kampf," *Neue Rheinische Zeitung,* Jan. 13, 1849; *MEW* 6; p. 171. Also Engels, "Der demokratische Panslavismus," *Neue Rheinische Zeitung,* Feb. 15 and 16, 1849; *MEW* 6, pp. 270–86.

views Engels propagated were conceived of as the political manifesto of an ideal European revolutionary party whose scientific doctrine of civilization would oblige and entitle it to make sovereign decisions about the historical future of those peoples and races under the yoke of the Austrian monarchy. Engels took it to be self-evident that "from among all the nations and principalities included in Austria" only three were still viable as "bearers of progress" and therefore (potentially) revolutionary: the Germans, the Poles, and the Hungarians. "The mission of all other tribes and peoples, large and small, is simply to perish in the world-wide revolutionary tempest. Therefore, they are now counter-revolutionary."[72] To Engels the principal sign of national viability was a wealthy industrial bourgeoisie; only such a bourgeoisie would have the historical initiative – Engels here provisionally excluded the proletariat altogether! – vis à vis the backward nations that Pan-Slavism wished to bring under the power of the "Russian knout."[73] Even Bakunin's democratic Pan-Slavism, which never went beyond the realm of purely moral categories, found no favor in Engels's Hegelian eyes, although he looked approvingly, for example, upon the civilizing conquests of the "American people" who had saved "magnificent California from the lazy Mexicans who did not know what to do with it."[74] The brutal manner in which Engels concluded his diatribe against Bakunin may explain the uncompromising attitude he later took toward Alexander Herzen's socialist "Pan-Slavism":

In answer to the sentimental phrases of brotherhood offered here [in Bakunin's *Appeal to the Slavs*] in the name of the most counter-revolutionary European nations, we reply that Russophobia was and still is the *primary revolutionary passion* of the Germans, that since the revolution hatred of the Czechs and Croats has been added and that we, together with the Poles and the Magyars, can guarantee the

[72]*MEW* 6, p. 168. See also Engels's contrasting view (letter to Marx, May 23, 1851) that the Poles are *"une nation foutue,"* to whom the Germans owe only reestablishment "with suitable boundaries ... provided there be an agrarian revolution." Engels was certain "that this revolution will be fully achieved in Russia more likely than in Poland because of the Russian national character and the more developed bourgeois elements there" (*MEW* 27; pp. 266 ff).

[73]Engels, "Der magyarische Kampf"; *MEW* 6, p. 171.

[74]Engels, "Democratic Panslavism," in *The Russian Menace to Europe*, Paul Blackstock and Bert F. Hoselitz, eds. (Glencoe, Ill.: Free Press, 1952), p. 71. Earlier, Engels based himself on Hegel in seeing the Slavic peoples as "debris" subjected to the merciless course of history. Their whole existence is "nothing more than a protest against a great historical revolution" (p. 63).

revolution only by carrying out the most decisive terrorism against these Slavic peoples . . . battle, "an unrelenting battle to the death" [Engels here quotes Bakunin who used this phrase to express his support for a great and free Slavdom] against the Slavs, the betrayers of the revolution; a war of extermination and ruthless terrorism – not in the interests of Germany but in the interests of the Revolution![75]

Recognizable in these lines is the more or less conscious refusal of the "Marx party" to join in the debate over Russia and Europe that was stirred up among philosophers of history in Western Europe during the late 1840s and early 1850s.[76] To Marx and Engels matters like the anticipated revolution in France and the crisis provoked by Russia in the Orient must have seemed much too important to allow them to concern themselves seriously with Alexander Herzen's anti-Occidental campaign, for example, with its plea for Russia's "primitive socialism."[77] Even after Herzen's emigration to London in 1852 Marx and Engels were hardly willing to take note of a Russian writer who in their estimation deserved at most a place in the *chronique scandaleuse* of the parti-colored political emigration. Engels was chiefly preoccupied with the conditions and prospects of a war led by the Holy Alliance against revolutionary France, a war in which the "half barbarian" Russian troops would form, by sheer weight of numbers, "the core and mainstay, the pivot" of the coalition army.[78] It was only in this connection that Engels had occasion to mention Herzen, whose book, *Du Développement des idées révolutionnaires en Russie,* he had received through Marx.[79] Assuming a conflict between Europe and czarist abolutism to be imminent, Engels was interested in "what would

[75] Ibid., p. 286.

[76] Cf. Groh, *Russland . . . ,* pp. 206 ff.

[77] An opposing view is presented in the exchange between Moses Hess and Herzen: Moses Hess, *Briefwechsel,* ed. E. Silberner (The Hague: 1959), pp. 234 ff and 277 ff. In *Vom anderen Ufer,* a book published anonymously in Hamburg in 1850, Herzen prophesized that the Slavic family of peoples would be heir to the senile European. Hess replied (ca. Feb. 1850): "I admit that the Slavs are a modern Byzantium, an occidental China, but I don't think that they can make of our Europe a social-democratic republic, if Europe cannot liberate itself" (p. 245). Cf. Groh, *Russland . . . ,* pp. 253 ff.

[78] According to the manuscript published in *MEW* 7, pp. 468 ff. Concerning the Russian army see Ibid., pp. 476 ff. "General" Engels apparently had no scruples about commanding the proletarian revolution to use the means and methods of modern warfare discovered by the bourgeoisie.

[79] Marx to Engels, Jan. 21, Jan. 29, and Feb. 23, 1853; *MEW* 28, pp. 207, 209, 216.

be required of a revolutionary army in case of the welcome offensive against Russia."[80]

Apart from the strategic side of this problem Engels estimated the possibility of internal turmoil within Russia. He stressed that "among the possible prospects" would be "an aristocratic-bourgeois revolution in Petersburg with subsequent civil war in the interior." Referring to Herzen's work, he wrote: "Herr Herzen has simplified that for himself by inventing, in Hegelian fashion, a democratic-social-communist-Proudhonian republic of Russia under the triumvirate of Bakunin-Herzen-Golovin, so that absolutely nothing is lacking."[81] When the Pan-Slavic influence began to be noticeable in the Anglo-American press, Marx lost his temper with the "miserable Russians" for harping on the theme that "the Russian *people* are thoroughly democratic and that official Russia (the emperor and the bureaucracy), as well as the aristocracy, is German."[82] He urged Engels to attack the "idiotic idea" that Germany was to be fought in Russia and not Russia in Germany, recalling the "Teutonic asses" who "blamed the German despotism of Friedrich II, etc. on the French, as if backward slaves did not always need civilized slaves to keep them in line."[83] Marx presumably noted as well that not only the Russian Herzen but also German authors were debating the question of Russia's world-historical role because the ranks of the latter included his former fellow student and combatant Bruno Bauer. Bauer had been the target of caustic polemics in *The German Ideology,* where Marx and Engels attacked him as a "critical critic" and as a young Hegelian who despised the masses.[84] Like Herzen before him, Bauer's image of Russia was fashioned in the early 1850s with the help of the Westphalian baron August von Haxthausen's *Studien* concerning Russia's internal conditions and rural structure, published in 1847 and 1852.[85] To Bauer Russian absolutism represented the rebirth of Roman statesmanship, a religiously conditioned life-principle appropriate for the masses, which he contrasted with the democratic liberalism of the decaying Western bourgeoisie. He consoled a divided "Teutonism" with the rich pros-

[80]Engels to Joseph Weydemeyer, Apr. 12, 1853; *MEW* 28, p. 577.
[81]Ibid.
[82]Marx to Engels, Sept. 7, 1853; Ibid., p. 287.
[83]Ibid.
[84]Cf. Marx and Engels, *The Holy Family* (1844) and *The German Ideology* (1845–1846).
[85]Cf. Groh, *Russland . . . ,* p. 265 ff.

pect of sharing its anticipated security as a nation with a people "which since Peter the Great has deduced from his unity of purpose a scorn for all half-measures," a people "destined by its gigantic talent to upset the axioms and dogmas of the West."[86]

Even before Marx learned of Bruno Bauer's other pamphlets, which were written in the same reactionary spirit, he urged Engels to speak out against that growing Russomania that made a mockery of their own theory of history and civilization.[87] Engels earnestly set about accomplishing this task. His unfinished, unpublished writing on *Germanen- und Slawentum* consisted primarily of a sharp criticism of Alexander Herzen's messianic belief in Russia's socialist calling, a belief that resembled that of Bauer in its denunciation of the bourgeois-democratic and proletarian-revolutionary West.[88] Engels treated Herzen as one of those Pan-Slavists who longed for Slavic conquest of Europe and who dreamed of the thousand-year Reich of the Russian village commune. He accused Herzen of plagiarizing Haxthausen and ridiculed the boastful dilettantism of the Russian intelligentsia: "As the individual, so the nation. Just impress Europe. Behind that the bad conscience of inner barbarism."[89] Engels had developed, together with Marx, a "theory" of Asiatic despotism that held the absence of private property to be the key to the political and religious history of the entire Orient. "Engels took up this line of thought in his pamphlet *Germanen- und Slawentum* in which he stressed, while conceding to Haxthausen that czarism supplemented communal democracy, that the entire Orient lacked private property, the link between the community and the state and that, by contrast, the Teutonic *Gau* system of government signified an organic advance."[90]

[86]Cf. Bruno Bauer, *Russland und das Germanenthum* (Charlottenburg: 1853), pp. 117 ff.

[87]Marx to Engels, Dec. 8, 1854; *MEW* 28, p. 419.

[88]For details on Engels's unfinished pamphlet *Germanen- und das Slawentum*, cf. Gustav Mayer, *Friedrich Engels. Eine Biographie* (The Hague: 1934), vol. 2, pp. 54 ff. The manuscript was originally in the literary archives of Marx and Engels now maintained by the International Institute for Social History in Amsterdam. Helmut Krause conjectures that it was "taken along back to Moscow by Riazanov" (*Marx und Engels* . . . , p. 90). Cf. on this N. Riazanov's note in *Gesammelte Schriften von Marx/Engels* . . . , (Stuttgart: 1920), vol. 2, p. 520.

[89]G. Mayer, *Friedrich Engels*, vol. 2, p. 57.

[90]Ibid., p. 58. See also Engels, "Deutschland und der Panslawismus," *Neue Oder-Zeitung*, Apr. 21 and 24, 1855; *MEW* 11, p. 193 ff.; in English: "Panslavism and the Crimean War," in *The Russian Menace to Europe*, Paul Blackstock and Bert F. Hoselitz, eds. (Glencoe, Ill.: Free Press, 1952), pp. 84–90. Marx comments on these articles to Moritz Elsner, Apr. 17, 1855; *MEW* 28, p. 616.

The difficulties that Marx and Engels encountered in conducting a journalistic campaign against Herzen and Bauer now presumably prompted Marx to publish a writing of his own designed, in a certain sense, to demonstrate both that the development of Russian autocracy corresponded to a natural law and that Herzen's and Bauer's messianic Russophile pronouncements were utterly unfounded.[91] Marx apparently took this project seriously for, among other things, he refused to participate in an international meeting called by his Chartist friends and declared that "nowhere and never" did he want to "figure together" with Herzen and was not of a mind "to see old Europe renewed by Russian blood."[92] With regard to Bruno Bauer, Marx had every reason to refute the "pedantic old professor's"[93] metaphysical speculations on history with a myth-free interpretation of history based on rigorously empirical investigation. During one of his London visits, Bauer explained to Marx his standpoint on Russia as follows: ". . . the old state of affairs in the West must be overturned; this can only come from the Orient since the Oriental alone has real hate, namely, hate for the Occidental; and Russia, besides being the only European country where there is still cohesion, is the sole compact power of the Orient."[94]

As with many other of his important literary and scientific plans, Marx was only able to accomplish part of this project. The thirteen articles that he published in David Urquhart's London *Free Press* from August 16, 1856 to April 1, 1857 were conceived of as an introduction to a larger work whose aim was accurately described by David Riazanov: "[Marx] seeks in the distant past the solution to the riddle of Russia's colossal power and of the old Anglo-Russian slavery under whose yoke the whole of Europe groaned."[95] In his *Revelations on the Diplomatic History of the 18th Century*, Marx used his materialistic method as a means of critically under-

[91]Riazanov remarks on Marx's and Engels's anti-Pan-Slavic articles, which were not printed by the *New York Daily Tribune* because of "Russophilia," in his introduction to *Gesammelte Schriften*, vol. 1, pp. xxxv ff. See also *MEW* 28, p. 719 (note 454).

[92]Marx to Engels, Feb. 13, 1855; *MEW* 28, pp. 434 ff.

[93]Marx to Engels, Dec. 14, 1855; *MEW* 28, p. 466.

[94]Marx to Engels, Jan. 18, 1856; *MEW* 29, p. 6.

[95]D. Riazanov, "Karl Marx über den Ursprung der Vorherrschaft Russlands in Europa," *Ergänzungshefte zur Neuen Zeit*, no. 5 (Mar. 5, 1909), 11. Cf. *Marx's Secret Diplomatic History of the 18th Century*, ed. Lester Hutchinson (London: 1969), pp. 108–21.

standing history, far exceeding both the monumental and the antiquarian approaches to history – to use Nietzsche's distinction. He possessed that power of subjectivity needed "to shatter and dissolve a past,"[96] which Nietzsche required of the historian who serves life, that is, defends certain values of life by pronouncing a judgment on the past, carefully investigating, and finally condemning it.

When he received Bruno Bauer's pamphlets on Russia Marx was again motivated to take up the Russian problem.[97] Just as he had attacked the "critical critic's" thoughts on philosophy of history more than twelve years earlier, in *The Holy Family*, he began now to examine closely the world-political opinions advanced by this apologist of Russian dictatorship; but his interest in Bauer's Russomaniac eschatology did not last.[98] He and Engels would soon perceive that Russian society, ostensibly condemned to inertia, was exposed to internal tensions, and that it was therefore possible to treat the relations between the Russian state and Russian society in terms of the materialist conception of history.[99]

The founders' bequest to Russia

The Russian Revolution of 1917 is a unique example of an event of immense historical importance that is held to conform to a scientific theory or formula. This claim is strengthened in that the "Russian October" has come to signify the beginning of the era of consciously "made" revolutions and therefore of that social form that, according to Karl Marx, concludes "the prehistory of human society."[100] The myth of the Russian Com-

[96]Nietzsche, *Vom Nutzen . . .* , p. 229.

[97]In late 1855 Bruno Bauer turned up at Marx's home in London and subsequently paid him numerous visits. See Marx's reports about the "old boy" in his letters to Engels, Dec. 14, 1855, Jan. 18, and Feb. 12, 1856; *MEW* 28, p. 466; *MEW* 29, pp. 6, 15. A year later Bauer sent Marx his pamphlets on Russia. "Weak and pretentious," was Marx's judgment (letter to Engels, Jan. 10, 1857; *MEW* 29, p. 93). He had seriously considered publishing an attack on Bauer, as is confirmed by a fragmentary writing found among his posthumous papers.

[98]Cf. Karl Marx, "Pamflety Bruno Bauera o russkom konflikte," *Letopisi marksizma*, vol. VI (1928), 52–61 (introduction by F. Schiller). To my knowledge, the original German version of Marx's manuscript has never been published. At any rate, it, as well as Engels's *Deutschland und das Slawentum*, has not been included in the volumes of *MEW*.

[99]For further details on Marx's and Engels's evaluation of Russian absolutism, especially after 1860, see Helmut Krause, *Marx und Engels . . .*

[100]*Critique of Political Economy*, 1859; *MEW* 13, p. 9.

mune is due chiefly to the two-fold merit of "scientific social-ism" – its universal validity both as an analytic theory of the "natural processes of history"[101] (as Marx would have us under-stand the development of economic social structures) and as a "guide to action" (as Engels stressed).[102] Yet precisely with re-spect to Russia, Marx and Engels formulated their theoretical legacy with such clarity that it became a veritable warning to their Russian followers. Social disturbances in czarist Russia, constantly more numerous and more severe, ultimately signaled the presence there of active revolutionary forces that inaugu-rated the spontaneous historical activity of the Russian masses; these forces rendered superfluous the use of any doctrinaire recipe derived from the experiences of the Western labor move-ment to attain their goal, the overthrow of czarist absolutism. The "founders" may well have had doubts about the populists' religious faith in the peasant communities, yet they were much closer to the revolutionary praxis of the populists, including their terrorism, than to the sectarian discords generated by the rival groups of Russian emigrés.[103] As spokesman for the Ge-neva-based Russian section of the International Workingmen's Association, Marx expected not a revolutionary or "Marxist" party platform, but cooperation in liberating Poland through elimination of Russian militarism "as the precondition for the universal liberation of the European proletariat."[104] Marx's ac-tivity in the General Council of the International, together with the publication of *Capital,* created even in Russian political and intellectual circles an attentive public whose efforts for reform he now had to take into account.[105] When he recognized that even czarist Russia was a class society entangled in antagonistic

[101]*Capital* I, preface to the first German edition (1867), p. 10.

[102]Engels to F. A. Sorge, Nov. 29, 1886: "Even the Germans ... do not understand the theory for the most part and treat it doctrinally and dogmatically as if it were something to be learned by heart ... It is for them a credo, not a guide to action" (*MEW* 36, p. 578).

[103]See Marx to Jenny Longuet, Apr. 11, 1881; *MEW* 35, pp. 178 ff.; and Engels, "Flüchtlingsliteratur, IV," *Volksstaat,* Mar. 28, 1875; *MEW* 18, pp. 546 ff. Cf. N. A. Morosov's memoirs of Marx in *Russkije sowremenniki o Markse i Engelse* (Moscow: 1969), pp. 78–86; L. N. Hartmann to N. A. Morosov, May 14, 1880, Ibid., pp. 180 ff.

[104]The General Council of the International Working Men's Association to the members of the committee of the Russian section in Geneva, Mar. 24, 1870; *MEW* 16, pp. 407 ff.

[105]Cf. A. L. Reuel, *Russkaja ekonomitscheskaja mysl 60–70 godow XXX weka i marksism* (Moscow: 1956). See Marx to Laura Lafargue, Dec. 14, 1882; *MEW* 35, p. 408; Engels to J. E. Papritz, June 26, 1884; *MEW* 36, p. 169.

interests, he began studying Russian in order to examine the source material concerning its economic and social situation.[106] More than a decade of research (which, as Engels irritably realized, prevented Marx from finishing *Capital*) led Marx to discover that the Russian peasantry was a potentially revolutionary element; the hope that communism would shape Russia's social future depended upon the preservation of the old village community, an arrangement widespread among the Slavic peoples and one that displayed their historical gift for comradely self-administration. This unexpected viewpoint, which Engels eventually came to share during Marx's lifetime, meant a reconciliation with Herzen and Bakunin (both of whom had died) inasmuch as Marx's and Engels's Russophobia now gave way to a positive – albeit qualified – valuation of the social tendencies of the Russian people.

Either Russian society would be regenerated through the resistance of the rural communities to the disintegrating impact of capitalism, *or* it would adapt more or less rapidly in its economic and social facets to the capitalist modes of production already strongly rooted in the West: These were the rigorously pondered alternatives that Marx recommended to his Russian followers as a kind of theoretical guide for their political action. Engels abandoned his friend's Russian legacy when he realized that the *Obschina* was condemned to extinction; he believed himself authorized to console Russian socialists with the one remaining prospect – that the blessings of capitalism outweighed by far the advantages of the peasant community. Engels challenged the *Narodniki* to give up their belief in any special "spontaneously communist" mission of Russia and at every opportunity he condemned the doctrinaire and sectarian attitude of the first Russian Marxists. He warned them that not only would "profane Russia" have to assume the difficult process of transforming its economy, but it would also have to be prepared for a long bourgeois-liberal period of political and cultural reeducation. The dissensions among those Russian followers in emigration especially exasperated Engels because of their mania for ascribing greater importance to scholarly interpretations of the Marxian writings – "as if they were texts taken from the classics or from the New Testament"[107] – than

---

[106]See Marx's letters; *MEW* 32, pp. 437, 443 ff., 656 ff.
[107]Engels to I. A. Gurvitsch, May 27, 1893; *MEW* 39, p. 75.

to the events occurring at all levels of Russian society itself, events that he, Engels, valued as signs of the inevitable bourgeois revolution in Russia patterned after the French Revolution of 1789.[108]

Apparently it was from a reading – perhaps only superficial – of Plekhanov's *Our Differences of Opinion* that Engels derived his understanding of the Russian Marxists: While recognizing the importance of capitalism as a school for the predominantly peasant population, they nevertheless underestimated the educative function of liberalism. The high esteem in which he and Marx held the revolutionary party of the "People's Will" is not unrelated to the fact that the manifesto published by the executive committee of the *Narodnaia Voliia* after Alexander II's assassination was inspired by a "statesmanlike" spirit completely alien to the Russian Marxists, who persisted in anti-*Narodniki* sectarianism.[109] Certainly the people who risked their lives planning and executing terrorist attacks knew much less of *The German Ideology* and *Capital* than did Plekhanov; but they were less estranged from the wishes and needs of the Russian masses than were the self-styled disciples of Marx who were wrangling about "organizational questions" and wanted to direct the Russian revolutionary movement from their Swiss exile. In their letter to Alexander III, the *Narodovoltsi* authors enumerated the conditions to be met before their revolutionary movement could be succeeded by peaceful action and stressed that these were not demands but necessary consequences of the events themselves that the executive committee was merely putting into writing:

First: General amnesty for all political offenders for having committed no crime but for having simply fulfilled their duty as citizens.

Second: Convocation of representatives of the entire people in order to deliberate on and reform social and political life according to the people's wishes and needs.

We feel it is necessary to point out, however, that power can be validated by representatives of the people only if the elections are completely free. Therefore, these elections must be held under the following conditions:

[108]Engels to Danielson, Oct. 17, 1893; *MEW* 39, pp. 148 ff.; see also pp. 36 ff.; Engels to Plekhanov, Feb. 26, 1895; *MEW* 39, p. 416.

[109]See Marx to Jenny Longuet, Apr. 11, 1881; *MEW* 35, pp. 178 ff.; Kautsky to Bernstein, June 30, 1885; *Eduard Bernsteins Briefwechsel mit Friedrich Engels*, ed. Helmut Hirsch (Assen: 1970), pp. 437 ff.

1. The deputies should be nominated from all classes without discrimination and in proportion to the population.
2. No restrictions of any kind are to be set either on the electors or on the elected.
3. The electoral campaign and the elections themselves must be completely free. The government must therefore allow provisionally, until a decision is taken by popular assembly:
   a. unrestricted freedom of the press
   b. unrestricted freedom of speech
   c. unrestricted freedom of assembly
   d. unrestricted freedom of electoral platforms.[110]

This program drawn up by the *Narodnaia Voliia* evidently inspired Engels's radical criticism of Plekhanov, who had attacked the terrorists from a doctrinaire Marxist standpoint. An examination of Engels's writings and correspondence in 1883 concerning the problems of the Russian revolutionary movement inspires this assumption. Expressing his outrage over Plekhanov's attack in the presence of a visitor, Alexander Voden, he also appeared to be astonished at Plekhanov's conception of the proletarian dictatorship.[111] Even if we question the credibility of Voden's report, it is hard to doubt Engels's ironic rejection of the notion that the proletarian dictatorship may be realized by the dictatorship of a Marxist intelligentsia. Thus, it is no exaggeration to say that essentially the legacy bequeathed by Marx and Engels to their Russian followers has proven to be prophetic indeed: In defending the independently creative initiative of all social levels oppressed by czarist absolutism, it implicitly condemns that party fetishism that was cultivated by all factions of Russian social democracy and has colored the history of the Soviet Union ever since the "Great October."

Charisma and political leadership

Switzerland, not Russia, is the birthplace of Russian Marxism. It was from Geneva that Plekhanov, Axelrod, Vera Zasulich,

[110]Cf. V. Gitermann, *Geschichte Russlands*, III, p. 619. "A struggle for a moderately liberal constitution – that was the objective meaning of the *Narodnaia Voliia's* legendary revolutionary work," according to Theodor Dan. See *The Origins of Bolshevism*, ed. and trans. Joel Carmichael (New York: Harper & Row, 1964), p. 125.

[111]On Voden's report see Na sare, "legalnovo Marksizma" (Is vozpominanii), *Letopisi Marksizma* IV (Moscow-Leningrad: 1927).

and Leo Deutsch tried to establish epistolary ties first with Marx and then with Engels. There they founded the "Liberation of Labor Group," a peculiar phenomenon whose history and development is more aptly studied in the context of religious sociology than political science.[112] The ideological and sectarian aspects of Russian social democracy did not escape Engels, but they reached full fruition only after his death, when Russian social democracy evolved into that hybrid of pseudoscience and pseudophilosophy that is labeled "Marxism" and proclaimed itself, louder than its sister parties in Western Europe, to be the one saving political theory. The exiled Russian Marxists lived on the periphery of Russia's industrial proletariat and the Russian peasant masses and could not find their place in the intellectual centers of European socialism. Their isolation was aggravated when, in the course of the revisionist quarrel provoked by Eduard Bernstein's "heretical" position, they sided with the Marxist orthodoxy and were thus compelled to distance themselves from the reform-oriented party and trade union praxis of the Western European social democrats. The orthodox Marxist line formulated by Plekhanov in the name of the "Liberation of Labor Group" continued to guide Russian social democracy in spite of all internal party struggles; in it Lenin discovered the essential traits of an avant garde ideology capable of supplying the indispensible theoretical justification for his party's hegemony before and after the revolution.[113]

In his first work as a follower of Marxian theories, *Socialism and Political Struggle* (1883), Plekhanov broke intellectually with his own revolutionary past. In an effort to achieve a critical understanding of the social problems of czarist Russia he drew on, indeed almost parodied, the main categories of Marx's political and economic theory, categories originally elaborated to explain the development of the Western capitalistic countries. Plekhanov coined the maxim, later appropri-

[112]Cf. P. Axelrod, "Gruppa 'Osvobozhdenis Truda'," *Letopisi Marksizma* VI (1928), 82–112; see Theodor Dan, *The Origins of Bolshevism*, pp. 164 ff.
[113]Cf. D. Geyer, *Lenin in der russischen Sozialdemokratie* (Köln/Graz: 1962), pp. 26 ff. Characteristic of the heterogeneous ways in which Marx was understood by the Russian students in the 1890s is the so-called legal Marxism, inspired by A. N. Potresov and Peter Struve. On Struve's pioneering work see Richard Pipes's recent biography, *Struve: Liberal on the Left. 1870–1905* (Cambridge, Mass.: Harvard University Press, 1970), and also his *Social Democracy and the St. Petersburg Labor Movement 1885–1897* (Cambridge, Mass.: Harvard University Press, 1963).

ated loyally by Lenin, that there can be "no revolutionary movement in the true sense of the word without revolutionary theory."[114] However, apparently neither of them was aware that this canonization of Marxism as a theory meant a complete reversal of the basic teaching of "scientific socialism" developed in *The Holy Family* and *The German Ideology* where the "classical thinkers" disputed the Young Hegelians' cult of ideas and elites. Whereas Marx and Engels admired for its political maturity the program elaborated by the executive committee of the *Narodnaia Voliia*, Plekhanov reproached the *Narodovoltsi*, his erstwhile party friends, for considering the urban workers to be only one element of the revolutionary movement, and not the sole revolutionary class historically commissioned to fight for the emancipation of the entire society, as is demonstrated in the *Communist Manifesto*. The concept of the spontaneous historical action of the industrial proletariat that Marx derived from his observations of Western European class struggles, was based upon the associational possibilities created for the industrial proletariat by the laws of bourgeois democracy. The elders of Russian Marxism applied this concept to a social reality that exhibited none of the sociological characteristics of Western Europe. In this as in other respects Plekhanov paved the ideological path for Lenin and for Bolshevism, even though Bolshevist organizational praxis owed less to the Geneva literary group than to the conspiratorial practices that had marked their country's revolutionary past.

Marx's Russian disciples were filled with an almost fanatical zeal to derive from the progress of the capitalist modes of production and commerce in Russia both the untenability of the doctrines held by the agrarian communists and the infallible advent of socialism as the necessary successor of capitalism. They were by no means averse to apologetics on behalf of capitalism or even to its glorification. No bourgeois Russian economist described the development of capitalism and its "historical mission" in Russia with as much expertise and optimism as did, for example, the Marxist-educated socialists, Plekhanov, Struve, and Lenin.[115] But they were just as inter-

---

[114]Plekhanov, *Sotsializm i politicheskaia bor'ba* (Geneva: 1883); here quoted from the French edition, *Oeuvres philosophiques*, Moscow, vol. I, p. 55. Lenin called this work "the first confession of faith of Russian socialism."

[115]Cf. Plekhanov, *Our Differences* (1883), chapters 2–4. Plekhanov bases his arguments against the various rival political tendencies – populists, anarchists, and Jacobins – on the progress of capitalism and the growth of the industrial proletariat in Russia. Cf. Lenin, *The Development of Capitalism in Russia* (St. Petersburg: 1899);

ested in anticipating the results of the slow process of capitalist maturation as they were in knowing the actual points of capitalism's strength in Russia. Consequently, the literati who agitated in the name of scientific socialism felt themselves sanctioned to assume the intellectual guardianship of the Russian factory worker, a newcomer on the historical stage: The tradeunionist strategy that pressed for immediate economic advantages had to be subordinated to a political goal. To use the classic formula coined by Lenin, as the student of Kautsky, "political class consciousness" had to be instilled "in the worker *from without*"; those who "spontaneously develop" only a "trade-unionist consciousness" had to be implanted with the philosophical, historical, and economic theories of socialism as elaborated by the "educated representatives" of the propertied classes, the intelligentsia.[116] In its simplest terms

CW 3; and Struve, *Kriticheskie zametki k voprosu ob ekonomi cheskom razyittii Rossii*. Vypusk I (St. Petersburg: 1894). The reader may also wish to consult Dietrich Geyer's *Lenin* . . . .

[116]Karl Kautsky's commentary on the suggested platform of the Austrian Social-Democratic Party, in *Neue Zeit* XX, 1 (1901–2) no. 3, pp. 79 ff: "Socialist consciousness is . . . something introduced into the proletarian class struggle, not something indigenous that arises spontaneously in it." In *What Is to Be Done?* (1902) Lenin quotes a lengthy passage from Kautsky's article in support of his own thesis that "the spontaneous working class movement is trade unionism pure and simple," while "the workers can acquire political class consciousness . . . *only from without*" (CW 5, p. 384). Prior to this passage, however, Lenin had quoted from the 1874 preface to *The Peasant War in Germany* in which Engels said of the German workers that "they belong to the most theoretical people of Europe and that they have retained that sense of theory which the so-called 'educated' classes of Germany have almost completely lost" (CW 5, p. 371; cf. SW 1, p. 590). Lenin immediately adopted Engels's statement concerning the German workers as the national task of the Russian socialist party, which could claim the role of vanguard if only because it was accompanied by a revolutionary, "progressive" theory (CW 5, p. 370); imperceptibly Lenin then transferred this postulate of a revolutionary calling from the party to the proletarian class, thereby divulging the charismatic character of this identification: "History has now given us [!] the immediate task which is the *most revolutionary* of all *immediate* tasks confronting the proletariat of any country whatsoever" (Ibid., p. 373). Lenin finally presents the following credo, an atrocity from the standpoint of the materialist theory of civilization: "The realization of this task, destruction of the most powerful bulwark not only of European but . . . also of Asiatic reaction, would make the Russian proletariat the avant garde of the international revolutionary proletariat" (Ibid.). Again Lenin's view was corroborated by Kautsky who wrote an essay especially for "Iskra" entitled *Die Slawen und die Revolution* (1902) in which he preached "that not only have the Slavs joined the ranks of revolutionary peoples but that the center of gravity of revolutionary thought and action is shifting more and more towards the Slavs . . . Russia has long since ceased to be simply the bulwark of reaction and absolutism for Western Europe. Indeed, the contrary is now the case. Western Europe is becoming the bulwark of reaction and of absolutism in Russia." Is it any wonder that eighteen years later Lenin triumphantly quoted these words of his former teacher—"when Kautsky was still a Marxist and no renegade?" Cf. " '*Left Wing' Communism, an Infantile Disorder*"; CW 31, p. 22.

Lenin's exceptional standpoint on the question of the revolutionary intelligentsia was this: His efforts were oriented
uniquely toward replacing the detested "cult of spontaneity"
with the cult of the ideologically indoctrinated party elite.
Thus, the Russian labor movement was instructed to rely less
on its own action of class struggle than on the political enlightenment of a self-assured elitist group of literati.

As a product of Western European thought, Russian Marxism exerted from the outset a charismatic aura of authority on
the groups of the Russian industrial proletariat then agitating
in the spirit of "economism." In the minds of the Marxists,
who thought in concepts provided by a dogmatic dialectic of
development, Russia's regrettable "historical backwardness,"
was in time seen as a salutary opportunity for "overtaking"
the West: Because capitalism—and therefore Russia's bourgeoisie and its proletariat—was only beginning to develop, the
rapidly growing working class could profit from all the experiences gained by the Western European proletariat in the economic and political class struggle; by avoiding the latter's mis-
takes it would to a certain extent be recognized by the rest of
the proletarian world as the prototype of *political* praxis.
Thus, history itself assigned leadership to the Russian workers
in two respects: First, as the true members of the revolutionary
class, they could claim and play a leading role even in Russia's
bourgeois revolution; second, by accelerating the process of
social development within their own country, they could spur
the workers' movement in the Western European nations to
decisive confrontations. The Marxism cultivated by certain
Russian political parties distinguishes itself through its unmis-
takeably *idealistic* conception of the almost universal calling of
the Russian proletariat. This conception provided the common
ideological foundation for the two main currents of Russian
social democracy, Menshevism and Bolshevism.[117] However,
the thesis that the bourgeois revolution was to be carried out
by a party ruling in the name of the industrial proletariat, and
thus *for* the peasant and petty bourgeois masses, could hardly
be reconciled with Marx's "materialist" theory of revolution.
After more than a half-century of modern Russian history this
"renovation" of Marx's theory by his Russian disciples has
certainly proved to be untenable.

[117]See Theodor Dan, *The Origins of Bolshevism*, p. 178.

Revolution: the social core, the political facade

Russia's spontaneous mass movements have demonstrated historically that the leadership claim of the various political factions that arose from the Marxist intelligentsia was largely ignored by the peasant and proletarian groups in establishing their goals and modes of action.[118] Through their rejection of purely political slogans during the great strikes of the 1890s and in the 1905 revolution, the Russian factory workers expressed above all their will to pressure for immediate improvements in their working and living conditions. Not until the strike movement came under the leadership of the spontaneously established workers' committees and led to the establishment of soviets composed of worker deputies did political-revolutionary goals find a place next to economic demands; this signified that the revolutionary initiative of the industrial workers had aroused all the active oppositional elements at other social levels. The working class itself thus confirmed the bourgeois democratic character of the 1905 revolution—without appealing to any doctrinaire party program—which received legal sanction from the czar in the "October Manifesto." "In the eyes of the majority of the Russian people that meant nothing less than the end of the old autocracy and the beginning of the constitutional parliamentarian era."[119]

Upon closer inspection and analysis all phases of Russian revolutionary history accord with Karl Marx's view of revolution, which despite its romantic orientation was no less socio-

---

[118]Seven years before the October revolution Trotsky drew the negative balance of social-democratic agitation among the Russian workers, accusing both Mensheviks and Bolsheviks of sectarianism, intellectualist individualism, ideological fetishism, and distortion of Marxism. Cf. L. Trotsky, "Die Entwicklungstendenzen der russischen Sozialdemokratie," *Die Neue Zeit*, Sept. 9, 1910, 860 ff. In 1916 Trotsky still had great reservations about collaborating with the sectarian "Leninists." Cf. L. J. van Rossum, "Ein unveröffentlicher Brief Trockijs von Anfang 1916," *International Review of Social History* XIV (1969) part 2, 251 ff. On the relations between Trotsky and Lenin before 1917 see Siegfried Bahne, "Der 'Trotskismus' in Geschichte und Gegenwart," *Vierteljahrshefte für Zeitgeschichte*, I (1967), pp. 68 ff. That Trotsky finally succumbed to Leninist party fetishism, although he stood for a "democratic centralism," should not be surprising because for both protagonists the party was "the highest expression of proletarian self-activity" (see Ibid., p. 72). Cf. also L. Trotsky's writing on *Terrorisme et communisme* (Paris: 1963); in this philippic, published in 1920 against Kautsky's similarly entitled writing (Berlin, 1919), Trotsky defended the communist party's prerogative to political representation of the proletarian dictatorship.

[119]Cf. Oskar Anweiler, *Die Rätebewegung in Russland. 1905–1921* (Leiden: 1958), p. 55.

logical in its analysis. Marx's historical study of the three great bourgeois revolutions, begun in Kreuznach in 1843, had had a decisive effect on the formation of his theory of revolution. His materialist, determinist point of view included from the start an idealizing and ethical element – even if this was not always openly avowed.[120] And it was the uprising of the Silesian weavers in the summer of 1844 that provided Marx with a historical occasion for empirically developing his revolutionary ideal. His pretext was an article by Arnold Ruge in which Germany's backwardness was held responsible for both the destructive fury of the starving weavers and the philanthropic Christian attitude of the Prussian king. Ruge concluded his article with a presentation of his basic thesis: "A social revolution without a political soul (i.e., without an organizational insight from the standpoint of the whole) is impossible. In this respect France and England will undoubtedly take the initiative, regardless of the Prussian King's insistence on new plans and great reforms."[121]

In order to grasp the full significance of Marx's refutation of this thesis we must remember that his first literary works of the Paris period contain no trace of any critical examination of contemporary nationalist economic theories. However, his two important essays from the Deutsch-Französischen Jahrbücher, namely, On the Jewish Question and Introduction to a Critique of Hegel's Philosophy of Right, contain the definitive value judgments that constitute the ethical foundation of the social conception Marx was later to term "materialist." His economic studies and insights, far from changing this table of values, contributed to its scientific underpinning. In On the Jewish Question Marx had dealt with the two basic evils inherent in the form of society produced by the bourgeois revolution: money and the state. In his Introduction to a Critique of Hegel's Philosophy of Right he mentioned that destructive and creative power that he felt was destined to remedy those evils and realize a truly human commune: the modern industrial proletariat. However premature and therefore erroneous Marx's estimation of the revolutionary perspectives in Germany, his conceptual prototype of an emancipatory and revolutionary class remains

---

[120]A precise description of the contents of Marx's Kreuznach notebooks (July–Oct. 1843) is given in MEGA I, 1/2, pp. 118–36.

[121]"Der König von Preussen und die Sozialreform." By a Prussian [Arnold Ruge], Vorwärts!, Paris, July 27, 1844.

valid. He derived his thesis on the revolutionary maturity of the German proletariat from the radicalism of "German theory," itself merely the philosophical expression of specific material circumstances, that is, a particular class relationship within bourgeois society. Radical theory is the correlate of universal suffering and absolute injustice as embodied in the proletariat and itself becomes a material power as soon as its demands correspond to the practical needs of the suffering masses. For "it is not enough that thought strives towards actualization, reality itself must feel the need for thought."[122]

In Marx's eyes the significance of the Silesian weavers' revolt far transcended the local context, because – in contrast to the first revolts of French and English workers – it "possessed a theoretical and conscious character," which the weavers manifested in destroying not only machines but also accounting books: They thereby announced violently and ruthlessly the opposition between the proletariat and private property. "The Silesian revolt *begins* precisely where the uprisings of the French and English workers *end*, with a consciousness of the essential nature of the proletariat."[123] Marx found literary confirmation for the intellectual superiority of the German worker in Wilhelm Weitling's "gifted" writings, which revealed Germany's "*classical* calling to *social* revolution"[124] no less than its incapacity for political revolution. However, Marx stressed, the disproportion between Germany's philosophical and its political development was no anomaly. "It is a necessary disproportion. Only in socialism can a philosophical people find its corresponding praxis, and thus only in the *proletariat* can it find the active element of its liberation."[125] To Marx a lack of political sense – with which Ruge reproached the Germans – was an eloquent proof of the universal *social* talent of the German proletariat. Ruge's demand for a social revolution that would be inspired by political demands amounted in fact to promoting the political community, that is, the state, to the status of a permanent social institution and therefore eternalizing human servitude. And here speaks Marx the anarchist, a Marx who today more than ever has drifted into oblivion –

[122]Marx, "Zur Kritik der Hegelschen Rechtsphilosophie. Einleitung." *Deutsch-Französische Jahrbücher*, 1844; *MEW* 1, p. 386.

[123]Marx, "Kritische Randglossen zu dem Artikel 'Der König von Preussen und die Sozialreform'," *Vorwärts!*, Aug. 10, 1844; *MEW* 1, p. 404.

[124]Ibid., pp. 404 ff.

[125]Ibid., p. 405.

"the existence of the state and the existence of slavery are inseparable."[126] Proof of this was given by the French Revolution whose heroes, imbued with more than enough political sense, imagined that they could eliminate social deficiencies by changing the form of the state. True, they did have the courage "to decree" the elimination of pauperism, but the Assembly's administrative and welfare measures were precisely of a political nature, that is, they left untouched the basis of the social malady. "Even radical and revolutionary politicians seek the source of the evil not in the *essence* of the state but in a particular *form of the state,* which they want to replace with *another* form of the state."[127] To Marx the expression "social revolution with political soul" meant only a purely political revolution, "just a revolution," that is, a spurious social upheaval that is not achieved "from the standpoint of the whole," a change in class rule at the expense of the society. What alone seemed meaningful was "a political revolution with a social soul," which implies the necessity of a political act aimed at overthrowing the old power. "But without *revolution socialism* cannot realize itself. It requires this *political* act insofar as it requires *destruction* and *dissolution.* But when its *organizational activity* begins, when its *inherent goal,* its *soul* emerges, socialism discards its *political* facade."[128]

In *The German Ideology,* written in collaboration with Engels, Marx modified and reduced the romanticism in this concept of revolution while developing the materialist basis of his conception of history. Here is a summary of the four theses formulated in that work as consequences of the materialist conception of history:

> 1. The development of the productive forces to purely pernicious forces of destruction (technology and money); correspondingly, the emergence of revolutionary proletarian masses that gradually educate themselves for a communist society ("a class that constitutes the majority of all members of society and that develops a consciousness of the necessity for a fundamental revolution,

---

[126]Ibid., p. 401 ff. This axiom still guided Marx twenty-seven years later when writing the Commune Address. Cf. "First Draft of 'The Civil War in France'," Karl Marx, *The Civil War in France* (Peking: Foreign Languages Press, 1966), pp. 105 ff.

[127]*MEW* 1, p. 401.

[128]Ibid., p. 409.

communist consciousness, which to be sure can develop in the other classes as well").[129]

2. The emergence of a power structure in which the class that possesses, and thus rules, also controls the instrument of power that is the state; the revolutionary struggle is directed against this class.

3. Abolition of wage labor, and so of classes and class conflicts, through a communist revolution carried out by the modern proletariat.

4. The necessity for a "massive transformation of men," above all the workers; communist consciousness and the realization of communism are linked to the revolutionary praxis of the "class that overthrows" and thereby demonstrates its capacity for self-liberation and for "a new founding of society."[130]

Norms derived from these theses determined Marx's orientation toward the Paris Commune more than a quarter of a century later. On the occasion of the 1871 Paris revolt, as on the occasion of the weavers' revolt in 1844, he idealized and glorified the revolutionary action of modern wage slaves, although he knew in both cases that there could be and was no question of "constructing socialism." And during the Commune it was not a "workers' *state*" that was created but a democratic workers' *government* that was to destroy the state. By abolishing the standing army, the political police, the bureaucracy, and the lawyers' caste and by separating education from both the state and the church all the attributes of the modern state were to be eliminated.[131]

[129]*The German Ideology; MEW* 3, p. 69.

[130]Ibid., p. 70.

[131]The characterization of the Commune as "the government of the working class" was based on the first proclamation of the Central Committee formed by the national guard (Mar. 20), which Marx extracted from French and English newspaper reports. Requested by the General Council of the International Working Men's Association to compose an address a few days before the Commune's fall, Marx used this expression in his first draft on "The Civil War in France." See Marx, *The Civil War in France* (Peking: 1966), pp. 150 ff., especially 184, as well as the newspaper material collected by Marx, published in *Archiv Marksa i Engelsa*, Moscow, III (VIII) 1934. However Marx was not satisfied with this fiery attack composed in the heat of events; after its publication he systematically collected further material about the Commune (published in *Archiv Marksa i Engelsa*, XV, 1963). His praise in 1876 for Lissagaray's *History of the Commune* of 1871 (Eng. trans. in 1886 by Eleanor Marx) indicates that

Marx's often subjective evaluation of the Paris uprising has led to the accusation that he authored a myth of the Commune. However, this should not make us forget that he created this "myth" in order to serve a cause whose success, for him, depended on the creative initiative of the oppressed and suffering masses — and not on the scientific enlightenment of a party leadership. Marx saw the Paris "titans" as *his* party, which nonetheless did not prevent him from reprimanding them for their "good natured" and "scrupulous" behavior.[132] The spontaneous action of the workers as a *class* ranked higher and was to him more important than the political genius of the working-class *leaders*. The latter he reckoned among the "coincidences" that occur in the general course of historical development and attributed to them merely an accelerating and/or retarding influence.[133] This conviction must not be forgotten in our critical examination of the myth of the Russian Commune of 1917.

Reality and myth of the Russian Commune

Marx and especially Engels made clear to their Russian followers that there was little chance of avoiding a bourgeois revolution in Russia and that its course would resemble that of its French precursor. Engels did not doubt that "once 1789 has begun . . . 1793 will not be far behind."[134] As if that were not enough, Marx and Engels evoked a third date in French revolutionary history, 1871, in order to strengthen the hopes of the Russian revolutionaries after the assassination of Czar Alex-

he had gravitated toward Lissagaray's thoroughly accurate presentation of the historical events, as well as the latter's interpretation of the Commune administration as an institution of chiefly petty-bourgeois character. Marx's letters to Wilhelm Bracke between Sept. 1876 and Aug. 1877 concerning the German edition of Lissagaray's book attest to this new turn of mind. Cf. Günter Grützner, *Die Pariser Kommune. Macht und Karriere einer politischen Legende. Die Auswirkungen auf das politische Denken in Deutschland* (Cologne/Opladen: 1963), pp. 49 ff. However, Grützner distorts the Marxian conception of the Commune in writing that to Marx was reserved the task of providing "the theoretical [?] basis for a real myth of the Paris revolt" (p. 42). Ten years after the event Marx wrote a more sober account of the Commune, the majority of whose members in no way were or could have been socialist, stating that it "could have achieved with a small quantum of common sense . . . a compromise with Versailles which would have been useful to all the popular masses — the only thing that could have been achieved at that time." Letter to F. Domela Nieuwenhuis, Feb. 22, 1881; *MEW* 35, p. 160.

[132] See Marx to Kugelmann, Apr. 12, 1871; *MEW* 33, p. 205.
[133] Marx to Kugelmann, Apr. 17, 1871; *MEW* 33, p. 209.
[134] Engels to Vera Zasulich, Apr. 23, 1885; *MEW* 36, pp. 303 ff.

ander II. In an address to a Slavic meeting called in London to celebrate the tenth anniversary of the Paris Commune they wrote: "When the Commune of Paris succumbed to the atrocious massacre organized by the defenders of Order, scarcely did the victors think that not ten years would elapse before there would occur in distant Petersburg an event which, perhaps after long and violent struggles, must ultimately and certainly lead to the establishment of a Russian Commune."[135]

It therefore seems most natural and logical that the leaders of Russian social democracy (before, during, and after the Revolution of 1917) did not hesitate to use these three important dates in French revolutionary history, together with two other moments of historical comparison—1830 and 1848.[136] At the outbreak of the February revolution the various Marxist political factions and their leadership, which had split back in 1903 over the problem of organization and the exercise of power, adopted conflicting viewpoints and attitudes depending upon which historical model they favored. At this time the Czar had been overthrown without their direct intervention, and workers' and soldiers' soviets had arisen first in Petrograd and soon after in the great provincial cities in opposition to the helpless provisional government.[137] From the beginning neither Mensheviks nor Bolsheviks doubted that the recent political upheaval had inaugurated the bourgeois-democratic phase of the revolutionary process in Russia and that therefore one could to a certain extent expect a repetition, on Russian soil and under specifically Russian conditions, of the French events of 1789 and 1793.

Although in his *April Theses* Lenin mentioned not these dates but the Paris Commune of 1871, the fact remains that neither his party nor the Menshevik leaders contemplated any "withering away" of the capitalist system of production and distribution in their country. What separated Lenin from the Mensheviks—and, at the beginning, even from the majority of his own party—was his demand for a "republic of soviets composed from the bottom up of deputies representing industrial

---

[135]*MEW* 19, p. 244.

[136]See for example Lenin, "The Immediate Tasks of the Soviet Government," *Izvestiya Ts IK,* Apr. 28, 1918; CW 27, p. 245; "Theses and Report on Bourgeois Democracy . . . , Mar. 4, 1919; CW 28, pp. 459 ff; " 'Left Wing' Communism—an Infantile Disorder," May 1920; CW 31, pp. 22 ff.

[137]Cf. O. Anweiler, *Die Rätebewegung . . .* , pp. 127 ff.

and agricultural workers throughout the entire country." In short—as he expressed himself two days later in his article *On Dual Power*—he demanded the immediate inauguration of a policy that would eventually produce a "state of the type characterized by the Paris Commune."[138] Hence Lenin did not neglect to stress that the creation of a proletarian state power did not mean the "introduction of socialism"; on the contrary, in his polemic against Plekhanov and Kautsky he insisted expressly upon the distinction between the "introduction of the commune" and the "introduction of socialism."[139] To Lenin the former signified the political maturity of the Russian people, who would create a temporary state apparatus to replace the bourgeois-capitalist state machine founded on the army, the police, and the bureaucracy; the "introduction of socialism," on the other hand, meant the organizational structure of a socialist economy and presupposed both well-developed economic conditions as well as a certain organizational experience acquired by the working masses. The "commune state" was to be the state form of proletarian rule during the transition from capitalism to socialism. The encroachments upon private property that it would undertake were thought of as the first economic steps toward socialism. As the highest form of the democratic state— yet, at the same time, "no longer a state in the real sense"—the Commune had taken a series of measures that indeed represented a break with the parliamentary bourgeois republic, yet it had never, contrary to the "countless lies and slanders" of bourgeois authors, attested to the intention and the will to "introduce" socialism immediately.[140]

Accordingly, the revolutionary program proposed by Lenin was from the beginning geared toward weakening private capitalism and accelerating the development of state capitalism; it called for the "nationalization of *all* land and soil—i.e., the transfer of all land and soil in the state to the central state power," and further, "the complete nationalization of all the banks and syndicates of capitalism, or at least the introduction of *immediate control* over them by the soviets..." Lenin stressed that these revolutionary measures certainly did not

[138]See Lenin's "April Theses"; CW 24, p. 23; "The Dual Power"; CW 24, p. 39; "The Tasks of the Proletariat in Our Revolution"; CW 24; p. 68.

[139]Lenin, "The Tasks of the Proletariat in our Revolution"; CW 24, pp. 68 ff., 73 ff.

[140]Ibid.

mean the "introduction of socialism" but were nevertheless "steps toward socialism."[141] He was much too familiar with the rudiments of Marx's theory of capital not to know that the most important step toward socialism is reached with the highest degree of concentration and accumulation of capital, at that historical moment when, according to the dialectics of negation, the monopoly of capital begins to fetter the mode of production and when the centralization of the means of production and the socialization of labor "become incompatible with their capitalist integument."[142] Russia's economic system fulfilled none of these conditions characteristic only of developed capitalism. The "negation of the negation" essentially presupposes, on the one hand, a social minority of usurpers who are monopolizing capital, and, on the other hand, a mass proletariat that satisfies capital's need to exploit. Lenin's program of nationalization masked that relation between economics and politics that Marx had disclosed in scientific terms. A party that took itself to be, as it were, the demiurge of social creations had the ambition to subordinate the "natural laws of capitalist production" to its own will to power and to make Marx's "economic law of motion of modern society"[143] the normative basis of a political program of reforms. In so doing, an ostensibly "proletarian" state apparatus controlled and manipulated by the party demiurge was to assume the socioeconomic functions of the dispossessed capitalist class. Lenin's conceptual formula, "bourgeois rule without the bourgeoisie," implied precisely such a sociopolitical exchange of functions, the transfer of a natural class role to a party that is conscious of its historical mission as an instrument of socioeconomic development.

Lenin never imagined that his suggested reforms for nationalization surpassed the limits of a capitalist economy; at the same time he was convinced that the Russian bourgeoisie was not mature enough to fulfill the tasks presented by an economic system modeled after Occidental economics and consistent with the rules of capitalist rationality. Thus, everything depended on establishing a socioeconomic system whose revolutionary ideology would abolish the contradiction between, on one hand, an economy to be based on both monopoly and force, and, on the other hand, the claim to political power of a

---

[141]Ibid., p. 74.
[142]*Capital* I (Moscow: 1959), p. 763.
[143]Ibid., pp. 8, 10.

party leadership that proclaimed itself as the dictatorship of the proletarian class. To this end the ambiguity of the epigones' particular conception of Marxism furnished them with an excellent device: Depending upon the situation of social conflict, they could adopt as their guideline for power politics either the Marxian economic theory of capital, or Marx's and Engels's political judgments and decisions (often the result of their emotional reactions to momentary impressions).

The political vacuum produced in Russia by the overthrow of czarism and the increasingly popular soviet movement enabled the quasimilitarist Bolshevik party to use the myth of the commune as an ideological weapon to secure for itself the necessary mass support for a rapid takeover of power in peasant Russia. However, the party's promises to end the war and to provide land and bread probably made a stronger and deeper impression on the Russian masses than did the slogan "all power to the soviets."[144]

Capitalist production relations and the communist ideology of domination

In a naïve but most significant passage in his history of the Russian revolution, Trotsky formulated the maxim that had guided the Bolshevik party in its role as ruling apparatus and enabled it to give its political theory – an ideology that masked Russia's real economic structure – the magical imprint of a Marxist doctrine of the state:

Yet precisely as a consequence of its retarded development Russia possessed new, most modern classes, parties and programs for the solution of these problems. And Russia needed Marx's ideas and methods in order to put an end to the ideas and methods of Rasputin.[145]

[144]Cf. Lenin, "Theses and Report on the Bourgeois Democracy . . . ," Mar. 4, 1919; CW 28, p. '473: "Our victory came more easily because in October we went with the peasantry, the whole peasantry. In this sense our revolution was a bourgeois revolution." Did Lenin mean to imply that if the Bolsheviks had at that time "gone" against the peasantry the revolution would have been . . . socialist? It is certain that this is the conclusion Stalin drew when he ordered the forced collectivization of Russian agriculture and in the space of one decade (1929–39) united 93.5 percent of all farms into kolkhozes. Stalin thus gave the lie to Plekhanov's opinion, expressed in 1883, that in the twentieth century an "Inka-communism" would be impossible "even in Eastern Europe." Cf. Plekhanov, *Oeuvres philosophiques*, vol. I, p. 66.

[145]L. Trotsky, *History of the Russian Revolution*, vol. III. Trans. Max Eastman (New York: Simon & Schuster, 1932), p. 54.

It did not occur to Trotsky that Marx never exercised any function at a czarist court and that only if he had might the comparison of his "ideas and methods" with those of Rasputin the magician somehow seem plausible. Nevertheless, in this passage the frustrated politician-turned-historian unconsciously betrays the secret of Bolshevik statesmanship. In order to justify in Marxist terminology the seizure of power by an oligarchy and the economic policies necessary to consolidate state capitalism, Marx's scientific theories were transformed into magical recipes that would enable Russia, in spite of its backwardness, to work a two-fold historical miracle: Politically, it would be the first nation in the world to tread the path of proletarian dictatorship; economically it would pioneer the construction of the socialist mode of production. When Vladimir Ilyitch Ulyanov-Lenin, chairman of the all-Bolshevist Council of the People's Commissars, opened the session of the Soviet Congress on October 25, 1917 with the declaration, "Now we are beginning with the construction of a socialist order,"[146] his words expressed not Marx's science but Marxist magic.

If intellectual honesty can be at all considered a moral criterion for political decisions, we may assume that Lenin made this declaration in absolute honesty. His constant, almost manic self-criticism attests to the measure of his political capacity for political adaptation and readaptation. No other Bolshevik statesman had been as conscious of Russia's economic and cultural backwardness – decisive factors from the standpoint of historical materialism (the basic principles of scientific socialism). No other Russian Marxist was so mindful of the warnings to be derived from Marx's and Engels's criticism of the "ideas and methods" advanced by Bakunin, Nechayev, or Tkachov, warnings that were no less valid for the praxis of the Bolshevik party. Who else remembered, as did Lenin in 1917, Engels's prophetic speculation as he occasionally reflected on the possibility of his "party's" premature seizure of power and the probable consequences? What Engels had written, for example, in 1850, about Thomas Münzer's insoluble dilemma during the German peasant war applied *mutatis mutandis* to Lenin and his party as well. What is even more striking, Engels himself could not help but establish a historical parallel with the defeat of the French proletariat in 1848. Engels, the revolutionary historian, depicted the organizational zeal of the

[146]Cf. V. Gitermann, *Geschichte Russlands*, III, p. 534.

prophet of revolution with admiration and sympathy, and it seems certain that a Lenin of his time would have aroused in him similar feelings. Three years later Engels was himself confronted with Münzer's dilemma, once German communism had, following the "socialist blunders" of 1848 and the Cologne communist trials of 1852, been given sufficient time to prepare for its "final examination."[147] The letter Engels wrote to his friend Weydemeyer, a German immigrant in New York, bears witness to this state of mind:

> Of course, all this is only a matter of theory. In practice we shall always be reduced to urging resolute measures and absolute ruthlessness above all else. And that's our misfortune. I have the vague feeling that our party, due to the perplexity and sluggishness of the others, will one fine day be forced into the government in order to carry out measures that are of no direct interest to us, but rather in the general interests of the revolution and in the specific interest of the petty bourgeoisie; then, driven by the proletarian populace and bound by our own published dictums and plans – more or less falsely interpreted and more or less passionately promoted during the party struggle – we shall be constrained to try communist experiments and sudden transitions which we know better than anyone else to be untimely . . . In a backward country like Germany, which possesses an advanced party and which is involved in an advanced revolution together with an advanced country like France, the advanced party must take over at the first serious conflict and as soon as any *real danger* occurs; and in any event that is prior to its normal time. However, this is really insignificant; should such an event occur the best thing for our party is to establish its historical rehabilitation in the party *literature*.[148]

In *The Peasant War* Engels anticipated such a literary rehabilitation in trying to interpret in the light of Marxian social theory the tragic destiny of Thomas Münzer who, in the Mühlhausen uprising of March 1525, advanced to the head of the newly elected "eternal council":

> The worst thing that can happen to the leader of an extremist party is to be forced to take over the government at a moment when the movement is not yet ripe either for the rule of the class which he represents or for the execution of the measures demanded by the rule of this class. What he *can* do depends, not on his will, but on the

---

[147]Engels to Joseph Weydemeyer, Apr. 12, 1853; *MEW* 28, p. 580.
[148]Ibid.

intensity of the opposition between the various classes and on the degree of development of the material conditions of existence, the modes of production and commerce that determine the degree to which class oppositions have developed at a given moment. . . Thus, he necessarily finds himself in an insoluble dilemma: what he *can* do contradicts all his previous actions, his principles and the immediate interests of his party; what he *ought* to do cannot be accomplished. In a word, he is forced to represent, not his party, not his class, but the class for whose rule the movement is ripe. In the interests of the movement itself he must realize the interests of an alien class and dismiss his own class with phrases and promises, with the protestation that the interests of that alien class are their own interests. Whoever falls into this false position is irrevocably lost. Even most recently we have witnessed examples of this; we need only recall the position taken by the representatives of the proletariat in the last French provincial government, although they themselves represented only a very low level of proletarian development. He who can still speculate about the possibility of official posts . . . after the experiences of the February regime must either have an inordinately one-track mind or belong to the extreme revolutionary party in name only.[149]

To apply Engels's general observations in their literal sense to the Russian Revolution of 1917 and to the role played in it by the Bolshevik party would of course be going too far. However, his words are of lasting value insofar as they are methodologically and sociologically applicable to any historical event of universal importance. At the basis of his reflections was Marx's "new materialism,"[150] in other words, the view that the relation between economic structure and political behavior can be rationally comprehended through dialectical understanding only if we presuppose that "the social, political and spiritual life process in its entirety . . . [depends] on the mode of production of material life."[151] Engels took every opportunity to dissuade his Russian disciples from their self-serving sectarian abuse of quotations from Marx's writings in

---

[149]F. Engels, *The Peasant War in Germany* (New York: 1926), pp. 135 ff. (German: "Der deutsche Bauernkrieg," *Neue Rheinische Zeitung-Politisch-ökonomische Revue; MEW* 7, pp. 400 ff.). "In fact," the social transformation envisaged by Münzer "never transcended a weak and unconscious attempt to establish prematurely an advanced bourgeois society" (Ibid., p. 402).

[150]K. Marx, *Theses on Feuerbach* (1845); *MEW* 3, p. 7.

[151]K. Marx, "Zur Kritik. . ."; *MEW* 13, pp. 8 ff.

political quarrels. His chief interest was to establish theoretically, in accordance with empirical knowledge of the general
social process in this predominantly agrarian country, the
revolutionary goals of both the *Narodniki* and their Marxist
opponents. He foresaw a "1789" for Russia, but did not ex-
clude the possibility that a party inspired by Blanquist methods
might succeed "in *making* a revolution, i.e. in overthrowing
with a small push an entire system whose equilibrium is more
than unstable . . . and in setting free, by an act meaningless in
itself, explosive forces that then could no longer be tamed."
He warned of that party's "illusions" and of the "superior
strength of will" that such illusions produce: "Those people
who prided themselves upon having *made* a revolution have
always seen the day after that they had not known what they
were doing, that the revolution they *made* did not at all resemble the revolution they wanted to make. Hegel called that
the irony of history, an irony which eludes few historical *dijat-
eli* (personalities)."[152]

Marx and Engels had a number of opportunities to observe
in themselves the psychological effect of revolutionary impatience and to examine it critically in the light of their own
theory. When Marx perceived the symptoms of a new economic crisis in the summer of 1852, he wrote to his friend:
"The revolution could come sooner than we wish. Nothing
worse than when revolutionaries have to be concerned with
supplying bread."[153]

The commune versus the state: an agelong dream

The working class did not expect miracles from the
Commune. They have no ready-made utopias to introduce *par décret du peuple*. They know that in
order to work out their own emancipation, and
along with it that higher form to which present society is irresistably tending by its own economical
agencies, they will have to pass through long strug-

---

[152]Engels to Vera Zasulich, Apr. 23, 1885; *MEW* 36, pp. 303 ff. More than thirty
years had passed since Engels had imparted to his friend Marx his views about their
party as a "band of asses who swear by us because they take us for their own kind,"
and about revolution as "a phenomenon of nature purely and simply." "And as soon
as one appears publically as the representative of a party, one is sucked into this
whirlpool of irresistible natural necessity." Letter of Feb. 13, 1851; *MEW* 27, p. 190.

[153]Letter of Aug. 19, 1852; *MEW* 28, p. 112.

gles, through a series of historic processes, transforming circumstances and men. They have no ideas
to realize, but to set free the elements of the new
society with which old collapsing bourgeois society
itself is pregnant.

> Karl Marx, *The Civil War in France*, Peking, 1966,
> p. 73

Like his historical work on the February Revolution, *The
Eighteenth Brumaire of Louis Bonaparte* (1852), Marx's address on the Paris Commune, written upon request of the General Council of the International Workingmen's Association,
was not the creation of a disinterested and unbiased scientist,
but the belligerent act of a revolutionary who sat in judgment
upon the modern class state and interceded on behalf of the
workers' future struggles. In neither of these writings did Marx
advocate a "new type of state" or a "workers' state." On the
contrary, his entire thinking was oriented toward proving an
absolute antinomy between the state and society, and toward
demonstrating that the creative spontaneity of the members of
society will mean emancipation from all of the authoritarian
institutions of the state. Marx had considered the revolt of the
Silesian weavers to be a gesture of anarchism and had raised it
to a symbol of the working class's instinct for freedom.
Twenty-seven years later he promoted the short-lived deed of
the Paris Commune to an event of universal emancipatory
significance. In both cases he was intent upon avoiding a mythological glorification of heroic traditions, for he believed
that the anticipated social revolution would derive "its poetry
not from the past . . . but from the future."[154] The vehemence
shown by Versailles in its barbaric repression of Paris must
have proved conclusively to the indignant journalist that the
Commune, the government of the working class, was no
mythical fiction, that in spite of its momentary helplessness it
contained the seed of future triumphs. The portent of the
Commune was felt even more by the conquerors than by the
conquered: The slaughter of the communists appeared to be an
anticipatory act of revenge for future defeats. They wiped out
not the real Paris Commune but what it virtually symbolized.
Marx circumscribed its symbolic meaning in one of his drafts
of *The Civil War in France:*

[154]Marx, *The Eighteenth Brumaire of Louis Bonapart* (1852); SW 1, p. 227.

[The Commune] was, therefore, a Revolution not against this or that legitimate, constitutional, republican or Imperialist form of State Power. It was a Revolution against the *State* itself . . . this supernaturalist abortion of society, a resumption by the people for the people of its own social life. It was not a revolution to transfer it from one fraction of the ruling classes to the other, but a Revolution to break down this horrid machinery of Class domination itself.[155]

The revolution that began with the overthrow of czarism in February 1917, in the midst of the war, was no surprise to anyone well-acquainted with Russian history, least of all to observers schooled in Marxism or to politically active Marxists who thought or imagined themselves masters of a sociological theory that would enable them to control both in theory and in praxis the further course of this upheaval. Both Bolsheviks and Mensheviks agreed that their country was still far from completing the historical phase of capitalist and therefore bourgeois development and that the principal beneficiary of the revolution would be the peasantry, not the industrial proletariat. In February 1917 no Russian Marxist thought that a "proletarian" or even a "socialist" revolution was possible for contemporary Russia. Those "coincidences"[156] that Marx had praised apropos of the Paris Commune, namely, the appearance of charismatic personalities of uncommon stature, were needed to set the definitive tempo of Russia's social and economic development and to justify this tumultuous process and gloss over it ideologically with references to and phantoms of the past. A Lenin was needed to claim a debased, mythicized version of the Paris Commune as the model for the dictatorship of his party.[157] Finally, a "coincidence" like Stalin was necessary to implement with perfect consistency Lenin's policy of usurping power from the workers', peasants', and soldiers' soviets and to pass off the process of transforming the Russian masses into a proletariat (something Marx had foreseen) as the realization of the first socialist commune. In 1917 Lenin derived his theoretical weapons for the planned seizure of power from a text in which Marx projected the image of a rational

---

[155]First draft (Peking: 1966), p. 166.

[156]Marx to Kugelmann, Apr. 17, 1871; *MEW* 33, p. 209.

[157]The comparison between the Paris Commune and the Soviet was not Lenin's own inspiration; social revolutionary Maximalists and anarchists had already made good propagandistic use of it in 1905 and 1906. Cf. O. Anweiler, *Die Rätebewegung* . . . , pp. 114 ff.

utopia, a stateless society, and explained the impossibility of actualizing that dream in the France of 1871.[158] But what was then impossible for France was to be achieved forty-six years later in revolutionary Russia thanks precisely to the unsuccessful experience of the Commune and to Marx's remarks on the weaknesses of its political leadership. Neither theory nor praxis failed to prevent the new commune from ending in catastrophe: In June 1917 the Bolsheviks, represented by their spokesman Lenin, were introduced to the first all-Russian Congress of the Soviets of the Workers' and Soldiers' Deputies as that party that was prepared "to assume all power . . . at any moment."[159]

If any one dogma may be considered as the perennial leitmotiv of Bolshevik politics, it is the one established by Lenin: *His party, as the governing power, is the organizational and organic embodiment of the "dictatorship of the proletariat."*[160] This maxim makes plausible how Lenin, after scarcely six months in power, was able to employ a political phraseology that marked him as the student not of Marx – but of Nietzsche! At that time his goal was to surpass the Western European revolutions, to secure victory over the bourgeoisie by exterminating it. Russia had not only attained the level of the French revolutions of 1793 and 1871 but had gone a step further: It (Lenin used the pronoun "we") had "decreed and established the supreme *type* of state, soviet power."[161] The transition to socialism had now begun, he said, and the material preconditions for the construction of socialism were to be

[158]In the first draft of the Commune Address Marx underlined the identity of the goals shared by the socialists who had been politically active in the International and the founders of utopian sects: "the suppression of the wage-system of labor with all its conditions of class rule" (Peking: 1966), p. 183.

[159]See Lenin's speech of June 4, 1917, concerning his position on the provisional government; CW 25, p. 20.

[160]Lenin's party fetishism, which implied in practice that "economic force" that Marx demonstrated to be, in the form of state power, "the midwife of every old society pregnant with a new one" (*Capital*, I, p. 751), comes to expression most clearly in his tirade against "leftism," published in June 1920 (CW 31, pp. 17–118). Lenin had no qualms about labeling the power structure of his party's central committee oligarchical, but he was careful enough to put the term "oligarchy" in quotation marks, probably to indicate that he used it in the figurative sense. In fact, however, the quotation marks concealed Lenin's feeling for identifications that often attained the intensity of self-hypnosis: "We refuse to understand that when we say 'state' we mean ourselves, the proletariat, the vanguard of the working class." Speech at the eleventh Party Conference, Mar. 27, 1922; CW 33, p. 278.

[161]"The Immediate Tasks of the Soviet Government"; CW 27, p. 245.

met by destroying private capital; it would be necessary to organize "accounting and controls over production and distribution of products to be carried out by the whole people"[162] and to increase the productivity of labor through the development of heavy industry, through a rise in the educational and cultural level of the masses, through the introduction of strict discipline over labor, and so on.

Lenin's speech, which begins as an apology for the Commune, gradually assumes the line of thought of an organizational specialist, of a highly gifted industrial manager whose ambition is to replace the system of private capital with that of state capital. He in fact left untouched the hierarchical social structure that Marx defined as the "relations of capital," adeptly using "dialectics" to justify the party's claim to undivided power—to a "dictatorship of insight," to use Lassalle's term: "Socialism is nothing other than a state capitalist monopoly which *is employed for the benefit of the whole people* and thus *has ceased* to be a capitalist monopoly."[163] Lenin did not hesitate to employ the term "state capitalism" in preference to the concept of "state socialism,"[164] which is untenable from the standpoint of Marx's theory, nor was he reticent in giving the "big word," dictatorship, a definition that not only ruptured forever his own myth of the Commune but also furthered the Stalinism to which he was definitely averse: "The indisputable experience of history attests that in the course of revolutionary movements the dictatorship of individuals has very often expressed, carried, and executed the dictatorship of the revolutionary classes."[165] Oblivious to that "poetry of the future," Lenin sought his historical models in the past, in what for

---

[162]Ibid., p. 253.

[163]"The Impending Catastrophe and How to Combat it"; CW 25, p. 358. In 1921, when the collapse of the Russian economy forced him to recall the fundamentals of Marx's *Capital* and to speak of the "paradox" that private and state capitalism is the forerunner of socialism, Lenin referred to that writing composed four years earlier "so that the reader may be convinced that this is by no means the first time I have valued state capitalism 'highly' but that I did so even *before* the Bolsheviks seized power" ("The Tax in Kind"; CW 32, p. 336).

[164]"The Immediate Tasks of the Soviet Government"; CW 27, p. 267.

[165]Ibid., p. 267. In these lines, which must seem incredible to a proletarian disciple of Marx, we detect the spirit of that leadership cult that Engels pilloried in 1850: "The whole view [of Thomas Carlyle] of the historic development process flattens into the dull triviality which typified the wisdom of the illuminati and the freemasons a century ago, to the simple morality of the 'Magic Flute' and to an infinitely degenerated and tedious Saint-Simonism. This naturally entails the old question of who then really

Marx was the stage of human prehistory. Disclaiming any sympathy for anarchism—which had been Marx's fundamental position in the Commune Address[166]—while defending the necessity of the state as the transitional political structure between capitalism and socialism, Lenin maintained that there was "not the least contradiction in principle between the soviet (i.e. the socialist) democracy" and the "use of dictatorial power by individuals." Similarly, there was no reason to reject the exercise of dictatorial power by individuals in large-scale enterprises where *one* central will guides the work "of thousands and tens of thousands of people." "But how can the strict unity of will be assured? By subordinating the wills of thousands to the will of one."[167]

Three years later, after having secured their power by their bloody suppression of the Cronstadt uprising and by stifling all opposition—which they branded as "anarchico-syndicalist factionalism"[168]—Lenin and his party could afford to decree the New Economic Policy (NEP) as the "period of economic transition," in order to transform "petty bourgeois capitalism" into "large-scale state capitalism."[169] Until the day of victory for "world socialism" and for the German revolution in particular, a regression to state capitalism seemed reasonable and would permit them later to advance all the more certainly and swiftly. It also seemed reasonable for them to learn their trade from the most advanced capitalist nations: "Should the revolution still be slow to erupt in Germany, then it will be our task

ought to rule, a question which is discussed at great length with pompous insipidity; the answer is finally given that the noble, the wise and the knowledgeable should rule, with the spontaneous conclusion that there must be a great deal of government, that there can never be too much government, since indeed governing is the constant disclosure and validation of the natural law vis-a-vis the masses." Review of Thomas Carlyle's *Latter-Day Pamphlets*, in *Neue Rheinische Zeitung-Politisch-ökonomische Revue*, Apr. 4, 1850; MEW 7, p. 261.

[166]Cf. Hans Kelsen, "Marx oder Lassalle. Wandlungen in der politischen Theorie des Marxismus," *Archiv für Geschichte des Sozialismus und der Arbeiterbewegung* XI (1925), 261 ff.: "Political theory as Marx and Engels developed it *is* pure anarchism" (p. 264).

[167]"The Immediate Tasks of the Soviet Government"; CW 27, p. 269.

[168]See Lenin's "Preliminary Draft Resolution of the Tenth Party Congress," Mar. 8–16, 1921; CW 32, pp. 241 ff. and 245 ff.

[169]"The proletarian state must become a careful, cautious, prudent landlord, a regular *wholesale merchant*—otherwise it cannot put this country of small farmers back on its feet economically. . . But this is precisely one of those contradictions which leads in real life from small-scale rural economy by way of state capitalism to socialism." "Fourth Anniversary of the October Revolution"; CW 33, p. 59.

to *learn* state capitalism from the Germans, to adopt it *with all our might,* to shun no dictatorial methods in hastening this transfer of western culture to barbarian Russia and not to fear using barbarian methods of war against barbarism."[170]

In keeping with his personal ethics of revolution Lenin imposed the use of barbarian methods on the members of the apparatus of state control, which he and his party had established in order to build in Russia a modern civilization that would emulate its bourgeois capitalist model; these new procedures required a rather different ideological justification than an appeal to Marx's Commune Address. No Bolshevik party leader recognized this as clearly as did Lenin's successor, Josef V. Stalin, who derived his political wisdom from a much more important work of Marx – *Capital.* Stalin was the leader who drew the logical conclusion from the four-year debate on industrialization and erected the disputed law of the so-called primitive socialist accumulation[171] into a norm of his political economics by decree. The methods followed by Stalin are summed up in *Capital* as follows: "But they all . . . employ *State Power,* the concentrated and organized power of society, to hasten, as in a hothouse, the process of transforming feudal into capitalist modes of production and to shorten the transition period. Force is the *midwife of every old society pregnant with a new one. It itself is an economic power.*"[172]

Insofar as the social and economic development of the Soviet Union, now in its seventh decade of existence, can'be analyzed using Marx's sociological theory, we may consider it to be a rather special example of that historical process characterized by the capitalist economic system and the era of bourgeois social formations.[173] From this standpoint, Bolshevism appears

---

[170]"The Tax in Kind"; CW 32, p. 335.

[171]Cf. Alexander Erlich, *The Soviet Industrialization Debate, 1922–1928* (Cambridge, Mass.: Harvard Univ. Press, 1960). Yevgeni A. Preobrazhenskyi, at that time a member of the left opposition led by Trotsky, was the principal defender of socialism's capitalist law of accumulation borrowed from *Capital* and rechristened for the purposes of Russia's economic development (pp. 31 ff.).

[172]*Capital* I (Moscow: 1959), p. 751.

[173]The statistical proof, so to speak, of this thesis was furnished by a non-Marxist author who took as the criterion of his investigation Marx's analysis of capitalism. The result was the "surprising realization that in fact the Bolsheviks could justly appeal to Marx – although not of course to the Marx who predicted the supplanting of capitalist society by socialism, but to the Marx who had described capitalism in *Capital.*" Cf. Günter Wagenlehner, *Das sowjetische Wirtschaftssystem und Karl Marx* (Cologne/Berlin: 1960), p. 15.

as a historical power with the dual functions of a proletarian economic order and a state economic power: Its task is to form a nationwide industry and a national proletariat. By no means can "Stalinism," as the most consistent power factor in this process of social transformation, be appraised as "a special phenomenon of early socialist society."[174] Rather, it must be seen as the adequate political expression of an economic system based on state capitalist exploitation, sharing many of the fundamental irrational traits of private capitalism in its classical and modern forms. From the standpoint of Marx's proletarian ethics—that is, the doctrine of the self-emancipation and self-realization of the immense majority of men in the interest of all—false socialism no less than genuine capitalism is, thanks to its use of modern technology and methods of warfare, a threat to the material and moral existence of the human species. In both systems, rivals though they may be, profit and power are the primordial values whose ubiquity is concealed by sophisms and myths.

The foregoing lines of censure, written to disclose the Russian Commune as the myth of a totalitarian state and of wage slavery, are dedicated to the memory of the vanquished members of the Paris Commune who fell more than one hundred years ago, those men whose poetry was inspired by a yet unfulfilled dream of the future.

[174]Cf. Werner Hofmann, *Stalinismus und Antikommunismus: Zur Soziologie des Ost-West-Konflikts* (Frankfurt am Main: 1969), p. 40. The same author furnished the refutation of this "phenomenology of Soviet Stalinism" in an earlier work: *Die Arbeitsverfassung der Sowjetunion* (Berlin: 1956). Hofmann's most recent statements on the praxis of party power and "democratic centralism" have nothing to do with Marx's sociology, but rather with that party mysticism most brilliantly represented by Georg Lukács. Lukács is the source of the thesis that absolutely negates Marx's ethics of self-emancipation: "The communist party is, with respect to the revolution, an autonomous form of proletarian class consciousness." *Geschichte und Klassenbewusstsein: Studien über materialistische Dialektik* (Berlin: 1923), p. 333. Lukács quotes the passage from the *Communist Manifesto* where the communists, in contrast to the rest of the proletariat, are said to possess theoretical insight into the process and universal results of the working-class movement, in support of the following hierocratic vision: "In other words they [the communists] are *the class consciousness of the proletariat made visible.*" Cf. G. Lukács, *Lenin: Studie über den Zusammenhang seiner Gedanken* (Vienna: 1924), p. 25. In these "other words" he displays Bolshevism's charismatic claim to leadership as the bourgeois ideology of domination in the Soviet party and state.

A bibliography of the writings of Maximilien Rubel

Editions

Karl Marx. *Pages choisies pour une éthique socialiste*. Ed. and trans. with notes and intro. by Maximilien Rubel. Paris: M. Rivière, 1948. (lv, 379 pp.) Reprinted as *Pages de Karl Marx pour une éthique socialiste;* Vol. 1, "Sociologie critique"; Vol. 2, "Révolution et socialisme." Paris: Payot, 1970. (302 pp.; 290 pp.)

Karl Marx. *Selected Writings in Sociology and Social Philosophy*. Ed. with intro. and notes by T. B. Bottomore and Maximilien Rubel. London: Watts, 1956. (xiii, 268 pp.) American edition, with foreword by Erich Fromm. New York: McGraw-Hill, 1964. (xviii, 268 pp.)

Karl Marx. *Oeuvres*. Edition established by Maximilien Rubel. (Bibliothèque de la Pléiade.)

    Economie Vol. I. Ed. with intro., notes, and appendixes by M. Rubel; preface by François Perroux. Paris: Gallimard, 1963. 5th ed. revised and corrected, 1977. (clxxvi, 1821 pp.)

    Economie Vol. II. Ed. with preface, intro., notes, and appendixes by M. Rubel. Paris: Gallimard, 1968. 2d ed. revised and corrected, 1972. (cxxxii, 1968 pp.)

    Philosophie. Ed. with preface, intro., and notes by M. Rubel. Paris: Gallimard, in press.

Jules Andrieu. *Notes pour servir à l'histoire de la Commune de Paris en 1871*. Ed. by M. Rubel and L. Janover. Paris: Payot, 1971. (xi, 267 pp.)

Karl Marx/Friedrich Engels. *Die russische Kommune. Kritik eines Mythos*. Ed. with postscript by M. Rubel. Munich: Carl Hanser Verlag, 1972. (381 pp.)

Books

Bibliographie des oeuvres de Karl Marx. Avec en appendice un répertoire des oeuvres de F. Engels. Paris: M. Rivière, 1956. (272 pp.)

Karl Marx. Essai de biographie intellectuelle. Paris: M. Rivière, 1957. (463 pp.) 2d ed. revised and corrected, 1971. (xii, 460 pp.)

Supplément à la Bibliographie des oeuvres de Karl Marx. Paris: M. Rivière, 1960. (74 pp.)

Karl Marx devant le bonapartisme. The Hague: Mouton, 1960. (167 pp.)

Marx-Chronik. Daten zu Leben und Werk. Munich: Hanser Verlag, 1968.
(163 pp.) 3d ed. revised and corrected, 1975. (155 pp.) [German version
of the "Chronologie de Marx" in Karl Marx. *Oeuvres. Economie Vol. I.*]
Marx critique du marxisme. Essais. Paris: Payot, 1974. (451 pp.) [This
collection contains the articles noted below, together with a forty-page
postscript written especially for the volume.]
Josef W. Stalin in Selbstzeugnissen und Bilddokumenten. Reinbek bei Ham-
burg: Rowohlt, 1975. (158 pp.)
Marx Without Myth. A Chronological Study of His Life and Work. (Co-
author – Margaret Manale.) Oxford: Basil Blackwell, 1975; New York:
Harper & Row, 1976. (xv, 368 pp.)
Marx Chronicle. Trans. by Mary Bottomore. London: Macmillan, in press.
[English version of the "Chronologie de Marx" in Karl Marx. *Oeuvres.
Economie Vol. I.*]
Lexique de Marx (Coauthor – Louis Janover). Paris: Editions du Seuil, in
preparation.

Articles

Marxology

"Karl Marx et Flora Tristan," *La Nef* (Jan. 1946), 68–76.
"Marx Lecteur (Les carnets d'extraits de Paris, 1844–45)," *La Revue socia-
liste* (Nov. 1946), 529–39.
"Un inédit de Karl Marx: Le travail aliéné," *La Revue socialiste* (Feb. 1947),
154–68.
"Karl Marx: Le travail salarie," in R. Aron et al., *De Marx au marxisme
1848–1948.* Paris: Editions de Flore, 1948, pp. 304–17 (with F.
Berthelot).
"La Bourgeoisie et la contre-révolution, par Karl Marx," *La Revue socialiste*
(May 1948), 451–59; (June–July 1948), 104–19.
"La vie posthume de Karl Marx (Textes inédits. . .)," *La Nef* (June 1948),
48–69 (with R. Meignez).
"Fragments d'un journal de voyage par F. Engels (de Paris à Berne, octobre–
novembre 1848)," *La Revue socialiste* (Apr. 1949), 271–80.
"Un échange de lettres entre Lassalle et Marx," *La Revue socialiste* (Dec.
1949), 434–47.
"Pour une biographie monumentale de Karl Marx," *La Revue socialiste*
(Oct. 1950), 309–21.
"Contribution à l'histoire de la genèse du *Capital:* les manuscrits économico-
politiques de Karl Marx (1857–1858)," *Revue d'Histoire économique
et sociale*, no. 2 (1950), 169–85.
"Karl Marx, auteur maudit en U.R.S.S.? I. l'Edition fantome," *Preuves I*, no.
7 (Sept. 1951), 14–16; "II. l'Edition censurée," Ibid., no. 8 (Oct. 1951),

11–13, with appendix (Karl Marx, Révélations sur l'histoire de la Russie), 13–14.

"Le sort de l'oeuvre de Marx et d'Engels en U.R.S.S.," *La Revue socialiste* (Apr. 1952), 327–49.

"L'Occident doit à Marx et à Engels une édition monumentale de leurs oeuvres," *La Revue socialiste* (July 1952), 113–14 (with Bracke-Desrousseaux).

"Les cahiers d'étude de Karl Marx. I. 1840–1853," *International Review of Social History* 2, part 3 (1957), 392–420. Reprinted in *Marx critique du marxisme*, pp. 301–25.

"A propos d'une bibliographie de Karl Marx," *Les temps modernes* (Jan.-Feb. 1958), 1525–7.

"Trois lettres inédites de Karl Marx," *l'Actualité de l'histoire*, no. 25 (Oct., Nov., Dec. 1958), 22–32.

"Les premières lectures économiques de Karl Marx (I)," *Etudes de marxologie* (Cahiers de l'Institut de Sciences économiques appliquées, "Economies et Sociétés," Series S), no. 1 (Jan. 1959), 5–8.

"Les premières lectures économiques de Karl Marx (II)," *Etudes de marxologie*, no. 2 (Oct. 1959), 51–72.

"Les cahiers d'étude de Karl Marx. II. 1853–1856," *International Review of Social History* 5, part 1 (1960), 39–76. Reprinted in *Marx critique du marxisme*, pp. 325–59.

"Karl Marx et la Première Internationale. Une chronologie-I (1864–1869)," *Etudes de marxologie*, no. 8 (Aug. 1964), 9–82.

"Karl Marx et la Première Internationale. Une chronologie-II (1870–1876)," *Etudes de marxologie*, no. 9 (Aug. 1965), 5–70.

"De la philosophie à l'économie politique," *Etudes de marxologie*, no. 11 (June 1967), 7–48.

"La première édition du *Capital*. Note sur sa diffusion," *Revue historique*, no. 239, part 1 (Jan.-Mar. 1968), 101–10. Reprinted in *Marx critique du marxisme*, pp. 360–8.

"La légende de Marx ou Engels fondateur," *Etudes de marxologie*, no. 15 (Dec. 1972), 2189–99. Reprinted in *Marx critique du marxisme*, pp. 17–24. In English: "Friedrich Engels – Marxism's Founding Father: Nine Premises to a Theme," in *Varieties of Marxism*, ed. S. Avineri. The Hague: M. Nijhoff, 1977, pp. 43–52.

"Plan et methode de l'Economie," *Etudes de marxologie*, no. 16 (Oct. 1973), 1777–1820. Reprinted in *Marx critique du marxisme*, pp. 369–401.

"Marx à la rencontre de Spinoza," *Cahiers Spinoza* 1 (Summer 1977), 7–28. Reprinted with additions in ·*Etudes de marxologie*, no. 19–20 (Jan.-Feb. 1978), 239–65.

"Matériaux pour un lexique de Marx: I. Etat II. Anarchisme," *Etudes de marxologie*, no. 19–20 (Jan.-Feb. 1978), 7–161 (with L. Janover).

"Marx et la nation," *Mondes en développement* (Cahiers de l'I.S.M.E.A. [formerly I.S.E.A.]), in press (with L. Janover).

Political Sociology

"La pensée maîtresse du Manifeste communiste," *La Revue socialiste* (Jan.– Feb. 1948), 1–19.
"Réflexions sur la société directoriale," *La Revue socialiste* (Feb. 1951), 181–94.
Karl Marx et le problème paysan," *Revue d'histoire économique et sociale* 32 (1954), 98–100.
"Fragments sociologiques dans le inédits de Marx," *Cahiers internationaux de Sociologie XXII* (1957), 128–46.
"Remarques sur le concept de parti prolétarien chez Marx," *Revue française de Sociologie II,* no. 3 (July–Sept. 1961), 166–76. Reprinted in *Marx critique du marxisme,* pp. 183–92.
"Premiers contacts des sociologues du XIXe siècle avec la pensée de Marx," *Cahiers internationaux de Sociologie XXXI* (1961), 175–84.
"De Marx au bolchévisme: partis et conseils," *Arguments VI,* no. 25–6 (1962), 31–9. Reprinted in *Marx critique du marxisme,* pp. 200–13.
"Le concept de démocratie chez Marx," *Le contrat social VI,* no. 4 (1962), 214–20. Reprinted in *Marx critique du marxisme,* pp. 171–82.
"Notes on Marx's Conception of Democracy," *New Politics I,* no. 2 (1962), 78–90.
"Deux interviews de Karl Marx sur la Commune," *Le Mouvement social,* no. 38 (Jan.–Mar. 1962), 3–27.
"La conception du prolétariat chez Marx," *Actes du cinquième Congrès mondial de sociologie,* Washington, D.C., Sept. 2–8, 1962. Vol. 4. Association internationale de sociologie, 1964. Reprinted in *Marx critique du marxisme,* pp. 193–9.
"La charte de la Première Internationale. Essai sur le marxisme dans l'A.I.T.," *Le Mouvement social,* no. 51 (Apr.–June 1965), 3–22. Reprinted in *Marx critique du marxisme,* pp. 25–41.
"Aux origines de l'Internationale. (Documents)," *Le Mouvement social,* no. 51 (Apr.–June 1965), 47–74.
"Reflections on Utopia and Revolution," in *Socialist Humanism: an International Symposium.* Ed. Erich Fromm. New York: Doubleday, 1965, pp. 192–9. In French ("Utopie et révolution") in *Marx critique du marxisme,* pp. 290–8.
"Science, éthique et idéologie," *Cahiers internationaux de Sociologie XLII* (1967), 133–43. Reprinted in *Marx critique du marxisme,* pp. 217–27.
"Did the Proletariat Need Marx and Did Marxism Help the Proletariat?", and "Marx and American Democracy," in *Marx and the Western World.* Ed. N. Lobkowicz. Notre Dame, Ind.: Notre Dame University Press, 1967, pp. 45–52, 217–28.

"Sociologie et utopie," *Année sociologique*, 3d series, no. 19 (1968), 243–52. Reprinted in *Marx critique du marxisme*, pp. 235–43.

"Révolte et utopie. Note critique à propos du livre de A. Tourraine, Le mouvement de mai ou le communisme utopique," *Revue française de Sociologie X*, no. 1 (Jan.–Mar. 1969), pp. 83–7. Reprinted in *Marx critique du marxisme*, pp. 228–34.

"Le communisme: de l'utopie à la mythologie," *Etudes de marxologie*, no. 14 (Nov. 1970), 2005–13. Reprinted in *Marx critique du marxisme*, pp. 244–51.

"Socialism and the Commune," in *Paradigm for Revolution? The Paris Commune 1871–1971*. Ed. Eugene Kamenka. Canberra: Australian National University Press, 1972, pp. 31–48. In French ("le Socialisme et la commune") in *Marx critique du marxisme*, pp. 272–89.

"Marx Théoricien de l'anarchisme," *L'Europe en formation*, no. 163–4 (Oct.–Nov. 1973), 39–54. Reprinted in *Marx critique du marxisme*, pp. 42–59.

"l'Autopraxis historique du prolétariat," *Etudes de marxologie*, no. 18 (Apr.–May 1976), 773–812.

"Le Parti de la mystification et la dictature du prolétariat," *Etudes de marxologie*, no. 19–20 (Jan.–Feb. 1978), 411–43.

Marx and Engels on Russia

"Karl Marx et le socialisme populiste russe," *La Revue socialiste* (May 1947), 544–59.

"La Russie dans l'oeuvre de Marx et d'Engels. Leur correspondance avec Danielson," *La Revue socialiste* (Apr. 1950), 327–49.

"La Russie dans l'oeuvre de Marx et d'Engels. *La Nouvelle Gazette rhénane* et la Russie (1848–1849)," *La Revue socialiste* (July 1951), 219–35.

"F. Engels et le socialisme messianique russe," *La Revue socialiste* (Nov. 1951), 450–64.

"Staline jugé par Marx," *Preuves* no. 12 (1952), 41–2.

"Staline et Cie. devant le verdict d'Engels," *La Revue socialiste* (Jan. 1953), 64–74.

"Les écrits de Karl Marx sur la Russie tsariste," *Revue d'histoire économique et sociale XXXIII*, no. 1 (1955), 113–21.

"La croissance du capital en URSS. Essai de confrontation critique," *Economie appliquée* (Archives de l'I.S.E.A.), X (Apr.–Sept. 1957), 363–408. Reprinted in *Marx critique du marxisme*, pp. 63–100.

"The Relationship of Bolshevism to Marxism," in *Revolutionary Russia*. Ed. Richard Pipes. Cambridge, Mass.: Harvard University Press, 1968, pp. 301–32. In French ("Bolchevisme et marxisme") in *Marx critique du marxisme*, pp. 101–20.

"Russland und die russische Revolution im Denken von Karl Marx," *Schriften aus dem Karl-Marx-Haus, Trier*, Heft 2 (1969).

'La Société de transition. Note critique sur *le Nouveau Léviathan* de P. Naville," *Sociologie du travail XIII*, no. 4 (Oct.–Dec. 1971), 416–25. Reprinted in *Marx critique du marxisme*, pp. 121–32.

"Le Chainon le plus faible (A propos de la 'loi du développement inégal')," *Mondes en développement* (Cahiers de l'I.S.M.E.A.), no. 1 (1973), 93–115. Reprinted in *Marx critique du marxisme*, pp. 146–68.

Miscellaneous

"Le magnum opus de Karl Kautsky: *La conception matérialiste de l'histoire*," *La Revue socialiste* (Jan. 1955), 4–14; (Mar. 1955), 275–91.

Karl Korsch, "Dix thèses sur le marxisme aujourd'hui," trans. by M. Rubel and L. Evrard, intro. by M. Rubel, *Arguments III*, no. 16 (1959), 26–8.

"Robert Owen à Paris en 1848," *l'Actualité de l'histoire*, no. 30 (Jan.–Mar. 1960), 3–14.

"Karl Marx," in *International Encyclopedia of Social Sciences*. New York: Macmillan and The Free Press, 1968. Vol. 10, pp. 34–40.

"Karl Marx," in *Sowjetsystem und demokratische Gesellschaft. Eine vergleichende Enzyklopädie*. Freiburg/Basel/Vienna: Herder, 1970. Vol. IV, pp. 301–30. In the English version: *Marxism, Communism and Western Society. A Comparative Encyclopedia*. Ed. C. D. Kernig. New York: Herder and Herder, 1972–3. Vol. 5, pp. 327–42.

"Saint-simonisme et marxisme," *Cahiers de l'Institute de Sciences économiques appliquées IV*, no. 6 ("Economies et Sociétés," Hors Série no. 9) (June 1970), 1069–94. Reprinted in *Marx critique du marxisme*, pp. 252–71.

"La fonction historique de la nouvelle bourgeoisie," *Praxis 1/2* (1971), 257–68. Reprinted in *Marx critique du marxisme*, pp. 133–45.

Introduction, in Thomas Hamilton, *Les Hommes et les moeurs aux Etats-Unis*. Geneva: Slatkine Reprints (Collection "Ressources"), 1979.

Bibliographies and Translations in Etudes de marxologie

"Bibliographie marxologique: Théorie économique I (1883–1914)," no. 1 (Jan. 1959), 37–40.

"Bibliographie marxologique: Théorie économique II (1915–1929)," no. 2 (Oct. 1959), 119–22.

"Bibliographie marxologique: Théorie économique III (1929–1945)," no. 3 (June 1960), 153–6.

"Bibliographie marxologique: Théorie économique IV (1945–1960)," no. 4 (Jan. 1961), 159–64.

"Bibliographie marxologique: Complément," no. 5 (Jan. 1962), 217–22.

"Bibliographie marxologique: Histoire et société (1893–1918)," no. 6 (Sept. 1962), 177–82.

"Bibliographie marxologique: Histoire et société (1893–1918)," no. 7 (Aug. 1963), 247–50.

"Bibliographie de la Première Internationale," no. 8 (Aug. 1964), 249–75.

"Supplément à la bibliographie de la Première Internationale," no. 9 (Aug. 1965), 255–60.

Karl Marx, "La Sprée et le Mincio," no. 3 (June 1960), 87–90 (with L. Evrard).

Karl Marx, "Formes précapitalistes de la production," no. 10 (Aug. 1966), 7–44.

Karl Marx, "Resultats immédiates de la production," no. 11 (June 1967), 125–76.

Karl Marx, "Notes sur l'aliénation (Manuscrits de 1844 et de 1858)," no. 12 (Dec. 1968), 2377–427.

Karl Marx, "L'affranchissement des paysans russes," no. 13 (July 1969), 1313–28.

Karl Marx, "La Pologne, la Russie et l'Europe," 1329–34 (with Y. Broutin).

F. Engels, "La politique extérieure du tsarisme," 1377–1420.

Marx/Engels, "Lettres et fragments divers," 1421–50 (with N. Rubel and Y. Broutin).

"Critique de Friedrich List. Un inédit de Karl Marx," no. 16 (Oct. 1973), 1821–57 (with Y. Broutin).

Index